THE WORD IN THE DESERT

THE WORD
IN THE DESERT

*Scripture and the Quest
for Holiness in Early
Christian Monasticism*

DOUGLAS BURTON-CHRISTIE

New York   Oxford
OXFORD UNIVERSITY PRESS
1993

Oxford University Press

Oxford   New York   Toronto
Delhi   Bombay   Calcutta   Madras   Karachi
Kuala Lumpur   Singapore   Hong Kong   Tokyo
Nairobi   Dar es Salaam   Cape Town
Melbourne   Auckland   Madrid

and associated companies in
Berlin   Ibadan

Copyright © 1993 by Douglas Burton-Christie

Published by Oxford University Press, Inc.
200 Madison Avenue, New York, NY 10016

Oxford is a registered trademark of Oxford University Press

Library of Congress Cataloging-in-Publication Data
Burton-Christie, Douglas.
The Word in the desert : scripture and the quest for holiness
in early Christian monasticism / Douglas Burton-Christie.
p.   cm.   Includes bibliographical references and index.
ISBN 0-19-506614-6
1. Monasticism and religious orders—Egypt—History.
2. Monasticism and religious orders—History—Early church, ca.
30–600.   3. Egypt—Church history.   I. Title.
BX2465.B87   1993
271'.00932—dc20   91-4150

3 5 7 9   8 6 4 2

Printed in the United States of America
on acid-free paper

For Mary Ellen

Preface

The desert fathers and mothers of fourth century Egypt created a spirituality of remarkable depth and enduring power from their reading and interpretation of Scripture. This book tells the story of early monastic spirituality in light of the hermeneutic that shaped it and within the context of the ascetical world of late antiquity.

The themes discussed here arose in my mind somewhat unexpectedly, the result of a happy convergence of two abiding interests: biblical interpretation and monastic culture. For some time, I had been interested in the question of how one determines meaning in the interpretation of biblical texts. In particular, I wondered whether it was possible to reconcile the diverse and often diametrically opposed approaches to biblical interpretation found in ancient and contemporary Christianity. The ancient and medieval Christian hermeneutical approaches posed a challenge: while they clearly did not establish the meaning of the text in the particular determinative way characterized by the contemporary historical-critical approach, they most certainly did establish meaning. The typological, allegorical, and sometimes literal readings of Scripture in which these ancient interpreters were engaged all comprised attempts to derive meaning from the texts. And yet, what kind of meaning was it? Were their interpretations genuine responses to the text or merely whimsical creations utterly detached from the biblical text itself?

The early monastic world of Egypt presents an especially good place to examine these questions. Here is a culture steeped in Scripture, viewing it not simply as an object of study but as a source of real spiritual sustenance. Daily ruminating and imbibing the Word within the rounds of work and prayer, the monks sought to reshape their imaginations around the world of Scripture and to allow it to penetrate to the core of their beings and their communities. The *Sayings of the Desert Fathers* struck me as a particularly fruitful source for considering the character and aim of the early monastic hermeneutic. Not only are the stories and sayings themselves inherently interesting, filled as they are with a motley band of colorful characters, wild adventures, and stinging, memorable "one-liners"; they also present a consistent struggle on the part of the monks to realize in their lives the holiness to which they felt called by Scripture. Here is a hermeneutic firmly embedded within the practical challenges presented by the ascetical life the monks had taken up in the Egyptian desert: a hermeneutic that demands, ultimately, that the meaning of a text be expressed in a life.

In exploring the character and shape of the desert hermeneutic here, I want to suggest that this complex, sophisticated, and creative approach to Scripture, which has been so neglected in considerations of the history of biblical interpretation, deserves to be better known; and that it can stimulate further thought about the contributions ancient hermeneutical strategies can make to our contemporary understanding of how to derive meaning from texts. I want to suggest also that an elucidation of the early monastic hermeneutic can contribute to a better understanding of the religious experience of the early monks and can help to situate their religious aspirations more clearly within the broad quest for holiness in late antiquity. The reading and interpretation of texts played a crucial role in the ascetical world of late antiquity; this exploration of the desert monks' hermeneutic can add color and texture to our picture of that world.

It is a pleasure to thank those whose support and encouragement have made this book possible: my friends in the Christian Spirituality program at the Graduate Theological Union in Berkeley, whose kindness, lively interest in my work, and commitment to building community provided the rich soil in which the ideas for this book first took root; Donald Nicholl, my first teacher of religious studies and a close friend, who first posed the questions that led me to the study of spirituality; Rebecca Lyman, whose thoughtful criticism helped me to situate the desert monks more carefully within the world of the fourth century; William Short, O.F.M., whose good humor often lifted my spirits and whose attention to detail contributed greatly to the improvement of this study; Graham Gould, whose own work on the *Sayings* has considerably deepened my understanding of it; Peter Brown, in whose seminar "Monks and Philosophers" at the University of California at Berkeley many of the seeds of this study were first sown; Lucien Regnault, who graciously hosted me during a visit to Solesmes and who shared with me so much of his considerable knowledge of the desert fathers; Robert Wilken, whose careful reading of the manuscript helped me to rethink some fundamental issues; Sandra Schneiders, whose probing analysis of my work helped me to focus on the significant questions and whose example of engaged scholarship has provided a model of how to study spirituality; the monks of the Monastery of St. Macarius in Egypt, who revealed to me the continuing vitality of the ancient tradition of the desert fathers; the community of Cistercian nuns at Redwoods Monastery, whose generous hospitality provided me with a place of warmth and silence in which to think through some difficult questions.

I would also like to express my appreciation to Mike Foley and Georgia Frank, who scrutinized the proofs and provided numerous helpful suggestions for improvements; to Sylvia Coates, who prepared the indexes; to Stephen Privett, S.J., of Santa Clara University, who provided generous financial assistance that helped bring the book to completion; and to Cynthia Read and Paul Schlotthauer of Oxford University Press, whose interest in the book helped give it life, and whose perceptive critiques improved it immensely.

I would especially like to thank my wife, Mary Ellen, whose love, tenderness, and sense of play enrich my life more than I can say.

Oakland, California   D. B.-C.
June 1992

Contents

Abbreviations

AP	*Apophthegmata Patrum*
CSCO	*Corpus scriptorum Christianorum Orientalium*, Louvain.
DS	*Dictionnaire de spiritualité*, Paris.
JTS	*Journal of Theological Studies*, London.
Nau	Anonymous apophthegmata (numbered), ed. F. Nau, in *ROC:* 13, 14, 17, 18.
OCP	*Orientalia Christiana Periodica*, Rome.
OMC	Guillaumont, *Aux Origines du monachisme chrétien*, Bellefontaine.
PG	*Patrologia Graeca*, of Migne, Paris.
PGL	Lampe, *Patristic Greek Lexicon*, Oxford.
PL	*Patrologia Latina*, of Migne, Paris.
ROC	*Revue de l'Orient chrétien*, Paris.
RSR	*Recherches de science religieuse*, Paris.
Recherches	J.-C. Guy, *Recherches sur la tradition grecque des* Apophthegmata Patrum, Brussels.
SPAlph	*Les sentences des pères du désert, collection alphabétique*, Solesmes.
SPAn	*Les sentences des pères du désert, série des anonymes*, Solesmes and Bellefontaine.
SPN	*Les sentences des pères du désert, nouveau recueil*, Solesmes.
SPTr	*Les sentences des pères du désert, troisième recueil & tables*, Solesmes.
TU	*Texte und Untersuchungen zur Geschichte der altchristlichen Literatur.*
VA	*Vita Antonii, PG* 26, Paris.
VP	*Vita Plotinii*, trans. S. Mackenna, London.

Author's Note

In citing biblical texts found in the *Sayings,* parentheses are used to indicate direct biblical quotations or texts with close verbal similarities to the original biblical text; brackets are used to indicate allusions or biblical references whose verbal similarities with the original biblical text are less than exact.

English translations of biblical texts cited in the *Sayings* are for the most part taken from Benedicta Ward's English translation of the *Sayings.* In a few instances, as indicated in the notes, translations are either my own or from the Revised Standard Version.

I

THE DESERT HERMENEUTIC
IN ITS SETTING

1

Introduction:
Toward a Desert Hermeneutic

The retreat to the desert and growth of monasticism in fourth-century Egypt has long been recognized as one of the most significant and alluring moments of early Christianity. In the withdrawal from the mainstream of society and culture to the stark solitude of the desert, a vibrant and original spirituality was born which had a wide influence on both contemporaries and succeeding generations. It was a rich and varied movement, full of apparent contradictions and paradoxes. Although largely composed of persons from an oral, rural, peasant culture, desert monasticism also attracted many from a more literate, urban culture of the late Roman Empire. Characterized by a certain simplicity and even naiveté, the monks were nevertheless capable of subtle discernment regarding the complex forces in the human soul. In their solitude, they consciously removed themselves from ordinary contact with their fellow human beings and were often perceived as aloof and forbidding; yet they were also revered for their extraordinary depth of compassion. They audaciously battled the demons in the desert, but humbly refused to acknowledge their own power. They spoke words of authority, though it was often in their silence that they were most eloquent. Many of the desert monks refused to participate in the growing establishment of the church under Constantine, choosing instead to live on the margins of society under the direct guidance of the Spirit and the Word of God. Yet in spite of or perhaps because of their singular response to the issues of their time, they had a far reaching impact on contemporary society and church and left a rich and varied legacy.

It is not easy to account for this extraordinary flowering in the desert. What motivated the early desert monks? Why did they withdraw to the desert in the first place and what drove them to embrace the hardships and rigors of life there with such seeming abandon? What concerns filled their days and nights? Why did they exert such a powerful attraction upon their

3

contemporaries and succeeding generations? These and other basic questions about early desert monasticism press themselves insistently upon anyone who encounters the literature of this movement. And the questions have generated a variety of responses. Early monasticism has been said to have arisen as a quest for knowledge (gnosis); a flight from taxes; a refuge from the law; a new form of martyrdom; revival of an earlier Jewish ascetical movement; a rejection of classical culture; an expression of Manichean dualism; a response to a call from the Gospels. These are only *some* of the explanations which have been proposed over the years to account for the appearance of monasticism during the late third and early fourth century in Egypt and elsewhere. Each one has its merits and is helpful to varying degrees in shedding light on the inner life of early monasticism and its impact on the world. Indeed, if the study of early monasticism during the last generation has taught us anything, it is that this complex movement cannot be explained or accounted for by reference to any single cause or idea. Still, one means of coming to a better understanding of this mysterious world is to penetrate deeply into one of its primary impulses. An aspect of early monasticism which has particular promise for unveiling the world of the desert monks is their use and interpretation of Scripture—the "desert hermeneutic."

Of the diverse forces which gave rise to and defined the quest for holiness in early monasticism, Scripture stands as one of the most fundamental and influential. Certain key texts from the Scriptures, especially those having to do with renunciation and detachment, stood at the beginning of desert monasticism, serving as primary sources of inspiration for the whole movement. These and numerous other biblical texts filled the day-to-day existence of the desert monks, providing a horizon of meaning in light of which they understood their ongoing quest for salvation: the Scriptures were experienced as authoritative words which pierced the hearts of the monks, illuminated them concerning the central issues of their lives, protected and comforted them during dark times of struggle and anxiety, and provided practical help in their ongoing quest for holiness. The characteristic spirituality or expression of holiness which emerged in the desert movement was a fundamentally biblical one: the monks appropriated Scripture so deeply that they came to be seen by their contemporaries as living "bearers of the word." By looking at the spirituality of the desert monks—their words, gestures, silences—through the lens of their hermeneutic, we can bring the image of holiness in the desert movement into sharper focus. The central theme of this book, then, is how the use and interpretation of Scripture shaped the quest for holiness amongst the desert monks of early Christianity.

In fleshing out this question, it will be useful to bear in mind three main issues or perspectives. First there are *historical* issues. There has been considerable dispute among historians regarding the origins of monasticism, the major influences upon its rise and growth and its effects on the world within which it existed. A better understanding of the place of Scripture in early monasticism can help to clarify the extent and character of various influences upon the early monastic movement and to situate early monasticism more clearly within its world. It can also reveal the characteristic features of the pedagogy practiced in the desert and show how it differed from and agreed with the classical Greek pedagogical model. The investigation of the place of Scripture in the world of the desert can add a new dimension to our knowledge of its rich spirituality and provide a clearer historical picture of certain key facets of that world: it can help to shed new light on the meaning of such important dimensions of desert spirituality as renunciation, discernment of spirits, fighting the demons, the charismatic relationship between master and disciple, the gift of tears, freedom from care, humility, silence, purity of heart, and the extraordinary compassion that fills so much of this literature.

There are also *hermeneutical* issues to consider. Principally, this concerns the meaning of the patterns of biblical interpretation found in the desert literature. A close study of the interpretation of Scripture within early monasticism can tell us much about the place of biblical interpretation within the moral and spiritual lives of Christians living in late antiquity. As such, it can help to fill out an important but heretofore neglected chapter in the history of biblical interpretation. A consideration of the desert hermeneutic can also contribute significantly to our understanding of how human beings derive meaning from sacred texts and can provide a fruitful point of entry for a dialogue with contemporary hermeneutics. To take but one example, the desert hermeneutic offers an intriguing perspective regarding how "prejudices" or preunderstanding affect the interpretation of sacred texts: the monks' physical solitude and social marginality certainly affected their interpretation of Scripture in important ways. Similarly, silence, praxis, and purity of heart were seen as important moral preconditions for hearing and interpreting the Scriptures in all their fullness. Seen from this perspective, the study of the desert hermeneutic can contribute an important new chapter to the history of biblical interpretation and provide an intriguing stimulus to contemporary thinking about the interpretation of Scripture.

Finally, this book poses questions about the *meaning of holiness* within the ancient monastic movement and about the role Scripture played in bringing this quest for holiness to realization. These questions are related to the hermeneutical ones but are concerned more directly with understanding how interpretation of Scripture led the monks toward personal and communal transformation—toward the realization of holiness. What authority did sacred texts have in the spiritual life, and how was that authority experienced? What moral attitude or posture did the monks feel was most appropriate and fruitful for understanding and realizing the meaning of Scripture? What was the relationship between praxis and understanding of Scripture? What did it mean to fulfill the words of Scripture in one's life? These questions open out onto an even wider circle of questions about the meaning of holiness that the desert monks asked themselves: What did it mean to know the self, to live with integrity? How could one learn to contend with the seemingly uncontrollable forces that assaulted one from within and without? What was the possibility of achieving freedom from these forces and a sense of abiding peace? What did it mean to give oneself in love? These are the kinds of ultimate questions which the desert fathers put to Scripture and which helped to stimulate and give shape to the biblical spirituality of the desert.

Any number of early monastic texts could be used as a basis for exploring these questions. In this book, *The Sayings of the Desert Fathers* will provide the primary lens through which we examine the early monastic world.[1] A brief word is necessary about the choice of this text. Although the collection of sayings and stories known as the *Sayings* is not strictly speaking the earliest text from early Egyptian monasticism, its nevertheless provides us with some of the earliest testimony from that world. It is precisely its primitive, relatively unsophisticated quality that makes it among the most important and interesting texts for understanding the early eremetical and semi-eremetical monastic world and its spirituality. It contains, moreover, a wealth of evidence regarding the place and function of Scripture in the life of the desert. However, unlike some of the other major early monastic texts of the fourth and fifth century which come to us from the perspective of outsiders, the *Sayings* often presents a valuable "insider's view" of early monastic life and its concerns. In short, *The Sayings of the Desert Fathers* provides one of the best possible places to observe and analyze the hermeneutic of the early desert movement and its effects upon the monks' ongoing quest for holiness.

To begin this analysis, it is worth taking some time to think about the way desert monasticism has been perceived and interpreted from the earliest times until the present. The contemporary reader of the desert literature is faced with an "effective history," or accumulated weight of opinion, on this subject which has dictated to a very great extent the shape of the present discussion of desert spirituality. Therefore, an examination of this effective history is a first step in learning how the desert fathers come to us—and how we come to them. This means accounting for both the ongoing appeal of the desert ideal and literature—the retrieval of desert spirituality at different historical moments—as well as some of the major critiques which have been levelled against the desert movement. Such a sketch will help to bring into sharper focus the place of Scripture in the quest for holiness among the early desert monks.

The Desert Fathers' Legacy

Desert monasticism, as story and spirituality, caught the imagination of the ancient world, and its appeal has diminished little over the centuries. A movement of bold gestures and heroic figures, desert monasticism has included as part of its legacy a legion of admirers and imitators. Whether moved by the desert fathers' approach to prayer, or their example of withdrawal into solitude, or the penetrating psychological insights developed through the practice of discernment of spirits, those who have followed or admired the way of the desert have seen in it a way of life rooted in Scripture and the source for a humane spirituality of compassion. Still, the desert movement has also had its detractors and, although fewer in number, they have been strident in their criticism of it. The complaint against the desert movement has arisen for two main reasons: that in its growth and development desert monasticism fundamentally misunderstood and departed from the spirit of Jesus and the Gospels; and that in its extreme physical, social, and intellectual renunciation, desert spirituality had a debilitating effect on the growth of humane culture. A brief discussion of the legacy of desert monasticism from the perspectives of both its supporters and its detractors can help to provide a context for considering the significance of the desert hermeneutic.

The Desert Legacy Embraced

The positive legacy of desert literature in the traditions of both Western and Eastern Christianity has been truly impressive. From the very beginning, stories about the desert monks spread rapidly and widely. St. Athanasius, biographer of St. Antony and contemporary of the earliest movement by monks into the Egyptian desert, noted with amazement toward the end of his *Vita Antonii* how far word of Antony's life had already traveled by the time he wrote his story in the middle of the fourth century. Reflecting on the paradox that Antony's withdrawal into obscurity had produced such notoriety, Athanasius asked, "How is it that he was heard of, though concealed and sitting in a mountain, in Spain and Gaul, and in Rome and Africa . . . ?"[2] In a celebrated passage from his *Confessions*, Augustine tells us that the story had indeed spread to distant lands by the time he was in Milan and was widely known. He relates how he and his friend Alypius first heard of St. Antony from their friend Ponticianus and how deeply the story moved them. Augustine comments—noting both the capacity of the story to fire the imagination and its widespread currency—that all three of them were amazed at what they heard: "Alypius and I because the story was so remarkable, and Ponticianus because we had not heard it before!"[3] For Augustine, as for many others in late antiquity, the stories of St. Antony and the other desert monks touched a nerve. The sheer numbers who either followed Antony to the desert or, like Augustine, were provoked by his example into making other dramatic changes in their lives, testify to the power which the ascetic impulse had during late antiquity.

The ongoing appeal of desert literature as a major resource for Western medieval monastic spirituality was ensured in large part by St. Benedict's positive assessment of it. In his vastly influential *Rule,* Benedict exhorted his monks to read the *Conferences, Institutes,* and *Lives of the Fathers*—a clear reference to the writings of John Cassian on the desert movement.[4] In addition to the writings of Cassian, there is evidence that *The Sayings of the Desert Fathers* was well known and loved in medieval Benedictine monasteries.[5] The desert literature served not only as one of the main sources for medieval monastic *lectio divina* but also inspired many monastic and religious reform movements in the medieval West. These often looked back to a "desert ideal" and made a point of geographical withdrawal to inaccessible desertlike sites. During every monastic revival in the Middle Ages—in the Carolingian period, in the eleventh century at Monte Cassino, Cluny, Camaldoli, and in the twelfth century at Cîteaux—the desert ideal of Egypt, and in particular the example of Antony, would be recalled. In some cases, as with the Carmelites and the Capuchin Franciscans, the spirit of the desert was adapted and integrated into a form of religious life more closely involved with engagement in the world than that of the first monks. The resilience and adaptability of the desert ideal to different circumstances and different ways of life was in fact one of its chief virtues. As Jean Leclercq notes, regardless of the particular observance under which the medieval monks lived, the life of Antony and the other desert monks was "a living text, a means of formation of monastic life."[6]

In the modern West, the influence of the desert has been felt not only in religious revivals but also in literature and art. Recent scholarship has revealed the surprising extent to which desert spirituality affected such diverse religious renewal movements as the German Evangelicals and Pietists in Pennsylvania, the *Devotio Moderna* movement in France, and the Methodist revival in England.[7] There has also been considerable artistic response to the desert in the West, focused particularly on St. Antony. This response sometimes came from unlikely places, such as the figure of Flaubert, who made Antony the hero of his extravagant literary work, *La tentation de Saint Antoine.*[8] Yet there has been a consistent if varied return to the subject of Antony as a subject for the artistic imagination. Indeed, if we take the sheer *number* of times St. Antony appears as a subject throughout the history of Western art as a measure, his story would appear to have had one of the most enduring and powerful appeals to the Western artistic imagination.[9]

The legacy of the desert has been, perhaps, even stronger within Eastern Christianity than in the West, providing rich and enduring inspiration for its theology and spirituality. Partly because of the greater historical and cultural continuity of Byzantium, the sayings and writings of desert figures such as Antony, Macarius, Poemen, Evagrius, Cassian, and others have endured in a special way as classics of Eastern Christianity, inspiring theologians and spiritual writers alike.[10] The monasticism of Mt. Athos, which has been a source of spiritual inspiration in the Eastern church since the middle of the tenth century, drew upon both the teaching of St. Basil, the founder of monasticism in Cappadocia, and the early Egyptian tradition, to form its own characteristic spirituality. Early Russian monasticism, exemplified by such figures as St. Antony of Kiev—who with his disciples withdrew to live in the caves near Kiev in the early eleventh century—also owed a great deal to the inspiration of early desert monasticism.[11] In a variety of ways, Eastern Christian spirituality, including spiritual practices such as the Jesus prayer and schools of spirituality such as hesychasm, has been continuously nurtured from the rich soil of the desert.

The thread of desert spirituality has continued to weave its way through the fabric of Eastern Christianity in modern times. One of the reasons for the ongoing presence of the sayings and stories of the desert fathers was their inclusion in the *Philokalia,* a compendium of teachings on the spiritual life compiled by St. Nicodemus of the Holy Mountain at the end of eighteenth century. Among the most influential publications in Orthodox history, the *Philokalia* was instrumental, through its translation from Greek into Slavonic and Russian, in introducing the spirituality of the desert into nineteenth-century Russia, and helped to produce a spiritual reawakening there. One of the traces of this awakening can be seen in the nineteenth century Russian spiritual classic, *The Way of a Pilgrim,* which was inspired at least in part by the *Philokalia*'s interpretation of desert spirituality. The desert impulse penetrated deeply into one of the greatest of the modern Russian saints, Seraphim of Sarov, who clearly modeled his life on the pattern of St. Antony of Egypt. And, indirectly at least, the spirit of the desert passed from Seraphim to Dostoyevsky, where it breathed life into the memorable character of the starets Zosima in *The Brothers Karamazov.*[12]

In the contemporary era, the legacy of the desert continues to be taken up and expressed in various ways, through renewal movements in religious life based on a "return to the desert," through a growing number of scholarly studies on various aspects of desert spirituality, and through the development of contemporary spiritualities inspired by the desert. The lonely witness of Charles de Foucault in the desert of Algeria in the early part of this century motivated the experiments of the Little Brothers and Sisters of Jesus, who combine a serious and demanding contemplative life with work alongside the poor and the dispossessed. Since at least the time of the Second Vatican Council, contemplative religious orders such as the Benedictines and Cistercians have increasingly looked to the spirituality of the early desert experience in an attempt to reinvigorate and reinterpret contemporary monastic spirituality.[13] This renewed interest in desert spirituality has inspired various concrete attempts within the monastic world to make that spirituality a more integral part of the contemporary monastic experience. The American Cistercian monk Thomas Merton was led, through his attraction to a more solitary, eremetical form of monastic life, to explore the practice and spirituality of early desert monasticism. Largely through his efforts, the eremetical dimension has been restored to contemporary cenobitic monasticism. Another expression of the reintegration of the desert charism within monasticism has been the development of new monastic experiments, in both Eastern and Western Christianity, based on a return to the spirit of the desert.[14] During the last twenty-five years, for example, the ancient Coptic monasteries in Egypt have experienced a dramatic revival under the guidance of Matta El-Meskeen, who has inspired the renewal precisely by returning to and reappropriating the spirit of the primitive desert movement.[15]

The spirit of the desert has also fired the imagination of a broader audience of contemporary thinkers, including historians of spirituality, social historians of late antiquity, and contemporary writers on Christian spirituality. Specific aspects of the desert tradition have been explored at some depth by historians of spirituality, providing us with a better understanding of the inner world of monasticism. Among the more prominent aspects of early monasticism which have been the focus of serious study are the practice of discernment of spirits and spiritual direction,[16] the experience of *penthos* and the gift of tears,[17] the role of the master-disciple relationship,[18] and the tradition of prayer in the desert, especially the prayer of the heart.[19] Social historians have devoted considerable attention to locating early monasticism within the religious world of late antiquity and particularly within its social milieu.[20] Numerous contemporary writers on spirituality have noted the enduring power of the desert tradition and have made use of some of its insights to address critical moral and spiritual questions.[21] Thomas Merton has made an especially prominent contribution in retrieving for contemporary spirituality elements of the desert tradition such as silence, solitude, and purity of heart. Interestingly, in Merton's hands the recovery of the spirituality of the desert has proved useful not only for redefining the meaning of contemporary Christian spirituality but also for building bridges with other spiritual traditions: when Merton and the great Zen scholar D. T. Suzuki embarked on their Zen-Christian dialogue, the desert fathers served as the interlocutors.[22]

This brief survey testifies to the depth and diversity of the legacy of the desert movement, to its tenacious hold on the human imagination, and to the manifold ways in which its spirit has been revived across the ages. As Hausherr has noted: "If you study the history of spirituality or the spiritual life of the Church, you will find that each time that there is a spiritual renewal in the Church, the desert fathers are present."[23] Implicit in the esteem that the desert movement has enjoyed throughout the history of the Christian tradition has been a conviction that it was a genuinely Christian, deeply human, and biblical movement filled with enduring wisdom.

The Desert Legacy Scorned

Not all observers of the early monastic movement have seen it as a positive force in the world. Its critics have maintained, for a variety of reasons, that the whole movement was deeply flawed, even fundamentally misconceived. Two criticisms of early monasticism have been particularly important. Some have argued that the early monastic movement was antisocial and anticultural, thereby contributing notably to the decay of humane culture and civilization in late antiquity. Others have criticized early monasticism as being profoundly unbiblical. They charge that the monks misread the biblical message of salvation, either through ignorance, conscious manipulation, or the influence of heterodox thought. Because these critiques have influenced contemporary assessments of the character and significance of early monasticism they are worth examining further.

Almost from the beginning the desert monks had their critics. From the perspective of educated pagans like the Emperor Julian or Eunapius of Sardis, the monks were miscreants who had abandoned the way of the gods and refused to share in the burdens of society. To Eunapius, a Greek rhetorician and historiographer, the monks were "men in appearance, but led the lives of swine."[24] Even some Christians, such as the well educated Synesius of Cyrene, saw them as uncultured boors, whose way of life was so utterly bereft of the refinements of traditional *paideia* that their religious search appeared ludicrous.[25] For these contemporary critics of the desert fathers, the heart of their complaint was that monasticism had arisen outside of and even in opposition to the traditional *culture* of the Roman world, which was central to its understanding and practice of piety.[26]

A millennium later, Edward Gibbon extended and sharpened this criticism into the extraordinarily powerful indictment of monasticism found in the thirty-seventh chapter of his *The History of the Decline and Fall of the Roman Empire*. The twenty pages Gibbon devotes to the early monks constitute, as Henry Chadwick notes, "one of the most strident specimens of sustained invective and cold hatred to be found in English prose."[27] Gibbon characterized monks as individuals, who, "inspired by a savage enthusiasm which represents man as a criminal and God as a tyrant . . . embraced a life of misery as the price of eternal happiness." Moreover, Gibbon sweepingly asserted that "a cruel, unfeeling temper has distinguished the monks of every age and country."[28] Although it is true to say that Gibbon failed to distinguish between abuses of the ascetic ideal and the ideal itself, his complaint against monasticism ran so deep as to make such a distinction meaningless. As Chadwick points out, "The underlying axiom of Gibbon's objection is that the ascetic ideal makes people so otherworldly as to be of no use in this world."[29] Nor was Gibbon alone in his bitter denunciation of monasticism. W. E. H. Lecky, writing at the end of the nineteenth century, revealed, in his otherwise measured *History of European Morals,* the full weight of his contempt for the monastic rejection of the classical ideal. For Lecky, the monk was "a hideous, sordid, and emaciated maniac, without knowledge, without patriotism, without natural affection, passing his life in a long routine of useless and atrocious self-torture, and quailing before the ghastly phantoms of his delirious brain, [and] had become the ideal of nations which had known the writings of Plato and Cicero and the lives of Socrates and Cato."[30]

Such attitudes toward monasticism are important to note in the context of the present discussion because they helped to shape the common contemporary perception of the age in which monasticism emerged and paganism declined as one characterized by "a failure of nerve." This idea, which was given currency early in this century by the classical scholar Gilbert Murray, but which actually derives from Gibbon's editor, J. B. Bury, has influenced much of the modern discussion of religion in late antiquity. In particular, it has contributed to the perception of the monastic movement as part of a broad decay pervading the ancient world.[31] Thus E. R. Dodds, after cataloguing case after case of the ascetical extremes of the desert fathers, felt compelled to ask, incredulous and exasperated: "Where did all this madness come from?" He concluded that it was a sign that "a strong injection of fanatical rigorism had been absorbed into the Church's system. It lingered there like a slow poison. . . ."[32] Dodds' criticism of monasticism, while less fierce than Gibbon's, nevertheless reveals a similar perception of the early monks: they had given into the forces of the irrational and had squandered the gifts of ancient civilization.

A different kind of complaint arose from within the Christian tradition itself: early monasticism was unbiblical. This criticism has endured, influencing the negative perception of early monasticism within much of Christianity and assessments of early monasticism by certain modern and contemporary scholars. For the reformers, especially Wycliffe, Luther, and Melanchthon, one of the major problems with monasticism was that it was not rooted in Scripture. Nowhere in Scripture, they argued, was there any warrant either for the ideas underlying monasticism or for the way of life practiced by the monks. This complaint against early monasticism almost certainly owed something to the Reformers' own observation of late medieval monasticism; it had, by this time, lost even the few virtues it possessed in the beginning, namely simplicity and poverty. Now, according to Wycliffe, monks were "turned into lords of this world, most idle in God's travail."[33]

The Reformation's critique of monasticism has had a strong influence, especially among Protestant historians, on perceptions of the character of early monasticism. One of the effects of this critique has been a tendency among certain historians to assume that a movement filled with such strange practices and ideas simply could not have sprung from the pure soil of the Gospels. This assumption of the lack of a scriptural basis has led some scholars to search for the primary cause or inspiration of the monastic movement in non-Christian sources.[34] But the strongest effect of this view has been the residual perception that it represents a deeply flawed and misguided moment in the history of Christianity. This in turn has contributed to the tendentious and polemical attitudes that have often characterized modern and contemporary discussions of early monasticism. In such an atmosphere, it has been difficult to assess accurately and fairly either the religious significance of early monasticism or the place of Scripture within it. The deep gulf of misunderstanding which has often separated modern interpreters of early monasticism can be seen in the writings of two figures, one Catholic and the other Protestant.

Hans Lietzmann illustrates well the tendentious attitude which has sometimes characterized the Protestant approach towards monasticism and especially towards its use of Scripture. Speaking of the practice of memorization of Scripture in early monasticism, Lietzmann says, "It should of course be understood that this learning by heart was nothing more than a superficial

accomplishment, ascetic in character, a kind of weaving and mental matting.
. . . The mechanical memorization did not penetrate the heart; it gave indeed only the faintest biblical tinge to the world of ideas in which the monks
lived.'' For Lietzmann, early monasticism was barely Christian, and certainly not rooted in Scripture. He considers Christian the monks' conviction
that sin separates a person from God and can only be overcome by prayer
to God in his mercy. Beyond this, he says, monasticism ''has nothing more
than external relations with the Christian religion.''[35] This rather crude
judgment against early monasticism has its counterpart in the equally superficial, though perhaps more creative, defense of the monastic achievement
on the part of the Catholic writer, Count De Montalembert. Writing for
clearly apologetic purposes, he asserts—without really demonstrating—that
monasticism, far from being unbiblical, is actually found within Scripture!
For him, the example of the early monks and their response to call of the
Gospel to renounce everything (Mt 19:21) is ''proof'' of the fundamentally
evangelical character of monasticism. He goes further however and declares
that, ''governed by these words of the Gospel, the most illustrious fathers,
doctors, and councils, have declared religious life to be founded by Jesus
Christ himself, and first practised by His apostles. . . . We know with
certainty, by the narrative of the Acts of the Apostles, that the first Christians lived as the monks have lived since.''[36] This was neither a new argument—John Cassian had advanced a similar claim many centuries earlier—
nor a particularly convincing one. However it illustrates well the tendency
on the part of some to assert, in an uncritical fashion and without real evidence, the biblical roots of the monastic movement. Although neither of
these assessments can be taken entirely seriously as an account of the influence of Scripture upon early monasticism, they reveal the kind of polemical
attitudes which have so often obfuscated discussions of the origins and purpose of monasticism in the past. If we are to make our way through the
haze of such rhetoric to a clearer understanding of the desert hermeneutic,
we must carefully reconsider the evidence, and perhaps even develop a new
approach to the question.

Reassessing the Desert Legacy

Both of the critiques of early monasticism which we have noted—that it is
anticultural and that it has no foundation in Scripture—have exerted a strong
influence upon the way the early monastic movement has been perceived.
These critiques should be kept in mind as the book proceeds, for I suggest
that a careful examination of early monasticism according to the testimony
of *The Sayings of the Desert Fathers* reveals quite a different picture: not

only did Scripture shape early monasticism's growth and development, but the early monastic movement can be said to represent a distinctive and profound cultural achievement. The increased attention that has been given to early monasticism in contemporary scholarship has contributed to a better understanding of the place of Scripture within early monasticism and of the particular culture which developed within that world.

The polemical attitudes toward early monasticism discussed above have subsided somewhat in recent decades; one of the results is that scholars have begun to reassess the place of the Bible in the early monastic movement. Although no consensus has been reached on questions regarding the origins of monasticism,[37] a growing number of scholars have come to agree that Scripture played a central role in its formation and continuing growth. This has been demonstrated both in general works on early monasticism[38] and studies of particular monastic authors and texts.[39] Evidence has also begun to accumulate with regard to the *Sayings* that, in spite of the apparently meager number of actual citations of Scripture found there, the place and function of Scripture within this literature is highly significant.[40] The growing consensus on this issue suggests that primitive monasticism cannot adequately be understood apart from a consideration of the place of Scripture in its formation and ongoing life. However, in spite of the increased clarity regarding Scripture's role, we still do not have a completely satisfying portrait of this aspect of the early monastic world. This is due in part to the fact that the discussion and analysis of the issue thus far has been, for very good reasons, introductory, exploratory, and fragmentary. Because of the diverse questions and assumptions that have guided these various studies, we lack consistency and clarity of perspective regarding both the appropriate questions and the methods for exploring this issue. Also, because the question has yet to be adequately situated either within the history of the interpretation of Scripture or within the broader concerns and issues of the fourth-century world, the picture of the desert hermeneutic lacks depth and complexity. We still possess only a line drawing. One of the ways the picture can be filled out is by paying closer attention to how the interpretive process actually works—how human beings derive meaning from texts.

Hermeneutics and Desert Spirituality

The subject of this book is hermeneutics and holiness, an examination of how the early desert monks interpreted Scripture and how their approach to interpretation shaped their search for holiness. Since questions of interpretation figure so prominently, it is worth looking closely at some of the primary hermeneutical issues which confronted the early monks and which confront us as we try to understand their world. A dialogue between the ancient hermeneutic of the desert monks and some of the insights of contemporary hermeneutics can help to illuminate these issues. Contemporary hermeneutical thought has provided some useful categories for thinking about what it means to interpret a text; it can, if used carefully, help to illuminate the way in which the early monastic movement interpreted the Scriptures. However, a word is perhaps necessary about the possibilities and limits of such an approach. One cannot use contemporary hermeneutics as a rigid, artificial grid into which to force the questions and issues of early monasticism, nor should it be applied anachronistically to the desert literature. Such an approach would provide more distortion than clarity about the early monastic world. What can be done is to use contemporary hermeneutics tentatively and experimentally, as a heuristic aid to help explain what is present in the monastic literature and as a means of responding to the questions which the texts themselves raise. This should be understood in terms of the way interpretive models are employed in the natural sciences. A model in this sense is a particular, partial, and imaginative way of approaching a question or a problem so that it can be seen in a new light and given greater clarity.[41] The use of a hermeneutical model in relation to the desert monks' approach to Scripture can do just that: shed new light on the questions raised by the interpretation of Scripture in the early monastic world.

Why Hermeneutics?

Any encounter with words immediately raises questions of interpretation. If the words are familiar to us, close to us in time, culture, and language, the questions may not make themselves felt very sharply at first, since it is easy to take such words at face value. Yet even here we are confronted with basic questions of comprehension and meaning, sometimes deceptively subtle if the words appear familiar. If we are dealing with words from the past, which are fixed in an ancient text, the questions fairly leap out at us, for already in the act of translation one is made aware of the need for interpretation in passing from one language world to another. The more closely we read such a text, the clearer it becomes that we need not only to learn another language, we must somehow find a way of entering into and coming to grips with a completely different world. This recognition of the linguistic and historical distance between ourselves and an ancient text reveals the real depth and breadth of the interpretive task. It suggests that we must not only familiarize ourselves with the basic geography of that other world, we must also find a way of translating meaning from that world to our own. Such a translation, if it is to be viable, must find a way of bringing our world into dialogue with that other world, so that we can experience growth and new understanding. To use the metaphor of travel, imaginative interpretation means that it is possible to return from a visit to a foreign land with more than vague impressions of the strangeness of the place. One can in fact return from such an encounter transformed and with a new vision of one's own world.

These considerations help to suggest why in any encounter with an ancient text, one must pass through the long detour of hermeneutics in order to come to understanding. This applies, though in different ways, both to the modern person who wishes to interpret ancient texts from early desert monasticism and also to the ancient person, in this case the desert monk, who wished to interpret the Scriptures. For the modern person, such a hermeneutical detour is necessary in large part because of the great distance that separates our world from the world of early monasticism. For the monk who was interested in interpreting Scripture, the hermeneutical detour was also necessary, not because of his consciousness of the historical distance separating him from Scripture—there was in fact very little sense of distance for him—but because Scripture presented a world of meaning that demanded interpretation. Such a detour is necessary for any human being who would come to understanding because we do not experience the world immediately. Rather, because our whole existence is mediated to us through *language* and *history*, that existence demands interpretation.[42] We have no choice but to interpret our world and we must interpret it from the particular historical place that we occupy.

That the question of language has come to occupy such an important place in contemporary hermeneutics has been due in part to a growing realization that a human being simply has no grasp of existence apart from language; that "language belongs to the closest neighborhood of man's being"; that only language "enables man to be the living being he is."[43] This is because language and apprehension—at least that apprehension which can be articulated—arise together in the mind.[44] Nor is this intimate connection between language and understanding simply a matter of understanding how language works—the principles of language, as it were. Rather, we "understand through language."[45] And, because we come to language through a language tradition, our self-understanding is indirect and comes into being through our encounter with fixed expressions from the past.[46] Self-understanding is historical not only in the sense that one must arrive at it by interpreting historically inherited texts, but in the sense that one must understand texts against the horizon of one's own position in time and history. In this sense, it can be said that "meaning always stands in a horizonal context that stretches into the past and into the future."[47]

To understand what these mediations of language and history mean in terms of the questions raised by this book, an important qualification needs to be made concerning the word *text*. Although we are examining here the early monastic interpretation of the texts of Scripture, such terminology presents certain problems. Text implies words which are written and which must be read to be understood. However, this is somewhat misleading for, as paradoxical as it may seem, not all texts are written nor are all texts read. It is important to take seriously the notion of *oral texts*, that is, texts which exist primarily not as "fixed expressions" on the pages of a book, but as words in the minds and hearts of certain persons who on occasion utter those words to others. Such oral texts have a different character from written texts, in that they are not fixed expressions encountered through the act of reading but are by their very nature encountered only in the presence of a living mediator through an aural experience. Both written and oral texts were important for the desert fathers and, in the hermeneutical model I am sketching here, the presence of both kinds of texts is assumed.[48]

Hermeneutics and the Desert Hermeneutic

There are several particular ideas arising from contemporary hermeneutics which can help to illuminate the use of Scripture in the desert. It was suggested earlier that we understand "through language." Yet, what *happens* in this process of understanding? What is it that we come to understand?

First, it can be said that language mediates or discloses being to us: "[I]t is in words and language that things first come into being and are."[49] Language unveils what was previously shrouded in darkness. The disclosive power of language suggests something significant about the interpretive process and our part in it—that interpretation is a response to an address: "[I]t is language that speaks. Man first speaks when, and only when, he responds to language by listening to its appeal. . . . [L]anguage beckons us."[50] Especially powerful linguistic disclosures have been described as "Word Events." Language is said to take on the character of an event when it "sets something in motion," when it transcends the boundaries of a mere statement and becomes an address.[51] And "when word happens rightly, existence is illumined."[52] It was axiomatic for the desert fathers that the Word was one of the fundamental ordering realities under whose authority they placed themselves. Theirs was a primarily oral culture, and words were living things. Both the Word of God and the word of the elder carried this authority and burst forth in "events" of revelatory power. The concrete power of these "word events" can be seen in their effect on those who felt their full force: such words invariably moved them and pierced them to the depths of their heart, often relieving them of the terrible burdens that weighed them down, though sometimes revealing to them with shattering clarity the shallowness of their convictions or the duplicity of their motives. Word events transformed their lives.

Walter Ong has suggested why our literate bias makes it difficult for us to understand how powerful language is in oral cultures: "Deeply typographic folk forget to think of words as primarily oral, as events, and hence as necessarily powered: for them, words tend rather to be assimilated to things, 'out there' on a flat surface. Such 'things' . . . are not actions, but are in a radical sense dead, though subject to dynamic resurrection."[53] The desert fathers, however, experienced words as events. It would be no exaggeration to say that the word event stands as one of the key experiences in desert spirituality.

Texts, however, do not act upon us as a "pure event," addressed only to the will. They are also addressed to the mind—what Amos Wilder refers to as "the will instructed by truth"—and convey meaning.[54] An awareness of what Paul Ricoeur calls the "dialectic of event and meaning" helps to clarify the relationship between the capacity of language to act as event and endure as meaning.[55] Ricoeur maintains that while the dynamic event-character of discourse is indeed important, its meaning must also be recognized and grasped. Understanding happens not only in the fleeting event, but in the meaning which endures: "Just as language, by being actualized in discourse, surpasses itself as system, and realizes itself as event, so too discourse, by entering the process of understanding, surpasses itself as event and becomes meaning."[56] This distinction between language as event and language as meaning allows us to appreciate how the meaning of a text is able to endure through time. Another distinction, that of sense and reference, helps to explain how we derive meaning from a text, and how such a text can be said to *project a world*. The sense can be considered the "what" of discourse while the reference is the "about what." The sense is immanent to the discourse and has to do with the ideal structure of a sentence; the reference expresses the movement in which language transcends itself and expresses a world. The reference has to do with the truth value of language, its claims to express reality or truth, something to which one can give assent. These possibilities of meaning can be understood as the project of the text, the outline of a new way-of-being-in-the-world which the text projects ahead of itself. The challenge of interpretation is precisely to engage that project or world.

In the desert, there was a clear sense that the words from Scripture and from the elders transcended the limited scope of the "event" in which they were initially encountered and endured in meaning. And there is no doubt that both the words of Scripture and the words of the elders projected a "world of meaning" which the desert fathers sought to enter. The call to sell everything, give the proceeds to the poor, and follow the Gospel (Mt 19:21), the exhortation never to let the sun set on one's anger (Eph 4:25), the commandment to love: these texts shaped the lives of the desert fathers in a particular way and projected a "world of meaning" which they strove to appropriate. Holiness in the desert meant giving concrete shape to this world of possibilities stretching ahead of the sacred texts by interpreting them and appropriating them into one's life.

The possibilities for entering into the worlds projected by the texts are literally endless. Texts have, in this sense, an endless *surplus of meaning*. The reference reaches its full potential for meaning precisely through being fixed (usually by being written down, though this has its equivalent with oral texts). This process leads to what Ricoeur calls the "semantic autonomy of the text." The author's intention and the meaning of the text cease to coincide, and "[t]he text's career escapes the finite horizon lived by its author. What the text means now matters more than what the author meant when he wrote it."[57] Thus a text, especially a powerfully evocative text, has the capacity continually to mean more, to overflow in an excess or surplus of meaning. A text never simply "means" one thing but continues to unfold new possibilities of meaning.

How and where these possibilities of meaning endured is one of the most interesting facets of the desert hermeneutic. Because there was so much emphasis in the desert on practice, on living with integrity, the monks interpreted Scripture primarily by putting it into practice. In the desert, Scripture's surplus of meaning endured not in the form of commentaries or homilies but in acts and gestures, in lives of holiness transformed by dialogue with Scripture. The sacred texts continued to mean more not only to those who read or encountered the texts but also to those encountering the holy ones who had come to embody the texts. The holy person became a new text and a new object of interpretation.[58]

Beyond these considerations of language and the language event, it is important to note the dynamics of the interpretive response, in particular the openness of the interpreter to what is being revealed through that language. Interpretation can be described as a "helping of the language event itself to happen" and the means by which one enters into the world of meaning projected by the text.[59] Because the meaning of a text can be understood only through the interpretive act, it is worth examining some of the elements which govern the interpreter's approach to the text. The temporal distance between the text and the interpreter requires that the interpreter recognize his or her *prejudices* as an influential factor in understanding the text. Especially significant in this regard is what Gadamer calls "effective historical consciousness." Meaning is always situated by a past which involves us in an "effective history" of inherited meanings. Whether one is aware of it or not, this effective history "determines in advance both what seems . . . worth enquiring about and what will appear as an object of investigation. . . ."[60] The prejudices derived from each person's unique historical existence are not barriers to understanding, but the very means by which meaning is initially opened up to a person. "The historicity of our existence entails that prejudices, in the literal sense of the word, constitute the initial directedness of our whole ability to experience. Prejudices are biases of our openness to the world."[61] This recognition of the productive potential of the interests, concerns, and questions one brings to a text suggests that in an encounter with a classic text, meaning emerges, slowly, tentatively, and in terms determined to a great extent by the questions addressed to the text. As the historian Marc Bloch suggests, "Even those texts . . . which seem the clearest and most accommodating will speak only when they are properly questioned."[62]

In what ways did "effective historical consciousness" and "prejudices" influence the desert fathers' interpretation of the sacred texts? At first glance, it appears that the desert fathers did not exhibit an "effective historical consciousness." For them, as for other ancient interpreters of the Bible, Scripture was inspired and existed on a single historical plane. (There is evidence that the desert fathers thought of themselves as being on the same level as the figures and events of the sacred texts). However, in spite of this "flattening" of the Bible, the monks had to wrestle with the meaning of texts that came to them in particular situations and were mediated through a tradition. They brought to Scripture a general pre-understanding and certain prejudices arising out of their life and experiences. These prejudices influenced not only which texts they found particularly significant, but also how they treated those texts. For example, understanding how the probing light of solitude searched out the frailties of the human heart helps to explain why the monks focused so much attention on biblical texts about the need for humility and mercy. And knowing how highly the desert fathers valued integrity of words and actions sheds light on their reticence to engage in speculation about the meaning of Scripture and their strong commitment to put the texts into practice. Understanding how the monks' biases determined their use of and attitudes toward Scripture helps to clarify their sometimes tendentious or ingenious interpretations. An examination of the factors contributing to the interpretive process in the desert can provide not only understanding of the desert hermeneutic but also insight into larger issues of desert spirituality.

It is easy to see the propriety of using the image of a *conversation* as a model for the whole interpretive process.[63] To enter a conversation one must allow the question, the subject matter, the world opened up in front of the text, to assume primacy. This does not mean that one should suspend all ''suspicion'' regarding the text, for this too can be productive of meaning.[64] It does, however, imply taking a certain risk. When one allows oneself to be carried away by the subject matter and to enter into the back-and-forth movement of the conversation itself, we say that ''understanding happens.'' The fact that we speak of it as ''happening'' to us implies something important about the process of coming to understanding: it occurs not as the result of personal achievement, but through surrendering to the movement of the conversation.[65] New understanding or awareness can emerge from the interpretive conversation with the text because, once the claim made upon us by the text is recognized, and we enter into conversation with it, a *fusion of horizons* becomes possible. This is the formation of a complete horizon in which the limited horizons of text and interpreter are fused into a common view of the subject matter—the meaning—with which both are concerned.[66] In this model, neither the text nor the interpreter is a static object. Both are realities-in-process. The ''fusion of horizons'' suggests a dynamic, interactive understanding of interpretation in which the constantly expanding relationship of text and interpreter creates endless new possibilities of meaning, sometimes described as as *hermeneutical circle*. In this circular process, each new act of interpretation opens up new horizons of meaning and leads to an altered sense of self and of the text, which in turn leads to further opportunitiés for understanding from that new perspective.

These images of conversation, fusion of horizons, and the hermeneutical circle can be helpful in addressing certain questions about the approach to Scripture in the desert. At first sight it seems that the authority of the sacred texts and the words of the elders in the desert were so strong that submission or obedience rather than conversation was the rule. Indeed, conversation about almost any subject, but especially about the sacred texts, was positively discouraged! Yet in a sense real conversation did take place in the desert. The desert fathers show themselves again and again willing to enter into a risky conversation with the texts, to suspend their former understanding of the world, and to allow themselves to be ''taken up'' into the world of the sacred texts. One of the central dramas in the desert literature concerns how those who have come to the desert will allow their horizons to be expanded and changed by the horizon of the sacred text. It is at this moment of transformation that the meaning of a text is realized, and this realization largely determines how holiness was understood in the desert. The texts themselves, moreover, were transformed in the hands of these unusual interpreters. One often sees the more obvious meaning of a text suspended or superseded in an effort to push to a deeper level of meaning. Thus the "conversation" appears to have been genuine.

The notion of a hermeneutical circle can help us to understand the dynamic of experience and interpretation that existed in the desert. The desert fathers believed that only those with experience could adequately interpret the sacred texts. They considered discernment and self-knowledge essential for enabling the discourse of the text to continue in a new discourse. Another twist in the spiral is seen in the conviction that because the texts are holy, only a holy one—the one with experience—can properly interpret them. Yet because one becomes holy precisely through practicing the texts, those without the same experience must continue to practice, and become purified so they may enter more deeply into the world of the text. Similarly, prayer and the sacred texts mutually inform one another, prayer adding to the understanding of the texts and the texts feeding and deepening the experience of prayer.

A final dimension of the interpretive process worth considering is the transformation that occurs through praxis. Although it is usually said that we interpret the text, it is also true that a text can "interpret us." We not only read the text, but "are read" by it. In allowing ourselves to experience the claim of text in this way, we can be taken up, however briefly, into the world projected before it. There "we experience the challenge, often the shock of a greater reality than the everyday self, a reality . . . that transforms us." [67] The recognition that the risk of interpretation can bring about transformation suggests the importance of praxis or *applicatio*. It has been noted that *applicatio* is intrinsic, not extrinsic to interpretation. [68] This means that interpretation, if it is to be complete, must be understood as always involving praxis and leading to some form of transformation. [69] The desert fathers understood this. Not only did they courageously open themselves to the claims of the sacred texts, but they sought at every turn to put those texts into practice. Words were expressed in lives. They manifested what George Steiner has said is at the heart of interpretation: execution. "An interpreter . . . is, in essence, an executant, one who 'acts out' the material before him so as to give it intelligible life. Interpretation is to the largest possible degree, lived." [70] Because of this, interpretation for the desert fathers always involved the possibility of personal and communal transformation. Holiness in the desert was defined, finally, by how deeply a person allowed himself or herself to be transformed by the words of Scripture.

Notes

1. The question of the date and composition of these texts is taken up below in chapter 3. Note that the main collections of the *Sayings* as we now have them, while almost certainly having been "composed" at a later date than texts such as the *Vita Antonii,* contain much material from the earliest stages of the monastic tradition. The issue of what to call the early desert dwellers is a difficult one. "Desert fathers" is a traditional term, and it is for the most part descriptively accurate of the early desert movement: desert monasticism *was,* after all, a predominantly male movement. Still there were women in the desert, some important and influential, known as "ammas" and who are sometimes referred to as desert mothers. Yet the attempt to balance traditional nomenclature, historical accuracy, and contemporary sensibilities regarding gender presents real difficulties. For instance, more "inclusive" terms, such as "desert Christians" or "desert fathers and mothers," have their own problems. In most individual cases, the phrase "desert fathers and mothers" is not descriptively accurate: the great majority of the stories are about the desert *fathers.* Thus in most instances, using the expression "desert fathers and mothers" to refer to the subjects of a particular story or set of stories would be misleading: there are no mothers to be found. Using the expression "desert Christians" is a possibility, except that it omits a word which had great significance in early Egyptian monasticism. As Lucien Regnault points out, "Abba," father, had a particular, almost technical meaning among the monks, conveying not merely a person of the male sex, but someone whose long experience in the desert and consequent authority had earned him this name. Thus not all of the male monks dwelling in the desert, were, strictly speaking "desert fathers." Cf. Lucien Regnault, "Des pères toujours vivants," *La Vie Spirituelle* 140 (1986): 191–93.

In spite of these difficulties, I have made some attempt to use more inclusive language. I refer to the body of texts under consideration by one of its traditional names, *The Sayings of the Desert Fathers.* When referring to individual stories, I distinguish clearly between those about men and those about women. When speaking of the desert dwellers as a whole or as a group, I use a number of expressions interchangeably: elders (an inclusive term which can refer to men or women); desert monks (also capable of being understood as an inclusive term, referring to "monk" in its root meaning as "one who dwells alone"); the traditional term "desert fathers"; and "desert fathers and mothers."

2. *VA* 93 [*PG* 26: 972B]: *The Life of Antony and the Letter to Marcellinus,* trans. R. C. Gregg (New York: Paulist Press, 1980), 98–99. Doubt has been cast as to the Athanasian authorship of the *VA.* For a discussion of this question, see R. Draguet, ed., *La vie primitive de S. Antoine conservée en syriaque,* CSCO 417, *Scriptores Syri* 184 (Louvain: CSCO, 1980); T. D. Barnes, "Angel of Light or Mystic Initiate? The Problem of the *Life of Antony,*" *JTS,* n.s., 37 (1986): 353–68; A. Louth, "St. Athanasius and the Greek *Life of Antony,*" *JTS,* n.s., 39 (1988): 504–09.

3. Augustine, *Confessions,* VIII:6; translated with an introduction by R. S. Pine-Coffin (Baltimore: Penguin Books, 1961), 166–68.

4. T. Fry, ed., *The Rule of St. Benedict,* in Latin and English with notes (Collegeville, MN: The Liturgical Press, 1981), 296–97.

5. See Jean-Claude Guy, "Les *Apophthegmata Patrum,*" in *Théologie de la vie monastique,* ed. G. Lemaître (Paris: Aubier, 1961), 77. Guy notes, "The numerous examples which we possess of these 'Paterika' serving in the Middle Ages as refectory reading or as private spiritual reading in the monasteries under the authority of the Rule [of St. Benedict]. . . ."

6. See Jean Leclercq, O.S.B., *The Love of Learning and the Desire for God* (New York: Fordham University Press, 1961), 125. See also idem, "S. Antoine dans la tradition monastique médiévale," *Studia Anselmiana* 38 (1956): 229–47.

7. On the influence of the desert literature, especially the *Homilies of St. Macarius,* upon the Pietists, see E. Benz, "Littérature du désert chez les Evangéliques allemandes et les Piétistes de Pennsylvanie," *Irénikon* 51 (1978): 338–57. On the use of the *Lives of the Fathers* and the writings of Cassian by members of the *Devotio Moderna* movement, see E. Novelli, "Littérature du désert dans le renouveau catholique au début de l'époque moderne," *Irénikon* 51 (1978): 5–45. On the influence of the desert literature, especially the *Homilies of St. Macarius,* on John Wesley, see G. Wakefield, "La littérature du désert chez John Wesley," *Irénikon* 51 (1978): 155–70.

8. G. Flaubert, *La tentation de saint Antoine,* ed. R. Dumesnil (Paris: Les Belles-Lettres, 1940). Lucien Regnault, in *La vie quotidienne des pères du désert en Égypte au IVe siècle* (Paris: Hachette, 1990), notes: "Flaubert, who claimed to be free from all prejudice and all belief, was literally obsessed for more than thirty years by the person of Antony, and one can say that the work which he has devoted to him was the work of his entire life" (13).

9. The Princeton Art Index records at least 302 representations of St. Antony the Great. See O. Meinardus, *Monks and Monasteries of the Egyptian Desert* (Cairo: The American University of Cairo Press, 1961), 15. On the cult of St. Antony, see S. Chaleur, "Le culte de St. Antoine," *Bulletin de l'Institut des études coptes* 1 (1958): 31–41.

10. T. Špidlík shows in his systematic treatment of the spirituality of the Christian East how pervasive the influence of the desert has been there. *The Spirituality of the Christian East: A Systematic Handbook,* trans. A. P. Gythiel (Kalamazoo, MI: Cistercian Publications, 1986).

11. On the influence of the desert on early Russian monasticism, see H. Iswolsky, *Christ in Russia* (Milwaukee: Bruce, 1960), 181.

12. *The Way of the Pilgrim,* trans. R. M. French (New York: Seabury Press, 1965); on St. Seraphim and the desert, see V. Zander, *St. Seraphim of Sarov* (London: SPCK, 1975), 15.

13. The Cistercian monastery of Bellefontaine in France has undertaken the series "Spiritualité Orientale," devoted largely to the publication of texts and studies of primitive monasticism.

14. Christ in the Desert Monastery in New Mexico is one of the most notable examples in the United States. There is also a community of French Catholic monks,

living in 'Ein Kerem near Jerusalem, who have modeled their life upon the primitive monastic life characteristic of early monasticism in Palestine. And the ecumenical French monastic community of Taizé clearly has drawn much of its inspiration from the desert tradition.

15. An introduction to the spirituality of the contemporary Egyptian desert may be found in: Matthew the Poor, *The Communion of Love*, introduction by H. Nouwen (New York: St. Vladimir, 1984).

16. I. Hausherr, S. J., *Direction spirituelle en orient d'autrefois*. Orientalia Christiana Analecta 144 (Rome: Pontificium Institutum Studiorum Orientalum, 1955); Andrew Hamilton, "Spiritual Direction in the Apophthegmata," *Colloquium* 15 (1983): 31–38; Benedicta Ward, "Spiritual Direction in the Desert Fathers," *The Way* 24 (January 1984): 61–70; Joseph T. Lienhard, "On 'Discernment of Spirits' in the Early Church," *Theological Studies* 41 (1980): 505–29.

17. I. Hausherr, S. J., *Penthos: The Doctrine of Compunction in the Christian East*, trans. A Hufstader (Kalamazoo, MI: Cistercian Publications, 1982).

18. A. Louf, "Spiritual Fatherhood in the Literature of the Desert," in *Abba*, ed. J. R. Sommerfeldt (Kalamazoo, MI: Cistercian Publications, 1982); Thomas Merton, "The Spiritual Father in the Desert Tradition," *Cistercian Studies* 3 (1968): 2–23; François Neyt, "A Form of Charismatic Authority," *Eastern Churches Review* 6 (1974): 52–65.

19. A. Guillaumont, "The Jesus Prayer among the Monks of Egypt," *Eastern Churches Review* 6 (1974): 66–71; I. Hausherr, S. J., *Hésychasme et prière* (Rome: Pontificium Institutum Studiorum Orientalium, 1966); Lucien Regnault, "La prière continuelle *monologistos* dans les apophtegmes des Pères," *Irénikon* 47 (1974): 467–93; idem, "La prière de Jésus dans quelques apophtegmes conservés en arabe," *Irénikon* 52 (1979): 344–55.

20. Derwas J. Chitty's masterful study, *The Desert a City* (Oxford: Blackwell, 1966), has shown how central the story of the rise of monasticism was within the theological and ecclesiastical life of the church of late antiquity. The studies of Peter Brown have been particularly significant for highlighting the social dimensions of the monastic movement and for placing the life-world of early monasticism within the broader world of late antique society. See his "The Rise and Function of the Holy Man in Late Antiquity," *Journal of Roman Studies* 61 (1971): 80–101, reprinted with revisions in idem, *Society and the Holy in Late Antiquity* (Berkeley: University of California Press, 1982), 103–52. "The Philosopher and Society in Late Antiquity" (Colloquy 34, Center for Hermeneutical Studies, Berkeley, 1978); *The Making of Late Antiquity* (Cambridge: Harvard University Press, 1978). For detailed studies of two major figures in the monastic movement, see Philip Rousseau, *Ascetics, Authority, and the Church in the Age of Jerome and Cassian*, Oxford Historical Monographs (Oxford: Oxford University Press, 1978), and *Pachomius: The Making of a Community in Fourth-Century Egypt* (Berkeley: University of California Press, 1985).

21. R. Bondi, *To Love as God Loves: Conversations with the Early Church* (Philadelphia: Fortress Press, 1987); H. Nouwen, *The Way of the Heart* (New York:

Ballantine Books, 1981). The psychological insights of the desert monks have attracted particular attention; see A. Jones, *Soul Making: The Desert Way of Spirituality* (San Francisco: Harper and Row, 1985); G. M. Priestley, "Some Jungian Parallels to the Sayings of the Desert Fathers," *Cistercian Studies* 11 (1976): 102–23; C. N. Fisher, "Pain as Purgation: The Role of Pathologizing in the Life of the Mystic," *Pastoral Psychology* 27 (1978): 62–70; W. L. Walsh, S. J., "Reality Therapy and Spiritual Direction," *Review for Religious* 35 (1976): 372–85. For a probing discussion of the desert impulse from the Bible to T. S. Eliot, see A. Louth, *The Wilderness of God* (London: Darton, Longman and Todd, 1991).

22. Thomas Merton translated a small selection of *The Sayings of the Desert Fathers, with an engaging introduction to the spirituality of the desert*, in *The Wisdom of the Desert* (New York: New Directions, 1960); his dialogue with Suzuki is found in *Zen and the Birds of Appetite* (New York: New Directions, 1968), 99–141.

23. I. Hausherr, S. J. "Pour comprendre l'orient chrétien: La primauté du spirituel," *OCP* 33 (1967): 359.

24. On Eunapius's criticism of the monks, see Philostratus and Eunapius, *The Lives of the Sophists*, trans. W. C. Wright (London: William Heinemann, 1922), 422–25.

25. On Synesius's defense of a life of learning and the enjoyment of reasonable pleasures against the advocates of extreme asceticism, see Synesius of Cyrene, *Essays and Hymns: Letters*, ed. N. Terzaghi, trans. A. Fitzgerald (London: Oxford University Press, 1930), esp. *Dion* 7, 8; *Letters* 105, 154. See also Jay Bregman, *Synesius of Cyrene* (Berkeley: University of California Press, 1982), 128–34.

26. For further discussion of the different attitudes toward the practice of holiness which characterized monks and pagan philosophers, see chapter 2.

27. Henry Chadwick, "The Ascetic Ideal in the Early Church," in *Monks, Hermits and the Ascetic Tradition*, ed. W. J. Sheils (Oxford: Blackwell, 1985), 6.

28. E. Gibbon, *The History of the Decline and Fall of the Roman Empire*, 7 vols., ed. J. B. Bury (London: Methuen, 1896–1900), 4:57–75.

29. H. Chadwick, "The Ascetic Ideal," 7.

30. W. E. H. Lecky, *History of European Morals*, 3rd ed., rev. (New York: D. Appleton, 1895), 2:107.

31. See J. Pelikan, *The Excellent Empire* (San Francisco: Harper and Row, 1987), 88–89.

32. E. R. Dodds, *Pagan and Christian in an Age of Anxiety* (New York: W. W. Norton, 1965), 34. It is significant that Dodds cites examples mostly from the *Historia Lausiaca* of Palladius, one of the most hellenized and dualistic of the early monastic documents. He makes no distinction between the ascetical practices depicted there and the much more restrained and moderate picture presented by the *Sayings*. Robin Lane Fox, in his recent work *Pagans and Christians* (New York: Knopf, 1987), continues Dodd's legacy, portraying the complex Christian ascetic impulse as something that impoverishes human existence. Commenting on the ideal of virginity that lies behind much of early Christian asceticism, he says: "Virginity encouraged single-mindedness and dependence on God alone. . . . This praise of

simplicity and single-mindedness exalted human achievement by greatly limiting its scope. It denied man's capacity for living in complexity, for pursuing desirable ends which might not be mutually consistent, for enlarging his sympathies and own understanding by engaging in several pursuits at once. To return to a child-like Paradise was to exclude almost everything and understand next to nothing: 'single-mindedness' is a dangerous, enfeebling myth" (366).

33. Cited in H. Chadwick, "The Ascetic Ideal," 5; for Luther's critique of monasticism, see "Judgement on Monastic Vows," in D. Martin Luthers Werke. Kritische Gesamtausgabe (Weimar: Herman Böhlau, 1883–). 8:577ff. Chadwick, "The Ascetic Ideal," 4, raises a question regarding what is perhaps another source of the Reformers' discomfort regarding monasticism and the ascetic ideal: their extreme interpretation of the Augustinian legacy.

Is the full-blooded Augustinianism of Luther and Calvin at the root of the Protestant rejection of monasticism as an institution? Luther and Calvin understood justification sola fide sola gratia to mean that we may get to heaven exclusively on the ground of the imputation to us sinners of the righteousness of Christ, and used language which reduced to zero the role of human will in making any kind of offering to God or in making efforts to strive after goodness. They talked as if moral virtue is, to the justified, virtually effortless, a "necessary" outflow in which specific acts of will and intention had no part to play. . . . Is there some inherent conflict between ultra-Augustinian doctrines of grace and the quest for perfection through disciplined exercises . . . ?

It should be noted that there have been numerous more positive assessments of monasticism and the ascetic ideal within Protestantism. In modern German Lutheranism, the Berneuchen group has played an important part in restoring ascetic life lived under rule in community. The nineteenth-century Anglican monastic revival has been chronicled by A. M. Allchin, The Silent Rebellion: Anglican Religious Communities, 1845–1900 (London: SCM Press, 1958).

34. For a discussion of the effects of this critique, see Claude Peifer, "The Biblical Foundations of Monasticism," Cistercian Studies 12 (1972): 7–9. K. Heussi, Der Ursprung des Mönchtums (Tubingen: Mohr, 1936), 280–304, discusses a number of these theories about the origins of and influences upon early monasticism: the recluses of the temple of Serapis (Weingarten); the Buddhist monks and Jewish Therapeutae (Zöckler); the Stoics, Neo-Pythagoreans, and Neo-Platonists (Reitzenstein); heretical movements such as the Montanists and Encratites (Harnack). Wilhelm Bousset, an important interpreter of the desert literature from the early part of this century, saw the Apophthegmata largely in terms of the Greek world, including the mystery religions and Stoicism. For him, monasticism was only in some distant way influenced by the biblical tradition. (W. Bousset, Apophthegmata. Studien zur Geschichte des ältesten Mönchtums [Tübingen: Mohr, 1923]).

35. Hans Lietzmann, A History of the Early Church, vol. 4: The Era of the Church Fathers, trans. B. L. Woolf (London: Lutterworth, 1951), 153.

36. Comte Charles Forbes René de Tyron de Montalembert, The Monks of the West from St. Benedict to St. Bernard (New York: Kennedy, 1912), 169–70. He

indicates the unabashedly apologetic nature of his work in the dedication to Pope Pius IX: the work is "intended to vindicate the glory of one of the greatest institutions of Christianity [monasticism]. . . ." (iii).

37. On the question of monastic origins, see L. Bouyer, *La vie de S. Antoine: Essaie sur la spiritualité du monachisme primitif* (Bégrolles-en-Mauges: Bellefontaine, 1977); S. Rubenson, *The Letters of St. Antony: Origenist Theology, Monastic Tradition and the Making of a Saint* (Lund: Lund University Press, 1990); J. C. O'Neill, "The Origins of Monasticism," in, *The Making of Orthodoxy: Essays in Honor of Henry Chadwick*, ed. R. Williams (Cambridge: Cambridge University Press, 1989), 270–87; Graham Gould, "The *Life of Antony* and the Origins of Christian Monasticism in Fourth-Century Egypt," *Medieval History* 1 (1991): 3–11: J. R. Binns, "The Early Monasteries," *Medieval History* 1 (1991): 12–22.

38. K. Heussi and H. Dörries have supplied more positive judgments from the Protestant perspective on the place of the Bible in early monasticism. See Heussi, *Der Ursprung des Mönchtums*, 276; H. Dörries, "Die Bibel im ältesten Mönchtum," *Theologische Literaturzeitung* 72 (1947): 215–22; see also F. Bauer, "Die heilige Schrift bei den ältesten Mönchen des christlichen Altertums," *Theologie und Glaube* 17 (1925): 512–32; E. von Severus, "Zu den biblischen Grundlagen des benediktinischen Mönchtums," *Geist und Leben* 26 (1953): 113–22; Peifer, "The Biblical Foundations of Monasticism," 7–31; Jean-Claude Guy, "Écriture sainte et vie spirituelle," *DS* 4, cols. 159–64; G. Colombás, "La Biblia en la espiritualidad del monacato primitivo," *Yermo* 1 (1963): 3–20; 149–70; 271–86; 2 (1964): 3–14; 113–29.

39. On Cassian, see J.-C. Guy, *Jean Cassien: Vie et doctrine spirituelle* (Paris: P. Lethielleux, 1961), 44–50; "Écriture sainte et vie spirituelle," cols. 163–64; A. Kristensen, "Cassian's Use of Scripture," *American Benedictine Review* 28 (1977): 276–88; Soeur Camille de la Grâce-Dieu, "Jean Cassien: La sainte écriture dans la vie du moine," *Tamié 79, La Lectio Divina, Rencontre des Père-Maîtres et Mère-Maîtresses bénédictins et cisterciens du Nord et de l'Est de la France à l'Abbaye de Tamié (Savoie) du 22 au 27 janvier, 1979*. On Palladius's *Historia Lausiaca*, see Robert T. Meyer, "Lectio Divina in Palladius," *Kuriakon: Festschrift Johannes Quasten*, ed. P. Granfield and J. A. Jungman (Munster: Verlag Aschendorff, 1970), 580–84; idem, "Palladius and the Study of Scripture," *Studia Patristica* 13 (1971): 487–90. On the *Historia Monachorum*, see Benedicta Ward, "Signs and Wonders: Miracles in the Desert Tradition," *Studia Patristica* 17 (1982): 539–42. On the *Vita Antonii*, see G. Couilleau, "La liberté d'Antoine," in *Commandements du Seigneur et libération évangélique*, ed. Jean Gribomont, O.S.B. (Rome: Anselmiana, 1977), 13–40. On the Pachomian literature, see: Armand Veilleux, "L'Écriture sainte dans la Koinonia pachômienne," in *La liturgie dans le cénobitisme pachômien au quatrième siècle*, Studia Anselmiana 57 (Rome: Herder, 1968), 262–75; Eng. trans. "Holy Scripture in the Pachomian Koinonia," *Monastic Studies* 10 (1974): 143–54; Heinrich Bacht, "Vom Umgang mit der Bibel im ältesten Mönchtum," *Theologie und Philosophie* 41 (1966): 557–66; William A. Graham, *Beyond the Written Word: Oral Aspects of Scripture in the History of Religion* (Cambridge: Cambridge University Press, 1987), 126–40. On Evagrius, see J. Driscoll, O.S.B., The *"Ad Mona-*

chos" of *Evagrius Ponticus: Its Structure and a Select Commentary* (Rome: Studia Anselmiana, 1991), 323–59.

40. Lucien Regnault, "The Beatitudes in the Apophthegmata Patrum," *Eastern Churches Review* 6 (1974): 23–43; Louis Leloir, "La 'Lectio Divina,' " in *Désert et communion: témoignage des Pères du Désert, recueillis à partir des "Paterica" arméniens* (Bégrolles-en-Mauges: Bellefontaine, 1978), 237–84 English translation: "Lectio Divina and the Desert Fathers," *Liturgy* 23 (1989): 3–38.; idem, "Les Pères du Désert et la Bible," *La Vie Spirituelle* 140 (1986): 167–81; J.-P. Lemaire, "L'abbé Poemen et la Sainte Écriture" (licentiate thesis, University of Freiburg, 1971); Luciana Mortari, *Vita e detti dei padri del deserto* (Rome: Città Nuova, 1971), 1:7–67; Natalio Fernández Marcos, "La Biblia y los origenes del monaquismo," *Miscelánea Comillas* 41 (1983): 383–96; P.-Th. Camelot, "L'Évangile au désert?" *La Vie Spirituelle* 140 (1986): 362–79. Fairy von Lilienfeld, "Anthropos Pneumatikos—Pater Pneumatophoros: Neues Testament und Apophthegmata Patrum," *Studia Patristica* 5, *TU* 80 (Berlin: Akademie Verlag, 1962), 382–92; 'Die Christliche Unterweisung der Apophthegmata Patrum," *Bulletin de la Société d'Archéologie Copte* 20 (1971): 85–110; "Jesus-Logion und Vaterspruch," in *Studia Byzantina*, ed. Johannes Irmscher (Halled-Wittenberg, 1966), 169–83; "Paulus-Zitate und Paulinische Gedanken in den *Apophthegmata Patrum*," *Studia Evangelica* 5, *TU* 103 (Berlin: Akademie-Verlag, 1968), 286–95.

41. On the use of models, see S. McFague, *Metaphorical Theology,* (Philadelphia: Fortress Press, 1982), 67–102; idem, *Models of God* (Philadelphia: Fortress Press, 1987); see also M. Black, *Models and Metaphors* (Ithaca, NY: Cornell University Press, 1962).

42. David Tracy describes this hermeneutical approach as "an articulation of the only ground on which any one of us stand: the ground of real finitude and radical historicality of all hermeneutical understanding." See D. Tracy, *The Analogical Imagination* (New York: Crossroad, 1981), 103; see also P. Ricoeur, "Naming God," *Union Theological Seminary Quarterly Review* 34 (1979): 215–27, where he speaks of the importance of recognizing the contextuality of all understanding.

43. M. Heidegger, *Poetry, Language and Thought,* trans. A. Hofstadter (New York: Harper and Row, 1971), 189.

44. Ray Hart, *Unfinished Man and the Imagination* (New York: Seabury Press, 1979), 27.

45. G. Ebeling, *Word and Faith,* trans. J. W. Leitch (Philadelphia: Fortress Press, 1963), 318.

46. As Robert Funk suggests, these two mediations of language and history are closely connected: "Only where there is language is there world, and only where world predominates is there history. Language is the means by which man exists historically" (R. Funk, *Language, Hermeneutic and the Word of God* [New York: Harper and Row, 1966], 41).

47. R. Palmer, *Hermeneutics: Interpretation Theory in Schleiermacher, Dilthey, Heidegger, and Gadamer* (Evanston, IL: Northwestern University Press, 1969), 117.

48. On the notion of "oral texts," see Walter J. Ong, *Orality and Literacy: The Technologizing of the Word* (London: Methuen, 1982); W. H. Kelber, *The Oral and*

Written Gospel (Philadelphia: Fortress Press, 1983); S. D. Gill, "Nonliterate Traditions and Holy Books," in *The Holy Book in Comparative Perspective*, ed. F. M. Denny and R. L. Taylor (Columbia: University of South Carolina Press, 1985), 224–39; Graham, *Beyond the Written Word*, 1–44.

49. M. Heidegger, *Introduction to Metaphysics*, trans. Ralph Manheim (New Haven: Yale University Press, 1959); cited in Palmer, *Hermeneutics*, 135.

50. M. Heidegger, *Poetry, Language and Thought*, 215–16.

51. Ebeling, *Word and Faith*, 183.

52. G. Ebeling, "Word of God and the New Hermeneutic," in *The New Hermeneutic*, ed. J. M. Robinson and J. B. Cobb, Jr. (New York: Harper and Row, 1964), 104.

53. See Ong, *Orality and Literacy*, 32–33.

54. See A. Wilder, "The Word as Address and the Word as Meaning," in *The New Hermeneutic*, 202.

55. P. Ricoeur, *Interpretation Theory: Discourse and the Surplus of Meaning* (Fort Worth: Texas Christian University Press, 1976), 8–12.

56. P. Ricoeur, "The Hermeneutical Function of Distanciation," in *Hermeneutics and the Human Sciences*, ed., trans., intro. J. Thompson (Cambridge: Cambridge University Press, 1981), 134.

57. Ricoeur, *Interpretation Theory*, 30.

58. Ricoeur has suggested that important *actions*, like classic texts, can extend beyond their original situation and have enduring meaning. "An important action . . . develops meaning which can be actualized or fulfilled in situations other than the one in which this action occurred. . . . The meaning of an important event exceeds, overcomes, transcends the social conditions of its production. . . ." ("The Model of the Text: Meaningful Action Considered as a Text," in *Hermeneutics and the Human Sciences*, 207–8).

59. Palmer, *Hermeneutics*, 155.

60. H.-G. Gadamer, *Truth and Method* (New York: Crossroad, 1975), 267. He also notes in this regard that "historical objectivism, in appealing to its critical method, conceals the involvement of the historical consciousness itself in effective history."

61. H.-G. Gadamer, *Philosophical Hermeneutics* (Berkeley: University of California Press, 1976), 9.

62. Marc Bloch, *The Historian's Craft* (New York: Vintage Books, 1953), 64.

63. Gadamer, *Truth and Method*, 325–41.

64. On the place of a "hermeneutics of suspicion," see Tracy, *The Analogical Imagination*, 137, n. 16; 190, n. 71. For a critique of Gadamer's "optimistic concept of understanding," see W. G. Jeanrond, *Text and Interpretation as Categories of Theological Thinking*, trans. T. J. Wilson (New York: Crossroad, 1988), 22–34.

65. Tracy, *The Analogical Imagination*, 101.

66. Gadamer, *Truth and Method*, 289:

The horizon of the present is conceived in constant formation insofar as we must all constantly test our prejudices. . . . Hence, the horizon of the present does not take shape at all without the past. Understanding is always a process of fusing such horizons . . .

and in the working of tradition such fusion occurs constantly. For there, the old and new grow together again in living value without the one or the other ever being removed explicitly.

67. Tracy, *The Analogical Imagination*, 114.

68. Gadamer, *Truth and Method*, 274–305.

69. Tracy, *The Analogical Imagination*, 78: "There is never an authentic disclosure of truth which is not also transformative."

70. George Steiner, *Real Presences* (Chicago: University of Chicago Press, 1989), 7.

2

Scripture and the Quest for Holiness in Late Antiquity

The desert hermeneutic emerged in response to the pressing questions that filled the world of fourth-century Egypt. Two aspects of this world, the religious climate in which Egyptian monasticism was born and the quest for holiness that characterized the fourth century, are particularly important for situating the desert monks' approach to Scripture in its living context. This means, first of all, placing the desert hermeneutic in relation to early Egyptian Christianity and the rise of monasticism there. Given the cultural, social, and religious complexity of the Egypt in which Christianity arose, and the wide range of possible influences on Egyptian Christianity, it is impossible to provide a simple account of monasticism's rise and development. However, it is possible to make a rough sketch of some of the characteristic features of early Egyptian Christianity; such a picture can help to demonstrate the plausibility of strong biblical influence upon the birth and growth of Egyptian monasticism. In light of the many claims that have been made for the prominence of non-Christian influences on the origins of monasticism and for the irrelevance of the biblical tradition to the early monastic movement, such a reassessment is important and necessary. Second, we need to widen our field of vision to situate the desert hermeneutic within the debate on the holy between pagans and Christians in late antiquity. A comparison of their respective strategies for seeking holiness will reveal the extent to which the questions motivating the monastic quest were part of a larger conversation about the meaning of holiness in late antiquity. Such a comparison will also help to identify the characteristic features of the monastic quest for holiness and to suggest the significance of Scripture in shaping early monastic spirituality.

33

Situating the Early Monastic Movement

Early Christianity in Egypt

The world of Roman Egypt out of which Christianity emerged during the early part of the Common Era is generally acknowledged to have been one in which religious impulses from diverse cultures and traditions converged to form a rich synthesis. "We see a land in which the gods of three cultures—the native Egyptian; the Greek . . . and the Roman . . . rub shoulders without noticeable friction, sometimes retaining their separate identities, but more often merging in syncretistic identification or alliance."[1] H. I. Bell argues that the synthesis was even richer, suggesting that religious beliefs in Egypt were based not simply on the gods of Greece and Rome or Egypt and Asia as conceived in pre-Hellenistic days. Rather, there was a "new composite religion, whose ingredients were drawn from many sources, Greek, Egyptian, Iranian, Semitic (including Judaism) and Anatolian. . . ." It was, he says, "a religion basically monotheistic, despite its multiplicity of gods and daimones, and deeply tinged by philosophic thought."[2] Such comments reflect a widely held assumption among scholars regarding the diversity of religious possibilities that existed in Egypt at the time of Christianity's emergence there. While there is no reason for questioning the general outlines of this picture, one of the consequences of such a view remains problematic; because of the particularly rich synthesis of religious impulses which existed in Egypt, early Egyptian Christianity and early Egyptian monasticism have often been accused of being heterodox. Although there can be no doubt that they were affected by these various religious movements, it is not at all clear how extensive this influence was. We can help to clarify the kind of world into which early Christian monasticism entered and the likely place of the Bible in giving rise to it by highlighting some of the main characteristics of early Christianity in Egypt.

We know very little with certainty about the earliest arrival of Christianity in Egypt or for that matter much about the life of the Egyptian church up until the episcopacy of Bishop Demetrius of Alexandria (ca. 188/9–231 C.E.).[3] There is some evidence to suggest that Christianity was first introduced to Egypt by Greek speaking missionaries and that early converts were made among the Greek and Hellenized inhabitants of the country, especially the Hellenized Jews.[4] However, before long Christianity also began to find adherents outside the Hellenized part of the population.[5] It has been suggested that its reception among the non-Hellenized populace was facilitated by some of the elements Christianity had in common with traditional Egyptian religion, "most notably the belief in resurrection that was inherent, *inter alia,* in the highly emotional yearly celebration of Isis' restoring wholeness to the dismembered Osiris.''[6] Whatever the precise reason for Christianity's appeal to the local populace may have been, the relatively large number of papyrus fragments uncovered in recent years in which adherents to Christianity are mentioned would appear to confirm its growing popularity in Egypt during the second century. Although such fragments probably reflect the beliefs of only a fraction of the population, they suggest that "from the middle of the second century onwards there was a not inconsiderable Christian element in . . . Egypt.''[7] Still, for all this, Christianity probably remained, throughout the second century, a relatively small affair, with no strong, central authority and little formal organization.[8]

Although it is difficult to say with any precision when Christianity began making a really significant impression on the Egyptian-speaking people, it had almost certainly begun doing so before the middle of the third century.[9] Origen, writing in the early third century, alludes to the fact that many of the proselytes among the Egyptians—by which he most likely means native-born Egyptians—had accepted the Christian faith.[10] Later, in the mid-third century, during the reign of Decius (240–251 C.E.), a particularly systematic attempt was made to eradicate Christianity, an event which argues for Christianity's growing importance in the country by this time, including some among the Egyptian-speaking population. Bishop Dionysius of Alexandria, in a letter to Bishop Fabius of Rome during this persecution, made a point of distinguishing Greeks and Egyptians among the martyrs, the latter being recognizable by their Coptic names, such as Bêsa and Amûn.[11] About the year 300 C.E. we hear of the first Coptic scholar Hiercas, who wrote in Greek as well as in Coptic, and was said to be well versed in Scripture.[12] The early translations of the Scriptures into Coptic also argue for the growth of Christianity among the Egyptian-speaking people at a relatively early stage.[13] It would appear that by the end of the third century, Christianity in Egypt had moved from being a fairly small, marginal religious group to one that was coming to occupy an increasingly important role in that country. Moreover, it was no longer present only in the towns and cities, among the well educated, hellenized members of the populace, but also to an ever-greater extent in the villages and countryside, among less well educated, native Egyptians.[14]

It was during the fourth century that Christianity truly came into its own in Egypt, helped in no small part by the changes wrought by Constantine, by vigorous native ecclesiastical leadership, and by the growth of monasticism. In the period following Constantine's conversion to Christianity, there are increasing references to Christians (seen, for example, in a larger number of Christian names), to their churches, and to Christian leaders, all testifying to the enormous impact of this event upon the growth of Christianity in Egypt. Lane Fox comments,"[T]he great expansion of Christianity belongs where we would expect it, after Constantine's victories, not before." [15] This expansion was accompanied by the golden age of the expansion of Egyptian monasticism and by the growing prominence of the Egyptian church under the leadership of Athanasius. The fourth century represents, by all accounts, the zenith of Egyptian Christianity: "From the second quarter of the fourth century onwards, Egyptian Christianity comes into the full light of day; drawing on the resources of Egyptian nationalism, it gained enormous impetus and became the inspiration and teacher of the Christian world." [16]

This survey of early Egyptian Christianity reveals a movement which emerged slowly, taking hold first in urban centers, and only later in the countryside. It suggests a Christianity which was initially hellenized and which eventually adapted itself to Egyptian language and culture. And there are hints that the adaptation of Christianity to Egypt was facilitated in part by certain native religious beliefs and practices. Yet neither the particular character of Egyptian Christianity nor the extent to which it was influenced by the diverse cultural and religious forces already present in Egypt are entirely clear. These are questions of great importance for understanding early monasticism; depending on one's assessment of early Egyptian Christianity, monasticism may appear on the one hand as a heterodox movement, a product of "foreign," non-Christian elements, or on the other hand as a fundamentally Christian movement, rooted in the Scriptures. Although the reality is almost certainly more complex than either of these alternatives suggest, the question of monastic origins has often been framed in such polemical terms, with the conclusions coloring one's assessments of the value and significance of early monasticism. Therefore, a consideration of some of the possible influences on Egyptian Christianity and on early Egyptian monasticism in particular will help in assessing the relative weight of the forces said to be responsible for the flowering of monasticism in Egypt.

Birth of Monasticism in Egypt: Proposed Influences

The widely acknowledged presence of diverse religious and philosophical movements in Egypt, and the skepticism among many scholars concerning the biblical basis of monasticism, has resulted in the proposal of a large number of influences and precedents behind the growth of monasticism in Egypt in the late third and early fourth centuries. [17] Included among the major non-Christian sources suggested are ancient and distant influences such as wandering Buddhist monks, [18] local Egyptian figures such as the *katachoi* of the temple of Serapis,[19] Greek philosophical schools like the Stoics, the Neo-Pythagoreans, and the Neo-Platonists,[20] ancient Jewish ascetical movements, including the Therapeutae and the Essenes,[21] and widespread ascetical religious movements such as the Manichees[22] and the Gnostics. Although the plausibility of these movements having influenced the shape of early Christianity in Egypt and the growth of monasticism there varies from case to case, none of them can be dismissed outright. We simply do not know enough about the precise circumstances of the origins of monasticism to exclude any of these movements as possible influences upon early monasticism with any degree of confidence. On the other hand, there is no strong evidence to suggest that any *one* of these movements was responsible for the origins and development of early monasticism, at least to the extent of having had more effect than the likely Christian sources, including Scripture. Of all the proposed "foreign" influences upon early Egyptian Christianity and monasticism, it is perhaps gnosticism which has the strongest case. A brief examination of the claims made on its behalf can shed some light on the questions surrounding the religious atmosphere in which monasticism took root in Egypt.

The plausibility of gnosticism's influence upon early monasticism has derived in large part from the claim that Egyptian Christianity was itself heavily gnostic. There has been, until recently, a virtual consensus among scholars concerning the gnostic character of early Egyptian Christianity. Adolf Harnack's description of Egyptian Christianity is typical: "There was a local gospel, described by Clement of Alexandria and others as 'the gospel according to the Egyptians.' . . . The heretical asceticism and modalism which characterize it throw a peculiar light upon the idiosyncrasies of early Egyptian Christianity. Originally, it was used not merely by actually heretical parties, who retained it ever afterwards, but also by Egyptian Christians in general. . . ."[23] H. I. Bell concurs in this assessment, arguing that early Egyptian Christianity was steeped in gnosticism: "One of the most persistent of the heresies influenced by Egyptian ideas was Gnosticism, which was widespread in the ancient world but was particularly associated with Egypt. . . . [T]he Egyptian church was deeply affected by Gnosticism."[24] Robert Grant contends that the gnostic influence in Egypt was pervasive: "In the second century, as far as our knowledge goes, Christianity in Egypt was almost exclusively heterodox."[25] This alleged gnostic influence has been used to explain both why we know so little about the early Egyptian church and why monasticism eventually took off so strongly in Egypt. It has been suggested that because the Egyptian church was so overrun by gnosticism, "the earlier chapters of the Church's history were intentionally forgotten."[26] This all-pervasive gnostic presence in Egyptian Christianity has also been used to explain the emergence of monasticism in Egypt: "The implied condemnation of the sex relationship suggests the encratite or ascetic tendency, so common in gnosticism, which . . . characterized the early Egyptian Church and which was later to inspire the monastic movement."[27] Most of the direct evidence we have linking monasticism to gnosticism comes from Pachomian monasticism in upper Egypt. It has been argued that the Pachomian community, with its close proximity to Nag Hammadi, was especially open to gnostic influences.[28] The monastic attitude toward non-Christian literature has been described as "loose" and inclusive, opening the way to the inclusion of all kinds of influences: "[T]o the first monks, it seems, any guide to heaven and the vision of God was as good as another. It did not matter if the text was pagan, Christian or heretical, so long as it suited their piety and their aims."[29] However, there is evidence to suggest that such a picture of easy convergence between gnosticism and monasticism, as appealing as it may be, is open to serious question.

While gnosticism may indeed have left some mark upon Egyptian Christianity and upon early monasticism, evidence from recent scholarship suggests that the relationship between gnosticism and Egyptian Christianity was much more complex than has previously been imagined. C. H. Roberts, in particular, has challenged some of the earlier assumptions about the relationship between them, arguing that gnosticism, far from being a pervasive influence with early Egyptian Christianity, more likely existed *alongside* Christianity. Evidence from the papyri suggests that there were diverse centers of production of various kinds of literature, with gnostic groups working concurrently with orthodox centers. Moreover, he argues that the silence about early Christianity in Egypt was due less to the influence of gnosticism than to the widespread persecutions which Christians likely suffered at the hands of the Romans. Especially important for our purposes is the evidence for the use of Scripture in Egypt as early as the second century, which, Roberts contends, "points to more than a few scattered individuals holding orthodox beliefs." The picture of early Egyptian Christianity that emerges from Roberts's analysis is that of a " 'common core Christianity' . . . defined by its rejection of docetism, its acceptance of the Old Testament, and the belief that the revelation was available to all, not just to a spiritual elite. . . . [T]his embryonic orthodoxy [was] related to a common core of books accepted by most Christians."[30] While it would not be strictly accurate to call the early church in Egypt orthodox—both because orthodoxy was still in the process of being defined and because there were most certainly diverse heterodox strands within it—the evidence suggests that it was not nearly as heterodox as has often been maintained. In particular the influence of gnosticism upon Egyptian Christianity's growth and development would seem to be much less pervasive than previously imagined. In fact, there is now growing evidence pointing to the Jewish character of earliest Christianity in Egypt, something which has important implications for understanding early Egyptian monasticism. The Egyptian church into which monasticism was born appears to have been a diverse and varied body which, while not easily reducible to or explainable by one major influence or another, showed strong connections with its Jewish roots and the influence of the Bible.[31]

Although the extent of gnostic influence on early Egyptian Christianity and early Egyptian monasticism cannot be measured with any real precision, the lack of conclusive evidence suggests that it is perhaps worth looking more closely at sources of influence within the Christian tradition itself. In particular, this means examining the general context of the evolution of Christian asceticism during the first four centuries of the church. This phenomenon may help to account for the monastic phenomenon in Egypt more easily and plausibly.

Early Christian Asceticism and the Roots of Monasticism in Egypt

Egypt was neither the first or only place in which the ascetical ideal came to expression in early Christianity. Throughout the early Christian world, asceticism was a common way of expression Christian piety, and religious communities were organized in which groups of Christians could withdraw from the world to give their attention to divine matters in a concentrated fashion. What we have come to know as monasticism—that is the withdrawal of individuals or small groups of people toward the fringes of society in order to live lives of ascetical rigor and spiritual purity—came to expression more or less at the same time in Mesopotamia, Syria, Egypt, and Cappadocia as well as in the West. It did not spring up overnight, however, or as a radical departure from anything that had existed previously in the Christian world. Rather, it developed in continuity with the various ascetic currents that characterized the life of the early church, particularly in areas with a strong Jewish influence.[32] Of special importance in tracing the monastic origins in Egypt is the kind of asceticism that developed in second- and third-century Syria.[33] Already by the middle of the second century, there were two distinct ascetic currents there, one deriving from the type of Judaism developed in the diaspora, particularly by Philo, and the second influenced by Jewish Christianity and Judaism in Syria. Armand Veilleux argues that "it was the second of these two traditions that more influenced Christian monasticism, including the Egyptian one."[34] A brief glance at some of the characteristic features of this strand of early Syrian asceticism will help to make the plausibility of its connection with Egyptian monasticism clear.

The ascetical impulse expressed itself in different forms in Syria. There were fraternities of "sons (or daughters) of the covenant," who pledged themselves at baptism to a life of celibacy, prayer, and lay ministry.[35] A less formal tradition of *xeniteia,* voluntary exile or expatriation, also appears to have derived from this Jewish-Christian asceticism in Syria, and eventually emerges as a prominent theme in Egyptian monasticism. Since, as we have noted, Egyptian Christianity was in its origins strongly Jewish-Christian, it seems plausible to see in this tradition of *xeniteia* a link with Syrian asceticism. It is, in any case, this model, together with the example of the apostles, to which the Egyptian monks themselves refer most readily.[36] Another connection with Syrian asceticism can be seen in the use of the Greek word *monachos* by early Egyptian monasticism. This word, which was accepted as it stood by the Coptic dialects and which became the primary word used to refer to the solitaries of Egyptian monasticism, is very likely a rendering of a technical Syrian word, *īhīdāyā,* meaning "sole" or "single." Guillaumont has shown that while the word refers to one who lives a celibate life, its primary meaning has to do with being undivided, attaining an inner unity, being free from care. Furthermore, the word has strong connections with certain biblical texts referring to renunciation, such as 1 Cor 7 and Mt 19:21.[37] The correspondence of early Syrian ascetical vocabulary with biblical texts such as these helps to underscore the connection between the broad Jewish-Christian ascetical tradition and the emergence of monasticism and provides us with important hints regarding one of the probable sources of the early monastic movement in Egypt. Similar language and attitudes among the early ascetics in Egypt suggest that among the diverse influences that affected the rise of monasticism there, the Syrian Jewish-Christian ascetical tradition, with its strong biblical roots, may have been among the most important.

The presence of a strong ascetical tradition within early Syrian Christianity and the connections between Syrian and Egyptian Christianity make the presence of ascetical activity connected with mainstream Egyptian Christianity at a relatively early date entirely plausible. In fact there is evidence from papyrus fragments as well as from some of the early monastic documents that various kinds of ascetics lived in Egypt before monasticism took dramatic hold there in the fourth century.[38] Although we have little detailed information about these ascetics, we know that toward the end of the third century, increasing numbers of people had begun to abandon their villages in a conscious act of *anachōrēsis* or withdrawal and to take up a solitary life in the nearby desert. A consideration of the social and religious meanings associated with this act of withdrawal can help to reveal some of the motivations behind the origins of monasticism in Egypt.

One of the most basic motives for withdrawal into the desert was flight from troubles of various kinds. *Anachōrēsis,* whether as an act of desperation by people who could not pay their debts, or as flight from the overwhelming burden of taxation, or as a refuge from other heavy responsibilities, was a common feature in the life of Roman Egypt. It was "traditionally the Egyptian peasantry's last resort when conditions became intolerable."[39] Although the efficiency which the Romans had brought to the collecting of taxes had helped to increase revenues, it had also brought increased levels of economic distress for many in Egypt by the third century. Gradually, those standing higher on the social ladder fled to the ultimate refuge of the desert, with the result that absences from village life became longer and sometimes even permanent. Small farmers, whose economic viability was increasingly strained by inexorable fiscal demands, were often forced to abandon cultivation completely and flee their villages. This in turn increased the tax burden on the population that remained. As more and more of those left behind found themselves constrained by an impossible situation, whole villages came to be deserted, especially near the desert's edge. "All through the centuries of Roman rule, and no doubt especially in the troubled times of the third century, men continued to flee their homes when their fiscal burden was increased by the last straw."[40] Questions put to an oracle by despairing farmers during this period reflect the intensity of these concerns: "Shall I flee? When shall my flight end? Am I to become a beggar?" The problem remained endemic.[41]

Certain changes in the social and economic landscape in fourth-century Roman Egypt accelerated the process of withdrawal and can be seen as contributing to the atmosphere which stimulated the anchoritic movement. By the time Antony withdrew to the desert (ca. 305 C.E.), the Egyptian villages had experienced two particular shifts which are important for understanding what *anachōrēsis* meant for at least some of the early monks. First, the villages had been brought more directly under the authority of distant state officials. Second, the Romans, in an effort to stimulate the economy and encourage more local involvement, had suppressed absentee ownership of large estates, appropriating large tracts of fertile land which could be let or sold to peasants or anyone who wanted to become a small local landowner. This increased "privatization" helped to make villages more self-contained, and benefited the ambitious small landowner by giving him more room to maneuver. However, it also increased social tensions in the village. The growing social and economic tensions felt by small farmers under the weight of these reforms coincide with and very likely contributed to the withdrawal to the desert by some of those in the first generation of anchorites. *Anachōrēsis* as an act of disengagement was one of the responses of Egyptian farmers who felt themselves squeezed by the pressures of this period.[42] The pressures to withdraw thus came not only from a sense of economic desperation, but also, increasingly in the fourth century, from tensions between human beings. As Peter Brown has suggested, "[t]he overwhelming impression given by the literature of the early Egyptian ascetics, is that we are dealing with men who found themselves driven into the desert by a crisis in human relations."[43] The heavy economic pressures bearing down upon the Egyptian village made that already small world feel even more compressed. One response was to flee, either to the next village or into the desert. The ascetic message of the monks derived much of its cogency and its appeal from having resolved those tensions.

An appreciation of the strong social forces at work behind the practice of *anachōrēsis* helps one to see the limitations of a purely spiritual interpretation of desert monasticism.[44] Whatever the spiritual motives of the first anchorites may have been, they should not be distinguished too sharply from the social and economic conditions just described. At the same time, while these social and economic tensions provide a context in which the meaning of *anachōrēsis* can be understood more clearly, the withdrawal into the desert cannot be reduced to these factors. There were other, genuinely religious, motives behind the withdrawal into the desert by the first anchorites, which should not be discounted. We can include among these the atmosphere of asceticism which existed at the time, the influence of the martyrs, and a particular way of reading and responding to Scripture.

The *Vita Antonii* and the *Vita Pachomii* both mention the presence of ascetics living on the fringes of their local communities or in the desert near their villages, an indication that such a way of life was not uncommon in Upper and Lower Egypt before the time of Antony and Pachomius. This suggests that the life adopted by the first Egyptian monks was not a complete novelty but rather fit into an already established ascetical context. While these experiments in asceticism were being conducted, certain social and religious factors began to coalesce to help define the life of asceticism in a new way. As E. A. Judge has shown, the emergence of the *monachos*, or monk, known for the particular way of life that he had taken up on the fringes of society, is inextricably bound up with the phenomenon of withdrawal, or *anachōrēsis*.[45]

At least some of the roots of Christian *anachoresis* in Egypt can be traced to the response to persecution as early as the mid-third century. Dionysius of Alexandria tells us that during the Decian persecution (ca. 250 C.E.) many Christians fled to the deserts and mountains and lived there in solitude. Although he does not suggest that this was more than a temporary retreat for most, one can well imagine that some of these refugees, "tasting the sweetness of that solitude,'' would have continued to live in the desert even when the danger had passed.[46] While we know little about these persons who fled into the desert at this early date, we catch occasional hints in the literature of the connection between the martyrs and the first monks. Antony's first master, for example, is said to have been an elderly hermit surviving from the time of the persecutions.[47] It appears that the example and presence in the desert of such solitary figures did not go unnoticed by the first monks. The *Vita Pachomii* is more specific about the influence of the martyrs. Following the persecutions, the author tells us, ''faith increased greatly in the holy Churches in every land, and monasteries and places for ascetics began to appear, for those who were the first monks had seen the endurance of the martyrs.''[48] The monastic literature also testifies in a number of places that the movement into the desert was seen above all as a response to a call from God mediated through Scripture. To assess the plausibility of this picture, it will be helpful to examine briefly the place of books—especially Scripture— in the early Egyptian Christianity and within desert monasticism.

Scripture and Books in the Desert

What was the relationship of the desert fathers to books in general and to Scripture in particular? In what languages were the sacred texts available to them, and in what forms? How many monks would have learned of the Scriptures through reading written texts as opposed to oral transmission? Although we still know relatively little about the production and use of books in the early Christian era, a brief consideration of the place and function of the book in early Christianity can help to shed light on the meaning of statements regarding books in the early Egyptian monastic milieu.

No early Christian writer has told us anything about the way in which Christian or any other books were written and circulated. We know less than we would like about how books came to occupy such an important place in the early Christian community.[49] That books were important to early Christians, however, is not in doubt. In Rome several images in the burial chamber of the catacombs show Christians at the last judgment, grasping their books. A group of Christian prisoners, standing before the governor of Africa, replied, when asked what they had brought with them, ''Texts of Paul, a just man.'' The significance of this story lies not simply in the particular kind of texts that Christians brought with them, but in their bringing texts at all. As Lane Fox suggests, ''One of the fundamental contrasts between pagan cult and Christianity was the passage from an oral culture of myth and conjecture to one based firmly on written texts.''[50] Although such an observation does not take sufficient account of the extent to which Scripture lived on within the Christian community as oral discourse through liturgy and teaching, it is true that the written word had an unusually strong effect on the formation of early Christian spirituality. In turn, the strong connection Christians had with the word apparently influenced the way books and writing were perceived in late antiquity.

Early Christians made a significant break with contemporary habits of reading through their widespread use of the codex (pages) instead of the rotulus (roll). Though the precise origins of the codex as a book form and the reasons for its success are far from clear, there is evidence to suggest that the widespread use of the codex derived in large part from the early Christian community's view that it was the only acceptable form for the writing of its sacred texts. C. H. Roberts has shown that there was a strong connection between the rise of the importance of the codex and the growth of Christianity.[51] Though rough parchment codices had existed for some time and were used for everyday purposes as notebooks,[52] it was not until the idea emerged to create a *papyrus* codex that the codex began to surpass the roll as the most favored form for more formal writing. Roberts' careful analysis of the extant fragments of rolls and codices from the first three centuries of the Common Era has revealed that the prominence of the papyrus codex in late antiquity, and possibly even its invention, can be traced directly to the early Christian community.[53] Though the reasons for the shift from roll to codex are a matter of some debate, Roberts has shown that this change had probably occurred already in the first century and that Christianity was from its earliest moments identified with the codex. Although the papyrus codex was the most common form in the earliest period, it was eventually superseded by the parchment codex, though of a finer quality than had been common in earlier examples. By the beginning of the fourth century, when Diocletian imposed a freeze on prices and wages specifying maximum rates of pay for scribes writing on parchment codices, the codex had already become very common. In 332 C.E., Constantine ordered fifty parchment Bibles. As Skeat notes, "It is plain that by this date the parchment codex had come to be regarded as the supreme form of the Christian book."[54]

The prominence of the codex in early Christianity indicates how Christians, including those who lived in the Egyptian desert, understood and made use of the Scriptures and how these texts impinged upon their lives. The size, form, and appearance of the codex all reflected an attitude toward the book which set the Christian community apart from its pagan and Jewish counterparts in important ways. The relatively small size of the codex meant that it was very portable and easy to conceal. By the end of the third century, some pocket codices measured from 15×11 cm. to 7×5 cm.; these already-small codices were eventually made even smaller and came increasingly to be used for devotional purposes. Moreover, as Roberts notes, there was a great contrast between the "hieratic elegance of the Jewish rolls of the Law and the workaday appearance of the first Christian codices. . . . [T]he earliest Christian codices were essentially books *for use,* not, as Jewish rolls of the Law sometimes were, almost cult objects." [55] This usefulness was in part due to the *form* of the codex which, unlike the more cumbersome roll, allowed one to refer back and forth relatively easily between texts—facilitating the ability to read and use it.

The story of the development of the Christian codex supplies us with some useful information regarding the practical place and function of Scripture in the early Christian community and provides hints about how the desert fathers could have gained access to the Scriptures. It suggests that codices of the Scriptures were in wide circulation, and that their practical benefits of portability and accessibility enabled them to be read and used, at least by those members of the community who could read. But what texts were being read and in what versions or translations were they available in early Christian Egypt?

The desert fathers' access to the Bible was determined not only by the availability of codices, but also by the availability of translations they could understand. If, as seems likely, the majority of those who were part of the desert movement were native Egyptians, our understanding of the place of Scripture in that movement depends upon knowing when and to what extent the Scriptures were translated from Greek into Coptic. [56] The evidence suggests that the translation of Scripture into Coptic began fairly early and that the Scriptures were indeed available to the early Egyptian monks in their own language.

The development of Coptic versions of the Scriptures was directly related to the expansion of Christianity into the Egyptian countryside and was even hastened by the growth of monasticism. Bruce Metzger has described the process of translation as occurring in roughly three stages. In the first, "preclassical Sahidic" stage (before 250 C.E.), as the number of native Coptic Christians began to increase, various local communities needed to make available translations of one or another of the books of the Bible. During this period, some books were translated several times by different translators in varying styles, while other books were neglected entirely. In the second, "classical Sahidic" stage (ca. 250–300 C.E.), an "official Coptic Bible had come into being." It was in the Sahidic dialect, the only one which could be understood throughout the country. It was the work of a number of different translators and was subsequently revised by a commission of experts. This official version, while providing greater uniformity than earlier versions, did not manage to drive out the earlier, independent translations, some of which were no less excellent. The presence of this new standard text, together with the many older variations (known as "wild texts"), suggests a situation of great fluidity among biblical texts, in which the Coptic Bible was becoming increasingly well known. Finally, in the third, "preclassical Bohairic" stage (ca. 300–500 C.E.), the Coptic church, taking advantage of its newfound power in the post-Constantinian era, began to evangelize the countryside systematically. Because the Sahidic dialect was not understood well enough there, the classical Sahidic version had to be translated into the principal minor dialects.[57]

The existence of early Coptic translations of Scripture provides strong evidence that Egyptian monks would have had access to Scripture in their own language. In a papyrus inscription from the fourth century, we hear of a "reader" in a small Egyptian church who was "illiterate," presumably meaning he could not speak Greek, and who therefore read the Bible from the Coptic. His father's name, Copreus, meaning "off the dung heap," indicates that the reader was a person of humble status who had been exposed at birth but rescued by others from death.[58] It was for the sake of such a person, and many others like him who took up life in the desert, that the translations of the Scriptures into Coptic were so important. Thus the growth of Christianity in the Egyptian countryside during the late third and early fourth centuries, and especially the rapidly growing number of hermits and monks who imitated Antony (as well as those in upper Egypt who gathered around Pachomius), very likely provided a strong impetus for the further translation of the Scriptures into Coptic.[59] Though the educated among them would have been able to read and understand the Scriptures in Greek, it is likely that the majority of early monks would have had access to the Scriptures only through these Coptic translations. However, this does not mean that those for whom the Coptic Scriptures were translated were "literate" in the strict sense, even in Coptic. It is likely, rather, that the Scriptures were known by a large number of the monks mainly through oral transmission, especially by way of the liturgy. It is clear, however, that the Scriptures existed in Coptic translation at the time the desert movement began to grow, and that those who entered into the desert would have had access to these texts in their own language, through either the written or spoken word.

All of this helps to shed light on the famous call to the monastic life found at the beginning of the *Vita Antonii*. There we meet Antony, a young man eighteen to twenty years old, raised as Christian by parents who were "well born and prosperous" and who had a good piece of farming land (they had "three hundred fertile and very beautiful *arourae*" of land). Following his parents' deaths, Antony became responsible not only for the land but also for his younger sister. Walking through his village toward the church, he pondered his situation in light of some words from Scripture: "He considered while he walked along how the apostles, forsaking everything, followed the Savior (Mt 4:20), and how in Acts, some sold what they possessed and took the proceeds and placed them at the feet of the apostles for distribution among those in need (Acts 4:35)." Antony entered the church and, still mulling these things over in his mind, heard this text being read from the Gospel: "If you would be perfect, go, sell what you possess, and give it to the poor, and you will have treasure in heaven" (Mt 19:21). Antony responded immediately to the words, selling his possessions and leaving his settled life behind, first withdrawing to the edge of the village and then into the depths of the desert.[60]

Even accounting for the complex theological motives and sophisticated literary models that may lie behind the portrayal of Antony found in the *Vita Antonii,* there are reasons for taking seriously the picture of monastic origins revealed here.[61] Everything we know about the Egyptian church and Egyptian asceticism in the late third and early fourth centuries makes such a scene entirely plausible. The Bible, as we have seen, certainly existed in translation by this time, having been translated at least in part in order to reach persons like Antony. The particular subject of Antony's musings reflects the kind of concerns shared by other ascetics who lived in Egypt at that time. As Judge has shown, the most common term for ascetics in Egypt was renunciant (apotaktikos), a word derived from the command of Jesus that those who wished to follow him should renounce all possessions (Lk 14:33).[62] Thus the ascetic life was linked with certain pointed biblical texts calling for renunciation.[63] Even if the account we have in the *Vita Antonii* represents a polished, refined version of a much more complex set of circumstances, it is based in fact. The movement for ascetic renunciation was beginning to stir in fourth-century Egypt. A person of Antony's description may well have found himself faced with the very situation described in this narrative. Although we have no way of knowing whether Antony had any contact with the renunciants in Egypt at that time, it is neither improbable nor difficult to imagine, given the social and religious atmosphere in which he lived, that he should have been led to ponder such an act of renunciation himself.

I suggest that, given what we know of the social tensions in Roman Egypt, the presence of an emerging culture of asceticism, and the growth of a church in which Scripture figured prominently, the impact of Scripture on early monastic acts of renunciation should not be underestimated.[64] A closer examination of the early monastic texts which follows in the remainder of the book will provide further evidence for the centrality of Scripture to the entire monastic ethos.

Quest for Holiness in Fourth Century: Pagan and Christian Approaches

The period of late antiquity has been characterized as a time in which interest in religious questions became ever more prominent and pervasive. "The entire culture, pagan as well as Christian, was moving into a phase in which religion was to be coextensive with life, and the quest for God was to cast its shadow over all other human activities."[65] As Peter Brown has persuasively argued, this quest was marked above all by a significant change in the perception of where holiness was seen to reside; increasingly, the locus of holiness came to be associated with certain *individuals*.[66] This change has led Brown to suggest that "the rise of the holy man is the 'leitmotiv' of the religious revolution of Late Antiquity . . . [which] marked out Late Antiquity as a distinct phase of religious history."[67] This revolution evolved within the context of a lively "debate on the holy" between pagans and Christians. Christian monks and pagan philosophers contended over questions such as where one was to seek holiness, what means one should use to gain access to the divine, and what qualities could be said to reflect the realization of holiness in a human being.[68] While there were many shared assumptions between pagans and Christians regarding the meaning of holiness, a real sense in which they shared in a "Mediterranean-wide *koiné*," there were also substantial differences which were important for defining the precise scope and meaning of the quest for holiness in each group.[69] The significance of the desert hermeneutic within the world of late antiquity can be further clarified by placing it within the context of this debate. By situating the desert hermeneutic within the wider "debate on the holy" we shall see how much the use and interpretation of Scripture in early desert monasticism contributed toward defining the monastic identity and its particular approach to holiness.

The Neoplatonic philosopher Plotinus provides a particularly good point of departure for inquiring into the issues that defined the pagan philosopher's quest for holiness. Plotinus was at the very heart of the late antique succession of major interpreters of the philosophy of Plato and stands at the head of the Neoplatonic revival which was perpetuated in various forms by such luminous successors as Porphyry, Iamblichus, and Proclus.[70] The school of philosophy which emerged from Plotinus was to extend far beyond his own lifetime and influence the shape of pagan piety throughout late antiquity. In making comparisons between Plotinus and his school and the desert monks, it helps to keep in mind the location of pagan and Christian holy men within their respective social milieux. We can only understand the influence of these holy ones on their contemporaries by noting certain distinctive features of their respective worlds. "To contemporaries, the difference between the role that each [monk and philosopher] was called upon to play and the authority that each wielded, was sharply delineated on two issues: poverty and culture."[71] Although care needs to be taken not to draw such distinctions too sharply, an awareness of such differences can help in distinquishing what holiness meant for these two groups and how they sought it. In particular, it can help to highlight the significance of Scripture within the monastic quest for holiness.

The Pagan Philosopher's Quest for Holiness: Plotinus and his Circle

It is generally acknowledged that Greek philosophy became an increasingly religious endeavor during the period of late antiquity. By the second century C.E. the philosophical schools were not thought of merely as intellectual schools of *thought* but as something broader—*bioi* or *ways of life*.[72] In these philosophical schools, religious questions were central. "To the man in the street," Dodd says, "the term 'philosophy' came increasingly to *mean* the quest for God."[73] Hadot, having reviewed numerous schools of ancient Greek philosophy, concludes that "[t]rue philosophy is . . . 'spiritual exercise' . . . no longer [understood] as a theoretical construction, but as a method of forming a new way of living and of seeing the world, as an attempt to transform man."[74] These descriptions of the philosophical endeavor in late antiquity catch much of the spirit of Plotinus's own school. It was characterized by a particular way of life and a distinctly religious approach to philosophical questions.

The pagan philosopher was distinguished by a generally positive appraisal of his culture. We learn at the beginning of Porphyry's *Vita Plotinii* that a crucial turning point in Plotinus's life came with his conversion to philosophy and the decision to spend time studying with the philosopher Ammonius Saccas.[75] Conversion to philosophy meant then, as it had for some time in the Greek world, a profound inward reorientation in which one was, in a sense, reborn into a new awareness of everything most sublime in the cultural tradition. It was "a turning from luxury and self indulgence and superstition, to a life of discipline and sometimes to a life of contemplation, scientific or mystic."[76] This note concerning Plotinus's conversion to philosophy helps to situate Plotinus's quest for holiness within his culture and society. The pagan philosopher's attitude toward culture was, fundamentally, sanguine. "For Plotinus and his pagan successors, otherworldliness rose out of the traditional culture like the last icy peak of a mountain range: a training in classical literature and philosophy stood at the base of asceticism of the late Roman philosophy, as seemingly irremovable as the foothills of the Himalayas." [77] The pagan holy man drew from the heart of his cultural tradition in order to define the meaning of his quest for holiness. This positive attitude toward the cultural tradition had some significant practical implications. Certain people were, for all intents and purposes, excluded from this quest: "Familiarity with the divine world was in effect limited to those capable of standing on the shoulders of the giants of the past—in other words to the learned." [78]

The pagan philosopher's positive appraisal of culture and learning linked him inextricably to a particular social milieu and to a particular understanding of his vocation within that milieu. Generally, the pagan holy man lived in an urban setting and operated largely among the educated classes. [79] In the case of Plotinus, we know that, upon leaving Ammonius, he came to settle in Rome, [80] where he gathered a certain number of *zēlōtai,* or disciples, around himself. [81] The economic requirements to be a disciple were, like the educational requirements, quite high. To become one of the *zēlōtai* "required not just dedication, but leisure and financial security. . . . [M]ost holy men do seem to have come from prosperous backgrounds." [82] The social, economic, and educational profile of the pagan philosopher made it fairly easy for him to move within circles of power and influence in the Roman world. There is evidence to suggest that at least some pagan philosophers eschewed these circles of influence for a more marginal position in society, "one of essential non-involvement." [83] However, for Plotinus and many others, their position in society was an important part of their currency, which through wise trading, enabled them to exert considerable influence within their culture. Among the wider circle surrounding Plotinus were senators and noble women, and Plotinus is said to have acted as a guardian to children of "men and women of position." [84] Further, Porphyry describes Plotinus's familiarity with the emperor, who enlisted Plotinus's support for a proposed "platonopolis" or city of philosophers. [85] Plotinus's role as an "arbiter in many differences" [86] further attests to the influence that a pagan philosopher often played within his culture. It suggests that Plotinus should not be thought of as a marginal figure, an unknown and modest Alexandrian, but as someone who was known and admired by many of the most important and influential members of his society.

Plotinus's attitude toward the pagan cultural tradition and his influential

social location suggest the extent to which the philosopher's quest for holiness could be understood only within the world of traditional pagan values
and culture. The precise means through which the pagan philosopher pursued holiness varied widely. However, we can learn much about the meaning of holiness in this setting by examining what Hadot calls the *exercices
spirituels* of the philosopher. One of these *exercices* which is worth looking
at, especially because of the comparison it allows us to make with early
monasticism, is the reading and interpretation of texts—especially the philosophical texts of Plato.[87] The centrality of this aspect of the pagan *paideia*
in the philosophical schools suggests the importance accorded to learning—
especially of the pagan philosophical tradition—the philosopher's quest for
holiness. Also, Plotinus's characteristic method of interpreting Plato's writing among his circle of disciples, reveals what a religious exercise such
interpretation was. Meaningful interpretation of these texts depended on the
depth of the philosopher's religious experience and on his sensitivity as a
director of souls. It was only through plumbing the depths of a tradition
shared by their contemporaries that Plotinus and his circle came to enjoy
such prestige and power within their world.

A certain amount of preparation was required in order to be able to interpret the works of Plato properly. Central to this preparatory work was the
practice of asceticism and the cultivation of virtue. Asceticism meant the
practice of certain elements of the Pythagorean ideal, including vegetarian-
ism, refusal to bathe in public,[88] frugality, reduction of time of sleep,[89]
celibacy, and to some extent, simplicity with regard to material goods. This
practice of asceticism reveals a certain pessimism toward the body, something reflected in Porphyry's description of Plotinus that "he seemed ashamed
of being in the body."[90] The ascetic impulse also reflected a desire to overcome undue anxiety about the things of this world and the inward division
caused by such anxiety.[91] Virtue was understood to be that which leads one
to God, through the interior transformation of one's being. "Without virtue," Plotinus said, "God is only a word."[92] The practice of asceticism
and the cultivation of virtue, as Plotinus understood it, was meant to lead to
an extremely *simple* attitude. The goal of the philosophical life, then, was
not to remove oneself from society, but to be so transformed inwardly that
one was able to live within society with a freedom which came from a
simple regard for "the One."

Reading and interpreting the texts of Plato could help one cultivate this
simple regard. Plotinus considered his own approach to these texts essentially traditional: "These teachings are therefore, no novelties, no inventions
of today but long since stated if not stressed; our doctrine here is the explanation of an earlier one and we can show the antiquity of these opinions on

the testimony of Plato himself."[93] He saw himself as defending the thought
of the "ancient Greek school,"[94] and his contemporaries regarded him as
"amongst the Platonists."[95] Plotinus appears as a creative exegete of Plato,
bringing questions and concerns of his own day to the texts, both to allow
Plato to shed new light on the questions and to rethink Plato in the light of
these questions. As Hadot suggests, with Plotinus, "philosophy becomes
exegesis."[96]

The hermeneutical key to Plotinus's interpretation of the Platonic tradition
was his radical interiorization of Plato's world of forms. Plotinus claims that
"each of us is an intellectual cosmos,"[97] that the journey of the soul is "a
voyage of self-discovery. . . . [I]f we wish to know the Real, we have only
to look within ourselves."[98] Such self-exploration teaches one to distinguish
between a lower self-consciousness—the ego's awareness of its own
activity[99]—and a higher consciousness—the secret inner person who is
"continually in the intellectual realm."[100] Because the hidden center of this
inner self coincides with the center of all things, the self may hope at times
to achieve total unification, that is, "become God" or, as Plotinus says, to
be God.[101]

The goals of self-transformation and total unification between the self and
"the One" help explain why so much emphasis was placed on the necessity
of a personal, dialogical approach to interpreting Plato's text. The way of
inner dialectic was, by its very nature, an experimental task, a process of
discernment which required a guide. It is interesting and significant, then,
that Porphyry directs our attention more to the *style* of Plotinus's exposition
than the substance of his teaching. Plotinus appears as a spiritual master
who acted as a mediator of the philosophical tradition to his disciples. Porphyry testifies to Plotinus's power of expression and explanation, and especially of his "remarkable power of going to the heart of the subject."[102] He
recalls that Plotinus's discourses were "free from academic pomp," and that
"he never forced upon his hearers the severely logical substructure of his
thesis."[103] Rather, "he used to encourage his hearers to put questions, a
liberty which . . . led to a great deal of wandering and futile talk."[104] This
meandering style was not seen as a hindrance to the quest for truth but as a
necessary part of the process. Thus Porphyry remarks, with obvious approval, that Plotinus's "lectures sometimes had the air of conversation."[105]
He was willing to entertain all manner of questions and rather than constructing a formal system, preferred to address individual philosophical
problems as they arose.[106] When a certain visitor asked Plotinus—clearly
with a certain amount of irritation—to expound his theory in a set treatise
instead of continuing to answer Porphyry's multitude of questions, Plotinus
responded by posing a question to the visitor, "But if we cannot first solve

the difficulties Porphyry raises, what could go into the treatise?''[107] This reply expresses a principle of interpretation to which Plotinus firmly adhered: that reference to the ancients, however useful and helpful, must never become a pretext for dispensing with one's own reflection on difficult philosophical problems.[108] It was not sufficient simply to repeat Plato; it was necessary to elaborate and develop the truth implicit in the texts, so that each one might apprehend the truth in himself.

This conversational, dialogical style marks Plotinus's real genius as an interpreter of Plato. His interest in reading the ancient philosophical texts with his disciples stemmed from an attitude. He "didn't conceive of his courses of exegesis from the point of view of pure philological erudition. His goal was not only to clarify the text of Plato; he also wanted to raise up a valuable truth *hic et nunc.* . . . [T]he text upon which he commented was only a privileged help for reaching the truth.''[109] The work of interpreting the text of Plato was of value primarily as a means of putting the philosophical problematic in perspective and of drawing the inquirer more deeply into the world of contemplation. It was an "existential" approach to philosophy, learned from Ammonius, in which philosophy was considered not as something which could be easily learned and passed on to another, but as an entire way of life with a spiritual and mystical character.[110] Plotinus's approach to the interpretation of Plato was fundamentally religious in character. Although some aspects of his hermeneutic can no doubt be attributed to his own personal and intellectual idiosyncrasies, he exemplified well the religious approach to philosophy characteristic of this age. It was an approach which aimed always at that "formation of self, to that *paideia,* which will teach us to live, not conforming to the human prejudices and social conventions but conforming to the nature of man which is none other than reason.''[111] In teaching his disciples how to interpret the ancients with his characteristic "depth of penetration," Plotinus taught them much more than doctrine; he taught them how to discover the truth for themselves. By appropriating within himself the truth of the tradition, he became a conduit for the life-giving wellspring of the One, leading his disciples to make their own contact with the One and become transformed. The goal of such transformation was not complete withdrawal from others. Rather, as Plotinus himself exemplified, it was "being able to live at once within himself and for others.''[112]

This brief sketch suggests several aspects of the philosopher's approach to holiness that are worth noting. The philosopher's positive attitude toward culture determined both the day-to-day life within the philosophical school as well as the particular exercises followed in the quest for holiness. Plotinus and his circle practiced a traditional, moderate form of asceticism, which had as its goal the increasing attainment of virtue, both personal and civic, as the basis for acquiring self-knowledge. At the center of his circle's *exercices spirituels* was his penetrating dialogue with disciples based on an "existential" interpretation of the ancient philosophical texts, especially those of Plato. Plotinus encouraged among his disciples a rigorous inner dialectic the goal of which was self-knowledge and union with "the One." The inner freedom gained through this process enabled the pagan philosopher to occupy an important role in late antique society. Yet the pagan philosopher's position as a "saint" in late antiquity and his ability to act with power in that world derived not only from his spiritual achievement. It also depended upon on his place in his world, including his knowledge of its culture and his easy dealings with his peers. "He summed up in his person ideals shared by the educated classes as a whole, and was admired for having acted these out in such a way as to transcend and stand outside the inconsistencies and the conflicts that were the stuff of public life. . . . His mind was the most pure and so, in his dealings with others, his hand could be counted on as the most unsullied.[113] The pagan philosopher's position as a "saint" and as an "honest broker" within his world came both because of his spiritual achievement and because it was achieved from within the core of his culture.

The Approach to Holiness in Desert Monasticism

The quest for holiness in early monasticism shared many things in common with that of the pagan philosophers. Both sought detachment through an ascetical form of life. Both gave great attention to the search for self-knowledge through an experiential exploration of the inner world. Both achieved some freedom from the social bonds weighing down their contemporaries and expressed this freedom in their attitudes and actions. However, there were also some important differences between them. Unlike the pagan philosophers who engaged in the quest for holiness from within the heart of traditional Roman society, the monks' pursuit of holiness usually meant separation and removal from the mainstream of society. They were certainly not the first Christians to have developed a negative image of pagan culture and learning. However, the monks' dramatic act of withdrawal into the desert sent a particularly strong message regarding the social, cultural, and religious distance of this movement from the heart of traditional pagan culture. Their withdrawal implied a rejection of much that was valued and cherished in that culture, especially the traditional link between *paideia* and holiness. Theirs was a new *paideia,* born of the silence and solitude of the desert and of the Word of God. The social meaning of the act of withdrawal was also

significant. Unlike their pagan counterparts, who remained close to the urban centers and very much part of its social world, the monks were literally
living on the margins of society. This act was fraught with religious significance. By thus removing themselves, the desert dwellers showed that it was
possible to break the bonds which tied human beings to the dominant powers
of the world. In doing so, they revealed to themselves and to their contemporaries that it was possible to achieve a profound level of freedom. That
the means of achieving this freedom included a long and careful rumination
of Scripture provides a key to understanding the significance of the monastic
quest for holiness.

The physical locus of the monks differed significantly from that of their
pagan counterparts. Rather than dwelling in urban centers, the early monks
took up their life in the stark, wild, dry, hot, "uncivilized," desert. The
images of the desert and the cell shaped the imagination of the desert fathers
and determined the shape of their quest for holiness in a profound way. In
spite of romantic images that are sometimes associated with the monastic
flight to the desert, the desert was first of all a fearful place. It was home to
the demons with whom the monk engaged in fierce and constant battle.[114]
Yet it was not only a place which inspired fear. This battle against the
demons was, among other things, a struggle with the self, where one sought
and sometimes gained a new kind of freedom. It is understandable then,
why Abba Sisoes, who in his old age eventually departed from the remote
region near St. Antony's mountain where he had lived for many years, still
felt a painful longing for that place. "Was not the liberty of my spirit enough
for me in the desert?"[115] The particular place within the desert in which the
monks sought this freedom was the cell. Often hidden away in a remote
corner of the desert, this was the privileged place for anyone who would
learn the ways of the desert. The ethos of the whole monastic life was
summed up by Abba Poemen through a brief reference to the cell: "Let us
enter into our cell, and sitting there, remember our sins, and the Lord will
come and help us in everything."[116] To the monks, it was literally the
source of their life: "Just as fish die if they stay too long out of water, so
the monks who loiter outside their cells . . . lose the intimacy of inner
peace."[117] The cell was the symbolic center of the monastic life.[118] The
physical coordinates of this desert solitude remind us that this world was far
removed conceptually, culturally, and socially from that of the pagan philosophers. However, it was not only the place itself that distinguished the
desert monk from the pagan philosopher. The desert place where the monks
took up their dwelling also carried with it a particular social and religious
significance.

The movement into the desert represented among other things a radical break with society and a decision to take up a position on the margins of that society.[119] One of the causes of *anachōrēsis*, or withdrawal, was, as I have suggested above, a response to certain social and economic pressures. More than a few of the figures in the desert found their way there precisely as a result of these kinds of pressures. The retreat to the desert provided a means of working out some of the social tensions inherent in the towns and villages of the late fourth century. Traces of the attempts to resolve some of these tensions are in fact revealed in the *Sayings*. One story tells of a brother who could not control his tongue and was constantly condemning those around him. Abba Matoes instructed the brother: "Flee into solitude. For this is a sickness." Matoes confessed that he himself did not come to dwell in the desert through heroic virtue, but "through weakness." That is, he entered the desert in order to heal his sickness—his own compulsion to berate and condemn others. The significance of solitude, Matoes suggests to the brother, is that it helps the monk to rub off his rough edges, so that he may live peacefully with others: "He who dwells with his brethren must not be square, but round, so as to turn himself towards all."[120] Such a story helps illustrate the social and religious significance of *anachōrēsis* and suggests why those who broke with society in such a stark fashion appealed so strongly to the peasant culture of fourth-century Egypt. "In his act of *anachōrēsis*, [the monk] had summed up the logical resolution of a dilemma with which the average farmer could identify himself wholeheartedly. . . . [The monk's] powers and prestige came from acting out, heroically, before a society enmeshed in oppressive obligations and abrasive relationships, the role of the utterly self-dependent autarkic man."[121] In the solitude of the desert, the monk worked to resolve within himself some of the tensions that existed between friends, family members, and neighbors in the Egyptian towns and villages of this period. In an important sense, then, both the social location of the monk and the meaning which his contemporaries derived from it were quite different from that of the pagan holy man.

With such marked differences of place and of social location between monks and philosophers, it is not surprising that one should also find among the desert monks a very different attitude toward the importance of learning in the quest for holiness. There was, however, a genuine ambivalence on this question for the monks. The attitudes of Christians toward classical education and culture had always been ambiguous, and the desert fathers' position on this question must be seen within this broader context. For many Christians, especially those without aspirations or opportunities for education, the question simply never arose. This was because Christianity "did not, like Neoplatonism, demand education."[122] However, among the learned Christians the matter of how to relate to classical culture was more complex.

On the one hand there were persons such as the apologists, Clement of Alexandria, Origen, Jerome, and Augustine, who insisted on the importance of classical culture and education for Christianity.[123] Yet even such affirmation of pagan learning often carried with it the seeds of distrust toward pagan culture. It was not uncommon for well educated Christians to support the benefits of a classical education while condemning the broader ideals of paganism. "Adopting the classical system of education did not mean accepting the culture it subserved."[124] The ambivalence which some must have felt about this question is captured in Jerome's famous dream in which, having died, he appeared before the heavenly judge claiming, "Christianus sum." The judge, noting Jerome's undisguised love for the classics, retorted: "Ciceronianus es, non Christianus."[125] Many Christians had no ambivalence whatever about the matter and felt only suspicion and antagonism toward pagan culture. These could easily answer "Nothing" to Tertullian's famous question "What has Athens to do with Jerusalem?" To them, paganism was not simply a set of ideas which Christianity could graft onto itself selectively but a competing philosophy or world-view. "The whole trend of this [pagan] humanistic culture was to set itself up as a rival to the new religion, for it too in its own way claimed to solve the problem of human existence."[126] For this reason, many Christians regarded the old gods with fear and aversion and felt that "classical culture, permeated as it was with paganism, was to be rejected *in toto:* to study it was, if not sinful, playing with fire."[127] Christianity, they felt, needed to create its own culture, nourished not by the classics but by Scripture. The monastic quest for holiness was profoundly affected by this outlook.

The attitude in the desert literature toward traditional pagan culture and learning is complex. On one level, one encounters stories of genuinely simple monks who reflect the piety of those ignorant of the wider world of Greek philosophy and culture. Here one sees an unselfconscious rejection of pagan culture. On another level one finds, especially by the more learned of the desert monks, self-consciously polemical statements against Greek learning and culture. In these cases, the monastic quest for holiness was consciously portrayed in opposition to the models presented by the pagan world. Taken together, they reflect a generally negative attitude toward the importance of culture and learning in the pursuit of holiness. Contrary to the opinion held by most pagan philosophers of the period, the monks believed it was not only possible for the simplest of human beings to seek holiness, but that this simplicity was now something to which even the learned aspired. Much of this attitude can be explained by considering the social and educational profiles of the monastic movement. Although some who went into the desert were educated, and spoke and read Greek, most of the monks were uncultured in the traditional sense of the word—they were illiterate and had little formal education. This in itself presents a startling contrast to the pagan philosophers, when one considers how important education was in their pursuit of holiness. Still, there were some who came to the desert who possessed a classical education. Even these found themselves faced with a new *paideia*.

For those who came to the desert with education, one of the first things required of them was a renunciation of the old way. John Cassian, who was, as Marrou says, "less concerned with learning than with forgetting the poetry and secular knowledge [he] had picked up in the schools before [his] conversion," was indicative of this sensibility.[128] For him, the problem with the old learning was at least in part psychological: it prevented the mind from absorbing the new ethos of the Scriptures:

> A special hindrance to salvation is added by that knowledge of literature which I seem already to have in some slight measure attained, in which the efforts of my tutor, or my attention to continual reading have so weakened me that—now my mind is filled with those songs of the poets so that even at the hour of prayer it is thinking about those trifling fables, and the stories of battles with which from its earliest infancy it was stored by its childish lessons.[129]

Arsenius, another person of great learning and high social status who came to live in the desert, soon came to realize how little he knew of its new *paideia*:

> One day Abba Arsenius consulted an old Egyptian monk about his own thoughts. Someone noticed this and said to him, "Abba Arsenius, how is it that you with such a good Latin and Greek education [παίδευσιν ʽΡωμαικὴν καὶ ʽΕλληνικὴν] ask this peasant about your thoughts?" He replied, "I have indeed been taught Latin and Greek, but I do not know even the alphabet of this peasant [τὸν δὲ ἀλφάβητον τοῦ ἀγροίκου τούτου οὔπω μεμάθηκα]."[130]

There was a clear sense among the educated ones who came to the desert that learning would have to start over in this place. In the desert, a clear distinction was made between the kind of knowledge that could be acquired through "worldly education" and what could be gained through the hard work of the simple desert monks:

> [Evagrius] said to blessed Arsenius, "How is it that we, with all our education and our wisdom [παιδεύσεως καί σοφίας] have nothing, while these uncultured Egyptians [αγροικοι καὶ Αἰγύπτιοι] acquire so many virtues?" Abba Arsenius said to him, "We indeed get nothing from our worldly education [κόσμου παιδεύσεως], but these uncultured Egyptians have acquired the virtues by their own hard work."[131]

The change in sensibilities among the learned took place not only by observing the simple monks, but sometimes through confrontations with them regarding the assumptions the well-educated ones brought with them to the desert. Sometimes such confrontations reflected tensions between Greek-speaking and Egyptian-speaking monks. In one instance, we see Abba Evagrius, one of the most learned of those to come to the desert, presenting a teaching to some of the monks. Although we are not told the precise reason for the conflict, one of the monks gently but firmly rebukes Evagrius: " 'Abba, we know that if you were living in your own country, you would probably be a bishop and a great leader; but at present you sit here as a stranger.'' He was filled with compunction, but was not at all upset and bending his head he replied, 'I have spoken once and will not answer, twice but I will proceed no further.' '' [132] Such stories reflect the authority enjoyed by the simple Coptic monks and the adjustments which the most learned had to make in their apprenticeship in the desert. Evagrius for one showed himself eager to learn. However, he could not, in spite of himself, hide his astonishment at the new teaching he received. Upon receiving a teaching from one of the elders, he was "pierced to his depths by the word, and made a prostration, saying, 'I have read many books before, but never have I received such teaching.' '' [133]

Such attitudes are found not only in the *Sayings* but also in other early monastic texts. A distinctly polemical note is heard in a description of Didymus the Blind contained in the *Historia Lausiaca*. We are told that, although he never learned to read or write, with his conscience as his teacher, "he surpassed all the ancients in knowledge.'' [134] Sozomen, in his *Historia Ecclesiastica,* proudly describes the monks as people who

> neglect many branches of mathematics and the technicalities of dialectics, because they regard such studies as superfluous, and as a useless expenditure of time, seeing that they contribute nothing towards correct living. . . . They do not demonstrate virtue by argument, but practice it. . . . Their instructions, though clothed in modesty and prudence, and devoid of vain and meretricious eloquence, possessed power, like covering medicines, in healing the moral diseases of their audiences. [135]

These texts suggest the kind of sensibility toward culture and learning which took hold in the desert. The model of Greek *paideia* followed by pagan philosophers was rejected by the desert monks. A new *paideia* was proposed in its place, one which Guy has described as "an altogether original method of spiritual education.'' [136] Scripture was central to the new *paideia* of the desert.

There is a certain irony in the fact that the desert fathers eschewed learning as part of their quest for holiness, while exalting the place of a particular book. Yet there can be no doubt that they saw the words of this singular book as a key to the quest for holiness upon which they had embarked in the desert. Cassian, who, as we noted earlier was not at all sanguine about the place of pagan learning in the monastic life, became a strong advocate for replacing the old study of pagan literature with the new knowledge of Scripture. Abba Nestoros had advised Cassian that "a speedy and effectual remedy [for your addiction to pagan learning] may arise if only you will transfer to the reading of and meditation upon the writings of the Spirit [Scripture], the same diligence and earnestness which you say that you showed in those secular studies of yours." [137] Apparently Cassian took the advice completely to heart. Guy notes that "it is rather remarkable that Cassian, whose culture, both profane and religious, was so great, doesn't anywhere set out a program of spiritual reading for his monks; the only book recommended for reading is the Book *par excellence,* the Bible." [138] Elsewhere, we hear Palladius, in the letter introducing the *Historia Lausiaca,* describe apostasy as "to be full of learning and yet not desire the Word for which the soul of a lover of God hungers." [139] He goes on to fill his work with accounts of those, both learned and unlearned, who have made the Word of God the center of their life in the desert. [140] The *Historia Monachorum,* in a comment which reflects a distinctly Christian and monastic notion of what constitutes true asceticism, tells of a certain Patermuthius, who, though unlearned, had "attained the highest degree of *ascesis*"—being able to recite the Scriptures by heart. [141] In the *Vita Antonii,* Antony is shown to have modeled his entire life upon the Bible, from his initial call through his long years of solitude in the desert. His own knowledge of Scripture was said to be profound: "He paid such close attention to what was read that nothing from Scripture did he fail to take in—rather he grasped everything, and in him memory took the place of books." [142] He held the Scriptures to be "sufficient for instruction," [143] and he counseled his monks to "keep in mind the deeds of the saints, so that the soul, ever mindful of the commandments, might be educated by their ardor." [144] In his debates with philosophers, Antony criticized the Greeks for their syllogistic approach to knowledge and for their failure "to read the Scriptures honestly." [145] He proposed a new kind of wisdom based on the Scriptures and not requiring any special learning.

These comments suggest that one of the chief differences between the quest for holiness in the desert and the quest for holiness among pagan philosophers was the text which formed the basis of its *paideia.* The centrality of Scripture in the desert implied a reversal of expectations regarding the cultural requirements for seeking holiness; in some ways this paralleled the change of locus from the city to the desert. Not only could the unlearned become "versed" in this new *paideia,* but even the learned who came to the desert were expected to learn a "new alphabet" and adopt a new text in pursuit of holiness. Thus, while there were certainly some similarities in the ascetic goals and even practices between the monks and philosophers, the differences regarding place and culture were quite marked. For the pagan philosopher, living within traditional pagan culture and drawing upon its resources shaped his message and determined in a particular way his social and religious impact. For the desert monks, it was the act of disengaging themselves from the ties of society, and immersing themselves in a new culture of solitude and Scripture that shaped their spirituality and determined much of their appeal to their contemporaries.

Very little attention has been devoted to the question of how the monastic approach to Scripture is to be situated in relation to other early Christian approaches to biblical interpretation. The monastic hermeneutic, if discussed at all, is generally treated as a minor, derivative moment in the history of interpretation.[146] This lack of attention is understandable from one perspective. Neither the intense focus which the desert fathers placed on Scripture nor the methods which they used to interpret Scripture were particularly original within Christianity. To the contrary, the desert fathers stood within a well-established tradition of biblical interpretation and drew upon many of the hermeneutical methods (allegory, typology, *exempla,* literal and moral interpretation) which had been established by previous interpreters of Scripture. What was new and distinct in the desert hermeneutic was the peculiar combination of the *locus* of the desert and the questions that arose within the ascetical life there. The questions were shaped by the particular demands of the life; in turn these questions affected the hermeneutic, both in terms of its substance and its form.

The silence and solitude of the desert, for instance, which so clearly revealed the hidden motivations of the heart, focused the attention of the desert fathers upon moral, ascetical, and psychological questions in a particularly acute way. The practical orientation of the desert fathers means that interpretation of Scripture in the *Sayings* almost never occurs for its own sake but is imbedded in the life and concerns of the desert. Biblical interpretation is always encountered as part of a lifelike situation, appearing sometimes as the focus of a particular saying or narrative, other times as the backdrop. We see Scripture on the lips of the monks during prayer in the solitude of the desert, in the context of conversations between master and disciple, during battles with demons, and in encounters with prostitutes, pagan priests, and local villagers. Its use is almost always practical, spontaneous, informal, and full of vitality. What Charles Kannengiesser has suggested regarding the hermeneutical approach of Athanasius is also true to a large extent of the desert fathers: it was a pastoral-ethical-ascetical approach to the interpretation of Scripture. The desert hermeneutic represented the far side of a transition from the saving power of Scripture being mediated by an intellectual elite, to mediation of Scripture by the church and its pastors.[147]

It is to *The Sayings of the Desert Fathers* that one must look to find the fullest expression of this pastoral-ethical-ascetical approach to biblical interpretation in early monasticism. What one finds there is a hermeneutic expressed as a whole way of life centered upon a profound appropriation of Scripture.

Notes

1. Naphtali Lewis, *Life in Egypt under Roman Rule* (Oxford: Clarendon Press, 1983), 84.

2. Harold Idris Bell, *Cults and Creeds in Graeco-Roman Egypt* (New York: Philosophical Library, 1953), 70.

3. Eusebius reports from hearsay that Christianity was brought to Egypt by St. Mark sometime during the first century, though there is little other evidence to substantiate that claim. Eusebius, *Historia Ecclesiastica* II.16.1. Early biblical manuscripts provide some hints of the possible presence of Christianity in Alexandria at an early date. Bruce Metzger, *The Early Versions of the New Testament: Their Origin, Transmission, and Limitations* (Oxford: Clarendon Press, 1977), 99: A Western reading of Acts 18:25 suggests that Apollos, a Jewish Christian from Alexandria, "[h]ad been instructed *in his own country* in the word (or way) of the Lord." If this is correct, it would indicate that Christianity had arrived in Alexandria no later than 50 c.e. For a recent critical evaluation of the emergence and growth of early Egyptian Christianity, see: C. Wilfred Griggs, *Early Egyptian Christianity: From its Origins to 451 c.e.* (Leiden: E. J. Brill, 1990).

4. See A. F. J. Klijn, "Jewish Christianity in Egypt," in *The Roots of Egyptian Christianity*, ed. B. A. Pearson and J. E. Goehring (Philadelphia: Fortress Press, 1986), 165ff. For these more educated and intelligent persons, H. I. Bell suggests that "the way had been prepared by [a] syncretistic religion . . . which at its best, with its basic monotheism, its high moral standard, its redemptive and sacramental mysteries, and its hope in immortality, showed a striking resemblance to Christianity" Bell, *Cults and Creeds*, 87.

5. Metzger, *Early Versions*, 103; Bell, *Cults and Creeds*, 87. C. H. Roberts, *Manuscript, Society and Belief in Early Christian Egypt* (London: Oxford University Press, 1979), 66.

6. Lewis, *Life in Egypt*, 100.

7. On the papyrus findings, see Bell, *Cults and Creeds,* 81; Mario Naldini, *Il christianesimo in Egitto: Lettere private nei papiri dei secoli II–IV* (Florence: Le Monnier, 1968).

8. Phillip Rousseau, *Pachomius: The Making of a Community in Fourth-Century Egypt* (Berkeley: University of California Press, 1985), 22.

9. Some have argued that the birth and growth of monasticism was itself in large part responsible for the spread of Christianity to the native Egyptian populace, but the influence between the growth of monasticism appears to have been reciprocal. Bell (*Cults and Creeds,* 88) sees a strong connection between monasticism and the spread of Christianity among the Egyptian-speaking population; Roberts (*Manuscript, Society and Belief,* 66) disputes this connection.

10. Origen, *Hom. in Luc.* xii; cited in Metzger, *Early Versions,* 104.

11. Eusebius, *Historia ecclesiastica* VI.41; cited in Metzger, *Early Versions,* 104; Bell, *Cults and Creeds,* 85.

12. Epiphanius *Haer.* lxvii; cited in Metzger, *Early Versions,* 104; Roberts (*Manuscript, Society and Belief,* 66) suggests that a person such as Hiercas may well have trained some of the early Christian monks.

13. "While it is generally agreed that almost the entire New Testament and much of the Old Testament existed in the Sahidic dialect before at latest the end of the fourth century and that translations into other dialects were being made, how far back the translations reached and what was the relation of Sahidic to other dialects is very much a matter of debate among experts" (Roberts, *Manuscript, Society and Belief,* 64).

14. On the relative strength of Christianity in Egypt in the middle to late third century, see Bell, *Cults and Creeds,* 86; Roberts, *Manuscript, Society and Belief,* 66–68. For the contrary view, see Robin Lane Fox, *Pagans and Christians* (New York: Knopf, 1987), 270, who disputes this assessment, claiming that there is not enough evidence to argue for a significant Christian presence in Egypt at this time and that "statements by Christians about their 'growth' should be read with a very critical eye for the figures from which they begin." Lane Fox suggests that the Christians were at this time a "small, but extremely articulate minority."

15. Lane Fox, *Pagans and Christians,* 590.

16. Roberts, *Manuscript, Society and Belief,* 73.

17. These theories are discussed in: C. Peifer, "The Biblical Foundations of Monasticism," *Cistercian Studies* 12 (1972):7–31; see also K. Heussi, *Die Ursprung des Mönchtums* (Tubingen: Mohr, 1936), 280–304.

18. The historical implausibility of the presence of wandering Buddhist monks in third-century Egypt makes this the least likely of the possible non-Christian influences on early Christian monasticism.

19. The *katachoi* of the temple of Serapis, however, were not really recluses and did not renounce the world in any way, making it difficult to trace any kinship or connection between them and the early Christian monks. See: H. G. Evelyn-White, *The Monasteries of the Wâdi 'n Natrûn,* pt. 2, *The History of the Monasteries of Nitria and Scetis* (New York: Metropolitan Museum of Art, 1932), 5; Hans Lietz-

mann, *A History of the Early Church,* vol. 4: *The Era of the Church Fathers,* trans. B. L. Woolf (London: Lutterworth, 1951), 133.

20. The influence of the Greek philosophical schools on the *origins* of monasticism is hard to credit simply because most of the major early figures in the monastic movement such as Antony, Amoun, Pachomius, and Macarius were, if not illiterate, at least people of very limited education. Also, they would have had little opportunity to travel and would have had few chances for contact with pagan philosophers, who were generally located in the larger urban centers. The influence of Greek thought is certainly felt in the monastic literature as the movement developed during the fourth century, especially in works such as the *Historia Lausiaca* and the writings of Evagrius and Cassian. At the early stages of monastic development, however, there is simply no reason to believe that Greek philosophical thought would have played any significant role. (Evelyn-White, *The Monasteries of the Wâdi 'n Natrûn,* 4).

21. The possible influence of the Jewish ascetical movement of the Therapeutae upon early monasticism is still a matter of some dispute and is probably a question to which no definite answer can be given. Rousseau thinks it is clearly important that a way of life so similar to early monasticism existed within the Egyptian tradition. He suggests that references to village settlements, manual labor, a structured community with a hierarchy of authority, and discussions of sacred teachings under the guidance of a superior "cannot be dismissed as unconnected with later monastic patterns" (Rousseau, *Pachomius,* 1). While this may have some real bearing on the formation of the Pachomian cenobitic tradition, it is much less likely that Antony and the other founders of the eremetical life in lower Egypt had any example of a Therapeutic community before them to serve as a model (Evelyn-White, *The Monasteries of the Wâdi 'n Natrûn,* 9).

22. The Manichees lived an austere and celibate life and were a well-recognized presence in Egypt's Christian centers by ca. 300 C.E. "Like many Christian groups scattered throughout Egypt, Manichaeism emphasized an on-going Apocalyptic tradition, gnosis required for salvation, and a broad-based literary tradition. The spiritual climate of Egypt, even Christian Egypt, in the third century was conducive to the spread of Manichaeism, and remnants of the movement lingered on for some centuries. . . ." (Griggs, *Early Egyptian Christianity,* 97). Although contacts between monks and Manichees were common in fourth-century Egypt, the precise character of their relationship is difficult to determine. To Lane Fox, "direct derivation . . . of the monastic impulse from a hated rival heresy is quite implausible. At most it was a goad, provoking a yet more competitive effort" (Lane Fox, *Pagans and Christians,* 602). For an instance of the contact between Christian monks and Manichees, see *VA* 68.

23. A. Harnack, *The Mission and Expansion of Christianity in the First Three Centuries,* trans., ed. J. Moffatt, 2d rev. ed., vol. 2 (New York: Putnam, 1908), 160–161. Walter Bauer was an influential proponent of the theory that gnosticism pervaded early Egyptian Christianity. See Walter Bauer, *Orthodoxy and Heresy in Earliest Christianity,* trans. and ed. R. A. Kraft and G. Krodel (Philadelphia: Fortress Press, 1971).

24. Bell, *Cults and Creeds,* 91–94.

25. R. M. Grant, "The New Testament Canon," in *The Cambridge History of the Bible*, vol. 1: *From the Beginnings to Jerome*, ed. P. R. Ackroyd and C. F. Evans (Cambridge: Cambridge University Press, 1970), 1:298.

26. J. M. Creed, "Egypt and the Christian Church," in *The Legacy of Egypt*, ed. S. R. K. Glanville (Oxford: Clarendon Press, 1942), 312.

27. Bell, *Cults and Creeds*, 91–94.

28. J. E. Goehring, "New Frontiers in Pachomian Studies," in *Roots of Egyptian Christianity*, 246–52; F. Wisse, "Gnosticism and Early Monasticism in Egypt," in *Gnosis; Festschrift für Hans Jonas*, ed. B. Aland (Gottingen: Vandenhoeck and Ruprecht, 1978), 431–40.

29. Lane Fox, *Pagans and Christians*, 415–16.

30. Roberts, *Manuscript, Society and Belief*, 49–72; on this same question, see Tito Orlandi, "Coptic Literature," in *Roots of Egyptian Christianity*, 55.

31. B. A. Pearson, "Earliest Christianity in Egypt: Some Observations," in *Roots of Egyptian Christianity*, 145–54; idem, *Gnosticism, Judaism, and Egyptian Christianity* (Philadelphia: Fortress Press, 1990), 194–213. Klijn, "Jewish Christianity in Egypt," 167ff.; Rousseau, *Pachomius*, 15–16. See Griggs, *Early Egyptian Christianity*, 13–34, for a carefully nuanced assessment of the relationship between "orthodoxy" and "heresy" in earliest Egyptian Christianity. While acknowledging the presence of gnosticism in early Egyptian Christianity, he suggests that the whole question needs to be approached in a new way.

> Instead of pursuing the somewhat fruitless arguments (made fruitless by the fragmentary nature of the evidence) of Bauer, Telfer, and others about the orthodoxy or heresy of earliest Egyptian Christianity, the archaeological evidence rather seems to point toward an undifferentiated Christianity based on a literary tradition encompassing both canonical and non-canonical works (both categories being named here in light of their *later* status as defined by the Catholic tradition). The forces which caused the narrow geographical and literary outlook of the Western Church . . . do not appear to have been felt strongly in Egypt during the first two centuries of the Christian era. Bauer may be correct in asserting that what later heresiologists attacked as "gnosticism" in Egypt may have been simply "Christianity" to Egyptian Christians, but he does not pay sufficient heed to the evidence of so-called "orthodox Christianity" existing alongside it. . . . A Gnostic type of Christianity was apparently more prevalent in Egypt than in the West. . . . One must emphasize that this is not to argue that Gnosticism was predominant in Egypt, as some have done, or that Catholicism was absent. Rather, Egyptian Christianity was founded on a more broadly-based literary tradition and a less defined ecclesiastical tradition than was the same religion in the region from Syria to Rome (32–34).

32. T. D. Barnes (*Constantine and Eusebius* [Cambridge: Harvard University Press, 1981], 194–95) notes a striking passage in Eusebius's *Historia Ecclesiastica* (II.17. 3ff.) in which Eusebius quotes long extracts from Philo's description of the Therapeutae of the first century, who organized themselves in celibate communities of men and women. This leads Barnes to surmise that "some form of monastic life existed in Palestine when Eusebius wrote this passage."

33. On early Syrian Christianity and the growth of monasticism there, see: A. Vööbus, *A History of Asceticism in the Syrian Orient*, CSCO 184, subsidia 14 (Lou-

vain: CSCO, 1958), 3–108; R. Murray, *Symbols of Church and Kingdom: A Study in Early Syriac Tradition* (Cambridge: Cambridge University Press, 1975); W. H. C. Frend, *The Rise of Christianity* (Philadelphia: Fortress Press, 1984), 578; S. P. Brock, "Early Syrian Asceticism," *Numen* 20 (1973):1–19.

34. Armand Veilleux, "Monasticism and Gnosis in Egypt," in *Roots of Egyptian Christianity,* 300; see also L. Bouyer, *The Spirituality of the New Testament and the Fathers* (New York: Seabury Press, 1982), 306.

35. R. Murray, "The Exhortation to Candidates for Ascetical Vows at Baptism in the Ancient Syrian Churches," *New Testament Studies* 21 (1974):59–80; J. Gribomont, "Monasticism and Asceticism—Eastern Christianity," in *Christian Spirituality: Origins to the Twelfth Century,* ed. B. McGinn, J. Meyendorff, and J. Leclercq (New York: Crossroad, 1985), 90–91; Lane Fox, *Pagans and Christians,* 602.

36. A. Guillaumont, "Le dépaysement comme forme d'ascèse dans le monachisme ancien," in *École pratique des hautes études,* V section: *Sciences religieuses, Annuaire 1968–69,* 76 (1968): 31–58; Veilleux, "Monasticism and Gnosis in Egypt," 301–2; on exile in the *Sayings,* see Andrew 1 [*PG* 65:136B], Longinus 1 [*PG* 65:256C].

37. A. Guillaumont, "Monachisme et éthique judéo-chrétienne," *Judéo-Christianisme, Recherches historiques et théologiques offertes en hommage au Cardinal Daniélou, RSR* 60 (1972):199–218.

38. E. A. Judge, in "The Earliest Use of Monachos for 'Monk' (P. Coll. Youtie 77) and the Origins of Monasticism," *Jahrbuch für Antike und Christentum* 20 (1977):72–89, makes use of papyrus fragments to trace the development of the early ascetical communities in Egypt. He identifies the anchoritic moment as the time in which Christian monks began to become specifically identified.

39. Lewis, *Life in Egypt,* 108; see also H. Henne, "Documents et travaux sur l'Anachôrèsis," *Akten des VIII Internationalen Kongresses für Papyrologie. Wien 1955* (Vienna: Rudolf M. Rohner, 1956), 59–66.

40. Lewis, *Life in Egypt,* 160–64, 184; see also M. Rostovtzeff, *The Social and Economic History of the Roman Empire,* 2d ed., rev. by P. M. Fraser (Oxford: Clarendon Press, 1957), 1:298, 2:677.

41. *Oxyrhynchus Papyri 1477;* cited in Rostovtzeff, *Social and Economic History,* 479, 742; see also Lewis, *Life in Egypt,* 164.

42. For an example of the plight of Egyptian farmers during this period, see A. E. R. Boak, "An Egyptian Farmer of the Age of Diocletian and Constantine," *Byzantina Metabyzantina* 1 (1946):39–43; A. E. Boak ("Village Liturgies in Fourth-Century Karanis," *Akten des VIII Internationalen Kongresses für Papyrologie. Wien 1955* [Vienna: Rudolf M. Rohner, 1956], 40) comments: "The small landholders were laboring under the double burden of heavy taxation and compulsory public services. . . . [T]he burden became intolerable and led to the crushing out of the greater part of the small proprietors, the spread of abandoned lands. . . ." Rousseau (*Pachomius,* 9–10) questions this assessment of the willingness of Egyptians to abandon society in such a dramatic fashion: "One is dealing with an enclosed system. Everyone knew everyone else; everyone was expected to bear their fiscal and corporate responsibilities. If people had abandoned their locality, it was widely known where

they had gone. 'Flight' or 'withdrawal' in those cases was rarely to the stark alter-
native of the desert and most often to another community identical in social and
economic structure, usually close by.'' Such a view can serve as an important cor-
rective to an impression that all flight from responsibility led inevitably to the desert.
We know from the literature that many of the monastic communities kept close
contact with the towns and villages around them. See, for example, J. E. Goehring,
"The World Engaged: The Social and Economic World of Early Egyptian Monasticism,'' in *Gnosticism and the Early Christian World: In Honor of James M. Robinson*, ed. J. E. Goehring et al. (Sonoma, CA: Polebridge, 1990), 134–44. Nevertheless, this does not lessen the reality or starkness of the genuine flight into the desert
that did take place for a great number of the early anchorites.

43. Peter Brown, *The Making of Late Antiquity* (Cambridge: Harvard University
Press, 1978), 82.

44. Daniélou remarks that, while others might have fled to the desert for these
reasons, "the monk chose the desert for reasons of a spiritual nature.'' Such a view
must clearly be revised in light of the analysis by Brown and others. See J. Daniélou
and H. Marrou, *The Christian Centuries*, vol. 1, *The First Six Hundred Years*, trans.
V. Cronin (New York: McGraw-Hill, 1964), 270.

45. *VA* 3 [*PG* 26:844 BC–845 A]: "There were not yet many monasteries in
Egypt and no monk knew at all the great desert, but each of those wishing to give
attention to his life disciplined himself in isolation, not far from his own village''
(*The Life of Antony and the Letter to Marcellinus*, trans. R. C. Gregg [New York:
Paulist Press], 32). See also *Vita Pachomii* (Bohairic Life) 1:2: *Pachomian Koinonia*, vol. 1, trans. with an introduction by Armand Veilleux (Kalamazoo, MI.:
Cistercian Publications, 1980), 23–24: "[I]n Egypt and the Thebaid there had not
been many of them.'' E. R. Hardy, in *Christian Egypt: Church and People* (New
York: Oxford University Press, 1952), 39, notes that "a Bishop from Upper Egypt
who appeared at the Council of Nicea in 325 is said to have lived in an *asceticon*
(which probably means an ascetic cell) for many years, from which we can say that
there were probably anchorites in the Thebaid long before that time.'' Judge, in
"The Earliest Use of Monachos for Monk','' 83–86, argues that *monachos* was
first used to describe those who renounced ordinary domesticities while retaining a
place in local society; shortly it became associated "with Antony and his kind and
is correctly applied to them from the point at which they began to mark themselves
off openly from the community at large (ca. 305)'' (85).

46. Eusebius, *Historia ecclesiastica* VI.42; see: Evelyn-White, *The Monasteries
of the Wâdi 'n Natrûn*, 12; Derwas J. Chitty, *The Desert a City* (Oxford: Blackwell,
1966), 7; Lane Fox, in *Pagans and Christians*, 610, suggests that one of the reasons
for the withdrawal into the desert may well have been the schisms that emerged from
lapsing during these persecutions: "We can well sympathize with those perfectionists
in Egypt who had begun to withdraw from their fellow Christians in order to pursue
their ideals in the desert.''

47. *VA* 3 [*PG* 26:844BC–845A]: "Now at that time in the neighboring village
there was an old man who had practiced from his youth the solitary life'' (Gregg,
Life of Antony, 32).

48. *Vita Pachomii* (Bohairic Life), 1 *Pachomian Koinonia*, 1:23–24. Veilleux (266) comments: "It is very interesting to see how the appearance of monasticism is presented here as a fruit of the increased faith of Christians after the time of the martyrs. This goes against the commonly held opinion that monasticism was a reaction to diminishing fervor in the Church after the persecution era."

49. T. C. Skeat, "Early Christian Book Production: Papyri and Manuscripts," in *The Cambridge History of the Bible*, Vol. 2: *The West from the Fathers to the Reformation*, ed. G. W. H. Lampe (Cambridge: Cambridge University Press, 1969), 54.

50. Lane Fox, *Pagans and Christians*, 304. Although this is to a large extent true, Lane Fox neglects to note the strong oral power that the Scriptures of Christianity possessed and the extent to which they circulated orally within large parts of the Christian community. See discussion, in chapter 4, on the oral dimension of Scripture in the desert. Also, there are examples in the pagan tradition of books that were revered as divinely inspired. See A. H. Armstrong, "The Ancient and Continuing Pieties of the Greek World," in *Classical and Mediterranean Spirituality*, ed. A. H. Armstrong (New York: Crossroad, 1986): "There were in the Greek world small (perhaps very small) groups of people who possessed a mass of books of poems which they claimed were divinely inspired compositions by Orpheus and other mythical singers of remote antiquity. They regarded these as a sort of inspired scripture. . . ." (98).

51. C. H. Roberts, "The Codex," *Proceedings of the British Academy* 40 (1954):169–204; Skeat, "Early Christian Book Production," 54–79; C. H. Roberts and T. C. Skeat, *The Birth of the Codex* (London: Oxford University Press, 1983).

52. Skeat, in "Early Christian Book Production," 66, notes that the evidence for these rough codices can be found throughout the Near East, from as early as the eighth century B.C.E., but that it was with the Romans that they came to be used more extensively. The author of 2 Timothy is presumably referring to rough codices such as these when he asks Timothy to "bring . . . the books, and above all the parchments [μεμβράνας]" (2 Tm 4:13). Skeat suggests that "his use of the Latin term confirms the theory that the parchment notebook was of Roman invention. . . ." The New English Bible captures the sense of the word in its translation, which reads, "the books, above all my notebooks."

53. Skeat, in "Early Christian Book Production," 68–69, has noted that in the case of pagan literature, the evidence suggests that the codex barely existed before 200 C.E. and did not achieve a sizeable proportion of all literature until after 250 C.E. Overall the proportion of codices to rolls is only 2.5 percent. The evidence from the Christian fragments and codices presents a startlingly different picture. Among the fragments which have been found in Egypt and which were produced up until the end of the fourth century C.E., over 99 percent are from codices. Moreover, of fourteen or fifteen biblical papyri which can be assigned to the second century, every one is a codex.

54. Skeat, "Early Christian Book Production," 75. Nevertheless, in Egypt especially, the papyrus codex remained in common use down to the sixth or seventh century.

55. Roberts, *Manuscript, Society and Belief*, 15 (emphasis mine). The issue of

the Bible as a sacred object in Egyptian monasticism is treated in chapter 4. Early Christianity was certainly not immune to the tendency toward "bibliomancy." The point here is that the early Christian codices generally had a very *practical* function within the Christian community. Roberts (20) notes also that there was no doubt some economic and social factors which contributed to the "common" appearance of the Christian codices: "[T]he earliest Christian communities may well not have had access to the services of skilled scribes such as the synagogue could command. . . . [T]his would mean that in their production economic and social factors as well as religious were at work and that the business-like hand of the early texts mirrors the character and circumstances of the communities that used them."

56. The fact that the *Sayings*, at least in the Alphabetico-Anonymous collection which forms the basis for this study, comes to us in Greek, means that those who committed the sayings and stories of the desert monks to writing would have had a closer relationship with the *LXX*, related Greek versions of the Old Testament, and the Greek New Testament than many of those who originally uttered the sayings.

57. Metzger, *Early Versions*, 126–29; see also C. S. C. Williams, "The History of the Text and Canon of the New Testament to Jerome," in *The Cambridge History of the Bible*, vol. 2: *The West from the Fathers to the Reformation*, ed. G. W. H. Lampe (Cambridge: Cambridge University Press, 1969), 27–53. Orlandi, "Coptic Literature,"' 63–64.

58. *Oxyrhynchus Papyri 2673;* cited in Lane Fox, *Pagans and Christians*, 282.

59. *VA* 1–3 [*PG* 26:840A–845A]; regarding Antony's ignorance of Greek, see Jerome, *De vir. ill.* lxxxviii: "Antonius monachus . . . misit aegyptiace ad diversa monasteria apostolici sensus sermonisque epistolas septem, *quae in graecum linguam translatae sunt*," cited in Metzger, *Early Versions*, 105.

60. *VA*, 2, 3 [*PG* 26:841B–45C]; Gregg, *The Life of Antony*, 31.

61. On the complex motives behind the *VA*, see R. Gregg and D. Groh, *Early Arianism: A View of Salvation* (Philadelphia: Fortress Press, 1981).

62. E. A. Judge, "Fourth Century Monasticism in the Papyri," in *Proceedings of the Sixteenth International Congress of Papyrologists*, ed. R. S. Bagnall et al. (Chico, CA: Scholar's Press, 1981), 616. Lk 14:33: "Whoever of you does not renounce [ἀποτάσσεται] all that he has cannot be my disciple."

63. Nor should one be persuaded by those who have argued that the monastic reading of the biblical texts regarding renunciation were fundamentally misguided. For example, Lietzmann, *Era of the Church Fathers*, 124–27; Lane Fox, in *Pagans and Christians*, 364–65, reduces an exceedingly complex matter to an oversimplified formula: "The influence of these texts (Mt 19:21; 1 Cor 7) and their *misunderstandings* were extremely important for first-class Christians" (emphasis mine).

64. As Veilleux has noted, "all the motivations that they themselves revealed to us in their writings came from Scripture. Do we have a right to pretend we know their secret motivations better than they did?" (Veilleux, "Monasticism and Gnosis in Egypt," 306).

65. E. R. Dodds, *Pagan and Christian in an Age of Anxiety* (New York: W. W. Norton, 1970), 101.

66. There was a growing sense, suggests Brown, that "certain concrete human

individuals are marked out by the supernatural by virtue of a peculiar intimacy thought to be enjoyed between themselves and the supernatural'' (Peter Brown, ''A Social Context to the Religious Crisis of the Third Century A.D.,'' Colloquy 14, Center for Hermeneutical Studies, Berkeley, 1975, 2–3).

67. Peter Brown, ''The Rise and Function of the Holy Man in Late Antiquity,'' *Journal of Roman Studies* 61 (1971):98–101; reprinted with revisions in idem, *Society and the Holy in Late Antiquity* (Berkeley: University of California Press, 1982), 148–51.

68. Peter Brown has coined the expression ''debate on the holy.'' See *The Making of Late Antiquity,* 1–26. ''Debate'' is used here to refer to the increasingly sharp definition of positions on the part of pagans and Christians regarding the means by which one was to pursue the holy. Although this ''debate'' took place largely in writing, it was occasionally expressed in face-to-face encounters between pagans and Christians. See, for example, Olympios 1 [*PG* 65:315 CD].

69. Brown, *The Making of Late Antiquity,* 82. For a helpful discussion of some of the convergences between paganism and Christianity in late antiquity, see G. W. Bowersock, *Hellenism in Late Antiquity* (Ann Arbor: University of Michigan Press, 1990).

70. Garth Fowden, ''The Pagan Holy Man in Late Antique Society,'' *Journal of Hellenic Studies,* 102 (1982):34.

71. Peter Brown, ''The Philosopher and Society in Late Antiquity,'' Colloquy 34. Center for Hermeneutical Studies, Berkeley, 1978, 13–14.

72. On the growth of Greek philosophical schools in the second century, see R. Wilken, *The Christians as the Romans Saw Them* (New Haven: Yale University Press, 1984), 72–77: ''(Lucian calls them *bioi*) similar to what we today would call religious movements.''

73. Dodds, *Pagan and Christian in an Age of Anxiety,* 92–93; see also Bell, *Cults and Creeds,* 71: ''Philosophy reinforced the tendency to a more personal and intimate form of religion and gave strength to the feeling that ceremonial purification is not enough, that the worshipper must have not only pure hands but a pure heart. . . .''

74. P. Hadot, *Exercices spirituels et philosophie antique* (Paris: Études Augustiniennes, 1981), 63, 68.

75. Porphyry, *Vita Plotinii [VP]* 3:5; in Plotinus, *The Enneads,* with Porphyry, *Life of Plotinus,* trans. S. Mackenna (London: Faber and Faber, 1963).

76. A. D. Nock, *Conversion* (London: Oxford University Press, 1933), 179.

77. P. Brown, *The World of Late Antiquity* (London: Thames and Hudson, 1971), 96.

78. Fowden, ''The Pagan Holy Man,'' 38.

79. Fowden, ''The Pagan Holy Man,'' 40.

80. *VP* 3:33.

81. *VP* 7:1–2. There were also listeners ἀκροαταί] who were more numerous, and who included, like many ancient philosophical schools, women.

82. Fowden, in ''The Pagan Holy Man,'' 48–49, notes that ''Porphyry pointedly distinguished the lover of wisdom from the athlete, the soldier, the sailor, the orator and in general from all those whose calling involved them in manual labour or the

world of affairs; and Eunapios makes clear that he regards any intellectual from a genuinely poor background as an exceptional and noteworthy phenomenon."

83. On the increasingly marginal positions of some pagan philosophers in late antiquity, see Fowden, "The Pagan Holy Man," 54ff; for an alternate view, see Brown, "The Philosopher and Society," 3, 7–10.

84. Senators: *VP* 7:29–30; women: *VP* 9:1–5.

85. *VP* 12:1.

86. *VP* 9:16–18.

87. Although Plotinus cannot be said to have been the head of a "school" in Rome, he was a *diadokē*, a teacher of a philosophical tradition or "school of thought," who interpreted the views of one of the more classical philosophers of old. In Plotinus's case, Plato was the philosopher whose work was the primary object of interpretation. On Plotinus as a *diadokē*, see *Porphyre: La vie de Plotin, travaux préliminaires*, ed. L. Brisson et al. (Paris: J. Vrin, 1982), 251.

88. *VP* 2:3–6.

89. *VP* 8:21–22.

90. *VP* 1:1.

91. *Enneads* IV.8.4.

92. *Enneads* II.9.15.39. By virtue, Plotinus meant primarily the purificatory virtues, which prepared the soul for contemplation; see *Enneads* VI.7.36.6: "Purification has the Good for goal; so the virtues, all right ordering, ascent within the Intellectual, settlement therein, banqueting upon the divine—by these methods one becomes, to self and all else, at once seen and seer; identical with Being and Intellectual—Principle and the entire living all, we no longer see the supreme as external; we are near now, the next is That and it is close at hand, radiant above the intellectual." He also included social virtues in this process of purification and maintained that they must never be separated. For other examples of the place of virtues in the pursuit of philosophy, see Wilken, *The Christians as the Romans Saw Them*, 80.

93. *Enneads* V. 1, 8, 10.

94. *Enneads* II. 9, 6, 24–26.

95. *VP* 20:30; E. R. Dodds, in "Tradition and Personal Achievement in Plotinus," *Journal of Roman Studies* 50 (1960):1–2, points out that one should be wary of taking this too literally, for to some extent at least, Plotinus used the Platonic texts as "authority" for his own speculations. This is a helpful qualification in the sense that it keeps us from thinking of Plotinus as slavishly copying Plato. However, Dodds goes too far in saying that had Plato never lived, Plotinus's thought would have taken the same structure and direction. Plotinus's thought is so steeped in Plato that it is difficult to imagine what shape his thinking would have taken without his great predecessor.

96. Pierre Hadot, *Plotin, ou la simplicité du regard* (Paris: Librairie Plon, 1963), 12.

97. *Enneads* III.4.3.22.

98. Dodds, *Pagan and Christian in an Age of Anxiety*, 84.

99. *Enneads* I.4.10.

100. *Enneads* IV.8.8.
101. *Enneads* VI.9.9.59: "Thus we have all the vision that may be of Him and of ourselves; but it is a self wrought to splendor, brimmed with the Intellectual light, become that light, pure buoyant, unburdened, raised to Godhood or, better, knowing its Godhood, all aflame them."
102. *VP* 13:1.
103. *VP* 18:6–8.
104. *VP* 3:35.
105. *VP* 18:2.
106. *VP* 4:10–11.
107. *VP* 13:15–16.
108. *Enneads* III.7 1.7–16.
109. Marie-Odile Goulet-Cazé, "Plotin, professeur de philosophie," in *Porphyre: La vie de Plotin*, 265.
110. Goulet-Cazé, "Plotin, professeur de philosophie," 266.
111. Hadot, "Exercices spirituels," 48.
112. *VP* 8:8.
113. Brown, "The Philosopher and Society," 17.
114. On Egyptian attitudes toward the desert as the home of the demonic forces, see L. Keiner, "L'horreur des Égyptiens pour les démons du désert," *Bulletin de l'Institut d'Égypte* 26 (1943–1944):135–47; see also A. Guillaumont ("La conception du désert chez les moines d'Egypte," in *Aux origines du monachisme chrétien* [Bégrolles-en-Mauges: Bellefontaine, 1979], 69–87), who contrasts the idealized notion of the desert held by some nonmonastic writers with the far more sober attitude toward the desert found in the early monastic literature. For the early monks, the desert was a place of terror, filled with demons.
115. Sisoes 26 [*PG* 65:400D–401A]. There is some evidence of questions arising among the monks about the usefulness of withdrawal into the desert and of tensions which sometimes existed between those who lived in complete solitude and those who lived in monasteries or small semieremetical communities. It was not withdrawal to the desert itself which guaranteed success but something more intangible—how one approached the life. Abba John, who was the abbot of a great monastery, asked Abba Paësius, who had been living for forty years in a remote region of the desert, " 'What good have you done by living here in retreat for so long, and not being easily disturbed by anyone?' He replied, 'Since I lived in solitude the sun has never seen me eating.' Abba John said to him, 'As for me, it has never seen me angry' " (Cassian 4 [*PG* 65:244CD–245A]).
116. Poemen 189 [*PG* 65:361B]. See also the statement of Evagrius on what is necessary in the monastic life: "Sit in your cell, collecting your thoughts." Evagrius 1 [*PG* 65:173A]. The regime of the cell included both its outer and inner necessities: "Living in your cell clearly means manual work, eating only once a day, silence, meditation; but really making progress in the cell means to experience contempt for yourself wherever you go, not to neglect the hours of prayer and to pray secretly" (Poemen 168 [*PG* 65:361CD]).

117. Antony 10 [*PG* 65:77C]. The cell was a place of refuge from temptations: John Colobos 12 [*PG* 65:208B].

118. It was not the cell itself which was important but what the cell taught the monk. The mindfulness of God which the monk sought to cultivate in the cell was meant to extend beyond it also: "God is in the cell, and on the other hand, he is outside also" (Daniel 5 [*PG* 65:156B]). For this reason, the dangers of self-delusion which came from false reliance upon the cell were carefully noted: "Abba Ammonas said, 'A man may remain for a hundred years in his cell without learning how to live in the cell' " (Poemen 96 [*PG* 65:345B]).

119. The tensions between desert and city are reflected in the following saying: "Abba Macarius said to the brethren, 'When you see a cell built close to the marsh, know that the devastation of Scetis is near; when you see trees, know that it is at the doors" (Macarius the Great 5 [*PG* 65:264D]).

120. Matoes 13 [*PG* 65:293C]. See also Theodore of Pherme 14 [*PG* 65:189D–192A]: "The man who has learned the sweetness of the cell flees from his neighbor but not as though he despised him."

121. Brown, *The Making of Late Antiquity*, 83–86: Agathon, one of the earliest (and youngest) to have withdrawn into the desert, is said to have "provided everything he needed for himself, in manual work, food, and clothing," and provides a picture of just this kind of man (Agathon 10, [*PG* 65:112C]).

122. Dodds, *Pagan and Christian in an Age of Anxiety*, 134.

123. Ibid., 106: "Clement of Alexandria had perceived that if Christianity was to be more than a religion for the uneducated, it must come to terms with Greek philosophy and Greek science; simple minded Christians must no longer 'fear philosophy as children fear a scarecrow.' (*Strom.* 6:80)"; see also Jean Leclercq, O.S.B., *The Love of Learning and the Desire for God* (New York: Fordham University Press, 1961): "St. Jerome quoted the *auctores*, praised their virtues, compared the Prophets' figures of speech with the hyperboles and apostrophes of Virgil, called attention to the fact that Solomon recommends the study of philosophy and that St. Paul quotes verses by Epimenides, Menander and Aratus. St. Augustine likewise pointed out that the sacred authors used the same literary methods as the pagan authors of antiquity" (145–49).

124. H. I. Marrou, *A History of Education in Antiquity*, trans. G. Lamb (Madison: University of Wisconsin Press, 1982), 320.

125. Jerome, *Epistle* xxii, ch. 30, in *Selected Letters of St. Jerome*, trans. F. A. Wright (London: Heinemann, 1933), 126–27.

126. Marrou, *A History of Education*: "Even the most educated of them, those who remained most faithful to classical art and classical thought—St. Augustine for example—share the spontaneous reaction of the simple and the ignorant, and condemn the old culture for being an independent ideal hostile to the Christian revelation" (319–320). Bowersock, in *Hellenism in Late Antiquity*, offers the helpful reminder that "[p]aganism as a rival to Christianity was essentially a Christian perception. For the pagans, coexistence with another cult, however popular it might be, was always a real possibility" (6).

127. A. H. M. Jones, "The Social Background of the Struggle between Paganism and Christianity," in *The Conflict between Paganism and Christianity in the Fourth Century*, ed. A. Momigliano (Oxford: Clarendon Press, 1963), 20.

128. Marrou, *A History of Education*, 330.

129. Cassian, *Conferences* 14:12, in Edgar C. S. Gibson, trans., *Library of Nicene and Post-Nicene Fathers*, 2d ser., vol. 11 (Oxford: Parker, 1894), 441. Cassian's attitude is a good example of a polemic which masks another reality. In spite of his pessimism regarding classical literature, his writings as a whole present a carefully wrought synthesis of classical and Christian thought.

130. Arsenius 6 [*PG* 65:89A], [m].

131. Arsenius 5 [*PG* 65:88D–89A], [m]. Such stories seem to convey, as Fernández Marcos suggests, "a nostalgia" among the monks for a primitive Christian praxis uncontaminated by the culture of the world. Natalio Fernández Marcos, "La Biblia y los origenes del monaquismo," *Miscelánea Comillas* 41 (1983):387.

132. Evagrius 7 [*PG* 65:178A].

133. Euprepius 7 [*PG* 65:172D], [m]. The saying is contained under the name of Euprepius in the Alphabetico-Anonymous collection, but there is strong evidence from other manuscripts that the saying comes from Evagrius. See Regnault's remarks in *SPAlph*, 91.

134. Palladius, *Historia Lausiaca* 4:1–2, in Robert T. Meyer, trans., *The Lausic History*, (Westminster, MD: Newman Press, 1965), 35.

135. Sozomen, *Historia ecclesiastica* I:12 [*PG* 67:890–93]; *Nicene and Post-Nicene Fathers*, trans. Chester D. Hartranft, 2d ser., vol. 2 (Grand Rapids, MI: Eerdmans, 1979), 247–48.

136. Jean-Claude Guy, "Educational Innovation in the Desert Fathers," *Eastern Churches Review* 6 (1974):45.

137. Cassian, *Conferences* 14:13, in Gibson, *Nicene and Post-Nicene Fathers*, 441.

138. Jean-Claude Guy, *Jean Cassien: Vie et doctrine spirituelle* (Paris: P. Lethielleux, 1961), 44.

139. Palladius, *Historia Lausiaca*, "Letter to Lausus," 3; Meyer, *Lausiac History*, 22.

140. Palladius, *Historia Lausiaca* 11:4; 18:25; 26:3; 32:12; 37:1; 58:1.

141. *Historia Monachorum in Aegypto* 10:7; trans. Norman Russell, introd. Benedicta Ward *The Lives of the Desert Fathers* (London: Mowbray, 1980), 83.

142. *VA* 3 [*PG* 26:844BC–845A]; Gregg, *Life of Antony*, 32.

143. *VA* 16 [*PG* 26:865C–868B]; Gregg, *Life of Antony*, 43. Much of what we hear in the *VA* clearly reflects the opinions of Athanasius.

144. *VA* 55 [*PG* 26:921BC–925A]; Gregg, *Life of Antony*, 72.

145. *VA* 72–80 [*PG* 26:944B–956A]; Gregg, *Life of Antony*, 86.

146. R. M. Grant, with D. Tracy, *A Short History of the Interpretation of the Bible*, 2d ed., rev. and enl. (Philadelphia: Fortress Press, 1984), 3–83; J. Kugel and R. A. Greer, *Early Biblical Interpretation* (Philadelphia: Westminster Press, 1986); K. Froehlich, *Biblical Interpretation in the Early Church* (Philadelphia: Fortress Press, 1984); B. Margerie, S. J., *Introduction à l'histoire de l'exégèse. I: Les pères grecs*

et orientaux (Paris: Cerf, 1980); C. Mondésert, ed., *Le Monde grec ancien et la Bible* (Paris: Beauchesne, 1984); S. M. Schneiders, "Scripture and Spirituality," in *Christian Spirituality: Origins to the Twelfth Century,* 1–20; R. P. C. Hanson, "Biblical Exegesis in the Early Church," in *The Cambridge History of the Bible,* 1:412–53; An exception is J. Biarne, "La Bible dans la vie monastique," in *Le Monde latin antique et la Bible,* ed. Jacques Fontaine and Charles Pietri (Paris: Beauchesne, 1985), 409–29.

147. C. Kannengiesser, *Early Christian Spirituality* (Philadelphia: Fortress Press, 1986), 10–15. See also K. Torjeson, "Review of *Early Christian Spirituality,*" *Patristics* 16 (1988):7–8.

3

The Sayings of the Desert Fathers

The Sayings of the Desert Fathers is among the most vital and engaging texts to emerge from the early Christian world. It was immensely popular among the early monks, who began at a relatively early date to collect and preserve the more memorable stories and sayings of their revered elders. The very qualities that guaranteed the preservation of these sayings also stimulated an abundant growth in the number and variety of collections and in the variations of sayings within those collections; because of this, the number and complexity of critical problems related to the *Sayings* is extraordinarily high.[1] While we are still far from being able to resolve all of these problems satisfactorily, a careful exploration of some of the more important critical questions the *Sayings* presents to us will contribute greatly toward our understanding of the hermeneutic and the spirituality of the early monks.

Setting, Origin and Growth of the *Sayings*

It is difficult to escape the feeling, when reading *The Sayings of the Desert Fathers*, that one is listening in on a conversation. The request for a "word" on the part of a monk, the sometimes gentle, sometimes sharp, often ironic responses from the elder, the subsequent questions or complaints from the monks—these "conversations" comprise the basic stuff of the *Sayings*. Yet, certain questions arise from hearing these conversations. How close is one to the desert monks in these texts? Are these genuine conversations or merely literary creations? What motivated the early monks to commit these conversations to memory and to pass them on to others? How and why did they come to be written down? Such questions are almost impossible to answer with any certainty; yet they are worth exploring. For by developing a sense of how such conversations came to be and how and why they were transmitted to others—both orally and in writing—we can gain a better understanding of the meaning and purpose of early monastic dialogue and of the place of Scripture within that dialogue.

The Origin of the Sayings: *Words in Response to Questions*

The great majority of the "words" and stories found in the *Sayings* emerged from the give-and-take of everyday life in the largely eremetical and semi-eremetical monastic movement of Scetis in lower Egypt.[2] These words were originally spoken and heard—probably in the Coptic tongue—rather than written and read. The oral character of life in the desert had a profound effect on the pedagogy of the desert monks and on their experience of the power of words. It also meant that transmission of the words from one to another during the earliest period was done almost entirely by word-of-mouth, only later being passed on as written texts.[3] The intimate relationship between a master and disciple and, in particular, the request for a "word" of power and salvation on the part of the disciple composed the setting in which the *Sayings* originated. In contrast to the cenobitic monastic world of Pachomius in upper Egypt, where a clear structure or "pedagogy of the rule" came to guide the spiritual formation and direction of monks, the eremetical world relied largely upon a "pedagogy of spiritual direction," based on personal experience, and the exchange of words between an elder and disciple.[4]

The terminology used in the *Sayings* to describe these exchanges reveals the dynamic character of the conversations which took place in the desert and provides some hints as to why and how they came to be preserved.[5] The word *apophthegma,* in spite of its use as part of the title of one collection of *Sayings* (the *Apophthegmata Patrum*), is neither the oldest nor most frequently used word for designating the teaching of the elders of the desert. *Logos, logion,* and above all, *rhēma* are the words most often used in the *Sayings* to convey that which is sought and received by those who came to the desert with their questions. A common expression is: "Abba, speak a word [*rhēma*] to me."*[6] The word *rhēma* corresponds to the Hebrew *dabar* and has a similar connotation of a deed or an "event" which is announced by a word. It expresses both the close relation between life and action which characterized these words as well as the weight and authority they possessed. Furthermore, it was commonly understood in the desert that one did not speak these words apart from an inspiration from God, nor did one

---

*Although in rendering the *Sayings* into English I have made regular use of the English translations of Benedicta Ward, I have sometimes modified her translations substantially. This is indicated with the symbol [m].

convey such a word to a listener unless that person showed a willingness to put the word into action. *The Sayings of the Desert Fathers* emerged and gained currency as words of power, life, and salvation addressed to particular persons in concrete situations.

Such an understanding of early pedagogy in the desert also sheds light on why and how the words of the elders began to be collected and transmitted.[7] We can see this process at work in the snatches of early monastic conversations preserved within the literature. The elders' words were cherished, collected, and transmitted because of the power and meaning they had in the ongoing life of the early desert community.[8] Yet the selection of the sayings was very personal. The words which came to be preserved were kept precisely because they had meaning for a specific person, to whom they were addressed in particular (and probably memorable) circumstances. The transmission of the elders' words from one monk to another also had a personal character, taking place in the context of the relationship between a master and a disciple. Often, when an elder was asked for a "word" from a certain monk, he would respond with a saying or story which he had heard from another elder. For instance, we hear how a certain brother, who was "troubled in his thoughts," approached Abba Poemen, asking him for a word. Poemen searched his memory and responded, not with a word of his own, but with a saying of another monk, Dioscorus, which he thought might soothe the brother's mind. In a similar case, a brother questioned an elder asking what good work he should do to gain salvation. The elder responded by passing on to him the "word" of another monk, this time that of Abba Nisterus.[9] In such exchanges, we catch glimpses of the manner in which the stories and sayings of the elders were passed on during the early moments of the desert movement and of the very practical motivation behind their transmission from one to another. Transmission of sayings, like the words themselves, arose in response to personal requests for words from the elders.

Yet, even these examples are probably somewhat removed from the earliest monastic experience. In the cases cited, there are rarely more than two figures involved in the transmission, something Lucien Regnault takes as an indication that a certain polishing and refining of the tradition had already taken place.[10] Examples of an earlier, rougher, and more extended process of transmission of sayings can be found by looking at a small collection of sayings preserved in Ethiopian. The compiler of this collection has preserved indications of this successive chain of transmission at the head of numerous sayings: "A brother said to me: Abba Paphnutius, copyist at Scetis, said to me also that Abba Ammoes had said. . . ." In another case, we hear: "A brother said to me: Abba Isaac said to me: I visited Abba Sisoes of Petra, the disciple of Abba Antony and I asked him: 'Speak to me a word.' "[11] This living chain of words suggests how vigorous the oral tradition of the sayings was and how vital it was to the ongoing spiritual life of the desert. The transmission of sayings was motivated not by the need to develop an accurate historical record of the early stages of the monastic tradition, but rather by the desire to maintain living contact with the early, founding members of the tradition and to perpetuate their words of life for the sake of others.

Transition from Oral to Early Written Sayings

The desire to keep alive the wisdom from the golden age of desert monasticism eventually led to the preservation of some of the sayings in written form. Just how soon the sayings of the desert fathers began to be written down is not entirely clear. There is some evidence that by the end of the fourth century there were small written collections of sayings in circulation.[12] Although the earliest stages of written transmission are for the most part hidden from our view, we do have some hints from the final collections of *Sayings* as well as from other, earlier collections of sayings regarding the manner through which the words of the elders passed from oral discourse into writing.

Two collections of sayings from the early fifth century, the Ethiopian Collection, known as the *Collectio Monastica,* and the *Asceticon* of Abba Isaiah, are of particular interest for what they reveal about the manner of the transmission of the sayings from oral to written form.[13] The value of these two collections derives from their position in midst of the transition between the oral and written tradition. In them, we can hear the deliberations which led the sayings to be written down for the first time. In the *Asceticon* for example, Isaiah introduces a formula through which he grounds the written accounts in his *Asceticon* in the authority of the desert's oral tradition: "Brothers, that which I have seen and heard from the ancients, I report to you. . . ."[14] Isaiah is not describing here a process of assembling written documents or collections which already existed, as the compilers of the later collections of *Sayings* were to do. Rather, he has gathered together his own personal memories of the words and actions of monks whom he has known and begun putting them into writing. We read of a similar process in the *Collectio Monastica.* The author calls attention to both the connection with the living oral tradition of the elders and the importance of the transition into written form: "Here are the words and actions of the ancients: May their prayer and their blessing be with the one who has put them into writing. . . ."[15]

These examples provide some evidence that the transition from oral to written sayings took place relatively close to the early tradition of the desert fathers. This is seen in one of the characteristic features of these early collections—that whole groups of sayings are gathered by the same person, who either heard them himself or collected them from the first-hand testimony of several witnesses. The collector or the witness usually expresses himself in the first person (''A brother said *to me* . . .''), an indication of how close he is to the speaker of the saying. Another sign of the closeness of these early collections to the primitive desert tradition is that they contain only sayings from the Egyptian monastic milieu, as distinct from the later ''great collections,'' which draw on material from diverse regions. These small, early collections have all the hallmarks of the earliest stages in the process by which the sayings from the desert were written down, gathered into collections, and passed from one person or group to the next. And although the precise reasons behind the decision to begin committing the sayings to writing are not entirely clear, it could well be due to two factors which were later to influence the production of the ''great collections''—the dispersion of the monks from Scetis and the desire to prevent the fervor of ancient monasticism from fading.[16]

Whatever the exact reasons for the shift to writing, the subtle changes it effected are worth noting. These can be seen in the terminology of the *Sayings*. The meaning of the term *apophthegma,* for example, is bound up in a specific way with the transcription of the sayings in written form. Thus, whereas *rhēma* refers to the character and content of a word which is primarily spoken, *apophthegma* designates the literary form of the saying. The *apophthegma* retains an organic relationship with the dynamic quality of the *rhēma,* while at the same time representing a movement away from the living quality of the oral tradition to a more formal transcription into written form. *Apophthegma* was a word used in classical antiquity and was distinguished in that tradition from the *gnomē,* or sentence, and from the *chreia,* or narrative. The *gnomē* was a wise maxim, enunciated in the abstract, which would be written down without having been pronounced. The *chréia* was a description of the circumstances of an event through words, in which the words, while important, did not comprise a special focus of attention. In the *apophthegma,* however, ''the word is essential and this word is reported along with the circumstances in which it has been pronounced and which clarify its meaning.''[17] The characteristic features of the *apophthegma* as a literary genre are the dynamic words of power which retain their quality as an event and the concrete circumstances which surround that event and provide the context for its meaning. The written sayings are, for the most part, rarely far removed from the particular circumstances and concerns of the life of the desert and can only be understood in relation to those circumstances.

This way of understanding the *Sayings* as a literary genre is significant for two reasons. In the first place it suggests a certain consistency in the process of transmission of sayings: the manner in which they were first uttered, came to be passed on, and were eventually written down was part of a continuous pattern. It also suggests that the genre of *apophthegma*, with its attention to words and the events surrounding them, should not be restricted, as some have suggested, to the shortest (and presumably earliest) sayings. Rather, *apophthegma* should be understood as being inclusive of numerous variations in form and substance.

Growth of the *Sayings* and Scripture

Two related questions—what is meant by the term *apophthegma* and how the sayings grew and developed—have a direct bearing on one of the central issues of this book: the extent to which we can find in the *Sayings* an accurate account of what the earliest desert monks thought about Scripture. Jean-Claude Guy has defined the word *apophthegma* fairly narrowly and has argued that the stages of growth in the tradition of the *Sayings* can be accurately identified by certain characteristic features. By paying attention to these features one can trace the process of growth from "early" (and implicitly more authentic) sayings to "later" (and implicitly less authentic) ones. Much of what the desert fathers have to say about Scripture appears in the sayings which Guy has characterized as "later." If Guy's schema is correct, it would suggest that we do not really have much access to what the earliest desert monks thought about Scripture. Therefore, it is worth examining his arguments more closely.

Guy has argued that the genre of the *Sayings* developed in three main stages, moving from simple pronouncements to longer speeches, narratives, or discussions.[18] The first stage is represented by sayings in which a disciple asks his Abba a question, to which the elder replies with a brief *logos* or *rhēma* deriving from the elder's gift of "discernment of spirits" and "charism" of his word. While this word may eventually be transmitted to others, it is at first a personal word, relevant only to the disciple's particular need at the moment, and has no narrative or discussion surrounding it. In the second stage, according to Guy, such *logoi* are generalized and perhaps combined or elaborated, becoming in the process sayings about the nature of the monastic life more widely applicable than the original word of the Abba to the disciple. Finally, in the third stage, the sayings are incorporated into narratives and supplemented by stories and anecdotes. These longer and more developed stories make up the majority of the sayings in the collections which have come down to us. Implied in this analysis is a belief that the short, piercing, charismatic sayings uttered in response to a particular question are the more "genuine" and that the longer narratives must be considered later, less authentic developments from the original. Although Guy admits here to a certain gray area in which the boundaries of the genre cannot accurately be discerned, still he clearly believes that the generalization of the *logos* is the first step towards the use of the material for which it was not intended—the development of systematic doctrines on the spiritual life such as one finds in the writings of John Cassian. Such a line of development alters the sayings, Guy argues, in such a way that their original simplicity and pungency is lost. It gives to the sayings an intellectual and speculative character which would have been unrecognizable to those who first uttered them.

There are reasons for questioning such a strict understanding of the development of the genre and especially the implications regarding which sayings are to be considered genuine.[19] Guy's claim that only the "simple" saying truly belongs to the genre of *apophthegma* is too narrow and does not sufficiently take into account the complex character of this literature. As Lucien Regnault has noted, the so-called simple sayings are not that numerous even in the small, early collections of *Sayings*. The relative paucity of simple sayings in these early collections raises questions as to the indisputably primitive character of such sayings. Regnault has also pointed out that the desert fathers' obvious appreciation for living examples of virtue and holiness which is found throughout the literature suggests that one should be cautious about discounting the presence of narratives in the earliest strata of material.[20] Rather than rejecting all narratives as secondary, it makes more sense to distinguish between those narratives which are likely to have been part of the earliest desert traditions and those which represent later additions. Such a distinction is especially useful for understanding the place of Scripture within the *Sayings*. One of the objections to the inclusion of the narratives as part of the earliest tradition of sayings has been based on the assumption that the relatively complex subject matter of the narratives, including questions about how to understand a virtue or a vice, or how to interpret a particular passage from Scripture, must represent a secondary development away from the "naked saying," the *rhēma* which the Abba uttered to the disciple. However, it can be argued, as Graham Gould has done, that "such matters did fall within the scope of the Abba's charismatic authority."

Pointing to some sayings from a section of the Systematic collection called *De Contemplatione* (from the Greek Περὶ διορατικῶν, meaning "on those who had the gift of vision"), Gould notes that the "vision" spoken of in these sayings included not only an ability to "read hearts" but also a capacity to interpret Scripture. In the sayings in question, several passages of Scripture are interpreted, and they appear not to have any connection with "vision," unless that word includes the gift of interpreting the meaning of Scripture.[21] Such evidence leads Gould to the conclusion that "interpretation of Scripture is part of the responsibility of the Abba as spiritual father and instructor of his disciples, and by no means to be seen as secondary to the utterance of 'moral pronouncements.' "[22] This suggests that the criteria by which one determines whether a saying is early or late needs to be revised considerably if we are to take account of the diversity and richness of this literature. This is especially important for understanding how Scripture functions in the *Sayings,* for it is often within the narratives that questions about the meaning of Scripture figure most prominently. These longer sayings should not necessarily be considered as later developments which do not reflect the spirituality of primitive desert monasticism. Rather, we need to recognize that many of them accurately reflect elements of the practice of the early desert monks and in particular their hermeneutic.

Another reason for questioning Guy's assumptions regarding the development of the longer narratives in the *Sayings* is that it is likely that the development of narratives was at least partly an oral—and thus an early—phenomenon. The works of Abba Isaiah provide a good picture of the oral dimension of the development and transmission of narratives among the desert monks. Isaiah's testimony is significant for, as we noted earlier, he represents an important link in the transmission of primitive desert traditions. He recounts a number of them which contain a good deal of narrative. In one of these sayings, someone questions Abba Abraham, asking him how he ought to live among his brothers. Abraham responds: "[Y]ou ought to live among them as if you were a stranger," and then goes on to illustrate this saying with a long story about his teacher Agathon.[23] This saying, with its piercing word and its more elaborate narrative, has verisimilitude—it is just the kind of situation in which a story would naturally have arisen. And given the close relationship which we know existed between Abraham and Agathon, there is every reason to think that the story originated not as a later addition but with Abraham in the situation described. From what we know about the oral process of transmission, it is very likely that such a story would have been passed along orally many different times before being committed to writing. There is, in fact, no reason to assume that all narratives must have originated in literary form, nor that a narrative cannot have been just as much a part of an elder's teaching repertoire as a "simple saying."

If the narratives were after all a part of the teaching of the desert elders, the reason they were transmitted along with the elders' shorter "words" becomes clear. Narratives were passed on not just because they were interesting or useful for teaching but because they were necessary for giving a context to the words of an elder and for making those words comprehensible. Many examples of this can be given, but a saying of John Colobos serves to illustrate the point: "[Abba John] was sitting in church one day and he sighed, not knowing that there was someone behind him. When he realized it he lay prostrate before him, saying, 'Forgive me, Abba, for I have not yet made a beginning.' "[24] The "word" in this case—"I have not yet made a beginning"—comes at the end of the saying. According to Guy's schema, it would represent the "primitive core" of the saying to which the previous narrative element was added later. However, it is difficult to believe in this case that the narrative is a secondary addition to the word which is spoken in this saying. Here, as in many other instances, the word or short saying receives its meaning in no small part through being part of a credible, lifelike and very concrete "story." * The narrative, then, is more than simply a vehicle which carries the saying. Rather, the saying and the narrative form a unity which must be read as a whole. Instead of viewing all narratives in the *Sayings* as secondary and implicitly less valuable as testimony to the early monastic tradition, narratives deserve to be considered as genuine expressions of the earliest monastic world and as foundational elements of the literature.

This more positive assessment of the role of narrative in the *Sayings* and its place in the world of primitive monasticism is especially important for understanding the role of Scripture in the *Sayings*. Not only is the citation of, allusion to, and interpretation of Scripture most often found within a narrative setting, but it is precisely because the interpretation of Scripture is found within a narrative setting, is surrounded by the events and questions of life, that we are able to learn so much about the early monastic attitudes toward Scripture, that we can observe the monks' hermeneutical strategies firsthand, and that we can see how they strove to enter into the world projected by the sacred texts. Although this analysis of the *Sayings'* early traditions leaves many questions unanswered, it has at least shown the extent to which we still have available to us in the *Sayings* much of the force and urgency of the original questions of early monasticism. It has also suggested that in the texts as we have them now, we have access to some of the questions regarding the interpretation of Scripture which occupied the minds

---

* Specifically, the narrative, with its veiled reference to an ecstatic or visionary religious experience, provides a credible and necessary context for the expression of humility that follows.

of the desert fathers. It remains, however, to examine the manner in which the sayings passed from the world of oral discourse and early written collections to the main written collections in which they took their final form.

Sayings Gathered into Collections

The *Sayings* has come down to us in at least two major forms, in many different languages, and in a huge number of manuscripts, only a fraction of which have been published. It will be useful at this point to describe the two main forms—the Systematic and the Alphabetical—and to provide a brief account of how they were compiled and the circumstances and motivations that helped forge these collections. By noting some of the principles that shaped them and the circumstances that gave rise to them, we can gain a better understanding of the *Sayings* as literature.

The modern discussion of the *Sayings* begins in the seventeenth century when two manuscripts, representing the two main forms of the sayings, were printed. The first manuscript, in Latin, was edited by the Jesuit Heribert Rosweyde in 1615 as part of his *Vitae Patrum,* and organized according to topic in twenty chapters.[25] Because of the topical arrangement, this edition of the *Sayings* has come to be referred to as the Systematic collection. The proper title, found in most early manuscripts, is *Adhortationes Patrum,* but the work has come to be known in the tradition of the Western church as the *Verba Seniorum.* This Latin text was itself a translation from a Greek manuscript (lost to us), done by two Roman clerics, the deacon Pelagius and the subdeacon John, sometime in middle of the sixth century. Much of the value of the *Verba Seniorum* to us today is due to the relatively early date at which this translation took place.[26] A second manuscript, this one in Greek, and with a different arrangement of the *Sayings,* was published by J. B. Cotelier in 1677 as part of his *Ecclesiae Graecae monumenta.* This collection is known as the *Apophthegmata Patrum,* or the *Paterikon,* the name more familiar to the Eastern church.[27] This edition, which contains much material also found in the *Verba Seniorum,* is arranged not topically but alphabetically, according to the names of the narrator or main protagonist of each saying. The prologue to the *Sayings* in Cotelier's text tells us that originally the work also included a group of anonymous sayings arranged in topical chapters that followed the text of the alphabetical sayings as a kind of appendix. Most of these anonymous sayings, which are missing from the manuscript published by Cotelier, are found in another manuscript (Coislin 126) of the same arrangement and have been published by F. Nau.[28] The reconstructed text, with both alphabetical and anonymous sayings, has come to be known as the Alphabetico-Anonymous (hereafter referred to as Alphabetical) collection. The manuscripts of this collection derive mostly from the ninth to the twelfth centuries.

A number of versions or translations of these two main forms of the *Sayings* exist. Fragments of Sahidic sayings arranged in a topical form similar to that of the *Verba Seniorum* have been drawn together in one volume by Marius Chaîne.[29] Although this collection of the *Sayings* is preserved in the native language of the Egyptians and might be thought to represent the earliest written testimony of the desert traditions, Chaîne has shown that the Coptic is a translation dependent on a Greek text. A number of sayings preserved in Bohairic have been published by A. Amélineau, who has shown that they too represent a translation from the Greek.[30] We also have a Syriac version of the *Sayings,* which was translated from various sources by a Nestorian monk named "Anan-Isho" early in the seventh century. Although undoubtedly secondary in character, it retains a special importance due to the early manuscripts that "Anan-Isho" had access to in compiling his work.[31] A Christian Palestinian Aramaic version also existed as can be seen from the fragments published by H. Duensing.[32] Two Armenian versions of the *Sayings* are extant, preserving both the alphabetical and systematic arrangements.[33] In addition to this, there are versions of the *Sayings* in Georgian, Arabic, and Ethiopian, each of which contributes something additional to the overall corpus of *The Sayings of the Desert Fathers.*[34]

This brief survey indicates the vastness and diversity of the tradition of sayings which has emerged from fourth century Egyptian monasticism. It also suggests why it is necessary to narrow the field of inquiry for the present study to a particular part of that tradition. Although the precise nature of the relationship among the various versions is far from clear, it is generally acknowledged by scholars today that in one form or another the sayings were first committed to writing in the Greek language.[35] Because of this, and because the Greek Alphabetical collection is the only one which is available to us in a relatively complete form, it forms the primary basis of this study.[36] A more detailed analysis of this particular collection, including the date of its composition, the likely location of its birth, and the circumstances in which it came into being will reveal some of its characteristic features and will help to show why it is such an appropriate text for the purposes of this study.

The Birth of the Major Collections

It is reasonably certain that the Alphabetical collection was compiled sometime during the first half of the sixth century.[37] Regarding the location in which it was compiled, most evidence points to Palestine, and specifically the region of Gaza, as the place most likely to have seen the rise of the major collections.[38] Numerous allusions to the *Sayings* found in other monastic literature from the region of Palestine such as the *Vita* of Melania the Younger, the *Correspondence* of Barsanuphius and John, and the *Discourses* of Dorotheus of Gaza indicate the broad diffusion of the sayings in Palestine during the fifth and sixth centuries. In addition to this, there are more than sixty sayings of monks who were either born in Palestine or who had adopted it as their home included in the *Sayings,* representing a significant change from the predominantly Egyptian character of the Ethiopian collection alluded to earlier. Reference to St. Basil in the *Sayings* provides further evidence for the Palestinian origin of the great collections, for while it is unlikely that the great Cappadocian bishop was widely known and honored in Egypt, he was certainly read and appreciated in the sixth-century Palestinian monastic milieux. A Palestinian origin for the great collections would also help to explain the rapid translation of the *Sayings* into all the major languages of Christianity. Palestine, which had always been a crossroads of peoples, had become, since the fourth century, the "chosen land" for the monks of all regions, not only Egyptians, but Greeks, Latins, Syrians, Armenians, and Georgians. All of this leads us to conclude, with Regnault, that "the first collection of the Alphabetico-Anonymous type was formed in Palestine rather than in Egypt."[39] The Palestinian setting also helps to shed light on the motivations for the compilation of the major collections.

The dispersion of great numbers of monks from Egypt to Palestine and the permanent loss of that world, the break of the Egyptian Monophysite monks from the orthodox cause, the growth of a large literate population of monks who could benefit from reading the words of the ancient monks, and the perception that the ancient fervor was waning, combined to motivate certain Palestinian monks to gather the disparate sayings together into one large collection. The presence of great numbers of monks in Palestine was due largely to the devastation of Scetis, the center of eremetical monasticism in Egypt, and the dispersion of its monks from there during the fifth century. The majority of the words and stories in the *Sayings* are from those who were at Scetis and there are several allusions in the text to their forced departure from that famous place.[40] After numerous attacks by hostile tribes, Scetis eventually became completely deserted. This dispersion, together with the refusal of the majority of Egyptian monks to accept the Council of Chalcedon and their decision to organize themselves along ethnic lines, no doubt quickened the realization on the part of some that Egyptian monastic heritage was in danger of being lost. If the spirit and memory of the remarkable flowering of the anchoritic movement in Egypt was to be preserved for the next generation, some attempt had to be made to collect the sayings systematically.

The circumstances of monasticism in Palestine were ripe for such a project. Cenobitic monasticism in Palestine, well developed by the late fifth and early sixth centuries, was literate and needed a literature for meditation. However, within this movement there was a perception that the ancient fervor from the early days of monasticism was being lost.[41] What better way to revive and renew monasticism in its diaspora and in particular within orthodox monastic circles than to gather together the sayings of the greatest of the Egyptian heroes, supplemented with other heroes of the faith such as Basil, Gregory, and Epiphanius, whose names were without any trace of heresy? Both a sense of urgency about the need to preserve the words of the Egyptian monks as well as what Chitty calls a certain "wistfulness" contributed to the desire to gather together the memories of an earlier time: "Physical insecurity and a sense of moral decay now gave impetus to the work, with the fear lest the great Old Men and their times should be forgotten."[42] The decision to collect these sayings, which had circulated freely in the oral tradition and in various shorter written forms, into a large inclusive anthology was a momentous step, one which would have a great impact not only on the immediate generation but on later generations as well. Indeed as Regnault says, "It is evidently this commitment of the sayings of the Egyptian anchorites to writing that has assured their perpetuity and their universal diffusion."[43] This diffusion, which began slowly with the small collections to which we have already referred, increased dramatically with the appearance of the great collections. Although the great collections themselves did not remain static, but grew and developed as they were used within a living monastic tradition, the Alphabetical and Systematic collections that emerged in the early sixth century remained the standard forms in which the sayings were read and pondered.

The Character of the *Sayings*

Our discussion of the *Sayings'* evolution from its beginnings as oral proclamations in the early eremetical movement in Egypt, to the first small written collections, and finally to the anthologies compiled to meet the needs of a later age, has revealed the complexity of the process which lay behind the growth of these sayings into the form in which we now have them. This raises further questions about what *kind* of text *The Sayings of the Desert Fathers* is and how to read it. Should it be read as a single text, with certain characteristic features of form and content which allow us to distinguish it from other early monastic texts? Or is it better seen simply as a composite text, influenced by diverse literary sources and reflecting the points of view of a patchwork of early monastic figures? I would suggest that a critical reading of the *Sayings* and of the place of Scripture within it requires taking both of these dimensions seriously. We must recognize the diverse sources which lie behind the final collection of *Sayings* and the different levels at which a reading of this text can be done. At the same time the *Sayings* has a particular character, an integrity of outlook which allows us to distinguish it from other early monastic documents. By paying attention to the diversity of the text as well as its integrity we will be better able to understand the particular way in which we meet monasticism in the *Sayings* and be in a position to evaluate the approach to the interpretation of Scripture found there.

Diversity in the Sayings

The diverse character of the *Sayings* would not be apparent from a cursory reading of the prologue. There, the editor sets out to provide an explanation of the purpose or intent of the collection:

> Those, however, who were industrious about these matters have handed down in writing some small account of these words and works which they produced, not so much to praise them as to raise successors to their zeal. Many, then, through various times have set forth in the form of a narrative in simple and unpolished speech these words and deeds of the holy elders. They were looking to one purpose only, to be of benefit to many.[44]

In general terms this is an accurate description of the Alphabetical collection as we know it. The great majority of the sayings do reflect the simple and unpolished speech of the anchorites who comprised the earliest generation of Egyptian monasticism. Also, it is largely true that the sayings are very practical in character and encourage imitation rather than reflection and speculation. The editor has emphasized this by noting that the primary purpose of the sayings is not to "teach" or "instruct" the ones seeking a word, but rather to "help" them.[45]

At the same time, if taken at face value, the prologue is somewhat misleading. However true it may be that we hear the voices of the earliest anchoritic tradition echoing through the pages of the *Sayings,* it is equally true that these early anchorites cannot be presumed to have spoken in some of the literary forms which are found there. While the units that comprise the *Sayings* preserve much of the original spirit of the early monastic world, they have nevertheless come into being as *literature.* Care should therefore be taken to read the sayings in terms of the genres into which they were formed by scribes and editors who consciously presented them to a reading world as texts. Also, although it is fair to characterize the *Sayings* as practical, helpful, and calling forth imitation, such a general characterization does not do justice to the specific character of individual sayings and to the diverse and often conflicting issues and themes addressed by them. In short, although it is possible to speak of the characteristics of the *Sayings* as a whole, it must always be done with a clear appreciation of the real diversity of the material which comprises the collection. Thus Frazer concludes that the "composite nature of the [*Sayings*] renders it inappropriate as an expression of a single coordinated view of fourth and fifth century monastic thought or experience."[46] Guy concurs, saying that this inherent diversity of the *Sayings* means that "there is no single theology of the monastic life which is expressed in the *Apophthegmata Patrum* . . . but many theologies of the monastic life."[47] This should not be taken to mean that one cannot speak of the thought or the spirituality of the *Sayings* in general terms for, as I will suggest, it is indeed possible to point to characteristic features of the *Sayings* which distinguish it from other literary expressions of early monasticism. Rather, these observations are meant to serve as a caution against the tendency to view the literature too simply. In assessing the *Sayings* as literature, one must take into account the diversity and richness of its literary expressions and the dynamic, reciprocal relationship that existed between it and other early monastic texts.

We can grasp the diversity of the *Sayings* best by noting some of the different literary genres that are present there. I have already noted that it is not helpful to view the genres within the *Sayings* as having developed in a clear and consistent way from early, simple expressions, or *logia,* to later, more elaborate narratives. Nor is it possible to paint a perfectly clear picture of the directions of literary influence in the *Sayings*. It is likely that besides being influenced by some early monastic texts, the *Sayings* also exerted its own influence on many of those same texts.[48] In most cases with the *Sayings,* we are looking at sayings or stories which arose from the experience of the desert and were shaped to a greater or lesser extent by certain literary models from the fourth-century world. What follows, then, are tentative suggestions regarding some of the influences behind the diverse literary expressions within the *Sayings*. In making these suggestions, I hope to clarify the multitude of settings in which one encounters the desert hermeneutic.

One of the most significant influences on the early literary expressions of the *Sayings* was the *Vita Antonii* of Athanasius.[49] The didactic modes introduced by Athanasius into the *Vita* from his own acquaintance with Hellenistic and ecclesiastical models are, Frazer says, "among the earliest known literary expressions of the desert ideals and tradition.''[50] In the *Vita,* all the sayings of Antony known to Athanasius were enclosed in a work of literary form with specific pedagogical intent. There were sections of *exhortations* and detailed instructions to the monastic population, sections of *exposition* seen in propaganda against the Arians and in interpretation of the Scriptures, and sections which recorded details of the hermit's life in the form of a brief *eulogy.*[51] The *Vita,* which was certainly known to the early anchoritic community as depicted in the *Sayings,*[52] became an important "model for monastic encouragement" and a "precedent for the formation of the tradition that proceeded from Nitria and Scete," which was to emerge in final form in the *Sayings.*[53] These three forms of exhortation, exposition, and eulogy, developed by Athanasius in his literary portrayal of Antony, became established as viable models for the perpetuation of monastic ideals of thought and action.

Exhortation, as it is found in the *Sayings,* often expresses the thought of the earliest settlers in Nitria and Scetis and is addressed to an immediate monastic audience, usually to an individual. This form reflects the intensely personal character of the early monastic impulse. Faced with the need to help resolve the personal inner conflicts of those who came to the abbas for help, a personal response was called for. This central goal of personal salvation produced a large number of "salvation sayings" consisting of a variety of personal responses related directly to the needs of an individual. These highly personal encounters were not isolated from broader social issues for, as we shall see, a great number of sayings came as responses to tensions and questions arising precisely from social concerns. In some cases, these concrete and personal words arising from an eremetical setting were adapted gradually to meet the needs of an expanding monastic community.[54]

Exposition often resulted from the need to interpret or clarify a "word" or an event and represents a common motivation for the expression of an anchorite.[55] There is usually very little polemic to be found in such sayings, even when they touch upon doctrinal matters. Rather, the address is directed to the petitioner and his quest for the words that lead to salvation. Almost always there is found within the elder's exposition a challenge for action of some kind. Though expositions may sometimes focus on a passing event or a casual piece of conversation, usually it is the characteristic or action of a particular anchorite that calls for comment.[56] A frequent subject of the expositions found in the *Sayings* is the meaning of Scripture. Although there is no unified hermeneutical pattern which accounts for all the various uses of Scripture in the *Sayings,* most accounts in which questions about Scripture are found concern how the sacred text is to be "realized" or "applied" in the life of the monk.

Eulogy in the *Sayings* takes the form of expressions of the praiseworthy qualities and accomplishments of the heroes of the desert movement. This is found in the numerous miniature "character sketches" in the *Sayings,* the purpose of which corresponds closely with that of the stated intention of the editor of the collection: to inspire similar zeal among those committed to the anchoritic life. These sayings usually commend to the monk and to the reader a reasonably attainable virtue while at the same time praising the performer of such deeds.[57] The eulogies found in the *Sayings* are for the most part spare and unspectacular.[58] Still, these modest examples of the "sanctification" of the desert heroes which are found in the *Sayings* reflect the growing recognition among the early monastic communities of the presence in their midst of holy exemplars.[59] As I will show in great detail below, the eulogies contained in the *Sayings* reveal the extent to which the holiness of the elders was seen as deriving from their conformity to Scripture. Imitation of these holy exemplars became in a sense the appropriation of the "world" projected by this new, living text.

These three forms of exhortation, exposition, and eulogy reflect the influence of the literary forms of such early monastic texts such as the *Vita Antonii* upon the growth of literary expressions found in the *Sayings.* Although these different expressions in the *Sayings* reflect certain elements of the early eremetical experience, they also indicate the extent to which that experience was shaped and influenced by other early monastic texts. They also show the diverse didactic purposes at work in the collection and serve as a reminder of the need to recognize the variety of questions being addressed in the different genres of the text.

In light of what has been said above, it will be clear that it is not entirely appropriate or accurate to speak about the overall character of the *Sayings,* as though it were the product of a single author or even of a single school. As an anthology, it represents a rich variety of personalities, geographical locations, and genres. Moreover, it addresses several distinct social settings and audiences across several generations. The *Sayings* projects a spectrum of worlds, and any attempt to reduce their outlook to one or two main characteristics would be misleading. Nevertheless, there is a sense in which it is appropriate to speak of certain general characteristics, or a shared worldview of the *Sayings.*

The Integrity of the Sayings

The *Sayings* is one text, an integral collection of sayings and stories, which has been read as such for centuries. In spite of its anthological structure, it has been edited in a conscious way by the early monastic community and can be said to have a coherent and fairly consistent overall world view. In spite of the different factors that have influenced the final shape of the collection, most of the sayings did emerge from the same world and share a similar vocabulary and ethos. Perhaps the best way of indicating the characteristic features of the *Sayings* is to distinguish it from some of the other early monastic texts.

This is not easy to do. The reciprocal literary influences among the various texts from the world of early monasticism make it difficult to find the seams between the different writings. I have already suggested the probability of the *Vita Antonii*'s influence on the *Sayings*. It is very likely that other early monastic writers, such as Evagrius, also helped shape certain features. However, the influence also operated in the other direction. Because the units of the *Sayings* were self-contained, they often became detached from their place in anthologies and were absorbed into larger, more intricately crafted works of monastic history and spirituality. Obvious parallels to many of the sayings can be found in such works as Cassian's *Collationes*, Evagrius's *Praktikos*, Palladius's *Historia Lausiaca*, the *Vita Antonii* of Athanasius, and Socrates's *Historia Ecclesiastica*. Not only did other early monastic writers give shape to the *Sayings*, but they were in turn shaped by it. In the process of using material from the *Sayings* they reshaped it for their own purposes.[60] The changes undergone by the material from the *Sayings* were of various kinds: changes in the author's perspective; greater polishing of the material; changes in form; more emphasis upon speculative philosophical matters. These changes can help us to distinguish the characteristic features of the *Sayings*.

The form of the *Sayings* is easily distinguished from the artificial ''histories of voyages,'' such as the *Historia Lausiaca* and the *Historia Monachorum*, which trace journeys among the different monastic settlements. Beyond differences in form, one can see a very different spirit in these two histories. The *Historia Lausiaca* is one of the most deeply hellenized of the early monastic texts and reflects the influence of Evagrius's thought to a much greater extent than that of the *Sayings*. This is reflected in a generally more severe attitude toward the body and a greater leaning toward the practice of asceticism. The *Historia Monachorum* is a document taken for the most part from a different geographical locale than the *Sayings*—focusing on the Nile valley as it does, it could be said to reflect ''river-bed'' monasticism. It also contains a much greater emphasis on the ''signs and wonders'' of the monastic life than the *Sayings*. The overall perspective or point of view of both of these documents differs quite markedly from the *Sayings*. They come from the pens of monastic pilgrims or tourists and convey very much an outsider's perspective on and glorification of the early monastic world.[61] The *Sayings* can also be distinguished from the carefully crafted biographies such as the *Vita Antonii* or the *Vita Pachomii*. Although we have seen the extent to which certain forms from the *Vita Antonii* influenced the *Sayings,* there is nothing in them resembling Athanasius's polished biographical form or his overarching theological agenda.[62] The *Sayings* bear even less resemblance to collections of sentences such as the *Gnostic Centuries* of Evagrius or the treatises on the monastic life that are represented, in various forms, in the writings of John Cassian, Isaiah of Scetis, and Dorotheus of Gaza. To take just one example, one can see in Cassian's writings that many words and stories from the *Sayings* have been changed, probably under the influence of Evagrius, into sophisticated and highly intellectual theological and spiritual reflections. This is reflected in the *length* of the monologues delivered by Cassian's monks, something which distinguishes them very clearly from the reticent figures found in the *Sayings:* "In the *Apophthegmata* the master answered with a single pithy sentence. In a divine like Cassian he answered with an hour, or several pages of analysis."[63]

The different perspectives reflected in these early monastic documents provide some clues for understanding the characteristic features of the *Sayings*. Though the *Sayings* stands in a dependent or reciprocal relationship to some of these other early monastic texts, it has managed to preserve more of the primitive quality of early monasticism than the other major monastic documents. Contrasting the *Sayings* with the *Historia Monachorum* and Cassian's *Conferences,* Louis Bouyer notes: "These last two texts . . . already bear the marks of a later systematization. Here we can follow the transition from a primitive, popular monasticism, wholly evangelical and entirely ignorant of philosophical problems or influences, to the erudite monasticism which was to be its heir. . . ."[64] To a much greater extent than these more carefully constructed works, the diverse sayings and stories in the *Sayings* remain organically related to the monastic world whose life and thought they express. Most of the sayings and stories emerge directly from the rough-and-tumble life of early monasticism. In spite of some polishing, they retain their flavor as the *matériel brut* of early monasticism.[65] This is reflected in the form and the overall tone of the *Sayings*.

The anthological form of the *Sayings* precludes any artificial synthesis or systematization of the material. Rather than constructing a series of spiritual conferences as Cassian does, or recounting tales of a journey as Palladius does, the editors of the *Sayings* have simply compiled what Chitty calls "a corpus of 'case law' of the deserts."[66] These cases are left, in all their bewildering variety, to stand next to one another, relatively free of commentary. This exuberant polyphony of words is one of the real strengths and charms of the *Sayings* and is, I think, at least partially responsible for its enduring appeal. The constant blending and sometimes even clashing of different voices offers us a potentially endless combination of "musical styles." As Ricouer reminds us in relation to biblical literature, such a polyphony can bring with it a revelatory richness unequalled by a single voice.[67] This variety makes of the *Sayings,* perhaps more than any of the other early monastic texts, "une somme d'une richesse inégalée."[68] There is also a richness in tone in the *Sayings.* Perhaps the best way of characterizing this tone is to note that the authority and insight with which the desert monks addressed the concerns of their fellow human beings mark the *Sayings* as "the last and one of the greatest products of the Wisdom Literature of the ancient Near East."[69] Its character as a kind of Wisdom literature is seen in the concrete manner with which the monks faced questions of all kinds. This text does not originate from theorizing or speculating on the nature of the spiritual life or holiness but, like ancient Wisdom sayings, is born from experience and gives practical, earthy, and specific advice on how to live.[70] Although the sayings had a teaching function, their primary orientation was not so much to "teach" in a narrow sense as to edify and help those who came to seek "a word." Many of the sayings convey the revelatory shock of parables and had the effect of drawing their hearers into a new world and transforming them. Finally a word should be said about the "audiovisual quality" of the *Sayings.* Chitty has noted that the name *Apophthegmata Patrum* is "a term convenient enough but for the fact that the collection is hardly less occupied with the actions of the fathers than with their sayings."[71] The *Sayings* constitutes, as Regnault reminds us, "une galerie de portraits," "un montage audiovisuel." As such the *Sayings* brings us in touch not only with the words of the desert monks but also with their countenances.[72] It is important to keep this "double character" of the *Sayings* in mind, for it is often in the movements, gestures, and faces of the holy exemplars that we are led to understand the way in which they have engaged the project of the sacred texts. Taken altogether, these diverse qualities of the *Sayings* lead one to agree with Benedicta Ward that "it is in the [*Sayings*] of the fathers, the collections of their words, that the spirit of the desert can best be found."[73]

How Much Scripture in the *Sayings?*

Although it is clear, as I have pointed out above, that questions about Scripture were frequently posed in the desert, it is not easy to determine how often Scripture is actually quoted in the text of the *Sayings.* Opinions have varied widely on this question, from those who see almost no Scripture in the *Sayings* to those who see the *Sayings* filled with citations of and allusions to Scripture. Judgments about this question depend to a large extent on how one evaluates the various traces of Scripture found in the literature and how carefully one distinguishes between actual citations or quotations of Scripture and allusions to the sacred texts.

One way to approach the question of scriptural content in the *Sayings* is to compare the biblical references noted in the approximately one thousand sayings of Cotelier's edition of the Alphabetical collection with those in three contemporary translations of this collection in English, French, and Italian. Each of these works indicates the presence of biblical references within the text of the *Sayings,* and the French and Italian translations also include an index of biblical references reflecting the number of biblical citations and allusions the respective translators have detected in the *Sayings.* Neither in the Greek edition nor in any of the translations is a method or set of criteria proposed for determining the presence of biblical texts in the *Sayings,* or for distinguishing between biblical citations and allusions. The great discrepancy in the number of biblical references attested to in the different translations should be taken as an indication of how subjective such judgments are. Using the Alphabetical collection as a basis for comparison, we come up with surprisingly different numbers of biblical texts cited by the different translators.[74]

Jean-Claude Guy long ago noted the apparent paucity of biblical citations in Cotelier's Greek edition of the Alphabetical collection, where he counted only 150 biblical citations or allusions in the entire collection.[75] Benedicta Ward, in her English translation made in 1975, noted even fewer biblical references, citing only 93 biblical references altogether, with 45 from the Old Testament and 48 from the New Testament.[76] Lucien Regnault's 1985 French translation of the Alphabetical collection shows a larger number of biblical references than Guy and more than twice as many as Ward. He has noted 224 citations altogether, with 98 from the Old Testament and 126 from the New Testament.[77] Luciana Mortari, who translated the Alphabetical collection into Italian in 1971, has included far more biblical references in her translation than the others have, citing 832 biblical citations altogether, with 269 texts from the Old Testament and 563 texts from the New Testament.[78] The sharp differences in the number of biblical texts noted by these different scholars point to how difficult it is to be precise about identifying the number of biblical texts and the patterns of use in the *Sayings.* Mortari's much larger numbers suggest that she has taken biblical *allusions* more seriously than the others have done. This leaves unanswered, however, the question of what criteria one is to use in evaluating the presence of biblical allusions or echoes in the *Sayings.* Although it is not a simple matter of saying that the truth lies somewhere in between the two extremes, the large number of biblical texts cited in Mortari's translation at least suggests that the generally low estimate of the number of biblical texts in the *Sayings* that has prevailed for so long among scholars should be revised upward.

Notwithstanding the inherent ambiguity of the question of how many biblical texts are to be found in the *Sayings,* some tentative suggestions can be made based on both the agreements and differences among Cotelier and the different translations regarding the patterns of biblical use in the *Sayings*. In the first place Cotelier and all three of the translators agree that the New Testament is cited more frequently than the Old Testament in the *Sayings*. For Cotelier, Ward, and Regnault the difference between them is relatively small, while Mortari notes that more than twice as many texts are cited from the New Testament than from the Old Testament. All agree that the most frequently cited Old Testament texts are the Psalms, followed by the books of Genesis and Isaiah, while the higher numbers cited by Mortari suggest that these two texts occupied an especially prominent place in the desert. In addition, Mortari claims that both Exodus and Ezekiel figure in a prominent way, something not noted by the others.

With regard to the New Testament, all are agreed that the Gospels are the most frequently cited texts, accounting for more than half of all the New Testament texts found in the *Sayings*. All are also agreed that, among the Gospels, Matthew is the most often cited, accounting for approximately a third of all the New Testament texts in the *Sayings*. Cotelier, Mortari, and Regnault note a significant number of citations from the Gospel of Luke while Mortari alone sees a large number of citations from the Gospel of John. The only other pattern of New Testament citations that emerges is due primarily to the generally larger numbers which Mortari finds overall. She sees high numbers of texts cited from Paul's writings as well as from Hebrews, James, and Revelation.

These numbers provide us with what is at best an approximate account of the overall patterns of use of Scripture in the *Sayings*. The range of opinions regarding how much and which kinds of Scripture are found in the *Sayings* attests to the difficulty of resolving this question with any certitude. However, even this ambiguity may be instructive as to the extent to which Scripture influenced both the desert monks as well as the literature of the desert. We would do well in this regard to keep in mind Benedicta Ward's comment that "the language of the writings of the desert was so formed by the meditation of the scriptures that it is almost impossible to say where quotation ends and comments begin."[79] This inherent ambiguity notwithstanding, the rough approximations of Scriptural use presented here do suggest some of the broad patterns of use of Scripture in the *Sayings*. Just how the monks used Scripture in the day-to-day life of the desert is the question to which we must now turn.

Notes

1. The critical difficulties associated with the *Sayings* are legendary. In his critical introduction to the Pachomian corpus of writings (which itself presents no end of critical problems), Armand Veilleux has stated that, in comparison to the *Sayings,* the Pachomian literature is "un tout homogène!" See Armand Veilleux, *La liturgie dans le cénobitisme pachômien au quatrième siècle* Studia Anselmiana 57, (Rome: Herder, 1968), 11. On the critical work that has been done on the *Apophthegmata* (or *Sayings*) and the difficulties or problems that remain, see W. Bousset, *Apophthegmata. Studien zur Geschichte des ältesten Mönchtums* (Tübingen: Mohr, 1923); Jean-Claude Guy, *Recherches sur la tradition grecque des Apophthegmata Patrum,* Subsidia Hagiographica 36 (Brussels: Société des Bollandistes, 1962). See Ruth Frazer, "The Morphology of Desert Wisdom in the *Apophthegmata Patrum*" (Ph.D. diss., University of Chicago, 1977), for a careful analysis of the structure and form of the *Sayings* and of some of the more difficult literary questions underlying them. See also Graham Gould, "A Note on the *Apophthegmata Patrum,*" *JTS,* n.s., 37 (1986):133–38. Gould's critique of Guy's work and its bearing on understanding the desert hermeneutic is discussed in detail below. See also F. Cavallera ("Apophtegmes," *DS,* vol. I, col. 768); who aptly describes what is still, unfortunately, the state of our knowledge of the *Sayings:* "It is impossible to provide a definitive solution to the majority of the questions posed by the existence of the diverse collections [of the *Sayings*]." One result of the complex character of the tradition is that there is as yet no critical text of the *Sayings.* (This will soon change with the forthcoming publication of a critical edition from *Sources chrétiennes,* prepared in large part by the late Jean-Claude Guy).

2. See Derwas J. Chitty, *The Desert a City* (Oxford: Blackwell, 1966), 67: "The *Apophthegmata Patrum* belong primarily to Scetis." This does not mean that one does not find sayings from other milieux in the *Sayings.* It simply suggests that Scetis is the geographical center of the sayings.

3. See Hans Lietzmann, *A History of the Early Church,* Vol. 4: The Era of the Church Fathers, trans. B. L. Woolf (London: Lutterworth, 1951), 140: "In the first instance, the tradition was of an oral character and in the Coptic language. It was later translated into Greek and written down." See also K. Heussi, *Der Ursprung des Mönchtums* (Tubingen: Mohr, 1936), 145, 158.

4. Jean-Claude Guy, "Les *Apophthegmata Patrum,*" in *Théologie de la vie monastique* (Paris: Aubier, 1961), 75. This is not to say the master-disciple relationship was unimportant in Pachomian monasticism. It simply did not play the same role as it did in eremetical and semieremetical monasticism.

5. See Lucien Regnault, "Aux origines des Apophtegmes," in *Les Pères du désert à travers leurs Apophtegmes* (Sablé-sur-Sarthe: Solesmes, 1987), 57–58.

6. For example, Ammonas 1 [PG 65:120A]: Εἰπέ μοι ῥῆμα. In citing from the *Sayings*, I refer to the source of the Greek text in Migne [*PG* 65] or in Nau [*ROC* 13, 14, 17, 18] and to the supplementary texts found in Guy [*Recherches*]. In addition, I occasionally refer to texts taken from other collections [J, Pa, etc.], which are found in the French collection of sayings published by Solesmes and Bellefontaine. For a full account of these texts, consult the table of abbreviations in *SPTr*.

7. In what follows, I am indebted to the discussion of L. Regnault, in "Aux origines des Apophtegmes," 57–63.

8. This is not meant to imply that the earliest stages of the tradition necessarily consisted of brief, piercing words and that other, longer narratives developed from them as a later form, a question which will be dealt with in more detail below. At this point I am simply pointing to the fact that these sayings grew out of a concrete setting in which "words" of power were addressed to genuine questions.

9. Dioscorus 2 [*PG* 65:160D–161A]; Nisterus 2[*PG* 65:307D–308A].

10. Lucien Regnault, "La transmission des Apophtegmes," in *Les pères du désert*, 66–67.

11. *Collectio Monastica,* 13:36, p. 63; 14:64, p. 92.

12. As Chitty suggests, "[I]t is not improbable that both Palladius and Evagrius had some such written records to draw from" (*The Desert a City,* 67).

13. For the *Collectio Monastica*, see n. 34; for the *Asceticon*, see n. 23.

14. *Asceticon, CSCO* 293, 28.

15. *Collectio Monastica, CSCO* 238, 126; *CSCO* 239, 93.

16. Regnault, "La transmission des Apophtegmes," 69.

17. Regnault, "Aux origines des Apophtegmes," 58.

18. Jean-Claude Guy, "Remarques sur le texte des *Apophthegmata Patrum*," *RSR* 63 (1955):252–58.

19. For much of what follows I am indebted to Gould, "Note on the *Apophthegmata Patrum*," 133–38.

20. Lucien Regnault, *Les sentences des pères du désert Recueil de Pélage et Jean*. Introd. Lucien Regnault. Trans. Jean Dion and Guy Oury (Sablé-sur-Sarthe: Solesmes, 1966), 4–11.

21. *Vitae Patrum* V. 18, nos. 17, 18 [*PL* 73:985–86]; VI. 1, nos. 2, 4, 6 [*PL* 73:993–94].

22. Gould, "Note on the *Apophthegmata Patrum*," 135. He points also to a long list of virtues included in a saying of John Colobos (34), suggesting that while "such a listing of virtues might well not be appropriate if addressed to an individual brother in need of guidance on a specific matter, in an assembly, as part of an address to a group of monks, it would be fully in place" (136).

23. Abba Isaiah, Logos VI, *Les cinq recensions de l'ascéticon syriaque d'Abba Isaïe I: Introductino au problème isaïen. Version des Logoi I–XIII avec des parallèles grecs et latins,* ed. René Draguet, *CSCO* 293, Scriptores Syri 122 (Louvain: CSCO, 1968), 27–81. See Gould, "Note on the Apophthegmata Patrum," 136.

24. John Colobos 23 [*PG* 65:212D–213A]. Other examples include: Abraham 3; Isaiah 6; Theodore of Pherme 6; Poemen 61.

25. H. Rosweyde, *Vitae Patrum* V, VI (Antwerp: 1615); reprint ed., Migne, *PL* 73:855–1022.

26. Lucien Regnault (*Les sentences des pères du désert, Recueil de Pélage and Jean,* intro. L. Regnault, trans. J. Dion and G. Oury [Sablé-sur-Sarthe: Solesmes, 1966]) comments: "Its value comes above all from the fact that all the pieces which it contains certainly go back to at least the fifth century, while the other collections have been enlarged from later sayings" (23). See also Owen Chadwick (*Western Asceticism* [Philadelphia: Westminster Press, 1958], who notes that the *Verba Seniorum* "was the most influential of all the collections upon the history of monasticism in the west" (35). Manuscripts containing the Greek text of this systematic or topical arrangement were rediscovered by Jean-Claude Guy at a fairly recent date. Cf. *Recherches,* 118.

27. J. B. Cotelier, *Ecclesiae Graecae monumenta I* (Paris: Muguet, 1677) 338–712. Reprinted in Migne, *PG* 65:71–440.

28. F. Nau, "Histoire des solitaires égyptiens" (MS Coislin 126, fol 158f.) nos. 133–369: *ROC,* 13 (1908):47–57; 14 (1909):357–79; 17 (1912):204–22, 294–301; 18 (1913):137–40.

29. M. Chaîne, *Le manuscrit de la version copte en dialecte sahidique des "Apophthegmata Patrum,"* Bibliothèque d'études Coptes 6 (Cairo: Institut Français d'Archéologie Orientale, 1960); idem, "Le texte originale des Apophtegmes des pères," *Mélanges de la Faculté orientale,* vol. 5, pt. 2 (Beirut: Université St. Joseph, 1912), 541–69.

30. A. Amélineau, *Monuments pour servir à l'histoire de l'Égypte chrétienne: Histoire des monastères de la Basse-Egypte,* Annales du Musée Guimet, vol. 25 (Paris: Leroux, 1894).

31. E. A. Wallis Budge, *The Book of Paradise, being the Histories and Sayings of the Monks and Ascetics of the Egyptian Desert according to the Rescension of 'Anan-Isho' of Beth Abbe,* vol. 2 (London: Printed for Lady Mieux by Drugulin, 1904).

32. H. Duensing, ed., "Neue christlich-palästinisch-aramäische Fragmente," *Nachrichten von der Akademie der Wissenschaften in Göttingen aus dem Jahre 1944,* Philologische-historische Klasse (Göttingen: Vandenhoeck and Ruprecht, 1944), 215–27.

33. Louis Leloir, ed. *Paterica Armeniaca a P. P. Mechitaristis edita (1855) nunc latine reddita,* CCSO 353, 361, 371, 379. (Louvain: CSCO, 1974–76).

34. M. Dvali, *Anciennes traductions georgiennes de récits du moyen âge,* vol. 1, *Traduction par Euthyme l'Hagiorite d'une ancienne recension du Patericon, d'après un manuscrit du XIe siècle* (Tiflis: Institut des manuscrits, 1966); J. M. Sauget, "Le Paterikon du ms. Mingana Christian Arabic 120a," *OCP* 28 (1962):402–17; idem, "La collection d'Apophthègmes du ms. 4225 de la Bibliothèque de Strasbourg," *OCP* 30 (1964):495–500; *Collectio monastica,* Ethiopian text and Latin translation by V. Arras, *CSCO* 238–39 (Louvain: CSCO, 1963); *Ethiopian Paterikon,* Ethiopian text and Latin trans. by V. Arras, *CSCO* 277–78 (Louvain: CSCO, 1967); M. van Esbroeck, "Les apophtegmes dans les versions orientales," *Analecta Bollandiana* 93 (1975): 381–89.

35. See the evidence cited by Chaîne and Amélineau, above; Guy *(Recherches)* has based his entire research into the Greek manuscript tradition on this assumption.

36. This should not be taken to mean that the Greek Alphabetico-Anonymous collection contains only the most primitive material or that the other collections are of less value. In spite of the linguistic priority of this Greek collection, the manuscripts we possess of the Greek collections are relatively late, coming for the most part from the eleventh and twelfth centuries. For this reason, the various versions or translations of the sayings retain their value as witnesses to important variants in the tradition.

37. There is considerable internal evidence to support this. See Frazer, "Morphology," 85–87.

38. Lucien Regnault, "Les Apophtegmes en Palestine aux Ve–VIe siècles," *Irénikon* 54 (1981):320–30, reprinted in *Les pères du désert,* 73–83. Derwas J. Chitty, "The Books of the Old Men," *Eastern Churches Review* 6 (1974): "The Gaza milieu . . . is likely to have seen the emergence of the first great collection of *Apophthegmata*— a region of high intellectual calibre to which leading monks of Egypt withdrew at a time when in dogma as in politics Christians were weighed down with a sense of impending disaster. . ." (20).

39. Regnault, "Les Apophtegmes en Palestine": "La première collection de type alphabético-anonyme a été formée en Palestine plutôt qu'en Égypte" (81).

40. *Collectio Monastica,* 13:35; 13:36; 13:79; 14:33.

41. The Ethiopian Collection contains numerous sayings which speak of a general relaxation among the monks: *Collectio Monastica* 13:22; 13:47; 13:70. On the disenchantment of some of the monks, see *Collectio Monastica,* 13:15; 13:16.

42. Chitty, *The Desert a City,* 67.

43. Regnault, "La transmission des Apophtegmes": "C'est évidemment cette mise par écrit des apophtegmes des anachorètes égyptiens qui va assurer leur perennité et leur diffusion universelle" (70).

44. *PG* 65:73AB, trans. Frazer, "Morphology," 115–16.

45. Guy, "Les *Apophthegmata Patrum*,": "The *Apophthegmata Patrum* [is] not conceived as an 'instructive' book, but as a 'useful' book . . . one doesn't find there διδασκαλιᾶ but ὠφελια" (81). The prologue uses this language to describe the purpose of the *Sayings:* ὠφελῆσαι τοὺς πολλούς [*PG* 65:73A].

46. Frazer, "Morphology," 178.

47. Guy, "Les *Apophthegmata Patrum,*" 79.

48. See Guy ("Les *Apophthegmata Patrum,*" 78), who shows the depth of the influence of *Sayings* on other early monastic texts.

49. The relationship between the words of Antony found in the *Sayings,* in his letters, and in the *VA* is complex. In proposing that the *VA* influenced the *Sayings,* I am not arguing that the picture of Antony found in the *VA* is earlier or more authentic than the words found in the *Sayings.* Rather the influence must be seen as reciprocal, with the "Antony Tradition" of sayings shaping Athanasius's depiction of him, and Athanasius in turn influencing the literary form, not only of the words of Antony in the *Sayings* but the collection as a whole. On this question, see: Samuel Rubenson,

The Letters of St. Antony: Origenist Theology, Monastic Tradition and the Making of a Saint (Lund: Lund University Press, 1990).

50. Frazer, "Morphology," 175.

51. Athanasius, *VA*, Exhortation and instruction: 69, 72–80, 25, 55; Exposition:15–43; Eulogy: passim.

52. See Sisoes 25 [*PG* 65:400D]; Peter of Dios 1 [*PG* 65:385C].

53. Frazer, "Morphology," 117–29.

54. The signs of this adaptation can be found in a number of sayings. For example, Macarius 22 [*PG* 65:272B]; Daniel 6 [*PG* 65:156BC].

55. These expositions are not all to be thought of, as we have shown above, as representing a later or more developed form. We have shown how exposition and teaching as commmentary on a saying could well comprise part of an original saying. The point here is to acknowledge the extent to which this form was polished and refined under the influence of Athanasius's *VA*.

56. In these cases, sometimes the characteristics or action itself is the focus of attention, while at other times the explanation or *logion* is more prominent. See, for example, Macarius 12, regarding Macarius's practice of fasting.

57. Frazer ("Morphology," 124) notes that these items are "retrospective in their original form, representing traditions that are already secondary to the action itself."

58. This is especially clear when comparing the *Sayings* with the exaggerated style of the early hagiographical literature of the Coptic church. Exceptions in the *Sayings* themselves to this rule of sobriety include Paul 1 [*PG* 65:380D–381A]; Bessarion 2 [*PG* 65:140A].

59. See, for example, Antony 28 [*PG* 65:85D–85A]; Pambo 12 [*PG* 65:372A].

60. Frazer, "Morphology," 10; Bousset, *Apophthegmata*, 71–76. Although it is impossible to state with any certainty the exact manner in which the sayings were absorbed into these larger works, it is clear that the sayings were known and used by these authors in different and earlier forms than the ones we possess now. The writings mentioned above were all published before the middle of the fifth century, while the *Sayings*, as we have seen, was probably not completed before the end of the fifth century.

61. On the influence of Evagrius on the *Historia Lausiaca* and the *Historia Monachorum*, see J. Daniélou and H. Marrou, *The Christian Centuries*, vol. 1, *The First Six Hundred Years*, trans. V. Cronin (New York: McGraw-Hill, 1964), 274; L. Bouyer, *The Spirituality of the New Testament and the Fathers* (New York: Seabury Press, 1982), 424; on the limitations of the *Historia Monachorum*, see Chitty, *The Desert a City*, 51; on the sympathy of the author of the *Historia Monachorum* for the Origenist party, see H. G. Evelyn-White, *The Monasteries of the Wadî'n Natrûn*, pt. 2, *The History of the Monasteries of Nitria and Scetis*, ed. W. Hauser (New York: Metropolitan Museum of Art, 1932), 92–93.

62. For an analysis of the anti-Arian interests in the *VA*, see R. Gregg and D. Groh, *Early Arianism: A View of Salvation* (Philadelphia: Fortress Press, 1982); especially chapter 4, "Claims on the Life of St. Antony."

63. See Owen Chadwick, *John Cassian,* 2d ed. (Cambridge: Cambridge University Press, 1968), 3.

64. Bouyer, *Spirituality of the New Testament,* 307. Although Bouyer somewhat overstates the contrast, his main point is on the whole accurate.

65. Jean-Claude Guy, "Écriture sainte et vie spirituelle," *DS* 4, col. 161.

66. Chitty, *The Desert a City,* 67.

67. P. Ricoeur, *Essays on Biblical Interpretation,* edited with an introduction by Lewis S. Mudge (Philadelphia: Fortress Press, 1980), 73–118.

68. Guy, "Les *Apophthegmata Patrum,*" 82.

69. Peter Brown, *The Making of Late Antiquity* (Cambridge: Harvard University Press, 1978), 82.

70. Guy, "Les *Apophthegmata Patrum,*" 80.

71. Chitty, "The Books of the Old Men," 17.

72. Lucien Regnault, *Les sentences des pères du désert. Série des anonymes* (Sablé-sur-Sarthe/Bégrolles-en-Mauges: Solesmes/Bellefontaine, 1985), 7.

73. Benedicta Ward, "Spiritual Direction in the Desert Fathers," *The Way* 24 (January 1984): 10. See also Chadwick *(Cassian):* "No document brings us nearer to the earliest monks than these sayings. No other source is quite so alive" (3).

74. For a comparison of the number of biblical references cited in each of three modern translations of the *Sayings,* see Appendix I.

75. *DS* 4, col. 161. My own count of Cotelier's Greek text yields 145 biblical references.

76. Benedicta Ward, *The Sayings of the Desert Fathers: The Alphabetical Collection* (London: Mowbrays, 1975). Ward includes no index of biblical references.

77. Lucien Regnault, *Les sentences des pères du désert* (Sablé-sur-Sarthe: Solesmes, 1981); Regnault includes an index in *SPTr,* 309–17.

78. Luciana Mortari, *Vita e detti dei padri del deserto* (Rome: Città Nuova, 1971). Mortari includes a biblical index in vol. 2: 289–96, and extensive notes on the use of the Bible throughout the text.

79. Ward, "Spiritual Direction in the Desert Fathers," 64–65.

II

APPROACHES TO THE WORD
IN THE DESERT

4

The Use of Scripture in the Desert

The apparent paucity of explicit biblical citations in the *Sayings,* the general reticence toward speaking about or commenting on Scripture found there, the high level of illiteracy among the monks, and the firm resistance on the part of many monks to reading or owning books have raised questions about how deeply Scripture penetrated the early eremetical movement. Indeed, some commentators have concluded that, apart from the proclamation of the Word at the weekly *synaxis* or gathering, the monks would have had hardly any contact with or knowledge of Scripture at all.[1] However, a closer look at the literature reveals that while Scripture certainly provoked diverse and ambivalent responses from the monks, it was nevertheless central to their spirituality.[2]

The high esteem in which the words of Scripture were held by the monks as well as the frequent recommendations to memorize and recite the sacred texts suggest the presence within desert monasticism of a culture nourished in significant ways on the Scriptures. Besides its place in the public *synaxis,* Scripture also played a key part in the life of the cells, where it was recited, ruminated, and meditated upon both in small groups of monks and by individuals in solitude. Scripture enjoyed great authority in the desert, and when someone asked an elder for a ''word,'' it was often a word from Scripture that he received in reply. Yet there *was* a real reticence among many of the monks to speak about Scripture and strong resistance in some quarters to owning books, including the sacred texts themselves. This reticence should not necessarily be taken to imply indifference or antagonism toward Scripture on the part of the monks. Rather, it should be understood as a natural result of tensions which often develop within oral cultures making the transition toward greater dependence upon written texts. We see among the desert monks a religious culture which was nourished to a very great degree on an encounter with the Word; yet it was more of an aural than a visual encounter. Still, as we have already seen, the central place of Scripture within Christianity meant that books in general, and especially books of

Scripture, gained increasing significance in the Christian world throughout this period.

This tension between an oral and a written approach to the word impinged itself upon the world of the desert and affected the way monks encountered and responded to Scripture. The ambivalent attitudes toward Scripture which we encounter in the *Sayings* can be best understood in light of this shift in emphasis from oral to written discourse. An examination of the oral and written approaches to Scripture among the monks will help to show how deeply Scripture penetrated into the world of the desert and how varied the apprehension of the word was. Before pursuing this question, however, it will be useful to note the monks' sense of the *value* of the Word in all its forms.

The Value of the Word: Scripture and the Elder

The great authority of Scripture and its centrality in the quest for salvation is reflected throughout the *Sayings*. The understanding of what constituted a sacred text was fluid and the authority of Scripture was experienced not only as something *written* but also as something *spoken*. Also, because the words of the leaders were valued so highly in the desert, there was no clear distinction between the words which came from the sacred texts and the words which came from the holy exemplars. The value of Scripture was almost always seen in very practical terms, relating to the help it provided in the discovery of salvation and self-knowledge. The words of Scripture and the worlds of the elders were seen as the preeminent guides to be followed.

Numerous sayings refer to the authority of Scripture and its importance for the life of the monk. Epiphanius, a bishop for whom reading and study were more important than for many of the simple monks, insisted that to be without knowledge of the Scriptures [τῶν Γραφῶν ἡ ἄγνοια] was to be in "a precipice and a deep abyss."[3] "To know nothing of the divine law [μηδένα τῶν θείων νόμων εἰδέναι]," he said, was a "betrayal of salvation."[4] The same matter-of-fact attitude toward the authority of Scripture is reflected in a response by Antony to some brothers who came seeking a "word" to help them discover how to be saved. Antony felt it sufficient to answer, "You have heard Scripture [ἠκούσατε τὴν γραφήν]. That should teach you how."[5] This simple response is revealing—regarding not only the authority of Scripture, but also the manner in which the monks often encountered it. Antony's brusque reply to the brothers' question speaks clearly about where he felt that clues to salvation were to be found; he neither refers to a particular text, nor engages in any commentary, but simply points the brothers in the direction of Scripture. However, he does not necessarily send the brothers away to *read* Scripture. Antony makes no assumption that his listeners will have studied or read Scripture or even have the ability to do so. Clearly, the authority and message of Scripture could be received through *hearing*. Antony suggests to the brothers that they have heard these words but have not really taken them in. He encourages his questioners to *listen* more carefully in the future to the words from Scripture.

Increased attentiveness to Scripture is also the subject of another saying of Antony's. To a brother who asked what he must do in order to please God, Antony replies with a double command, "Wherever you go, always have God before your eyes; whatever you do, have [before you] the testimony of the holy Scriptures."[6] In this telling comparison, Antony suggests that having the testimony of the Scriptures constantly before one is equivalent to being always in the presence of God. Scripture has that kind of power. Also, by reminding his listeners that they should have this testimony before them whatever they do, he indicates that Scripture is the surest guide for action. The call to look toward Scripture as a guide to salvation did not remain simply a general one, however. The monks often answered questions directly with quotations from or allusions to a Scriptural text. Epiphanius, for example, responded to someone who put a question to him about the meaning of righteousness by quoting a text from Jeremiah.[7] In another case, when a brother asked simply for a "word," Cronius gave him, without any hesitation, a word from Scripture and its interpretation.[8] The manner in which this was done leaves no doubt that it is the authoritative word which the questioner was seeking and that it is a word to be obeyed. The general exhortations to look toward Scripture and the specific quotations cited in response to particular questions testify to a common belief among the desert monks in the value of the Scripture—both as written word and as oral word—and of the need to follow in its way.

Still, there were also other words of power in desert, which should not be too sharply distinguished from the words of Scripture, and these came from the elders themselves, usually in response to a request for "a word" of salvation. The responses to these requests were varied, consisting sometimes of a short saying or story, sometimes of quotations from Scripture, and still other times of silence or of a symbolic action. Whatever the response, however, the words of the elders were often seen as carrying the same weight of authority as those of Scripture. The power of these utterances or actions was held to derive from the great purity of the holy one who was at their source. This moral purity gave the elder the authority to speak with power:

"It was axiomatic that the words of one who lived so close to God would be inspired."[9] The words of the holy ones were seen as participating in and continuing the discourse of the authoritative words of Scripture.

The words of elders and of Scripture constituted a double tradition of authority for those living in the desert. Abba Poemen alludes to this in his teaching about the place of tears and compunction. Weeping, he says, is "the way the Scriptures and our Fathers give us," an indication that both are important sources of spiritual authority.[10] An anonymous saying concerning obedience echoes this sentiment. One of the elders says that God asks two kinds of obedience of the monks: that they "obey the holy Scriptures, and obey their . . . spiritual fathers."[11] That the relationship between these two sources of authority was not always clear can be seen in the continuation of the saying of Antony alluded to earlier. The brothers who asked Antony for a word were told, "You have heard the Scriptures. That should teach you how." But they pressed him, saying, "We want to hear from *you too*, father."[12] While the brothers were not necessarily disputing the authority of the words of Scripture, it is clear that they also wanted to hear the authoritative words which Antony would utter. Such a request on the part of the brothers reflects not only the fluid relationship between Scripture and the words of the elder, but also the kinds of words most valued—whether from Scripture or the elder—words that were intimate, direct, and personal.

In some cases, the words of the elder appear to have had an authority which went beyond that of Scripture. One saying tells of Poemen citing a passage from Proverbs, prefacing his citation with the authoritative phrase "it is written." In this particular instance, however, Poemen felt the need to go beyond what was stated in the biblical text, in order to warn the brothers about the dangers of self-delusion. In doing so, he expressed the authority of his own words in a startling way, introducing his comments on the text with the very same expression Jesus used in the Sermon on the Mount (Mt 5:22) to announce his new authority: "but *I* say to you [ἐγὼ δὲ λέγω ὑμῖν] . . ."[13] Poemen's use of this expression is not reflective of a cavalier attitude toward Scripture. Rather, it expresses the "freedom of speech" which characterized the elders of the desert and the authority their words enjoyed. We see a symbolic expression of the importance attached to such authoritative, charismatic teaching in the desert in a story concerning what is required to be accorded the title "abba." When some of the brothers questioned Poemen about why Agathon, who was very young, should be called abba, Poemen replied, "because his mouth makes him worthy to be called abba."[14] In spite of his young age, Agathon's mouth—his words and teaching—were pure and authoritative and gave him the right to be called "abba."

Words, then, written and spoken, from Scripture and the elders, were basic to the quest for salvation in the desert. It is worth remembering the different sources of words—Scripture and the elders—as we proceed. When we hear of monks reciting or meditating upon words, it is likely that these are words from Scripture. However, the charismatic authority enjoyed by the words of the elders made them, in the minds of many of the monks, just as worthy of remembrance and meditation. In the same way, if we are to understand how the words of salvation—whether those of Scripture or of the elders—penetrated the imagination of the desert monks, we need to distinguish the two main ways the monks encountered these words: through written and oral discourse.

The Written Word

One way the desert Christians encountered Scripture was through the written word, or texts. Although it is likely that the majority of those who lived the semieremetical life in Lower Egypt could not read, the literature indicates that there was a good number for whom reading was one of the primary means of learning Scripture. For them, the culture of the book—especially the Bible, the book *par excellence*—was highly valued. Nevertheless, there was a genuine ambivalence in the desert toward possessing and reading books. In a predominantly oral culture, books were seen by many as presenting a threat to the spiritual life proclaimed by Scripture. This was especially true in cases where books came to be viewed not as mediators of the Word but as ends in themselves. Still, such doubts about the value of books did not entirely preclude the monks' use of written texts.

The presence of books in the everyday life of the desert is seen in numerous places in the *Sayings,* an indication that, although books may not have been common in the desert, neither were they entirely absent. Recalling that the great codices were produced during this era, we should not be surprised that some of them would have found their way into the desert communities. We hear of Abba Gelasius, who possessed a beautiful, and extremely valuable copy of the Bible in parchment (Βιβλίον ἐν δέρμασιν), said to contain the whole of the Old and New Testaments.[15] In a similar vein, we hear that Theodore of Pherme is said to have possessed "three good books [τρία Βιβλία καλά]" from which he and his brothers derived much profit.[16] And Abba Ammoes tells of some monks who possessed "books of parchment [Βιβλίων μεμβράνων]" in their cells.[17] While the precise character of these books and the use to which they were put is not easy to determine, it is likely that at least some of them would have included Bibles for use by the community at the weekly *synaxis*. These were Bibles which belonged to the "household," though in some cases the monk would have been allowed to keep them in his cell for personal use. There is also evidence that some of the monks made use of small, personal copies of the Bible (or parts of the Bible). Serapion is said to have possessed "a Psalter [τὸ ψαλτήριον]" and a copy of Paul's epistles, these probably being just the kind of small, portable codices whose widespread existence we have already noted.[18] There were also some larger and more expensive codices in the desert. These were apparently highly coveted in the desert, since we hear that they were frequently stolen.[19] One can see, then, that there were at least some books for liturgical as well as personal use to be found in the desert. While it remains difficult to be precise about how widely available books were, the frequent mention of literary activities among the monks, such as writing and reading, provides further evidence that the use of books was not uncommon.

The mention of writing, especially copying, implies that there was some demand for copies of the Bible. We hear for instance of Abba Mark, who sat for long hours in his cell writing in a book, copying from another text. Although we are not told what he copied, a likely focus of his efforts would have been Scripture.[20] In another instance we are told of a scribe at Scetis who worked in his cell copying books for the brothers. He is portrayed as being very skilled and well known for his ability as a scribe, implying that the demand for written copies of the sacred texts was not unusual.[21] The importance of books in the desert is also indicated by the frequent mention of *reading*. Although for many of the monks the primary source of the Word was what they heard at the weekly *synaxis,* there is evidence that a good number also practiced reading in their cells, which implies that at least some of them had books there. The practice of reading was important enough to Sisoes, that, when asked for a word, he could simply refer to his own practice of *reading* Scripture: "What shall I say to you? I *read* the New Testament, and I turn to the Old."[22] Similarly, we hear that Abba John Colobos regularly gave himself over to "prayers, *readings,* and meditations of the Holy Scriptures."[23]

The reading of Scripture was felt by the monks to have numerous practical spiritual benefits. Implicit in this belief was a sense of the power of the sacred text to keep evil at bay. Thus, reading was believed to "terrify the demons."[24] For Epiphanius, "reading the Scriptures is a great safeguard against sin."[25] In a more positive vein, reading Scripture was felt to provide important nourishment for the soul.[26] Because of this, one brother confidently asserted that happiness comes to the soul "by means of assiduous *reading* of the Scriptures."[27] Such reading of Scripture was not a guarantee against disturbance, however, but could sometimes even attract trouble. In one story, we hear of an old man who, according to his custom, was sitting in his cell reading from Scripture. In the midst of his reading, he was suddenly interrupted by a demon who wanted to engage him in a contest to prove that his knowledge of Scripture was greater than the monk's![28] The power of Scripture implied in these stories was evident in other, more mundane ways as well. Reading Scripture aloud, for example, could enable one to persuade or comfort another person. Serapion found it useful in his attempt to win over a prostitute to read to her from a Psalter and from "the Apostle" (Paul).[29] Reading aloud could also be useful for providing comfort to those who were too ill to read for themselves or meditate, or attend the *synaxis*. Thus, we hear that while Agathon and another brother were lying ill in their cell, a brother read to them from the book of Genesis.[30] In a variety of ways, reading played an important role in giving the monks knowledge of the Scripture. It helped them to avoid certain temptations, served as a source of personal encouragement, and played a role in their interpersonal relationships.

Beyond these practical benefits of reading, there was a real sense for many of the monks that the Bible was to be revered as a sacred object. The Bible clearly had a powerful talismanic effect on the imagination of the early desert dwellers beyond any consideration of the meaning of its words.[31] Abba Epiphanius expressed this well, indicating his belief that merely *seeing* sacred books can help bring one to salvation: "The acquisition of Christian books is necessary for those who can use them. For the mere *sight* of these books renders us less inclined to sin, and incites us to believe more firmly in righteousness."[32] A further indication of the symbolic power of the written word in the desert imagination is found in a story told about Abba Ephrem, depicting the presentation to him of a sacred scroll. A brother had a vision in which a band of angels was seen coming from heaven, holding in their hands a small piece of papyrus scroll (κεφαλίδα), covered with writing. After some discussion among themselves about whom they should give it to, it was agreed that no one but Ephrem was worthy to receive it. Ephrem was given the scroll and immediately afterwards, the brother saw a fountain flowing from Ephrem's lips, a confirmation that the words coming from his mouth were from the Holy Spirit.[33] The story, the main point of which is to comment upon the inspired language of Ephrem, nevertheless reveals indirectly the symbolic significance of the written text for the monks. It is the presence of this sacred text, after all, and its solemn presentation to Ephrem, which confirms the inspired character of Ephrem's words.

Perhaps the best illustration of the holiness attributed to the Bible by the desert fathers is found in a story which appears, on the surface, to denigrate Scripture. An elder, wishing to test the obedience of one of his disciples, ordered him to seize a valuable Bible used in the liturgical assembly and pitch it into the flaming furnace. The disciple did so without hesitation, and immediately the fire was extinguished.[34] The story at first glance appears to condone a careless or deprecatory attitude toward the Bible. However, as Fernandez Marcos notes, the pedagogical point of the story—to show that obedience is the "ladder to the kingdom of heaven"—only becomes clear if one recognizes how precious and dear the Bible was to the brother who was ordered to throw it into the furnace. We can see this better by comparing this story with a similar one found elsewhere in the *Sayings*, in which the disciple in question was suffering from depression. When the elder asked him why he was depressed, the brother told him that he missed his three children whom he had left behind in the city, and wanted to bring them to the monastery. The abba ordered him to do so. Upon reaching the city, the brother discovered that his two oldest children were dead, so he took his youngest with him and returned to the monastery. They went to the bakery to see the abba, who took the child in his arms and covered him with kisses. Then he asked the child's father: "Do you love him?" The father said that he did. "Do you love him very much?" the abba asked him. He answered, "Yes." Then the abba, wishing to test the faith of the disciple, ordered him to throw his child into the flames. Without a moment's hesitation, the father did so. Again, as in the first story, the fire was immediately quenched, becoming "like dew, full of freshness," and no harm came to the child. In an indication of the parallel with the story of Abraham and Isaac, we are told that "through this act he received glory like the patriarch Abraham."[35] The comparison of the two stories reveals the true significance of the command to cast the Bible into the furnace. The reverence accorded to Scripture made that command one of the severest tests of obedience imaginable, and its fulfillment a dramatic statement about the importance of obedience. The story gains even more poignancy when it is remembered that in the fourth century it was considered a grave sin in the Christian community to destroy or even mutilate a copy of the Bible. In an era not far removed from the ravages of persecution, the monks would not likely have forgotten that the reverence shown toward the sacred texts by both Christians and Jews had led to the regular requisition and destruction of books by authorities at times of persecution.[36] Like the stories in the Acts of the Martyrs, in which sacred books are seen to miraculously extinguish the fire which they are thrown, this story affirms the strength, power, and sacredness of the Bible as written word in the experience and imagination of the desert fathers.

The Oral Word

Critique of the Bible as "Sacred Object"

While there can be no doubt that the written word occupied a significant place in the life of the desert monks, there is evidence that many of the desert fathers believed that too much reliance on books, even the most sacred, could lead to trouble. The *Sayings* is filled with stories which reveal the recurring problem of the tendency to make the written text an end in itself. The desert fathers were acutely aware of a problem that plagues any community which places so much emphasis on a sacred text: "The fixing of the holy word in writing always carries with it potential threats to the original spontaneity and living quality of the scriptural text, for it places it ever in danger of becoming only a 'dead letter' rather than the 'living word.' " [37] The monks were astute and perceptive observers of the manifold ways the Word could be relegated to a thing. Because they sensed that allowing these tendencies to spread would mean the death of the Word, they were vigorous in their opposition to such attitudes.

The elders could be blunt in their response to those who seemed to place too much faith in their knowledge or mastery of the written word while neglecting to carry out what that word enjoined. In one case, a brother proudly told an old man at Scetis that he had copied with his own hand the whole of the Old and New Testaments. Unimpressed, the old man responded drily, "You have filled the cupboards with paper." [38] Other sayings, especially those dealing with the propriety of owning books, seem to arise form a similar concern—that too much emphasis on the written word would lead to a failure to pay sufficient attention to what the text actually said. For some of those living in the desert, the question of whether or not to possess books—including the Bible itself—was a serious moral issue. With a biting irony characteristic of the desert, some elders declared that the possession of a copy of the sacred texts was in direct conflict with the words of Scripture itself, which required one to renounce everything for the sake of the kingdom. Thus we hear of a brother who "owned only a book of the Gospels." Inspired by the gospel call, he sold it and gave away the money for the support of the poor saying, "I have sold the very word which speaks to me saying: 'Sell your possessions and give to the poor' (Mt. 19:21)." [39] Theodore of Pherme, who as we have seen possessed some "excellent books," was troubled enough about owning them to approach Abba Macarius for advice on the matter. He told Macarius that although he and his brothers derived great profit from the books, he was uncertain whether he should keep them or sell them and give the money to the poor. Macarius answered him with startling directness: "Your actions are good," he said, "but it is best of all to possess nothing." Hearing this, Theodore went immediately and sold the books, giving the money away to the poor.[40]

Possessing books was seen as problematic not only because it could distract one from adhering to the gospel call to renunciation, but also because it could blind one to the demands of charity and justice. Some of the desert fathers felt that the accumulation of books was tantamount to robbing the poor. Abba Serapion expressed this sentiment when, during a visit to the cell of a particular brother, he was asked by the brother for "a word." Looking around the cell gave Serapion pause, and he hesitated in responding to the brother. " 'What shall I say to you? You have taken the living of the widows and orphans and put it on your shelves.' For he saw them full of books."[41] Serapion is certainly not implying in these comments that possessing books is in itself immoral, for he himself made good use of books on occasion. What he appears to be criticizing is rather the desire among some monks merely to collect and accumulate books, allowing them to become useless objects. As he perceptively noted, such practice could lead the monks to turn the Word from a command to be fulfilled to a thing to be stored. Monks who allowed such an attitude to take hold in them would, he felt, become increasingly oblivious to the vulnerable and needy in their midst. We catch hints in the *Sayings* that just such a hardening of attitudes, and "objectification" of the Word, did take place among some monks, at least from the perspective of later generations. A group of monks who were reflecting on the earliest period in the desert lamented the great loss that resulted from failure to treat the Word as a living thing. The process of reification of the Word is described this way: "The prophets wrote books. Then came our Fathers who put them into practice. Those who came after them learnt them by heart. Then came the present generation, who have written them out and put them into their window seats without using them."[42]

We see here the ambiguity and tension over the place and function of books among those who came to live in the desert. Although the sacred book was highly esteemed and was a central part of the life of the desert, the recognition that the Word could too easily become a reified object of veneration or a "collector's item," whose power was scarcely felt, and whose meaning was too little grasped, led to a profound suspicion of books. This suspicion reflects a recognition on the part of the desert fathers that the Word is a living, dynamic force. It also reflects their desire to grapple with the *meaning* of Scripture and to appropriate that meaning as far as possible in their lives.

Reciting Synaxis

While it is clear that Scripture as a written word served as an important formative influence upon many of the desert fathers, it is likely that for the majority of them this was not the primary means of access to the sacred texts. Rather, the monks most often encountered and appropriated the Word through *hearing* the Scriptures at the weekly *synaxis* and from the lips of the elders. Beyond this, the monks were encouraged to prolong the encounter with the Word beyond the time of the *synaxis* through memorization, continual recitation, meditation, and rumination, appropriating the Word at the deepest level of their being.

The structure of public and private recitation of Scripture in the desert cannot be reconstructed with complete certainty.[43] We know that there were weekly public gatherings at which Scripture was recited and to which all the monks in the vicinity were invited. Further, it was common to meditate and recite Scripture in private or in small groups during the week. However, there were enough significant variations in these practices that it would be inaccurate to speak of a single commonly accepted routine followed by the semieremetical monks of Lower Egypt. Nevertheless, we can identify the more common practices and assess their significance.

Synaxis, which means a gathering together, is the most common word used in the *Sayings* to describe both the public and private occasions when Scripture was recited. Though we have little detailed description of the public *synaxis* in the *Sayings,* the routine manner in which it is described confirms the impression gained elsewhere that it was a common and widely accepted ritual in the desert. Abba Paul the Simple, a disciple of Antony, tells of coming to a monastery (presumably from his cell) where, "after the customary conference, the brothers entered the holy church of God to perform the *synaxis* there, as was their custom."[44] Elsewhere, Abba Marcellin is described as going out every week on Sunday for the *synaxis.*[45] It is here that the monks heard and recited the Scriptures on a regular basis, afterwards departing to their more solitary life in the cells, taking the words they had heard away with them.[46]

One of the means of prolonging the encounter with the Word which occurred at the weekly public *synaxis* was through the daily *synaxis,* or recitation of Scripture, in the cells of the monks.[47] This was performed either in solitude or in a small group of monks and was usually, though not always, observed at two main times of the day, in the early evening and during the night. The monastic day normally began at or soon after midnight with a recitation of Scripture privately observed in the cells, a practice which may owe something to Antony's injunction to "sing psalms before sleep and after sleep, and take to heart the precepts in the Scriptures."[48] Gelasius speaks routinely of the "hour of the night psalmody [νυκτερινῆς ψαλμῶας], when the brothers gathered."[49] A saying of Macarius notes two brothers who arose in the night to "recite the twelve Psalms [Βάλωμεν τοὺς δώδεκα ψαλμούς]." There was apparently an accepted order to this process, for the younger of the two began by "chanting five psalms in groups of six verses and an alleluia."[50] Regarding the evening *synaxis,* Palladius tells us that it was "at about the ninth hour," or about three o'clock, that the psalmody could be heard proceeding from each cell at the Mount of Nitria.[51] At the first meeting of Paul the Simple and Antony, the two are said to have recited psalms together both in the evening and during the night, a practice which appears already to be customary.[52] Elsewhere, Arsenius refers routinely to his practice of reciting "the twelve psalms" at morning and in the evening.[53] Apart from these night and early evening recitations of Scripture, which were for the most part observed by small groups of monks reciting together, there were also other, less clearly defined practices.

There appears to have been considerable flexibility concerning the time and manner in which the recitation of Scripture took place. We hear in various places that the reciting of the psalms began simply "when it was late [ὡς ἐγένετο ὀψὲ]," that is, in the early evening, an indication that there was no fixed hour for the observance of the evening *synaxis.*[54] And there are cases where the reciting of psalms at night could sometimes extend until dawn.[55] Nor were the two customary times for reciting Scripture the only occasions in which monks engaged in this practice. We hear Paphnutius tell a brother who is tempted to leave the life of solitude for the monastery to practice prayer three times a day: "Go and stay in your cell; make only one prayer in the morning, one in the evening and one at night."[56] Some monks apparently had their own individual practices, apart from the customary ones. Abba Lot speaks of reciting "my little *synaxis* [μιχράν μου σύναξιν]," which appears to be a practice he engaged in alone, and may or may not be related to the two offices mentioned.[57] Isidore the Priest recalls that when he was younger, he remained in his cell and "had no limit to *synaxis* [μέτρον συνάξεως οὐκ εἶχον]. The night was for me as much the time of *synaxis* as the day."[58] We see in these stories indications that while there were certain customary ways and times of reciting the Scriptures in the desert, these were not observed rigidly or universally. The point of reciting the Scriptures was to become absorbed in the world of the texts, and desert fathers worked at this assiduously.

The variations in the practice of Scripture recitation which we find in the *Sayings* reveal not only the slight differences in the practices between different monks or between different groups of monks but also the significant tensions regarding the purpose and meaning of reciting Scripture that sometimes surfaced. Thus, we hear of rivalries between cenobites and anchorites about how long the *synaxis* should be, questions about the exact procedure to observe when saying the *synaxis,* as well as more mundane concerns about oversleeping and missing the *synaxis* altogether. All of these issues reflect, in one way or another, the desire on the part of the monks to move beyond the surface meaning of Scripture recitation to a more profound understanding of the practice.

The first step in this direction often involved abandoning certain preconceived notions regarding the purpose of *synaxis* and how it was to be observed. For some the desire to observe the *synaxis* in the precise and correct way actually prevented them from experiencing the Word as a living force within them. One such instance is described in a story of an abba from a monastery in Palestine who came to visit Abba Epiphanius. The visitor thanked Epiphanius for all his prayers and said that because of them, he and his disciples never neglected their appointed round of psalmody but were always "very careful to recite terce, sext and none." But Epiphanius was puzzled by this comment, and, with barely concealed irony in his voice, responded to the visitor: "It is clear that you do not trouble about the other hours of the day, if you cease from prayer. The true monk should have unceasing prayer and psalmody in his heart."[59] For Epiphanius, too much emphasis on precise observance of the ritual of *synaxis* could actually preclude openness to continual prayer. The recitation of the text was best understood not as a perfunctory duty to be carried out only at discrete times but as an ongoing process leading toward the continual recitation of the text in one's heart. Expectations regarding the need for correct observance of the *synaxis* could also produce—especially when expectations were not met—a sense of shame and discouragement and a belief that it was better not to engage in the recitation of the texts at all. A brother told one of the elders that on occasions when he was overcome by sleep and missed the time of the night *synaxis,* he felt too ashamed to get up and say the *synaxis* in front of his brothers after the usual time. The elder sought to ease the brother's sense of shame and provide him with a practical solution to his dilemma, telling him that if he did happen to oversleep, he should simply get up, shut his door and his window, and say the *synaxis* alone. And to give the brother added confidence that such practice was acceptable before God, he alluded to Scripture: "The day is yours and the night is yours also (Ps 74:16). In truth, God is glorified at all times. [1 Pt 4:11]."[60] Such episodes convey the sense that for the desert fathers scruples about correct observance of *synaxis* should never be allowed to obscure the realization that Scripture could be recited at any time. Such an awareness would, it was hoped, lead to the continual presence of the Word in the heart of the monk.

Tensions over the proper way to observe the *synaxis* also occasionally surfaced between monks living different ways of life. Cenobites and anchorites sometimes clashed over the issue of how long and rigorous the *synaxis* should be, and how much Scripture should be recited there. These stories reveal an awareness on the part of the desert fathers of the dangers of rigorism and the realization that giving in to an extremist mentality could cause them to lose sight of the whole purpose of Scripture recitation. One story, told from the perspective of the anchorites, tells of some brothers from a cenobitic community who went to the desert to visit a certain anchorite. When evening came, the anchorite and his visitors joined together and "recited the twelve psalms, and likewise during the night." After they had finished, the anchorite, unbeknownst to the brothers, continued privately to "keep vigil" long into the night. While he was keeping vigil, the anchorite overheard the brothers talking amongst themselves, remarking on how short and easy the anchorite's *synaxis* was and on how much softer the anchorite's way of life was then their own life in the monastery. The anchorite did not let his visitors know he had overheard them and did not say anything to them at that point. But the next morning, as his visitors were preparing to depart, he decided to enlist the aid of a friend to help dispel their illusions about the anchoritic life and to teach them some humility. He knew they were planning to visit another anchorite near by and asked them to greet him with the words: "Do not water the vegetables." When the other anchorite heard this greeting, he understood immediately. He put his visitors to work and kept them hard at work until evening at which time he began to recite the "great *synaxis* [μεγάλην σύναξιν]." After reciting for a while he paused and said to his visitors, "Let us stop now, for you are tired." He then told them, "It is not our custom to eat every day, but for your sakes let us eat a little." He brought them dry bread and salt, saying, "For your sake we must celebrate"; and he poured a little vinegar on the salt. When they had finished eating, they continued reciting the *synaxis* until dawn. At that point, the old man said to them, "We cannot fulfil the whole rule [ὅλον τὸν κανόνα] on your account; you must take a little rest, for you come from far." When morning came, the brothers were completely worn out and desperately began seeking some pretext for escaping the place. But the anchorite begged them to stay longer, at least three days, as this was "the traditional custom of the desert." The brothers, realizing then that the old man would not send them away with his blessing, yet certain they could endure no more, "arose and fled secretly."[61] This story, which conveys a barely disguised polemic on the part of the anchorites against the cenobitic way of life, contains some interesting details about the practice of the *syn-axis* and the mentality that sometimes accompanied it. We see that the *syn-axis*, especially the "great *synaxis*" referred to here, could extend far into the night and tax the endurance of those who were not used to it. Though the story contains a barb against those following the cenobitic way of life and their relatively undemanding practice, it does reveal what was probably a significant discrepancy in the desert between the practice of some anchor-ites and that of the cenobitic communities. Whether it was a formal rule or not, the "canon" referred to by the anchorites appears to have included customs that may well have gone beyond the usual practices we have seen referred to elsewhere. However, the main point of the story is not to dem-onstrate the superiority of the anchoritic *ascesis*. Rather, it is meant to serve as a humorous reminder of the dangers and folly of giving into a rigorist mentality. The anchorites are shown as playing along with their visitors, who attempt to flaunt the strictness of their own ascetical regime, until they are eventually startled into the recognition of their superficial attitude toward ascetical practice. The picture of these proud monks withering before the everyday regime of the anchorite would have sent a clear message to others with misplaced aspirations toward heroic asceticism: the purpose of reciting *synaxis* (and of other ascetical practices) was not to scale ever greater heights but to ponder the words in simplicity and humility.

The capacity to recite *synaxis* with humility was considered especially important for preventing a superficially rigorous attitude toward Scripture from taking hold in the monastic life. It was not uncommon, as the previous stories testify, for monks to try to shield from their visitors' eyes the true extent of their ascetical practice. Stories of monks keeping their recitation of Scripture "hidden" point to the value they placed on humility. One story tells of Abba Eulogius, a "great ascetic," who was reputed to fast for days on end, coming to visit Abba Joseph at Panephysis. Joseph received him joyfully and offered him everything he had on hand to refresh him. Eulo-gius's disciples, however, coldly reminded Joseph of the strict regime ob-served by their master: "The priest eats only bread and salt." The visitors proceeded to spend three days with Joseph and his disciples, but "without hearing them chanting psalms or praying, for their activity was hidden." Eventually, being neither edified nor impressed by the way of life of Joseph and his disciples, the visitors decided to leave. Soon after they had departed it became dark and they lost their way, forcing them to make their way back to Abba Joseph's place. Upon arriving, they paused for a moment outside the cell of Joseph and his disciple, where "they heard them chanting psalms [ἤκουσαν αὐτῶν ψαλλόντων]." After finishing their "psalmody [ψαλμῳδίας]," Joseph and his disciples greeted the visitors with joy and again showed them every hospitality. The visitors, realizing that they had been mistaken about the brothers' practice of *synaxis*, soon saw that they had misjudged nearly every aspect of Abba Joseph's way of life. Their concern with ascetic exactitude and rigor had been so pervasive that they failed to perceive the depth of humility, compassion, and discernment in Joseph and his disciples. This story, as well as others like it, makes it clear that the recitation of the Scriptures should be approached with great care, a prayerful disposition, and, above all, humility.[62] The care toward recitation of *synaxis* reflected in such stories indicates how seriously the monks took the practice of recitation. They were convinced that there was an inherent power in Scripture and that verbal recitation could make that power available to them in their quest for salvation.

Meditation and Rumination of Scripture

The *Sayings* speaks often of the benefits of ruminating and meditating upon Scripture. These practices are described in the same general terms as the recitation of Scripture at the public or private *synaxis* and should not be too sharply distinguished from it. Such an approach to Scripture involved saying the words of a particular text, mulling them over in the mind, chewing on and slowly digesting the words. And it was a predominantly oral phenomenon. However, unlike the *synaxis*, meditation did not usually involve chanting. Also, whereas the *synaxis* usually involved recitation of Scripture in common on a regular basis, meditation generally referred to the more solitary and less regular practice of mulling over one or two verses of Scripture or a memorable saying of an elder in one's cell. The discussion of meditation in the *Sayings* suggests that it was a common, widespread practice in early monasticism and considered an indispensable part of the life of the monk. It is in relation to this practice that the monks expressed some of their most insightful comments regarding the practical, psychological benefits of Scripture recitation. We find here dramatic evidence of the power these texts had for the monks: for aiding them in their battle with the demons; for healing and encouragement; for helping them to draw disparate thoughts and energies into a contemplative union.

Numerous sayings testify to the central place of meditation in the life of the desert monks. Often meditation is included in a basic list of the practices which are believed to be fundamental to monastic *ascesis*. "The life of the monk is obedience, meditation, not judging, not slandering, not complaining."[63] Meditation is described as one of the foundations of the monastic life. When a brother asks one of the elders how to rebuild one's life after having succumbed to temptation, the elder reminds him that to rebuild a collapsed structure, one must begin from the ground up: "Meditation [τὴν μελέτην], psalmody, and manual work—these are the foundations."[64] Abba Poemen includes meditation among the activities which are indispensable for life in solitude: "Living in the cell means manual work, eating only once a day, silence, meditation."[65] Abba Iot describes his ascetic routine to Abba Joseph this way: "I say my little office, I fast a little, I pray and meditate, I live in peace as far as I can, I purify my thoughts."[66]

Meditation was not, as the word has come to imply today, an interior reflection on the meaning of certain words. It was first and foremost the utterance, or exclamation of words, which were gradually digested and interiorized. Meditation on Scripture was an oral phenomenon. We see this from the account of witnesses, who are said to both *hear* and *see* monks meditating on Scripture. In one story, Abba Ammoes relates that he went with a companion to see Abba Achilles: "We *heard* him meditating on this saying [ἠκούσαμεν αὐτοῦ μελετῶντος τὸν λόγον τοῦτον]. 'Do not fear, Jacob, to go down into Egypt' (Gen 46:3). For a long time, he remained, meditating on this word."[67] Elsewhere, a monk relates having "*seen* a brother meditating in his cell [εἶδον ἀδελφὸν μελετῶντα ἐν τῷ κελλίῳ αὐτοῦ]," presumably meaning he had seen him moving his lips as he recited the words.[68]

Such private, oral recitation of Scripture was viewed as one of the most effective means of protecting the monk against the snares of the evil one. The desert fathers had a keen sense of the multitude of traps that lay before them in the desert and of the power inherent in certain words to save them from these snares. Because of this they made use of short exclamations or bursts of prayer, using either words of Scripture or words modeled upon Scripture, to protect themselves from the most violent assaults which beset them. An elder imparted these words of advice to those struggling with the "impious": "Practice silence, care for nothing, pay attention to your meditation, lie down and get up in the fear of God, and you will not need to fear the assaults of the impious."[69] Macarius told one of his disciples that the best way to pray in the midst of any struggle was simply to cry out, "Lord, help."[70] In another instance, a monk was said to have been kept from being dragged from his cell by a demon by crying out, "Jesus save me."[71] Reflecting the extent to which the power of the New Covenant was perceived by the monks to have overcome the kingdom of Satan, we hear that the mere mention of the word "New" (in "New Testament") was enough to cause the demon to vanish.[72] Another story relates how a brother was meditating in his cell with the demons standing outside it. "While the brother was meditating, they were not able to enter, but when he stopped meditating, then the demons entered the cell and strove with him."[73] To gain such protection, it was not even necessary, claimed one elder, for the monk to understand the words upon which he was meditating. A brother who battled with impure thoughts was told: "Watch your thoughts, and every time they begin to say something to you, do not answer them, but rise and pray; kneel down, saying, 'Son of God, have mercy on me.' " But the brother protested, saying: "Look, abba, I meditate but there is no compunction in my heart because I do not understand the meaning of the words." The abba responded: "Be content to meditate. Indeed, I have heard that Abba Poemen and many other fathers uttered the following saying, 'The magician does not understand the meaning of the words which he pronounces, but the wild animal who hears it understands, submits and bows to it.' So it is with us also: even if we do not understand the meaning of the words we are saying, when the demons hear them, they take fright and go away." [74]

These stories convey a common conviction in the desert regarding the talismanic power of particular words from Scripture. While it is tempting to dismiss such attitudes as reflective of primitive credulity, we should be wary of doing so. It reflects a sense of language almost completely foreign to literate cultures but common to oral ones. As Walter Ong observes, "The fact that oral peoples commonly and in all likelihood universally consider words to have magical potency is clearly tied in, at least unconsciously, with the sense of the word as necessarily spoken, sounded, and hence power-driven." [75] This was certainly true of attitudes in the desert toward spoken words in general. It was especially true of the monks' attitudes toward words from Scripture.

The capacity of meditation upon Scripture to protect the monks from demonic assaults was not simply a matter of the "brute power" of the words. Meditation was an act which could have real psychological significance. It is important to note in this regard that the "battles with the demons" reflect the immense psychological challenges the monks experienced in their life in the desert. [76] The power of meditation to help the monk work through this interior struggle is related in a story told by Macarius about a brother who was beset by temptations. One day as he was watching the road by his cell, he met a demon who was "going to stir up the memories of the brothers [ἀπέρχομαι ὑπομνῆσαι τοὺς ἀδελφούς]." Upon his return the demon gloomily reported to Macarius that he had all but failed in his task. Only one of the brothers had succumbed to him. "When he sees me, he changes like the wind," the demon said. Upon hearing this, Macarius journeyed down to visit the brother to inquire about his welfare. The brother reported that all was well with him, but Macarius pressed him, asking "Do not your thoughts war against you?" The brother again replied that he was fine, because he was afraid to admit anything of his struggles. Macarius sensed this and changed his approach, telling the brother of his own troubles, of how even after so many years of living as an ascetic, he was still beset by temptations. Slowly the brother opened up to Macarius and began to admit the immensity of the struggles he faced. This enabled Macarius to offer him some advice: "Meditate [ἀποστήθιζε] on the Gospel and the other Scriptures, and if a thought arises within you, never look at it but always look upwards, and the Lord will come at once to your help." The brother followed the advice and eventually became liberated from the assaults of this demon.[77] This story provides us with a good sense for the kind of psychological relief which meditation on Scripture could bring to those who felt themselves beset by the demons. Here, as so often in the *Sayings,* the struggle with the demon symbolizes a profound psychological challenge.

From the beginning we see that the form that the assault takes is the "stirring up of memories." Although we are not told of what these consisted, there is ample evidence elsewhere in the *Sayings* for the kind of memories which plagued the monks. These were not simply recollections of their "former life in the world," although many were afflicted by questions about family and loved ones left behind. There were also memories of a lifetime of struggle—often laced with failure—to live in a certain way, and memories of remorse for words or actions which may have wounded another person. The story told by Macarius suggests the ways discouragement and despondency could affect the life of a monk plagued by such memories and thoughts. The advice Macarius offers to one caught in the web of such thoughts shows both wisdom and a genuinely Christian sense of hope. Meditation on Scripture—literally reciting it by heart—not only occupies the memory of the monk but creates a new, potentially healing reservoir of thoughts. Even so, old thoughts and memories will continue to arise from within, like putrid gases from a garbage heap. In such cases, the brother should avoid a "head on" confrontation with these thoughts. They are too strong. Instead, when these thoughts arise, the brother should "look upwards" to the Lord. Help will come at once. Such advice takes seriously the reality of the struggle with thoughts, and without advocating their repression, provides the monk with a practical strategy for avoiding their fiercest blows. More than this, there is a deeply Christian sense of hope which permeates these words. Meditation itself would not enable the monk to overcome the demons; only the attitude of abandonment to God cultivated through meditation could bring peace.

The struggle with the demons could lead beyond psychological depression and confusion, even resulting in physical illness. In such cases, the recitation of Scripture was experienced as a healing balm for the whole person.

However, as we have already seen, such healing was the result not only of the power of Scripture but also of the determination of the person to persevere in reciting Scripture even in the face of despair. Amma Theodora relates that while it was a good thing indeed for someone to choose the life of *hesychia,* or silent recollection, it was almost inevitable that immediately after making such a choice, "evil [would come] to weigh down the soul through *accidie,* faintheartedness and evil thoughts." Moreover, it would also attack the body through sickness, debility, weakening of the knees and all the members, so sapping the strength of the soul and body that one was no longer able to pray. In spite of this, Theodora asserted that the power of evil had limits and could be driven out through vigilant recitation of Scripture. She tells the story of a brother who suffered from cold, fever, and headaches every time he recited the *synaxis.* Depressed from this condition, and fearing that he was near death, the brother determined nevertheless to get up and recite the *synaxis* one last time before he died. But, "as the *synaxis* came to an end, so too the fever ceased from troubling him. . . . By reasoning in this way, the brother resisted, he recited the *synaxis,* and he conquered his thought[s]."[78] The recitation of Scripture —in particular the *decision* to recite in spite of the temptation to despair—is seen here as contributing to the health and well-being of one beset by trouble. The story suggests that, in spite of how difficult the struggles in solitude could be and how the psychological depression experienced in such struggles could even lead to physical illness, reciting Scripture with determination and hope could help restore one to health. Although we are not told which texts were recited or how the healing was effected, it is clear that on one level the simple decision to recite the texts in the face of death constituted an act of faith and hope. One can imagine any number of texts which, recited in faith, might initiate a process of psychological and physical healing. The struggle against sickness and depression depicted here was no doubt a common one in the solitude of the desert. Recitation of Scripture was one of the chief means of dealing with it. Amma Syncletica elsewhere affirms this, claiming that in the fight against *accidie,* that kind of grief or deep sadness so common to the desert, the psalms are one of the main sources of healing.[79]

Even in less extreme circumstances, if one's thoughts had simply become scattered during the course of the day, the recitation of Scripture was advocated as a means of restoring one to a certain equilibrium. Abba John Colobos apparently noticed how working everyday in the harvest had the effect of dissipating his attention, making him vulnerable to all kinds of thoughts. Because of this, whenever he returned from the harvest, he would give himself to "prayer, meditation and psalmody until his thoughts were reestablished in their previous order."[80] This saying suggests that one of the main purposes of meditation was the cultivation of simplicity, or unity within the mind and heart. Such attentiveness helped the monk avoid the kind of spiritual torpor which so often resulted when one became overwhelmed by a multitude of thoughts. The ability to remain attentive in this way, to *remember* the sayings of Scripture and not give way to forgetfulness was crucial to the health and well-being of the monk. One saying tells of a brother, who, while reciting the *synaxis* with one of the elders, "forgot and lost track of a word of the psalm." When the *synaxis* was finished, the elder, noticing the brother's lapse, told him of his own attitude during the recitation of *synaxis*. He thinks of himself as being on top of a burning fire: "My thoughts cannot stray right or left." He then asked the brother: "Where were your thoughts, when we were saying the *synaxis,* that the word of the psalm escaped you? Don't you know that you are standing in the presence of God and speaking to God?"[81] Attentiveness or mindfulness while reciting Scripture was crucial in the life of the monk. Carelessness in this regard not only led one to forget the words of Scripture, a relatively small problem in itself; more important, it made one oblivious to the presence of God mediated through the words of Scripture. It was this concern that led one of the elders to affirm: "If God reproaches us for carelessness in our prayers and distractions in our psalmody [αἰχμαλωσίας τὰς ἐν ταῖς ψαλμῳδίαις], we cannot be saved."[82]

cSuch concerns are echoed elsewhere in the early monastic literature, especially in Cassian's *Conferences*. In two different passages, which can be read as a kind of commentary on the saying of Abba John Colobos, we find further elaboration on the psychological benefits of meditation. In the first, Abba Moses compares the heart to a mill wheel, which is constantly turned around by a headlong rush of water. While one cannot stop the wheel from turning as long as it is driven by the force of the water, one is free to choose what kind of grain it will grind. So it is with the mind and thoughts:

> The mind, also through the trials of the present life, is driven about by the torrents of temptations pouring in upon it from all sides, and cannot be free from the flow of thoughts. But . . . if, as we said, we constantly recur to meditation on the Holy Scriptures and raise our memory toward the recollection of spiritual things . . . spiritual thoughts are sure to rise from this, and cause the mind to dwell on those things on which we have been meditating.

The emphasis here is on the question of what kind of grain the monk will grind in his heart and on the singleness of purpose with which the monk must run his mill. By grinding the good grain of Scripture, the monk will prevent a harvest of tares from springing up in his heart, and will be less easily overcome by worries and cares. By doing so with attentiveness and care, the torrent of thoughts which well up from within may be turned to good effect.[83] Elsewhere in the *Conferences,* Abba Isaac comments on the remarkable power that is available to the monk from ceaselessly reciting in the heart the verse from the psalms: "O God, make speed to save me: O Lord make haste to help me (Ps 69:2)." Although this is only one of many verses uttered by the monks for their meditation, it is particularly useful for illustrating the power of meditation:

> For it carries within it all the feelings of which human nature is capable. It can be adapted to every condition and can usefully be deployed against every temptation. It carries within it a cry of help to God in the face of every danger. It expresses the humility of a pious confession. It conveys the watchfulness born of unending worry and fear. It conveys a sense of our frailty, the assurance of being heard, the confidence in help that is always and everywhere present. . . . This is the voice of ardor and charity. This is the terrified cry of someone who sees the snares of the enemy, the cry of someone besieged day and night and exclaiming that he cannot escape unless his protector comes to the rescue. . . . This verse keeps us from despairing of our salvation since it reveals to us the One to whom we call. . . .[84]

These comments reflect how capacious Scripture was for the monks—deep enough to contain all the fears and longings they could pour into it. Yet Isaac goes on to suggest that the aim of such meditation was to move beyond the wealth of thoughts toward simplicity or poverty of intention. He says that the mind will go on grasping this single verse of Scripture "until it can cast away the wealth and multiplicity of other thoughts, and restore itself to the poverty of a single verse."[85] Thus the repetition of a Scripture was held to unify the mind, helping one to overcome the kind of dissipation and distraction which left one open to the diverse attacks of the demons.

Such stories conveying the power of meditation on Scripture for overcoming temptation, distraction, and illness no doubt derived from the experience of the desert fathers in their own struggles against the demons. As such, they had a definite pedagogical value. Others who struggled to avoid the depression and accompanying physical symptoms brought on by the demons would have been comforted by the testimony presented in these stories and would have been strengthened in their own attempts to be faithful to the practice of recitation and meditation upon Scripture. It was hoped that monks would learn to emulate such figures as Apollo, of whom it was said: "his prayer became his meditation day and night."[86] Nothing less than continuous meditation on the mysteries of judgment and redemption could create the conditions for realizing salvation. For Abba Ammonas, "the monk ought to give himself up at all times to accusing his own soul, saying 'unhappy wretch that I am, how shall I stand before the judgment seat of Christ [2

Cor 5:10]?' What shall I say in my defense?' If you meditate on this continually, you may be saved.''[87]

Clearly Scripture was valued very highly in the desert, both as written and spoken word. It played an important role in the day-to-day life of the desert and was cherished for its authority, power, and for its capacity to mediate God's presence and protection. Scripture contributed significantly to the psychological well-being of the monks who meditated upon it, encouraging those who were troubled and creating, amid conflicting thoughts and aspirations, a sense of serenity and unity and awareness of God's presence. Yet there was also a genuine ambivalence toward Scripture in the desert, arising from a concern that it not be reduced to a mere object of reverence. This ambivalence reflected the pervading belief among the desert fathers that words were living things and that the words of Scripture were meant to be taken in, practiced, manifested in one's life. To understand how the monks expressed this belief, we need now to turn our attention to two of the most remarkable and intriguing aspects of the desert hermeneutic—the attention to the power of language and the sense of the ethical imperatives of interpretation.

Notes

1. W. Bousset, *Apophthegmata: Studien zur Geschichte des ältesten Mönchtums* (Tübingen: Mohr, 1923), 82–83; K. Heussi, *Der Ursprung des Mönchthums* (Tübingen: Mohr, 1936), 276–77.
2. Jean-Claude Guy, in "Écriture sainte et vie spirituelle" (*DS* 4, 161), says, "[T]he assiduous use of the Bible appears as a common doctrine in all the monastic centers of lower Egypt." This is not only true of the *Sayings* but also appears in other sources such as the *VA* (3), the *Historia Monachorum* (2:5; 8:50, 11:5), the *Historia Lausiaca* (11, 18, 22, 37, 47, 58), and Cassian's *Conferences* (10).
3. Epiphanius 10 [*PG* 65:165B]. It should be noted that the attitude expressed in these sayings of Epiphanius reveals a greater concern with the *written* word than is found in most of the rest of the *Sayings*.
4. Epiphanius 11 [*PG* 65:165B].
5. Antony 19 [*PG* 65:81BC], [m].
6. Antony 3 [*PG* 65:76C], [m].
7. Epiphanius 14 [*PG* 65:165C].
8. Cronius 1 [*PG* 65:248AB]; the instances of this are too numerous to list, and in any case, are examined in greater detail below.
9. Henry Chadwick, *The Early Church* (Harmondsworth: Penguin, 1967), 178.
10. Poemen 119 [*PG* 65:353A].

11. Nau 388 [*ROC* 18:143]; see also N 592/37 [*SPAn*, 223–24]: we hear also that the words of the fathers and of Scripture are both sources of "the word of God."

12. Antony 19 [*PG* 65:81B].

13. Poemen 114 [*PG* 65:352A].

14. Poemen 61 [*PG* 65:336D], [m]. Abba Poemen himself was said to have "the gift of speaking," although interestingly, one of the characteristic aspects of this gift in his case was its relationship with silence; see Poemen 108 [*PG* 65:348D].

15. Gelasius 1 [*PG* 65:145CD].

16. Theodore of Pherme 1 [*PG* 65:188A].

17. Ammoes 5 [*PG* 65:128AB].

18. Serapion 1[*PG* 65:413D–416C].

19. See Theodore of Pherme 29 [*PG* 65:196AB]; see also Ammoes 5 [*PG* 65:128AB].

20. Mark, Disciple of Silvanus 1 [*PG* 65:295D–293A].

21. Abraham 3 [*PG* 65:132BC]; see also Nau 385 [*ROC* 18:143], the story in which a brother claims to have copied with his own hand the whole of the Old and New Testaments.

22. Sisoes 35 [*PG* 65:404B].

23. CSP I 2 [*SPTr*, 129].

24. XXI 44 [*SPTr*, 107].

25. Epiphanius 9 [*PG* 65:165B].

26. J 676 [*SPAn*, 289].

27. Pa 40, 1 [*SPN*, 212].

28. N 632 [*SPAn*, 632].

29. Serapion 1 [*PG* 65:413D–416C].

30. Agathon 22 [*PG* 65:116AB].

31. While such attitudes may strike the contemporary reader as hopelessly super-stitious, they reflect a sensibility not uncommon in the ancient world, where books were rarer and consequently more greatly cherished than they have been since the advent of modern printing. For a discussion of attitudes toward sacred texts in the ancient world, see William Graham, *Beyond the Written Word: Oral Aspects of Scripture in the History of Religion* (Cambridge: Cambridge University Press, 1987), 45–55; see especially 46:

> The casual familiarity with which we move among and handle books as a part of our everyday routine has bred in us its own kind of contempt for, or at least carelessness of, the unremarkable and ubiquitous printed page. In the specific case of scripture, the cheap and easy availability of myriad versions of the Jewish or Christian scriptures has done much to reduce the special quality of the physical text as an object of reverence and devotion in and of itself. . . . The tracing of manuscript traditions and collation of textual variants has improved our understanding of the growth of scriptural texts, but it has also taught us how to treat them only as simply historical documents. *Consequently, we have some difficulty empathizing with persons for whom a copy of a sacred text was or is a seldom and wonderful thing, perhaps a magical and awesome thing, to be handled with solicitude and to which the proper response is reverential deference or even worshipful veneration* (emphasis mine).

32. Epiphanius 8 [*PG* 65:165A] (emphasis mine).

33. Ephrem 2 [*PG* 65:168BC]. The κεφαλίς is a roll, forming part of a book, or a book in scroll form. It is interesting that whereas elsewhere in the desert the book is usually a codex, here it is a scroll. It is likely that the scroll in question was of the Old Testament scriptures, for which the word κεφαλίς is commonly used.

34. Nau 53 [*ROC* 12:179]; Natalio Fernández Marcos, "La Biblia y los orígenes del monaquismo," *Miscelánea Comillas* 41 (1983): 385–87.

35. Nau 295 [*ROC* 14:378].

36. Fernández Marcos, "La Biblia y los orígenes del monaquismo," 387; C. H. Roberts, *Manuscript, Society and Belief in Early Christian Egypt* (London: Oxford University Press, 1979), 7–8.

37. Graham, *Beyond the Written Word*, 59–60.

38. Nau 385 [*ROC* 18:143].

39. Nau 392 [*ROC* 18:144].

40. Theodore of Pherme 1 [*PG* 65:188A].

41. Serapion 2 [*PG* 65:416C].

42. Nau 228 [*ROC* 14:361]. The sacred books have become ἀργά, literally "useless."

43. On the question of the structure of the liturgical life of the Egyptian monks, see the helpful discussion in H. G. Evelyn-White, *The Monasteries of the Wâdi 'n Natrûn*, pt. 2, *The History of the Monasteries of Nitria and Scetis* (New York: Metropolitan Museum of Art, 1932), 184–98; Robert Taft, S.J. *The Liturgy of the Hours in East and West* (Collegeville, MN: The Liturgical Press, 1986), 57–73; Antoine Guillaumont, "Histoire des moines aux Kellia," *Orientalia Lovaniensia Periodica* 8 (Leuven, 1977): 187–203; reprinted in *Aux origines du monachisme chrétien. Pour une phénoménologie du monachisme*. Spiritualité orientale et vie monastique 30 (Bégrolles-en-Mauges: Bellefontaine, 1979), 151–67).

44. Paul the Simple 1 [*PG* 65:381C–385B], [m].

45. N567 [*SPAn,* 207]; see also Eth. Coll. 13, 13 [*SPN,* 290], in which a brother speaks of going to the "assembly."

46. For other allusions to this larger, public *synaxis,* see: Arsenius 16; Theodore of Pherme 29; Isaac the Theban 2; Cronius 5; Motius 1; Poemen 11; Poemen 32; Poemen 92.

47. On the practice of psalmody in the desert, see A. Davril, O.S.B., "La psalmodie chez les pères du désert," *Collectanea Cisterciensia* 49 (1987): 132– 39.

48. *VA* 55 [*PG* 26:921C].

49. Gelasius 3 [*PG* 65:149AB].

50. Macarius 33 [*PG* 65:273D–277B]. For another example of this pattern of twelve psalms chanted during the night, see Nau 229 [*ROC* 14:361]: Some brothers "recited twelve psalms . . . during the night."

51. *Historia Lausiaca* 7:5, in Meyer, *Lausiac History,* 41. Note the fact that the monks can be *heard;* see Meyer, *Lausiac History,* 175, n. 85, where he notes that Athanasius, in his *Letter to Marcellinus,* refers to *singing* of the psalms and says that this liturgical custom was introduced not for its musical effect but to give worshippers more time to meditate on its meaning.

52. *Historia Lausiaca* 22:8; Meyer, *Lausiac History*, 79.

53. An Abba of Rome 1 [*PG* 65:388D]. The saying is anonymous but it is almost certainly from Arsenius.

54. Abba of Rome 1 [*PG* 65:385C–389A]; Nau 229 [*ROC* 14:359]; Heraclides 1 [*PG* 65:185BD].

55. *Historia Lausiaca* 22:8 [Meyer, *Lausiac History*, 79]: "Antony got up then and prayed twelve prayers and sang twelve psalms. . . . At midnight he got up again to sing psalms till it was day."

56. Paphnutius 5 [*PG* 65:380BC]. The word used here, εὐχὴν (prayer), does not refer specifically to the practice of reciting of Scriptures but may have involved meditation on the sacred texts.

57. Joseph of Panephysis 7 [*PG* 65:229CD].

58. Isidore the Priest 4 [*PG* 65:220CD]; see also Macarius the Great 33 [*PG* 65:273D–277B].

59. Epiphanius 3 [*PG* 65:161B]. Cassian, in *Institutes* II. 4ff., tells us that Syrian and Palestinian monks differed in their observance of the hours of *synaxis*.

60. Nau 230 [*ROC* 14:361–62].

61. Nau 229 [*ROC* 14:361].

62. Eulogius the Priest 1 [*PG* 65:169CD], [m]; see also Macarius the Great 33 [*PG* 65:273D–277B].

63. Nau 225 [*ROC* 14:360].

64. Nau 168 [*ROC* 13:54].

65. Poemen 168 [*PG* 65:361CD].

66. Joseph of Panephysis 7 [*PG* 65:229CD].

67. Achilles 5 [*PG* 65:125AB] (emphasis mine).

68. Nau 366 [*ROC* 17:138] (emphasis mine); see also J 676 [*SPAn*, 289]: "[W]e must chew the good food but not the bad. . . . [T]he soul of him who loves God must always meditate on [the Scriptures]"; PA App 8 [*SPTr*, 127]: "After the meal sitting until evening, they meditate upon the holy Scriptures"; Eth. Coll. 13, 13 [*SPN*, 290]: A brother who asks whether he should meditate upon what he reads in the Scriptures is answered affirmatively by an old man, who tells him: "It is to the source of life that you are going."

69. Nau 274 [*ROC* 14:371]. Elsewhere, N 626 [*SPAn*, 269], it is said to be "good for a person to study the Sacred Scriptures against the attacks of the demons."

70. Macarius the Great 19 [*PG* 65:269C].

71. Elias 7 [*PG* 65:185A]. The reliance on the power of the Name of God has a long history in the Judeo-Christian tradition. In the Old Testament, as in other ancient cultures, there is a virtual identity between a person's soul and name. One's whole personality is present in one's name. To know a person's name was to gain a definite insight into his or her nature, and thereby to establish a relationship. In the Hebrew tradition, to do a thing *in the name* of another or to *invoke* and *call upon his name* are acts of the utmost weight and potency. As Kallistos Ware, in *The Power of the Name* (Oxford: Fairacres, 1974), suggests, "Everything that is true of human names is true to an incomparably higher degree of the divine Name. The power and glory of God are present and active in His Name. The Name of God is

numen praesens, God with us, *Emmanuel.* Attentively and deliberately to invoke God's Name is to place oneself in his presence, to open oneself to his energy, to offer oneself as an instrument and a living sacrifice in His hands'' (10).

72. N 632 [*SPAn,* 275].

73. Nau 366 [*ROC* 18:138–39].

74. Nau 184 [*ROC* 13:271–72].

75. Walter Ong, *Orality and Literacy: The Technologizing of the Word* (London: Methuen, 1982), 32.

76. See below, chapter 6.

77. Macarius the Great 3 [*PG* 65:261A–64A].

78. Theodora 3 [*PG* 65:201CD].

79. Syncletica 27 [Guy, *Recherches,* S10:35]; on *accidie,* see G. Bardy, *DS* 11: cols. 166–69.

80. John Colobos 35 [*PG* 65:216A].

81. Nau 146 [*ROC* 13:50], [m].

82. Theodore of Enaton 3 [*PG* 65:197A], [m]. The sense of the word $\alpha \grave{\imath} \chi \mu \alpha \lambda \omega \sigma \acute{\imath} \alpha$ is only partially conveyed by the word "distraction." Literally, it means to be led away into captivity. Here the sense is that carelessness and distraction can lead one literally to forget the meaning of salvation.

83. Cassian, *Conferences,* 1:18, in Gibson, *Nicene and Post-Nicene Fathers,* 303.

84. Cassian, *Conferences,* 10:10, in Colm Luibheid, trans., *John Cassian: Conferences* (New York: Paulist Press, 1985), 133.

85. Cassian, *Conferences,* 10:11, in Owen Chadwick, trans., *Western Asceticism* (Philadelphia: Westminister, 1958), 243.

86. Apollo 2 [*PG* 65:133C–136A].

87. Ammonas 1 [*PG* 65:120A].

5

Words and Praxis

Two constantly recurring questions found in the *Sayings* remind us of the inextricable bonds that connected words and praxis for the desert monks. The first—"Abba, give me a *word*"—is more of a plea than a question, but nevertheless implies a multitude of questions. The other—"Abba, what should I *do?*"—reveals the concrete and practical character of the monks' concerns and complements the first. Together, these two questions provide an entrée into a world characterized by an extraordinary sensitivity to words and their effects, both those of Scripture and those of the elders. Those who came to the elders seeking "a word" did so not because they wanted or needed an extended spiritual discourse. They sought instead to have their very particular needs and concerns addressed by direct, immediate words of salvation, power, truth, assurance, and even tenderness. "The answers were not intended to be general, universal prescriptions. Rather, they were originally concrete and precise keys to particular doors that had to be entered, at a given time, by given individuals. They had a practical and existential quality." [1] The elders themselves made it abundantly clear that these words were spoken only for the sake of being taken up and integrated into the hearts, minds, and actions of those who received them. Therefore, the question of how to realize or fulfill the meaning of these words became one of the paramount concerns of the desert. The concern for words of salvation and how to bring them to realization are the primary elements necessary for understanding how the culture of the Word was formed in the desert.

The desert fathers recognized that in order to appropriate the words of Scripture and weave them into the fabric of their lives, they needed to cultivate and maintain a sensitivity to language. The positive power of language was experienced in the capacity of words—both those of Scripture and those of the elders—to bring forth life and renewal. However, the monks were also acutely aware of the dangerous, wounding power of language. Used carelessly, words had the power to cause immense damage and destruction. The recognition of this prompted the elders to give careful and prolonged attention to language—examining the way words work, how and when one should speak, and above all how to develop integrity of life and words. Their concern with words also helps to explain why such importance was attached to silence in the desert. Silence not only prevented one from using language in a harmful way but also provided the fertile ground out of which words of power could grow and through which these words could bear fruit in lives of holiness.

The careful attention given to words in the desert was complemented by the importance attributed to praxis. Because the desert fathers held integrity of words and life to be so important, the question of how to bring one's life into conformity with Scripture became a burning question. They were convinced that only through *doing* what the text enjoined could one hope to gain any understanding of its meaning. The prospect of fulfilling Scripture in this way raised thorny questions, however. What was the personal, moral cost of trying to fulfill the texts? What were the pitfalls one was likely to encounter along the way? What were the benefits of trying to conform one's life to Scripture? In wrestling with these questions, the desert fathers signaled their commitment to eschew speculation in favor of a practical, ethical hermeneutic. An exploration of their two central concerns—words and praxis—will reveal how the elders developed this hermeneutic and what it meant to them to appropriate the meaning of the Scripture into their lives.

Words in the Desert

The desert fathers learned from experience that it was important to take care with words. Whether in the close proximity of village life, where words passed quickly from one to another, or in the solitude and silence of the desert, where the sound and effect of words could be greatly magnified, the monks showed themselves to be only too aware of the myriad ways in which words could be misunderstood and abused, and of the harm to others which so often resulted. In this sense, the issue of language reflects the social tensions that ran through early desert monasticism. Developing a shrewd, discerning understanding of how words work was part of the process of resolving those tensions—not only within the monastic community itself but also between the monks and those living in the surrounding villages. By examining the sources of their attachment to various kinds of verbal abuse, to slander, to carelessness with words, the desert fathers sought to heal some of the rifts which these habits produced. Yet, there was also an aspect of the monks' concern for language which had a more direct bearing on their interpretation of Scripture. The ethical responsibilities associated with speaking and hearing were believed to have a profound effect on one's capacity to interpret the words of Scripture and the words of power uttered by the elders. In particular, verbal purity and integrity were felt to be indispensable for engaging in meaningful interpretation. Even the absence of words itself—silence—was thought to be fruitful for interpretation. Silence was the soil in which words of life were cultivated.

Ambivalence Toward Words

Those in the desert who had experienced the healing power of the words of Scripture or the elders clearly recognized the power of words to accomplish good. Yet there was also a profound suspicion regarding words, about their capacity to be misused and be transformed into weapons, even in the most unlikely of circumstances. By learning to "test" the character of all words, the monks learned to distinguish between those which were destructive and those which brought life.

Numerous sayings express the desert fathers' awareness of the capacity of words to turn on them and of the need to take care in speaking. A story about Macarius the Great vividly illustrates the power of words to create conflict or sooth and heal. It concerned one of his disciples who, upon meeting a pagan priest traveling on the road, reviled him with a torrent of abusive words. The priest responded by beating the brother so severely that he nearly died. Later on, Macarius met this same priest but greeted him with such kind words that the priest was astonished. He was so touched by Macarius's greeting that he asked to become his disciple. Some of Macarius's disciples wondered aloud how such a transformation could have occurred and what to make of it. Macarius pointed toward the verbal significance of the episode, saying: "One evil word makes even the good evil, while one good word makes even the evil good." [2] Poemen also reminded his disciples of the ambiguous character of words and of the need to exercise great caution in speaking. Citing a text from Scripture, he said, "If a person remembered that it is written: 'By your words you will be justified and by your words you will be condemned' (Mt 12:37), he would choose to remain silent." [3] Another elder counseled his disciples to exercise discernment when it came to words. They should "not . . . agree with every word. Be slow to believe, quick to speak the truth." [4] Abba Xanthius indicated the ambiguous character of words through a telling comparison of the good thief and Judas. The thief on the cross, he says, was "justified by a single word," while Judas, through his words of treachery, "lost all his labor in one single night." [5] Words could lead to salvation or destruction. Such ambivalence about the character of words led in one case to a brother asking one of the monks whether it was worth the risk to speak at all or if one should remain silent. The monk answered that he should learn to distinguish between "useless words" and "good words." He was told that "if the words are useless [οἱ λόγοι ἀργοὶ], leave them alone, but if they are good [καλοὶ], give place to the good and speak." However, even discussion about good things was seen as potentially problematic. Since this so often led to trouble, it too should be moderated: "Even if [words] are good," he was told, he should exercise caution, and "not prolong speech, but terminate it quickly, and rest in tranquility [ἀνάπαυε]."[6] Refusal to be drawn into "useless" conversation could help one to cultivate the deep "rest" or "refreshment" associated with a pure heart.

The sense of the inherent ambiguity of language could sometimes lead to a wistful tone in the monks' reflections as they compared the past times when words had the effect of building up the community with the present moment when it seemed impossible to speak with integrity. One brother recalled the time when those in the desert met together and "spoke edifying things [ὠφελείας], encouraging one another. . . ." Now, he noted, "when we come together, we drag one another down with slander [καταλαλιὰν]."[7] The ability to distinguish between "good" or "edifying" words and "useless" or "slanderous" words was important, for the latter, when given free reign, had the power to drive out the "good" words. A vivid symbolic illustration of this is given in a story about a particularly talkative group of monks. While they were speaking of edifying things (ὠφελείας) they were surrounded by angels. However, when one of them began to speak of irrelevant things (ὁμιλία), the angels withdrew and some pigs came into their midst bringing a bad smell and dirtying everything. As soon as the monks returned to speaking about edifying things, the pigs withdrew and the angels returned.[8]

Such stories indicate that the desert fathers clearly understood the necessity of being able to ask questions and engage in conversation in order to explore meaningful issues. However they also reflect the monks' acute awareness of how difficult it was, while engaging in such dialogue, to keep from wandering into idle and even slanderous conversation. This very concern to find a way of using words carefully and responsibly may well have given rise to Sisoes's exclamation in the presence of his disciple, "O misery!" When his disciple asked him what was the matter, he replied, "I am seeking a man to speak to and I do not find one."[9] Finding a person with whom one could converse without wasting one's time was apparently not easy. One of the desert fathers' responses to this dearth of good words was to devote considerable attention to discerning the precise ways in which words worked their damage.

Negative Power of Words

Ethical questions were the central concern of the desert fathers as they sought to develop greater integrity in their use of words. They carefully scrutinized the various negative effects of words in order to learn how to discern the characteristic signs of abusive language and avoid the pitfalls associated with it. They paid especially close attention to the problems associated with the vehicles of language—the tongue and mouth—to the dangers of "loose" conversation, and to the damage inflicted by slander. This probing analysis of words created among the desert fathers a respect for language which contributed in significant ways to their ability to interpret Scripture.

The large number of sayings concerned with the tongue and mouth symbolizes the importance the desert fathers attached to words and the need to respond to their seemingly uncontrollable force. Basic questions often arose concerning the frustration of being unable to master these small but powerful parts of the body. Thus, Abba Joseph asks Abba Nisterus, "What should I do about my tongue [τί ποιήσω τῇ γλώσσῃ], for I cannot master it?" [10] Another monk's inability to control his tongue was so chronic that it led him to the edge of despair. He asked Abba Matoes, "What am I to do? My tongue afflicts me [ἡ γλῶσσά μου θλίβει με], and every time I go among men, I cannot control it, but I condemn them. . . ." Interestingly, Matoes does not attempt to comfort the brother but tells him honestly that his inability to control his speech is indeed "a sickness ['Ασθένεια]." The only cure is to "flee into solitude." [11] Sisoes affirmed how deeply rooted this enslavement to the tongue could be by explaining that for thirty years it had been his habit to repeat the same prayer to God: "Lord Jesus, shelter me from my tongue [σκέπασόν με ἀπὸ τῆς γλώσσης μου]." He admitted, however, that "until now every day, I fall because of it, and commit sin." [12]

For the desert fathers, the inability to control one's tongue was not simply a matter of lack of resolve but revealed how speech was driven and controlled by deeper passions. Agathon maintained that "no passion is worse than an uncontrolled tongue [παρρησία], because it is the mother of all the passions [γεννήτρια . . . πάντων τῶν παθῶν]." [13] Abba Hyperchius attested to the link between the tongue and the passions, saying that "he who cannot control his tongue in the time of anger will not control his passions either." [14] One elder suggested that even if a person could not keep the inner world in order, at least he or she could keep watch over the tongue in order to prevent the passions from gaining force through that channel: "[I]f the interior man is watchful, he can preserve the exterior man also; if this is not the case, let us guard our tongue [φυλάξωμεν τὴν γλῶσσαν] as much as we can." [15] So strongly did Sisoes feel about the need to "guard" the tongue

that he used one of the most evocative terms in early monasticism—exile—
to describe the level of inner detachment and freedom which should characterize a monk's attitudes toward words. He said that "exile [ξενητεία]
means that a man should control his mouth."[16] The attention given by the
desert fathers to the habits of the tongue and mouth reflect their deep and
abiding concern to keep these instruments of speech from enslaving them to
destructive or careless language.

One practical expression of this concern was the care the monks exercised
over the way they conversed with one another. While conversation between
an elder and a disciple about a matter of immediate concern was tolerated,
even this could become problematic when it led to wandering or malicious
speech. One story tells of some young brothers and "an old man" who were
traveling together to see Abba Antony. Along the way the young brothers
"were . . . speaking words of the Fathers, and from the Scriptures and
concerning the work of their hands. As for the old man, he remained silent." When they reached their destination, Antony commended the old man
for bringing such good brothers with him. The old man, who had spent a
good deal of time with the brothers, had formed his own opinion: " 'No
doubt they are good, but they do not have a door to their house and anyone
who wishes can enter the stable and loose the ass.' He meant that the brethren said whatever came into their mouths."[17] This rebuke reveals one of the
main reasons for the seriousness with which the desert fathers viewed loose
talk—it was seen as diluting and dissipating the power of all other words,
especially the precious words of Scripture.

We hear numerous instances of monks wrestling with how to respond to
ill-conceived, careless, or damaging words. It was generally recognized by
the elders that one would do well to avoid "alien" words. To one of the
elders, an important sign of one who had become a monk was that he was
"not to listen to alien words [μηδὲ ἀκούειν ἀλλότρια]."[18] Abba Or put
the matter in territorial terms to his disciple Paul: "Be careful never to let
an alien word [ἀλλότριον λόγον] come into this cell."[19] This issue was
actually tested on occasions, as when some brothers came to see whether
Abba John Colobos "would let his thoughts become unbalanced and speak
of the things of this world [πρᾶγμα τοῦ αἰῶ νος τούτου]." They proceeded
to engage in "small talk" regarding the great amount of rain there had been
that year, noting how this had caused the shoots of the palm trees to grow
vigorously and kept the brothers provided with work. However, Abba John
did not allow himself to be drawn into this "small talk" but quietly shifted
the discussion about the weather to another level. Comparing these events
with the movements of God within the human heart, he noted: "So it is
when the Holy Spirit descends into the hearts of men; they are renewed and

put forth leaves in the fear of God."[20] The matter of "loose talk" was not always resolved so deftly. Sometimes it pushed the elders to their limits. Sisoes, presumably exasperated by a talkative disciple, finally said to him, "Why do you compel me to speak unnecessarily [λαλῆσαι ἀργῶς]?"[21] Even when such talk was directed toward another, it could disrupt one's hard-won tranquility. Poemen complained that his brother "holds converse with someone and I have no rest [οὐκ ἀναπαύομαι]."[22] Sometimes, resisting the plague of words required distancing oneself from others. Abba Ammoes exercised such great caution with his words that if his disciple came to ask him about his thoughts, he would move away from him as soon as he had replied, saying to him, "It is for fear that, after edifying words, strange conversation [ξένη ὁμιλία] might slip in that I do not keep you with me."[23]

It should not be imagined that the desert fathers were fastidious in their use of words. To the contrary, the *Sayings* shows them to be willing to talk about almost anything. What we see in these stories is something different: a recognition of the intimate relationship between words and the desires, thoughts, and feelings behind them. While conversation about matters of general concern was not in itself problematic, it so easily opened the way to gossip or slander that real discernment was needed to tell the difference between them. And once the door to these kinds of words was opened, all manner of inner turmoil would inevitably follow. The caution exercised toward conversation was indeed aimed in part at the outward trappings of words in the monastic life. Yet such concerns reflect even more the clear sense of how much was at stake in the inner world of the monk—how dependence on words could grow to the point of displacing other more crucial desires of the heart. We see an illustration of this in a story of a monk whose ascetical prowess was bought at the price of addiction to words. Although this monk fasted to such a great degree that he was known far and wide simply as the "faster," he showed little or no ability to moderate his dependence on words. One day Abba Zeno asked the faster to come and see him. He did so, but even after he arrived at the place Zeno continued his work in silence. Because the faster was unable to engage Zeno in conversation, he became bored and decided to leave. Zeno asked him what was the matter, and the other told him that it was as if his heart were on fire. Nothing like this ever happened to him during his long fasts in the village. Zeno immediately recognized the source of the man's agitation. It was because, "In the village you fed yourself through your ears [ἐκ τῶν ὠτίων σου ἐτρέφου]."[24] Asked to go for even a short while in silence, the man now found himself out of his depth. One who was so addicted to words could hardly begin to make progress in the more complex process of rooting out the inner forces which drive them. All his fasting, Zeno suggests, had not taught him the first thing about silence or humility.

The seriousness with which the monks regarded the problem of carelessness with words reflects their perception that such looseness almost inevitably led to more serious and aggressive misuse of words in the form of slander. Among the most difficult challenges of their life in the desert was recognizing the effects of the biting wounds inflicted by such language and resisting the temptation to give into it themselves. The gravity of slander, for instance, was judged to be so great that it outweighed any infraction of the monks' ascetical code. Hyperchius uses a graphic comparison to drive the point home: "It is better to eat meat and drink wine and not to eat the flesh of one's brothers through slanderous words [μὴ φαγεῖν ἐν καταλαλιαῖς σάρκας ἀδελφῶν]."[25] Such a comparison was not mere hyperbole but reflected a conviction shared by many of the desert fathers that harmful words, if allowed to fester within, could inflict severe injury on a person. One story tells of an old man who came to see Abba Achilles and found him spitting blood from his mouth. When asked what was the matter, Achilles responded: "[T]he word of a brother grieved me, I struggled not to tell him so, and I prayed God to rid me of this word. So it became like blood in my mouth [γέγονεν ὁ λόγος ὡς αἷμα ἐν τῷ στόματί μου] and I have spat it out. Now I am in peace, having forgotten the matter."[26] To those in the desert who had spent time ruminating on the healing words of Scripture and the elders, the ironic truth of such a story would have been strikingly clear. Achilles, unwilling to "get rid of" the harmful word by responding in anger to the brother who uttered it, kept the word to himself, in effect ruminating it at great personal cost. Chewing on this slanderous word, far from having the healing effect of ruminating a word of the Scripture, apparently produced something like an ulcer within him. Achilles's discipline in keeping the word to himself reflects an admirable kindness and consideration on his part for the feelings of the brother. Yet the story makes another and equally important point about the psychology of healing. However virtuous it may have been for Achilles to hold this word within him and not seek retribution, healing and peace only came when he was able to leave the poisonous word behind and finally "forget" it. Other sayings express the recognition of how far reaching the effects of slanderous words could be, affecting not only the recipients of the words but also the ones who uttered them. Hyperchius makes this clear through an allusion to story of the fall: "It was through whispering that the serpent drove Eve out of paradise, so he who speaks against his neighbor [ὁ καταλαλῶν τοῦ πλησίον] will be like the serpent, for he corrupts the soul of him who listens to him and he does not save his own soul."[27] In spite of this potent comparison, and the widespread recognition of the evils of slander, the appreciation of the effects of slander seems to have been one of the most difficult lessons to learn. In one saying, a brother, seemingly bewildered at his own behavior, asks Abba John Colobos: "How is it that my soul, bruised with wounds [τραύματα], does not blush to speak against my neighbor [καταλαλεῖν τοῦ πλησίον]?"[28] Yet in spite of how deep-rooted this tendency to wound others through words may have been, the monks felt that there was recourse to such destructive patterns of behavior.

Abba Or provides simple, practical advice to one who has knowingly slandered another: "If you have spoken evil of your brother, and you are stricken with remorse, go and kneel down before him and say, 'I have spoken badly of you; let this be my surety that I will not spread this slander any further.' " Abba Or certainly recognized that humbling oneself in this way would not be easy. However, there was a sense of genuine urgency behind such commands. In a chilling reminder of how much was at stake, Or told his listeners: "Slander is death to the soul [θάνατος γάρ ἐστι τῆς ψυχῆς ἡ καταλαλιά]."[29] If, on the other hand, one was disturbed by the slanderous words uttered by others, there were certain strategies one could pursue for overcoming the pain and disorientation the words caused. John Colobos tells a story which recalls his own experience of being beset by vicious words and describes his strategy for rooting them out from his soul. At the church at Scetis, he "heard an argument [ἀντιλογίας] among some of his brothers, so he returned to his cell. He circled around it three times and then went in. Some brothers who had seen him wondered why he had done this and went to ask him. He said, "my ears were full of argument, so I circled round in order to purify them, and thus I entered my cell with my mind at rest [ἐν ἡσυχίᾳ]."[30]

An encounter between a brother and Abba Peter the Pionite regarding this very issue reveals the depth to which the desert fathers were prepared to go in overcoming the harmful effects of loose words. The brother complained to Abba Peter, "When I am in my cell, my soul is at peace [ἐν εἰρήνῃ], but if a brother comes to me and speaks to me of *external things* [τοὺς λόγους τῶν ἔξω my soul is disturbed [ταράσσεται ἡ ψυχή μου]." Abba Peter told him that his own teacher, Abba Lot, used to say to him, "Your key opens my door." By this he meant that one's own willingness to enter into conversation with others was the key that opened the floodgates of irrelevant or alien words. It was within each one's power to learn to make judicious use of the key. When the brother pressed him to explain how he could learn to use this key with greater care, Abba Peter responded: "Compunction is the absolute master. One cannot protect oneself where there is no compunction.'' Hearing this, the brother responded with an echo of his original complaint, acknowledging that ''when I am in my cell, compunction is with me, but if someone comes to see me or I go out of my cell, I do not have it any more.'' In a telling distinction, Abba Peter said to the brother, ''That means you do not really *have* compunction at all yet. It is merely that you practice it sometimes.''[31] This dialogue reveals the depth of purity required to resist the dangers of ''loose'' or careless words and the extent to which mastery of words was seen as depending on mastery of the self, in this case symbolized by compunction. An immense gulf separates those who ''practice it sometimes'' from those who have it. Such mastery cannot be superficial or occasional. Rather, in order to maintain freedom from the compul-sion to enter into idle or careless conversation, inner transformation is required.

In a similar way, Amma Theodora points to the inner change which is necessary for gaining freedom from ''sounds of the world.'' Someone asked her, ''If one is habitually listening to the sounds of the world [φωνὰς κοσμικὰς] how can one yet live for God alone?'' Theodora compares this situation to a banquet with many courses. She suggests that just as when you take some of the food out of politeness but without pleasure, ''so when worldly words [λόγοι κοσμικοί] come your way, have your heart turned toward God and, thanks to your disposition, you will hear them without pleasure, and they will not do you any harm.''[32] Only a clear determination to turn one's heart toward God, she suggests, will enable one to become free from domination by ''worldly conversation.''

Another indication of the level of freedom possible is illustrated by a story in which Abba Ammoun told Abba Poemen of a problem he had with words: ''[W]hen I go to my neighbor's cell, or when he comes to mine for some need or another, we are afraid of speaking together, for fear of slipping into strange conversation [ξένη ὁμιλία].'' The old man replied, ''[Y]ou are right, for young men need to be watchful.'' But Abba Ammoun, not understanding what Poemen meant, pressed him further, asking, ''But the elders, what do *they* do?'' Poemen replied, ''The elders, who have advanced in virtue, have nothing evil in them, nor anything strange in their mouths [οὐκ εἶχον ἐν αὐτοῖς ἕτερόν τι, ἢ ξένον ἐν τῷ στόματι], of which they could speak.''[33] The elders are shown to be ''incapable'' of misusing words because they have been purified of all false motivations and desires. The cumulative effect of such stories was to show that one *could* become free of the compulsions that drive malicious words. One could reach levels of integrity and self-knowledge such that the negative power of words no longer held sway in one's heart.

Words and Integrity

The desert monks' acute awareness of the dangers of careless speech and
slander led them to develop a spirituality in which integrity or purity of
speech was highly valued. Purity of speech was seen as flowing from and
reflecting purity of heart. Similarly, words were judged to have merit and
value to the extent that they issued from a life of integrity.

The monks spent considerable effort clarifying the relationship between
the heart and the mouth. A saying of Gregory Nazianzus included in the
Sayings suggests a concern for balance between the heart and the tongue.
He says that what God seeks most of all is a balance of the heart, the tongue
and the body: "right faith in the heart, truth on the tongue [ἀλήθειαν ἀπὸ
τῆς γλώσσης], and temperance in the body."[34] Abba Poemen encouraged
his disciples to consider the *reciprocal* influence of the heart and the mouth.
He exhorted them to "teach your mouth to say that which you have in your
heart [Δίδαξον τὸ στόμα σου λαλεῖν ἃ ἔχει ἡ καρδιά σου]"[35] *and* to
"teach your heart to guard that which your tongue teaches [δίδαξον τὴν
καρδίαν σου τηρεῖν ἃ διδάσκει ἡ γλῶσσά σου]."[36] Here we see evidence of the monks' strong conviction—no doubt based on long experience—that words of power and worth can only proceed from a heart that
has been tested and purified. The second statement is equally important,
though: because words have such power, the monk should exercise great
discernment over ("guard") what he says, how he says it, or even whether
he should speak at all. By guarding one's words in one's heart in this way,
the monk can assure himself that his words will not drift precariously far
from his life. We see this same sentiment echoed in an exchange between a
brother and Abba Sisoes. The brother came to Sisoes to ask him how to
"guard the heart." Interestingly, Sisoes directed the brother's attention not
toward the intricate workings of his heart but toward his mouth: "How,"
he asked, "can we keep watch over our hearts when our mouth . . . is
open?"[37] By leaving the gate of one's mouth carelessly ajar, Sisoes implies,
all of one's efforts to realize purity of heart could become dissipated.

Nor was it easy to avoid self-deception in these matters. Abba Poemen
noted that behavior which might appear to reflect genuine integrity of heart
and words could in fact mask deep inner contradictions. "A person may
seem to be silent, but if his heart is condemning others he is babbling ceaselessly. But there may be another who talks from morning till night and yet
he is truly silent; that is, he says nothing that is not profitable."[38] Silence,
that is, should not be thought of as merely a simple absence of words.
Rather, it should penetrate to the core of a person and be a reflection of a
transformed heart. Purity and integrity of speech could not be realized sim-

ply from the outward care taken with words. Only by cultivating a pure heart could one express oneself with integrity and authority. John Colobos believed such integrity was possible for the monk. He looked to Job as a model of integrity between the heart and mouth. Even though the devil touched Job's flesh, he "did not sin by any word that came out of his mouth" because "he had within his heart that which is of God, and he drew on that source unceasingly."[39]

If a pure heart was necessary for learning to speak with integrity, so was a life free from duplicity and guile. For the words of a monk to carry any weight, they had to be seen to be in conformity with a life. This was expressed in a variety of ways in the *Sayings,* but what is clear is that holiness was understood to involve the integration of one's life with one's words.[40] The integration of life with words was seen as a special responsibility of the teacher. This accounts for the numerous statements cautioning those who would teach not to fall prey to the most obvious hypocrisy—not practicing what they teach. Poemen held that "a person who teaches without doing what he teaches is like a spring which cleanses and gives drink to everyone, but is not able to purify itself."[41] According to Abba Moses, lack of integration of prayer and action was also disastrous: "If a person's deeds are not in harmony with his prayer, he labors in vain."[42] Echoing the concern expressed elsewhere that words should not be separated from work, Silvanus warns his listeners of the folly of having a reputation with no basis in reality. "Most unfortunate," he says, is "the one whose reputation exceeds his work."[43] A certain amount of detachment from one's words was necessary for effective teaching. As Poemen noted, only the one who is whole and without passions [ἀπαθοῦς] can instruct another.[44] The importance of having one's words tested by hard experience is confirmed by Amma Syncletica, who claims, "it is dangerous for anyone to teach who has not first been trained in the practical life [πρακτικοῦ βίου]."[45] Integrity implied not simply ethical purity, but also what one does with the body: "It is very hard to teach with the mouth that which one does not practice in the body."[46] In short, for words to bear fruit, they must have the proper culture in which to grow. There must be "work" to give them life: "[I]f the soul has the word but not the work, it is like a tree with leaves but no fruit. Just as a tree full of fruit also has beautiful foliage, so the word adapts itself well to the soul whose work is good."[47]

The witness of actual examples of such integrity was worth more than any number of sayings. This helps to account for the many occasions on which we hear the elders bear witness to their own integrity. These should not be taken as expressions of false pride, but as an example of witness, of testimony to a truth the desert fathers knew from experience. Such testimony helped to remove integrity from the realm of mere possibility or ideas and bring it to the level of concrete realization. The lives of holy exemplars provided evidence that it was actually possible for words to be bound up integrally with a life. For Cassian, integrity of speech meant that he could claim never to have "taught anything which I had not previously carried out."[48] Integrity of speech for Pambo meant that he could attest to the complete absence of any base or malicious motive in his words: "[B]y the grace of God, since I have left the world, I have not said one word of which I repented afterwards."[49] Abba Anoub makes such a statement more specific, claiming only that "[S]ince the day when the name of Christ was invoked upon me, no lie has come out of my mouth."[50] A word of testimony offered on behalf of Abba Or reveals the intimate connection between maintaining purity of actions and words. It was said of him that "he never lied, nor swore, nor hurt anyone, nor spoke without necessity."[51] The wholeness and integrity of life and words sought by the monks is summed up well in a saying of Isidore of Pelusia. He held that "to live without speaking is better than to speak without living. For the former is useful even by his silence, but the latter does no good even when he speaks. When words and life correspond to one another they are together the whole of philosophy."[52]

Silence

In spite of all these musings on words among the desert monks, the final word for them was . . . silence. The reasons for this are not difficult to grasp. With their acute awareness of the power of language—both the potential damage of words as well as a sense that words should flow from the depths of a pure heart—the desert fathers had a genuine appreciation of the practical value of silence. Not only was silence the quickest way to cut off the cancerous growth of slander and gossip, it was seen as the atmosphere in which a spirit of prayerful awareness of God could thrive. And it was recognized as the mysterious ground out of which the words of Scripture and the words of the holy ones emerged in their full revelatory power.

Silence, for Abba Epiphanius, was held to be the way to God recommended by Scripture itself: "the woman with the issue of blood is silent and she is called blessed [Lk 8]; the pharisee speaks and he is condemned [Mt 9]; the publican does not open his mouth and he is heard [Lk 18]."[53] There is a revealing inaccuracy in Epiphanius's recollection of the texts: the publican is not actually silent but utters a humble prayer for mercy. His attitude of total abandonment to God, like that of the woman with the hemorrhage, suggests the kind of humble disposition to which "the silent one" should aspire. To keep silence could also reflect the spirit of long-suffering. Abba Moses, for instance, was asked if he was not grieved at being insulted on account of his black skin. He responded echoing the Psalm, "I was grieved, but I kept silence (Ps 76:5)."[54] It was in order to cultivate attitudes of humility and long-suffering, rather than a pursuit of an abstract ascetical ideal, that the monks went to such lengths to learn silence: Abba Agathon is said to have gone for three years with a stone in his mouth so that he should learn silence.[55] Such discipline could produce abundant fruit in the lives of those who observed it, particularly because it created space for the Spirit to work: "If the soul keeps far away from all discourse and words, the Spirit of God will come to her and she who was barren will be fruitful."[56] Silence, in certain cases, was the only way of fulfilling "the commandment"—charity. In one instance, an elder who was insulted by someone refused to be drawn into retaliation: "I could say as much to you, but the commandment of God keeps my mouth shut."[57] Even in less explicit ways, silence could be an expression of love and tenderness and could effect a genuine change of heart in another. Sisoes tells a story of some brothers being led through the desert with a guide, who inadvertently led them astray all night. The brothers realized they were lost and each one struggled not to tell their guide, for fear of humiliating him. When day came and the guide realized he had lost his way, he admitted to the brothers that he had no idea where they were. They all said to him, "We knew this but we kept silence." Hearing this, the guide was filled with wonder and said, "Even to the point of death, the brothers control themselves so as not to speak."[58] While legitimate questions may be raised about the practicality of maintaining silence in such a situation, we see here the lengths to which the monks were willing to go to keep from injuring another person. Silence, in such cases, was an expression of tenderness.

Silence was also a privileged means of communicating the essence of the spiritual life. Abba Isaac relates the difficulties he had in learning to pay attention not only to the words of the elders but also to their *silence*. While he was living with Abba Theodore of Pherme, Isaac became frustrated at how little direction the elder gave him. He complained about this to some other elders, who took the matter to Abba Theodore himself. Theodore told them: "I do not tell him anything, but if he wishes he can do what he sees me doing." From that moment Isaac took the initiative and did what the old man was about to do. As for Theodore, Isaac reported, "what he did, he did in silence; so he taught me to work in silence."[59] Silence in this case was a pedagogical tool, a way of communicating the essentials of the eremetical life to a younger monk. Words were superfluous here: silent example was everything. Elsewhere in the *Sayings,* we hear of the numerous benefits of maintaining openness to the richness of silence. Abba Poemen reminded his listeners that keeping silence allows one to size up the situation and avoid speaking out of ignorance. Alluding to Proverbs 18:13 he says, " 'If one gives answer before he hears, it is his folly and shame.' If you are questioned, speak; if not, remain silent."[60] Poemen also contended that silence was powerful enough to bring victory over any affliction.[61] Because of this, he could assure his listeners, "If you are silent, you will have peace [ἀνάπαυσιν] wherever you live."[62] Finally, silence was an expression of a discerning patience, of insuring that one spoke only from inspiration. We see this in a story of some brothers who came to question Abba Pambo about their way of life, about whether they were proceeding toward salvation. Over the course of four days, they put all manner of questions to the old man but received not a single answer. They became discouraged and were preparing to leave when some of Pambo's companions approached them. "Do not be troubled, brothers. . . . It is the old man's custom not to speak readily until God inspires him." Eventually, Pambo *did* respond to the brothers, asking certain questions about their life and making some pointed observations. Upon hearing what he had to say, they "went away joyfully."[63] Silence in this sense provided perspective with which to really see things, space in which words of genuine inspiration might arise. Practicing this kind of discipline and restraint, it is no wonder that Pambo could say: "By the grace of God, since I left the world, I have not said one word of which I repented afterwards."[64]

The restraint with words and respect for silence which we see in these stories also influenced the monks' approach to Scripture. While they often raised questions about the meaning of a particular text, they recognized that there were times when silence was the most appropriate response to Scripture. A story of Abba Macarius and two "young strangers" illustrates this well. Two young men had heard of Macarius's reputation and had come to ask whether they could live with him in order to learn how to become monks. Seeing that the young men were "delicate and had been brought up in comfort," Macarius was dubious and did what he could to discourage them. However, when they reiterated their determination, he relented and told them they could build a cell nearby and begin to live the monastic life. He was certain they would soon depart because of the hardships of the life. Yet not only did they refuse to abandon their life in the desert, but never once in the course of three years did they come to see Macarius for advice or direction. Macarius knew nothing at all about their lives, except that they departed their cells once a week to go to church "in silence." He therefore decided to visit them to see if he could find out more about "their way of life." When he arrived at their door, they greeted him "in silence." At the time of the meal, one of the brothers put three small loaves on the table and stood "in silence." Macarius began to realize that their entire lives were permeated by silence and that a profound inner life lay hidden behind it. Later that night, unbeknownst to the two brothers, Macarius witnessed them engaged in fierce battle with the demons. The next morning, they mentioned nothing of this to Macarius but simply invited him to join them in chanting the psalms. The power of their silence and their whole way of life was confirmed in symbolic terms during this ritual. Macarius noticed that while the younger one chanted the psalms, a "tongue of flame came out of his mouth and ascended to heaven." When the elder one opened his mouth to chant, it was like "a column of fire which came forth and ascended to heaven." In contrast to this stunning display of power, Macarius adds, almost pitiably, "And I recited a little by heart." Moved by what he had seen, Macarius took his leave of the two, asking for their prayers. Characteristically, the brothers simply "bowed without saying a word." Later, after the two had died, Macarius took visitors to see where their "martyrdom" had occurred.[65] This is a curious story in many ways and is filled with more "wonders" than one finds in most episodes of the *Sayings*. On one level the story is about a "reversal": that things are not always as they seem. Macarius was chagrined to realize he had so badly misjudged the two young men but was grateful that he had come to recognize the impressive depth of their lives. The story also conveys the power of silence in the life of the monk and in particular the effect of silence on the recitation of Scripture. Silence is mentioned several times as characterizing the brothers' way of life and forms the backdrop to the dramatic scene of wrestling with the demons and chanting the psalms. The flames shooting forth from the brothers' mouths as they chanted the psalms symbolize the power which words—particularly the words of Scripture—can have when grounded in a life of humility and silence.

The significant amount of attention which the monks gave to questions of language reflects their respect for its power. Whether they were listening to words of Scripture or words of the elders, the monks learned to exercise caution and discernment in their responses to language. Their desire to avoid all manner of careless or slanderous talk reflects their healthy respect for the havoc words could wreak in the monastic community. Because of this, and because they recognized that words could also be a force for life and health, they gave considerable attention to cultivating integrity of speech and life. For certain monks, such integrity led them to a long and often difficult apprenticeship in the school of silence. All of this was part of a "culture of the word" which the monks created in the desert. The sensibilities toward language which the monks developed within this culture would have a profound influence on their approach to interpreting Scripture. In order to see how this manifested itself in particular cases, we need to turn to the second major question which occupied the monks: "Abba, what should I do?"

Praxis: Bringing Words to Life

A "practical ethos" permeated the desert monks' spirituality. We can see this in the urgent and practical character of the questions raised by the monks. The urgency—even desperation—of the questions which monks often put to the elders can be heard in the words of a brother who came seeking help from Abba Theodore. He cried out, "Speak a word to me, for I am perishing." [66] Behind such questions teemed a multitude of particular, concrete concerns about specific situations in the lives of the monks. This is reflected in the predominantly practical language which characterizes these questions. The questioners wanted to know, in one way or another, what they were to *do,* how they were to *act.* Their questions took various forms: "What should I do?" [67] "How should a person behave?" [68] "How should we conduct ourselves?" [69] "What good work should I do that I might live in it?" [70] These practical questions reveal the kind of concerns the monks brought to the elders. They sought not so much ideas about the spiritual life narrowly conceived, but rather a new way to live.

The practical character of the monks' aspirations also appears in the elders' responses to the questions put to them. Abba Isidore put the practical requirements of salvation in the form of a conditional statement: "If you desire salvation, do [ποίει] everything that leads you to it." [71] A similar attitude is reflected in a story about a struggle Abba Antony was engaged in with his thoughts. It was so severe that, in desperation, Antony cried out to God asking what he should do about this affliction. After a while, he went out of his cell, where he saw a man who was calmly alternating manual work and prayer. The man (who was an angel of God sent to help Antony) said to Antony: "Do this and you will be saved [Οὕτως ποίει, καὶ σώζῃ]." [72] Antony was encouraged by these words, and by following this simple advice managed to recover his balance. This practical approach was meant to penetrate the whole of one's life and to reflect an adherence to God's will. Abba Nisterus said that a monk should ask himself every night and every morning, "What have we done [ἐποιήσαμεν] that is as God wills and what have we left undone of that which he does not will? [73] Echoing the prophet Jeremiah, Abba Epiphanius spoke approvingly of the person "who does justice and righteousness [ἕνα ποιοῦντα κρῖμα καὶ δικαιοσύνην] (Jer 5:1)." [74] The opposite was also true: one refrains from engaging in practices which run contrary to the monastic way of life. Abba Moses cautioned a brother about the danger of allowing a rift to appear between one's practice and one's aims: "We should no longer *do* those things against which we pray."[75] Consistency in one's practice was the bedrock of desert spirituality.

Doing the Word

The practical ethos reflected in these questions and responses had a clear influence upon the monks' approach to the interpretation of Scripture. In fact, whether the monks were referring to the words of Scripture or the words of the elders, their primary emphasis was on "doing the word." This strong practical orientation helps to explain why the desert fathers were often reticent to enter into speculative discussion about the meaning of Scripture or even to speak about it at all. They were convinced that the practical, ethical demands of their life required their undivided attention. Only by focusing their attention on these primary demands, they believed, the meaning of words—those of Scripture as well as the elders—become clear.

The practical language used by the monks to describe how one should approach Scripture reveals their basic orientation to the text. Abba Gerontius exhorts his listeners to "do what is written [$\pi o \iota \epsilon \hat{\iota} \nu \ \tau \grave{o} \ \gamma \epsilon \gamma \rho \alpha \mu \mu \acute{\epsilon} \nu o \nu$]." Doing so was not a simple matter, however, and for this reason, Gerontius also advises that each one should "guard his own heart with all possible care."[76] "Doing what is written," that is, required vigilance and discernment. Abba Isidore contends it is through "obeying the truth [$\dot{\upsilon} \pi \alpha \kappa o \grave{\eta} \ \tau \hat{\eta} s \ \dot{\alpha} \lambda \eta \theta \epsilon \acute{\iota} \alpha s$]" and "following . . . the law of God [$\dot{\alpha} \kappa o \lambda o \upsilon \theta \epsilon \hat{\iota} \nu \ . . . \ \tau \hat{\wp} \ \nu o \mu \wp \ \tau o \hat{\upsilon} \ \theta \epsilon o \hat{\upsilon}$]—which appear to be nearly equivalent for him—that we realize our dignity as creatures made in the image and likeness of God.[77] The *Sayings* frequently allude to "keeping the commandments" or "fulfilling the commandments" as being keys to spiritual growth. We see this in the aspirations of the monks as well as the commands of the elders. A brother who came to Abba Theodore expressed his hopes this way: "I wish to fulfill the commandments [$\theta \acute{\epsilon} \lambda \omega \ \dot{\epsilon} \pi \iota \tau \epsilon \lambda \acute{\epsilon} \sigma \alpha \iota \ \tau \grave{\alpha} s \ \dot{\epsilon} \nu \tau o \lambda \acute{\alpha} s$]."[78] Abba Agathon would have found such a sentiment appropriate for the novice. He stated: "Unless a person keeps the commandments of God [$\phi \upsilon \lambda \alpha \kappa \hat{\eta} s \ \tau \hat{\omega} \nu \ \theta \epsilon \acute{\iota} \omega \nu \ \dot{\epsilon} \nu \tau o \lambda \hat{\omega} \nu$], he cannot make progress, not even in a single virtue."[79] The monk was to be mindful of his practical obligations in every situation. Abba Antony exhorted his disciples: "Whatever you do [$\pi \rho \acute{\alpha} \tau \tau \epsilon \iota s$], do it according to the testimony of the holy Scriptures."[80] Even on their deathbeds, the elders sought to remind their disciples of the need to fulfill the commands of Scripture. As Abba Benjamin was dying, he quoted a text from Scripture to his disciples. "Be joyful at all times, pray without ceasing, and give thanks for all things (1 Thes 5:16–18)." Then he said to them: "Do these things, and you can be saved [Ταῦτα ποιεῖτε, καὶ δύνασθε σωθῆναι]."[81] Such sayings suggest that the desert monks took seriously the ethical commitment required for understanding the biblical texts.

This ethical commitment also governed the way the monks responded to the words, commands, or lives of the elders. We see various indications in the *Sayings* of the authority of the elders' words. Sometimes they appear almost as the equivalent of Scripture, new words of power meant to be heard, put into practice, and passed on to others. Abba Pistus tells a story about the obedience of Abba Athres and Abba Or, and comments: "What I have seen [from the elders], I have done everything in my power to keep [φυλάξαι]."[82] In another instance a brother approached Abba Daniel, asking him for a word: "Give me a commandment and I will keep it [Δός μοι μίαν ἐντολὴν, καὶ φυλάξω αὐτήν]."[83] His language indicates how much authority the word of the elder had for him and how important it was to put that word into practice. This implicit trust in the elder's word and the importance of obeying it is conveyed in a saying of Abba Anoub, which reveals how such words could influence the daily routine of the monastic life. Abba Anoub, Abba Poemen, and others, forced to leave Scetis after it had been attacked in a raid, moved to Terenuthis, near the Nile. Abba Anoub proposed, "for love's sake," a way of life for them in their new place. They would each live alone and in quietness without meeting one another the whole week. They would strive, as far as possible, to avoid giving way to pride and anger. The brothers said to Abba Anoub, "We will *do* [ποιοῦμεν] as you wish, Father, and we will *listen* to what you say to us [ἀκούομεν ὡς λέγεις ἡμῖν]." Abba Poemen added, "Let us remain together for the rest of our time, working *according to the word* [κατὰ τὸν λόγον] which the old man has spoken to us. . . ."[84] The meaning of this story turns on the quality and authority of the elder's word. The phrase indicating Abba Anoub's motivation—"for love's sake"—suggests why his word had so much authority in this particular case. The brothers realized that Anoub had no "agenda" for their life together, wishing only to create an atmosphere conducive to their collective well-being. They recognized that by doing what he wished, and listening to what he said, they would be able to live with one another in peace. It was this sense of the truth and efficacy of Abba Anoub's "word" which led Poemen to urge the brothers to remain together "working according to the word of the old man."

The desert fathers' practical orientation toward Scripture and the words of the elders was not merely "blind obedience" to words of authority. Nor is it true that they somehow abdicated responsibility or choice in their response to these words. To the contrary, the monks clearly recognized how difficult it was to fulfill these commands and knew the risks involved in trying to do so. This is reflected in the language used to describe the process of responding to and appropriating a text. Several stories speak of the need to *attain* a saying from Scripture, an indication that the practice of Scripture should lead one to become or appropriate completely its message. This appropriation was seen as a difficult but necessary part of the process of coming truly to understand and realize the meaning the Scripture. Poemen, for instance, declared that when a person attains ($\phi\theta\acute{\alpha}\sigma\eta$) the word of the Apostle, "to the pure, everything is pure" (Ti 1:15), he sees himself less than all creatures. One of the brothers objected to this, because he felt the implication of this command to be absurd if not repulsive. "How can I deem myself less than a murderer?" he asked. Poemen responded, "[W]hen a person has really attained this saying, if he sees a man committing a murder, he says, 'he has only committed this one sin but I commit sins every day.' "[85] In a similar vein, a brother put a question to Abba Moses concerning what it meant to "die to one's neighbor." This idea, while not from Scripture itself, was an important part of Abba Moses' teaching and implied a wide range of thinking and experience. It meant weeping for oneself and one's sins, not judging others, not doing them any harm, not measuring oneself against others. It implied not cold indifference toward others but a level of detachment from petty concerns which made a real human relationship possible. Moses responded to the brother's question: "[I]f a man does not think in his heart that he is already three days dead in the tomb, he cannot attain this saying."[86] Attaining a saying from Scripture, realizing its truth within oneself, implied a deep moral and spiritual transformation. For Poemen, to attain a saying as opposed to merely understanding its meaning, one must in some sense *become* that of which the text speaks. In this particular case, the way to become pure (of heart) is by practicing humility and recognizing how deeply one shares in the struggles of all other creatures, even those of a murderer. In the case of Abba Moses, one could become "dead to one's neighbor" only by undergoing a costly process of detachment. Attaining a saying, then, meant nothing less than dying to oneself, to an old way of being in the world and entering into a new world—the world of possibilities projected by the text. In this way, the horizon of one's life could become fused with the horizon of the text.

The desert fathers certainly did not underestimate the difficulty of such practical appropriation of Scripture. Their strong emphasis on the need to practice the Scriptures served as a sobering reminder of the depth of commitment involved in interpretation. It was also a safeguard against pride. Thus one monk was counselled: "[E]very time a thought of superiority or vanity moves you, examine your conscience to see if you have kept all the commandments [εἰ πάσας τὰς ἐντολὰς ἐφύλαξας], if you love your enemies and are grieved at their sins, if you consider yourself as an unprofitable servant and the greatest sinner of all.''[87] Such advice reveals not only a recognition of how difficult it was to acquire or attain the truth of Scripture but also reflects an awareness of how constructive it could be to meditate upon the shortfall. Reflecting in this way on the gap between aspirations and reality instilled a healthy sense of humility which was itself an aid in learning to attain Scripture. Such a standard of practice also helped to keep from deception those who were inclined to equate intellectual knowledge of the written word with practical knowledge of it. A particular incident suggests that at least some of the tensions which existed around this question arose over differences between those for whom the Word was written and those for whom the Word was spoken and practiced. A certain brother was eager to have a scribe copy a book for him. The old man agreed to do so, and "wrote, omitting some phrases and [including] no punctuation." The brother noticed that some words were missing and, wishing to have the text punctuated and corrected, he returned to the old man and asked him to take care of it. The old man, however, must have discerned something in the brother's manner which disturbed him, for he refused to make the corrections. He simply told the brother pointedly: "Practice first that which is written, then come back and I will write the rest."[88] Such straight talk regarding the priority of practice served to remind all those who came to the desert that their primary responsibility regarding Scripture was to *do* something with the texts. W. H. C. Frend sees this insistence on practice as a new and important contribution made by the monastic movement: "Almost for the first time in three centuries the Lord's commands were being accepted literally by Christ's followers."[89] Although the historical accuracy of this statement is open to some question, Frend is nevertheless right to note the significance of the monks' practical approach to Scripture. For the desert fathers, Scripture existed in order to be put into practice and—little by little—to be woven into the fabric of their lives. And as the monks slowly *realized* the meaning of Scripture in their lives, they became better able to use it to shed light on the practical concerns of their day-to-day existence.

Reticence to Speak of Scripture

Precisely because of their practical orientation to Scripture, the monks were wary about speculating on its meaning or even talking about it at all. The numerous occasions on which the elders discouraged attempts to inquire into the meaning of a particular text reveal how seriously they took their responsibilities toward Scripture. The reasons for their refusal to discuss the texts were varied: a general sense that one was treading on holy ground, genuine humility in that it was beyond the competence of even the greatest of the elders to inquire into their meaning, and a sense that more words about the meaning of a particular text would not contribute as much toward clarifying its meaning as a humble attempt to practice it. It is clear, for instance, that conversation about Scripture was generally discouraged. When someone asked Amoun if it were better to talk about the sayings of the fathers or the Scriptures, he was told, "You had better talk about the sayings of the Fathers than about the Scriptures; it is not so dangerous."[90] Although Amoun does not say precisely what the source of the danger is, the implication is clear: excessive speculation on Scripture would inevitably lead one away from the simple exercise of putting the commands of the text into practice. While there might well be points of interpretation worth discussing, the advantages to be gained in such conversation would be outweighed by the erosion of the practical sensibility toward the text. Some apparently wondered whether Amoun and others like him refrained from talking about Scripture simply because of their ignorance. Abba Daniel attempted to refute this point of view with his testimony concerning Abba Arsenius: "He never wanted to reply to a question concerning the Scriptures, though he could well have done so had he wished. . . ."[91] It was not mere ignorance, then, which kept the elders from addressing questions about the Scriptures. Sometimes the elders themselves initiated conversation about Scripture. However, as we see in a story of Abba Antony and his disciples discussing a text from Scripture, the aim of such exercises was not to encourage speculation on the meaning of the text. Antony, wanting to test some of his disciples, suggested a saying from Scripture and, beginning with the youngest, asked them what it meant. Each gave his opinion as well as he could, but to each Antony said, "You have not discovered the meaning." Last of all, he asked Abba Joseph how he would interpret the saying, to which Joseph responded, "I do not know." To this response Antony commented, "Indeed, Abba Joseph has found the way, for he has said, 'I do not know.' "[92] Such celebrations of ignorance are, at first glance, perplexing. Was it really inappropriate to ask *any* questions at all about Scripture? Was there a kind of pigheadedness about such questions in the attitude of the elders? Clearly this was not the case. As we will see later, the elders fielded any number of questions on the meaning of Scripture and used it, with intelligence and subtlety, in their teaching. Stories like this which emphasized the need for silence before the text had a very particular pedagogical aim: to guide the one who would inquire into the meaning of Scripture into the humble way of practice.

We can gain further insight into this practical orientation by examining the attitude of Abba Pambo toward Scripture. Pambo was, like Amoun, reticent to speak about Scripture: "[I]f he was asked to interpret part of the Scriptures he would not reply immediately, but he would say he did not know that saying. If he was asked again, he would say no more."[93] We hear elsewhere that the reason for Pambo's silence before Scripture had to do with his strong conviction that words without practice were useless. Early in his monastic career, he went to one of the elders to learn a psalm. Having heard the first verse of Psalm 38 ("I said I will take heed to thy way, that I offend not with my tongue"), he departed without staying to hear the second verse. He said to himself: "[T]his one will suffice, if I can practically acquire it." More than six months passed before he returned to consult the elder again. When he did so, the old man reproved Pambo for staying away so long. But Pambo told him that the reason for his long absence was that he had been fully occupied with the verse he had been given. Even now, he said, "he had not yet learnt to practice the verse of the Psalm." Many years later, Pambo was asked by one of his companions whether he had finally mastered the verse. He responded, "I have scarcely succeeded in accomplishing it during nineteen years."[94] Such honesty and humility served as an example for anyone who wished to unlock the mysteries of Scripture: no amount of speculation and conversation about the text was as valuable as a silent and earnest effort to realize in one's life the meaning of even a single verse.

Another reason for the elders' reticence to speak about Scripture came from their uneasiness in talking about matters in which they had no experience. Abba Poemen, for one, was much happier talking about "earthly matters such as the passions of the soul, which he knew well, than he was speculating about the "spiritual and heavenly" subjects in Scripture, about which he felt he knew very little. We see this in a story telling of a great anchorite who came from a distant part of the desert to visit Abba Poemen. "The visitor began to speak of the Scriptures, concerning spiritual and heavenly things. But Abba Poemen turned his face away and did not give him a response." The anchorite, realizing that Poemen was not going to speak to him, departed, grieved and disappointed. When one of the brothers asked Poemen why he had treated his distinguished visitor in this way, he answered (somewhat nonplussed), "He is from above and speaks of heavenly things [ἐπουράνια] and I am from below and speak of earthly things [ἐπίγεια]. If he had spoken of the passions of the soul, I should have replied, but he speaks to me of spiritual things and I know nothing about that." Poemen's words were conveyed to the old anchorite, who, upon hearing them, returned at once. Now, he put a very different question to Poemen: " 'What should I do Abba, for the passions of the soul master me?'

The old man turned toward him and replied joyfully, 'This time you come as you should. Now open your mouth concerning this and I will fill it with good things.' "[95] The story sets up a contrast between "spiritual, heavenly things" about which Poemen feels unworthy and unwilling to speak, and "earthly things" which he is more than willing to discuss. Poemen's reluctance to speak of Scripture is due in part to his genuine sense of being "at a loss" in the realm of "heavenly things." He is more at home in the realm of "earthly things"—the passions of the soul—and can speak about these with some authority. However, we also see here evidence of Poemen's hard-won recognition of the priority of "earthly things." It is only through wrestling with the passions of the soul that one begins to come to a real knowledge of self, or, as the monks called it, purity of heart. A consistent focus on this long and difficult process, Poemen suggests, will produce a practical and enduring wisdom. The meaning of Scripture (and all other "heavenly things") will reveal itself as one grows in this wisdom. The contrast expressed in the story between the "heavenly things" and the "earthly things" indicates not a dualism, in which the things of the next world are favored over the things of this world, but a rejection of speculation in favor of practice.

Such stories indicate the kind of ambivalence which characterized monastic attitudes toward speaking about Scripture. It is clear on the one hand that the Scriptures were held in great esteem by the monks. However, precisely because of the great value attached to them, the monks generally refrained from speculating or inquiring too deeply into their theoretical meaning. Instead they often kept silence, preferring to focus their attention on the "earthly things," the practical demands of their life. They believed this was the best way to unleash the power of the word.

Willingness to Do the Word

The monks recognized that the fate of any given word—whether that of Scripture or the elders—depended upon the attitude of the one who heard it. While words clearly possessed a certain inherent power, their full meaning and force could only be realized through a sympathetic reception on the part of the hearer. Thus the *willingness* to carry out the words of Scripture or the elders without undue speculation was seen as a necessary precondition for the continued presence of words of power in the desert. The predisposition of those who came to hear a word from the elder deeply affected the kind and power of words which the elder would speak. Only those who showed a willingness to take the words seriously, to put them into practice, would find the verbal treasures they sought.

One of the greatest challenges facing the monks in this regard was trying to keep their words from getting ahead of themselves. We see an instance of this in the story of a brother who came to converse with Abba Theodore about a matter of some concern to him. He "began to speak with [Abba Theodore] and inquire about things which he had not yet put into practice." Theodore told the brother: "You have not yet found a ship nor put your cargo aboard it and before having sailed, you have already arrived at the city. When you have first done the work, you will then catch up to what you are now talking about."[96] Theodore's colorful imagery aptly conveys the brother's predicament: by trying to speak of matters about which he had no practical experience, he had effectively left himself bereft of "transportation." With his practical experience so far behind his words and ideas, the only hope the brother would have of learning the answers to his questions would be to reboard the ship and begin loading the cargo. This story indicates how important it was for the elders to be able to distinguish mere "traffickers" from those who came in earnest to ask for a word. In one case, we are told of a certain brother who stayed with Abba Theodore for three days, begging him for a word. Theodore refused to speak to him, and in the end the brother went away grieved. Theodore's disciple, who had witnessed all of this, asked him why he had refused to speak to the brother. He told him it was because "he is a trafficker [$\pi\rho\alpha\gamma\mu\alpha\tau\epsilon\upsilon\tau\dot{\eta}s$] [in words] who seeks to glorify himself through the words of others."[97] On the other hand, to those who showed that they took the words seriously, the elders opened themselves generously. We see this in a story of a brother who came to ask Abba Ares for "a word." Ares gave the brother some particularly difficult commands, which he received and attempted to carry out as well as he was able. Abba Abraham was visiting Ares at the time and noticed that to most of the others who came to him, Ares assigned much less strenuous tasks. He asked Ares why he prescribed relatively easy tasks for most of the brothers but placed such a heavy burden on this particular one. Ares responded: "How I send them away depends upon what the brothers came to seek. Now it is for the sake of God that this one comes to hear a word, for he is a hard worker and what I tell him, he carries out eagerly. It is because of this that I speak the Word of God to him."[98] We see here how important the attitude of the listener was for "releasing" words from the elders. Only when Ares realized how committed the brother was did he decide to share with him a word of such weight. It is intriguing to note the kind of discernment which was needed on the part of the elder for speaking words to those who came to him: Ares was not careless with his words, but in each case measured his speech in proportion to the needs and disposition of the listener.

A certain amount of discernment was also required of those who came seeking words from the elders, for the elders sometimes chose to speak in puzzles and riddles. A brother who came to see Abba Joseph of Panephysis complained that it was often impossible to understand the meaning of the elder's words. He had been commanded by Abba Joseph to eat some of the fruit of a nearby mulberry tree. But because it was a day of fasting, the brother hesitated, uncertain as to whether he ought to eat or not. After agonizing over this question for some time, he finally went to ask Joseph for an explanation. Why had he given him this command? Joseph told him: "[A]t the beginning the Fathers do not 'talk straight' to the brothers, but rather in a twisted manner. If they see that they do these twisted things, then they no longer speak like that, but tell them the truth knowing that they are obedient in all things." [99]

The elders and their disciples, it appears, took considerable care in "feeling one another out" over the matter of words. There were so many ways to be deceived in this regard that it was worth taking the trouble to find out if someone was really in earnest about their intentions. While the elders demanded evidence of real commitment on the part of those who asked them for words, they were also demanding of themselves. They expressed a healthy caution regarding their own authority and genuine detachment regarding their words. Thus when Abba Romanus was at the point of death and his disciples asked him how they ought to conduct themselves, he reminded them: "I do not think I have ever told one of you to do something, without having first made the decision not to get angry if what I said were not done." [100] This kind of detachment helped to ensure that fulfilling the commandments of Scripture or the elders did not become a pretext for blind authoritarianism or an excuse to express anger toward another if that person failed to carry out a particular command. It placed praxis in the proper light—as an undeniably valuable means toward integrity and understanding of the words of Scripture, but not as an end in itself.

There are strong indications, however, that the monks felt the whole of their life in the desert hinged on their capacity to respond to the words of the Scripture and the elders with the seriousness they deserved. This is expressed in a story which claims that the withdrawal of words of power from the desert was due to the monks' failure to put them into practice. Some brothers came to Abba Felix, begging him for a word. But he remained silent. They continued, beseeching him repeatedly to speak to them, and finally he asked them: "You wish to hear a word? . . . There are no more words nowadays. When the brothers used to consult the old men and when they did what was said to them, God showed them how to speak. But now since they ask without doing that which they hear, God has withdrawn the grace of the word from the old men and they do not find anything to say, because there are no longer any who carry their words out."[101] The chilling effect of these words would have been palpable to all who heard them. Although Felix was not sanguine about the possibilities for the future, his words would have had the effect of reinforcing a truth which had long been known among the desert monks. There was water in the well, but in order to release it from the ground, they needed to provide it with a means to the surface. The power and meaning of words could only be realized by those with a commitment to put them into practice. We see here a realization on the part of those who lived in the desert that without practical integrity, there is nothing to rely upon, no basis on which to make a judgment. That the absence of this integrity was perceived as a cause for the closing of the channels of the Word is an indication of its importance as a precondition for hearing the Word.

Hermeneutical Significance of Praxis

The monks' insistence on the importance of praxis had a direct influence on the way they approached the interpretation of Scripture. On the positive side, practice of Scripture was seen as illuminating the whole life of the monk. As one slowly and even with some hesitation and doubt began to incorporate the teaching of a particular text into one's life, a whole host of questions might well become clearer. On the other hand, the monks were well aware of the negative effects brought about from failure to put Scripture into practice. Numerous kinds of self-deception arose among the monks in their approach to Scripture which prevented them from realizing the meaning of the texts and from realizing the holiness they sought. The tension between these two poles reveals the end of the hermeneutical process as far as the monks were concerned: fulfillment or incorporation of the text in a life.

The practice of the commands of Scripture was seen first of all as a help in freeing the monks from some of the questions and temptations which tormented them. An example of this can be seen in the advice Abba Gerontius gave to some brothers who had deceived themselves at the deepest levels of their being, committing "fornication in their spirit," and "prostitution in their soul." He recommended that they "do that which is written [in the Scriptures], guarding the heart with all possible care (Prv 4:23)." If they followed this practice, they would be freed of the inner divisions which plagued them.[102] In a similar vein, Abba Or said that "practicing the commandments" was the key to overcoming "thoughts" and gaining purity of heart.[103] Abba Agathon knew from his own experience that when his thoughts were stirred up within him, urging him to pass judgment on someone, only the conscious refusal to give way to this temptation would restore his thoughts to a peaceful state.[104] Sometimes, of course, there were real doubts as to whether or not one should fulfill a particular command—whether from Scripture or the elders. Yet there was such confidence among the monks in the inherent power and value of these words that such doubts were usually overcome. One brother wondered whether he should keep the command of one of the elders even though there was the danger of temptation associated with it. Agathon said that he himself "would fulfill the commandment, and thus overcome the temptation."[105] Carrying out the words of Scripture and the elders thus gave the monks power in their struggle against the demons.

The benefits of putting the teaching of Scripture into practice were not equally apparent to all. A common and costly form of self-deception in this regard was to confuse attaining or practicing the texts with mere theoretical knowledge about them. In one story, two brothers came to an old man at Scetis and proclaimed to him their proficiency with the Bible. One of them proclaimed: "I have learned the Old and New Testaments by heart [$\dot{\alpha}\pi\dot{o}$ $\sigma\tau\dot{\eta}\theta o v s$]." To this, the old man replied: "You have filled the air with words [$\dot{\epsilon}\gamma\dot{\epsilon}\mu\iota\sigma\alpha s$ $\tau\dot{o}v$ $\dot{\alpha}\dot{\epsilon}\rho\alpha$ $\lambda\dot{o}\gamma\omega\nu$]."[106] One of the reasons for the elder's harsh response is that memorization, while valuable in itself, often became a substitute for genuine engagement with the message of the texts. A saying which illustrates this comes from a brother who ruefully admits that through lack of discernment, a division between knowledge and practice had emerged which has prevented his community from realizing the texts in their lives: "We know the Scriptures by heart, we complete all the Psalms of David, but we do not have that which God seeks: charity and humility."[107] In another story, the test of true knowledge of Scripture is reflected in the extent to which one has come to realize within oneself the meaning of the beatitudes. A woman came to Antony and declared that she had endured great fasting and had learned the entire Bible by heart. She wanted to know from Antony what more she should do. Antony was less sanguine about her accomplishments than she was and put a series of questions to her. He asked her, "Is contempt the same as honor to you?" She answered, "No." He then asked her, "Is loss as gain, strangers as your parents, poverty as abundance?" Again she answered "No." Antony said to her, "Thus you have neither fasted nor learned the Old and New Testament, but you have deceived yourself."[108] This kind of self-deception concerning the sacred texts had far-reaching effects in the lives of the monks. In a revealing comment about the source of the practical difficulties which so many of the monks encountered in their life in the desert, Poemen observed that the source of many of these difficulties was failure to do what Scripture enjoins: "We do not help our brother whom Scripture tells us to receive."[109]

Simple practice of Scripture, then, was a necessary first step for deepening one's grasp of the meaning of the monastic life. It was also an incomparable means for learning the meaning of those texts. We see this in an encounter that Antony had with some visitors who came to ask for a word. He began by telling them in a general way simply to look to the Scriptures for guidance. But when they pressed him for more specific advice, he told them they should follow the words of the Gospel of Matthew: "If anyone strikes you on one cheek, turn to him the other also (Mt 5:39)." The brothers protested: "We cannot do that [οὐ δυνάμεθα τοῦτο ποιῆσαι]." Antony then reduced the requirement somewhat, instructing them, "If you cannot do that, at least allow one cheek to be struck." The brothers again replied, "We cannot do that." So Antony revised his teaching a third time, say-ing, "If you are not able to do that, [at least] do not return evil for evil [Mt 5:39]." But once again, the brothers complained: "We cannot do that either." Antony, realizing the futility of this line of argument, refused to proceed any further. Instead, he instructed one of his disciples to "make . . . a little porridge," for the visitors—because "they are ill." Finally, he said to his visitors, "If you cannot do this, or that, what can I do for you? What you need is prayers." [110]

This episode reveals a great deal regarding the monks' attitude toward the practice of Scripture. In the first place, Antony, when pressed by the brothers to say something, refers to a specific text from Scripture and simply advises his listeners to put it into practice as well as they can. It is significant that the dialogue which ensues does not revolve around the meaning of the text, but on whether or not the brothers are able to *do* it, that is, put it into practice. Antony seems to be saying that the meaning of the text, as well as the answer to their original question about how to find salvation, will be revealed as they put one or another of these texts into practice. His unwillingness to go further with the discussion when the brothers confess on three successive occasions that they are incapable of putting even one text into practice and his decision to prepare some porridge for the brothers, suggest the balance Antony sought on this question of praxis. There was obviously no question of proceeding further with discussion of the text or its meaning, for, as he says, there is nothing more he can do for them if they will not engage in practice themselves. The preparation of the porridge revealed in symbolic terms the enfeebled condition of the brothers, who were not able to take even the smallest steps of scriptural practice on their own. Yet there is no harshness here. The preparation of porridge also manifested Antony's compassion for the brothers in their frail condition. He not only recognized their need to recover their health in small measures but expressed his own willingness to aid in that recovery. One element of this story stands out clearly: to the extent that the Scriptures reveal the way to salvation, something must be *done* with these texts if the meaning of salvation is to be realized in the monks' life.

We hear of instances in the desert when a fundamental misunderstanding of the meaning of a text prevented someone from practicing the text, much less fulfilling it. In such circumstances the elders were capable of indicating in a practical and ironical way what a particular text meant and what it might mean to fulfill it. In this way they helped to bring others along, to lead them into the world of the text so that they might begin to live there. In one story, we are told of a brother who went to see Abba Silvanus to seek his counsel. When he saw the brothers there working hard, he cited Scripture to Silvanus: " 'Do not labor for the food which perishes (Jn 6:27).' 'Mary has chosen the good portion (Lk 10:42).' " Silvanus then had one of his disciples give the visitor a book and take him to his cell where he could get on with his reading. When the ninth hour came, the visitor watched the door, expecting that someone would come to call him for the meal. However, when no one came, he went to find Silvanus, asking him, "Have the brothers not eaten today?" The old man replied that they had. Annoyed at having been forgotten, the visitor asked him, "Why did you not call me?" Silvanus replied, "Because you are a spiritual man and do not need that kind of food. We, being carnal, want to eat, and that is why we work. But you have chosen the good portion and read the whole day long and you do not want to eat carnal food." When he heard these words, the brother made a prostration, saying, "Forgive me, Abba." The old man then said to him, "Mary needs Martha. It is really thanks to Martha that Mary is praised."[111] This story suggests what was at stake in getting the meaning of a text wrong. In the case of Silvanus's young visitor, his misinterpretation of the Gospel texts led him to a view of the spiritual life that disparaged physical labor. Silvanus rejects this spiritual interpretation of the text and manages to communicate to the brother in a very practical way what it means to bring this text to life. It means, he shows him, living a life which is whole, in which the physical and spiritual, praxis and contemplation, are woven into a single fabric.

The same issue is raised in a slightly different way in a story which concerns what it means to fulfill the precept to "pray without ceasing." This story concerns some Euchites, who went to see Abba Lucius. When Lucius asked them about their work, they replied, "We do not touch manual work but as the Apostle says, we pray without ceasing (1 Thes 5:17)." Lucius was dubious about this reply and pressed his visitors to elaborate. He asked them whether they ever ate or slept. They replied that they did. Lucius then asked them how they prayed when they were eating or sleeping, but they could not find any answer to give him. Seeing this, he said to them, in language which expressed the depth of their misunderstanding of the biblical text, "Forgive me but you do not act as you speak." Lucius then proceeded to show them how, while doing his manual work, he prayed without ceasing. He told them: "I sit down with God, soaking my reeds and plaiting my ropes and saying to God, 'have mercy on me . . . save me from my sins.' " He asked them if this were not prayer and they replied that it was. Then he told them how he always put part of what he earned while praying and working outside his door. Whoever took the money would pray for Lucius while he was eating and sleeping. So, Lucius concludes, "By the grace of God I fulfill the precept to pray without ceasing." [112] The story is obviously meant to discourage the kind of dualistic and overspiritualized approach to prayer which characterized the attitudes of certain monks. However, it also says something important about the role of praxis in bringing biblical texts to fulfillment. In this particular case, the call to pray without ceasing was fulfilled not only by the practice of prayer but also by the practice of charity. By sharing the earnings from his labor in a generous manner, the fruit of Lucius's prayer and work became the seed for the prayer of another. And the recipient of his charity, by praying for the one who had so graced him, helped Lucius to complete the circle of unceasing prayer and thanksgiving. Like the previous story it reflects a vision of life as something which is whole and integrated. Prayer is not a separate category of the spiritual life: to fulfill the command to pray without ceasing means to pray in everything one does.

A remarkable story concerning a monk and a prostitute reveals the importance of right practice in being able to hear the Word of God in the first place and in its ultimate power to effect conversion. In this story, we are told that Abba Timothy went to ask the advice of Abba Poemen about a certain woman he knew who practiced fornication and gave her wages away in alms. Abba Poemen said: "She will not go on committing fornication, for the fruit of faith is appearing in her." Now it happened that Timothy's mother, who knew this woman, came to see her son, and he asked her, "Is that woman still living in fornication?" "Yes," she replied, "and she has increased the number of her lovers, but also the number of her alms." Abba Timothy told this to Poemen, who said, "She will not go on committing fornication." Finally, the prostitute told Timothy's mother that she wished to come and see him and have him pray over her. We are told that "when the woman saw him and heard the word of God from him, she was filled with compunction [ἀκούσασα παρ᾽ αὐτοῦ τὸν λόγον τοῦ θεοῦ, κατενύγη], and said to him, weeping, 'From this day forward I shall cling to

God. . . .' "[113] What is interesting about this story is how the woman "prepares the soil" for the word of God by giving away her earnings in alms. She was, in her generosity, already moving toward faith and this draws her to Timothy. The transforming power of the word is in a sense unleashed by the woman's praxis of compassion.

It was the practice of Scripture, then, that enabled those living in the desert to realize their deepest aspirations. Abba Evagrius agreed with Abba Lucius that the experience of true prayer was inextricably bound up with the concern to engage in praxis of certain key teachings of Scripture. He said: "Go, sell all that belongs to you and give it to the poor (Mt 19:21) and taking up your cross, deny yourself (Mt 16:24); in this way you will be able to pray without distraction." [114] This saying is notable for what it implies about the locus of true prayer for the monks. Evagrius, for whom prayer was usually described as imageless and wordless, does not conceive of prayer as a moment of mystical experience detached from all else. Rather, prayer arises through the practice of renunciation and—even more important—love. As Hausherr notes, for Evagrius: "La charité est la porte de la contemplation." [115] The same sentiment was expressed in a different way by Abba Poemen. He suggests that it is precisely the *act* of concealing or covering the faults of another that reveals to us the meaning of the mercy of the gospels. [116] And finally, it was the practice of mercy that brought about *parrhēsia*—that "freedom of speech" betokening a deep sense of intimacy with God. [117]

This survey of the evidence in the *Sayings* concerning words and praxis suggests the rich perspective the desert fathers brought to the interpretation of Scripture and how it influenced that interpretation. Their sensitivity toward the power of words led to a strong conviction that they should refrain from abusing words in any way. It also contributed to a belief in the importance of integrity of words and heart, words and life. This commitment to integrity with regard to language helps to explain why the desert fathers were so insistent on the importance of praxis. Consistency of practice was viewed in the desert as life-sustaining and as a check against which integrity could be tested. The seriousness with which the desert fathers viewed praxis also kept them from unnecessary speculation and futile talk about Scripture. In short, the monks' practical orientation to Scripture provided the key which opened up its worlds of meaning and led them toward lives of evangelical integrity and authenticity. The desert hermeneutic in this sense involved a hermeneutical circle or spiral—interpretation both derived from and led toward praxis. To understand the Scriptures, it was necessary to make some attempt to put them into practice. Having begun to practice them, even partially and imperfectly, understanding slowly broadened and deepened, leading to ever more profound levels of practice and understanding. Scripture was fulfilled through being transformed by praxis.

Interpretive Approaches

The concern to realize or fulfill the texts of Scripture within a life deter-mined to a great extent how the texts were selected and used by the monks. The informal narrative setting in which Scripture is generally found in the *Sayings* accurately reflects the circumstances in which discussions of the texts arose in the desert. As we have noted earlier, the biblical texts were encountered in life situations and were most often used as a way to address concrete questions and concerns raised by the monks. The monks' interests and predispositions influenced in a very clear way which texts they chose, how they used them, and what kind of meaning they found in them. In general, the desert fathers agreed with St. Paul that the Scriptures "are warnings for us . . . [and] were written down for our instruction" (1 Cor 10:6, 11).[118] The whole of the Scripture, both the Old Testament and New Testament, was focused sharply on the particular concerns that exercised the desert fathers. Everything in Scripture "referred" to that life and had the potential to shed light on its meaning. The texts were read, heard, scruti-nized, and ruminated by the monks chiefly for one purpose: to better under-stand how to pursue salvation and holiness.

There were several variations in the way Scripture was used and inter-preted. Roughly speaking, these can be divided into three main categories: exemplary, allegorical, and ethical. Exemplary interpretation refers to the monks' use of biblical exemplars as models for their own lives. Allegorical interpretation refers to the use of Scripture to point toward a "spiritual" reality, whether the celestial world or the inner world of the soul. Ethical interpretation refers to the use of Scripture as an ethical, moral model, pro-viding a guideline for action which was to be followed as closely as possible in practical, concrete terms.

Two initial observations should be made about the monks' use of these interpretive methods or approaches. First, there was nothing particularly original in their use of these methods; all of them had been in more-or-less constant use throughout early Christianity, and the monks added nothing substantially new. Our interest in the monks' use of these interpretive strat-egies lies less in their hermeneutical originality than in the particular way they applied them to the moral and religious questions they faced in their lives in the desert. Second, while it is useful to draw distinctions between the various hermeneutical methods used by the monks, in practice the methods were not always so different from one another. All three were colored by the practical approach to life which was characteristic of the monks' outlook. These categories, then, distinguish *moments* or *aspects* of a hermeneutical process that was by its very nature alive and changing. Here as elsewhere in early Christianity, hermeneutical categories often overlapped and influenced one another reciprocally. Exemplars could be types or even allegories as well as moral and spiritual models. Allegories could be partly typological and often, especially in the desert, contained a moral lesson. The ethical use of Scripture could slide over into allegory or typology.[119] These ambiguities should be kept in mind in the discussion which follows. They indicate that use of Scripture in the desert was a living, changing reality for the desert monks, determined by the exigencies of the moment.

Perhaps the primary means through which the Bible entered and affected the imaginations of those who took up life in the desert was the vivid images of holy exemplars from Scripture—that is, through exemplary interpretation. The biblical saints to whom the monks looked for guidance included figures from both the Old Testament and New Testament, the well known together with the obscure. Among these holy exemplars, though of course distinct from them in important ways, was the person of Christ, who figures prominently in the *Sayings*. Taken altogether, these holy exemplars contributed in significant ways to the development of the desert hermeneutic. They were experienced sometimes as awesome figures, remote in time and place, who were eminently worthy of emulation, and sometimes as near contemporaries who were intimately bound up with the destiny of those who sought their help. The desert fathers' relationship to these figures was as real to them as the air they breathed, and it was a relationship that worked, at least in part, because of the monks' attitude toward time. For the fourth-century person, "[m]oral exemplars of a thousand years previously had no built-in obsolescence: what was good for them could be good for you."[120] The particular concerns of the monks determined to a great extent which biblical exemplars figures most prominently and what values or virtues they were seen to embody. The figures selected and the themes associated with them thus provide a window through which we can observe those issues that were most significant in the desert and how these biblical exemplars were seen to have addressed these issues.

The texts in which holy exemplars appeared were interpreted in two main ways by the monks. In the most common approach, the texts were interpreted with a particular emphasis on how the biblical heroes had acted; by implication, this was how the monks themselves were now expected to act. This use of Scripture was characterized by directness, even literalness; biblical figures were taken to be exemplars of certain values or virtues rather than signs or allegories which represent something. This distinction was not rigorously maintained however, and both typology and allegory figured from time to time as part of the interpretation of biblical exemplars. Still, the primary function of the citation of the texts was to present an exemplar who showed the way, so that those who heard of them would know how to act. The biblical exemplars also served as primary points of reference for describing the kind of holiness found in the lives of the desert fathers themselves. So important were these exemplars to the self-understanding of the monks that, to a very large extent, the monks could explain their deepest aspirations and accomplishments only in terms of the virtues of the biblical saints.

The desert fathers were generally inclusive and expansive in their approach to interpreting biblical exemplars. They were willing to make room for a broad range of figures in their celestial hierarchy of saints and resisted the tendency to use the biblical exemplars in a narrow ideological way to support only certain virtues or qualities. One saying offers a veritable procession of saints from the Bible and shows the diversity of qualities admired by the monks in their biblical heroes. Someone asked Abba John the Persian whether the monks would inherit the kingdom of heaven after enduring so many afflictions during their life in the desert. He referred to his own experience and to the importance of the biblical exemplars in showing the way: "I have been hospitable like Abraham, meek like Moses, holy like Aaron, patient like Job, humble like David, a hermit like John, filled with compunction like Jeremiah, a master like Paul, full of faith like Peter, wise like Solomon." Then, alluding to the Good Thief of the Gospel, he indicated the quality that gave meaning to all the rest: "Like the thief, I trust that He who of his natural goodness has given me all that, will also grant me the kingdom." [121] Another saying reflects a similar diversity, while also expressing a resistance to an unnecessarily narrow interpretation of the qualities of the biblical exemplars. Someone asked Abba Nisterus: "What good work is there that I should do?" He responded with a question of his own: "Are not all actions equal?" He cited three examples presented by Scripture, consciously refusing to draw distinctions among them: "Scripture says that Abraham was hospitable [Gn 18] and God was with him. Elias loved interior peace [1 Kgs 17:5] and God was with him. David was humble [1 Sm 18:23] and God was with him. So, whatever you see that your soul desires according to God, do that, and guard your heart [Prv 4:23]." [122] As this saying indicates, the choice to imitate the way of the biblical heroes was highly subjective: the monk was to pay careful attention to the deepest desires of his own heart and respond to the particular model who best exemplified that to which he aspired. To follow or imitate this host of exemplars was ultimately a way of great diversity and of freedom.

The desert fathers showed a genuine ambivalence in their attitudes toward the biblical exemplars. They saw them as distant figures deserving of awe and respect due to their status as forerunners in the faith, and as intimate friends to whom they could address questions and converse as though they were contemporaries. We see this in a story about Abba Agathon and another brother listening to a reading of the account in Genesis of Jacob's lament at losing his sons, Joseph and Simeon (Gn 42:36, 38). The brother became irritated at Jacob and suddenly blurted out his complaint—directly to the Old Testament patriarch himself: "Are not the ten enough for you, Abba Jacob?" Agathon found himself in the position of having to defend Jacob. He said to the brother: "Let be, old man. If God is the God of the righteous, who shall condemn Jacob [Rom 8:33]?" [123] We see here the kind of tension that could arise between those who felt sufficiently at ease in the company of the biblical heroes to engage them in dialogue and even criticize them and those who were prepared to guard the status of their heroes. The brother addressed the patriarch as though he were sitting beside him, and his question, while evincing a strange lack of sympathy for Jacob's plight, nevertheless arose from a feeling that Jacob's sorrow was a palpable part of the present moment. Agathon, by contrast, sought to remind the brother that in God's eyes the patriarch was righteous and above reproach—at least by the present generation. We do not see in the story any kind of resolution to the tension between these two positions. Awe and intimacy are both seen as natural responses to the biblical predecessors.

The sense of intimacy with the biblical saints was sometimes seen to have direct hermeneutical benefits. On one occasion, some brothers came to Abba Antony to ask him for help in interpreting a difficult passage from Leviticus. Antony did not answer immediately but went out into the desert where he stood, "praying and crying in a loud voice: 'God, send Moses, that he may teach me the meaning of this passage [ἀπόστειλον τὸν Μωϋσῆν, καὶ διδάξει με τὸ ῥῆμα τοῦτο].' Then there came a voice speaking with him." Abba Ammonas, "knowing it was [Antony's] custom" to go into the desert at such times, had secretly followed him to the solitary place. He testified that although he heard the voice of Moses addressing Antony, he was not able to understand what it said. [124] This is a puzzling story. We do not know which text from Leviticus the brothers brought to Antony for advice, nor do we know what occurred when Antony withdrew into the desert or what "answer" he received from Moses. What we do know is that it was Antony's custom, when faced with difficult questions about Scripture, to retreat into solitude and to search out the answer there. His dialogue with Moses about the meaning of the biblical text appears entirely natural, a response born of long intimacy with the biblical exemplars. Whatever answer may have emerged from this discussion was far less important than the symbolism of Antony and Moses in dialogue. It expressed unambiguously the sense that certain persons enjoyed a real intimacy with the biblical exemplars, shared in their world, and could "call" upon them for help.

Such intimacy with their biblical predecessors sometimes helped the desert monks to escape real difficulties. A story tells of an elder said to be "a worker of miracles" to whom "all that he asked of God was revealed." However, Cyril, bishop of Alexandria, heard that this elder had expressed certain problematic opinions concerning Melchizedek, an Old Testament figure whose identity and significance were matters of some controversy. Knowing the old man's reputation for intimacy with God, Cyril sent someone to put a question to him about the identity of Melchizedek, so that he might be drawn out of his error. The old man was asked by one of Cyril's messengers: "Pray God to reveal to you what he is [a man or the Son of God]." The old man "said with confidence [εἶπε μετὰ παρρησίας], 'Give me three days. I will ask God about this matter and I will tell you who he is.'" After three days, he reported to Cyril that he had determined that Melchizedek was not the Son of God, but only a man. When asked how he knew this, the old man responded, "God has revealed to me all the patriarchs in such a way that each one, from Adam to Melchizedek, passed before me."[125] The story is primarily concerned with a particular point of biblical interpretation and a question of doctrine which rested upon it. However, what is interesting for our purposes is the elder's direct and matter-of-fact sense of relationship with the family of patriarchs. His difficulties with Melchizedek were resolved not through debate or discussion but through direct revelation. The elder's easy access to this world (παρρησίας) was the source of his authority and holiness. The intimacy which the desert fathers enjoyed with God and with the biblical exemplars in the courts of heaven explains a good deal of their appeal to the common person of late antiquity: "Byzantine piety had created the majestic figure of Christ the Lord of all enthroned in glory in the dome of the East Roman Churches, and before this unapproachable majesty yourself, your needs appeared as a very little thing: but a *saint* had access to the courts of heaven: he through his mediation (Πρεσβεία) would present your needs and requests."[126] Still, this was not the only means by which the desert fathers gained access to the world revealed by Scripture.

They also interpreted Scripture allegorically.[127] The presence of allegorical interpretation among the monks seems unremarkable when one remembers that it formed such a common part of the early church's general approach to scripture and that Alexandria was the home of the systematic development of the allegorical method. Origen, the greatest of the Alexandrian exponents of the allegorical approach, exerted a strong influence on monasticism and had many disciples in the desert.[128] It is nonetheless surprising that we see as much allegory among the desert monks as we do. Despite Origen's enormous influence, he was a controversial figure in the desert. His speculative theology and especially his allegorical approach to Scripture made him extremely unpopular with many of the simpler monks.[129]

The presence of allegory in the *Sayings,* in spite of the strong anti-Origenist sentiments in the desert, can be explained by a number of factors. In the first place, the *Sayings* represents diverse desert traditions, including Origen's sympathizers as well as his opponents. Second, allegory was not necessarily synonymous with Origenism and had a long history of use before the great Alexandrian made so much of it. Moreover, it appears that the monks were perfectly capable of opposing Origen's method in principle while using it for their own purposes. However it is to be explained, the allegorical approach to Scripture does occupy a significant place in the *Sayings* and represents one way the monks sought to bring Scripture to life. It was used to point to the underlying spiritual significance of certain biblical texts and to help the monk cultivate an awareness of the various levels at which challenges and questions could arise. It sometimes drew out a playful side to the monks' approach to Scripture: they used allegory to spin out the implications of certain verbal connections which they observed in the text. In whatever way it was used, though, allegorical interpretation always maintained a strong ethical dimension; it was one more way to encourage ethical engagement with the sacred texts.

This kind of engagement with Scripture was emphasized most strongly and most commonly through ethical interpretation.[130] Here the text was valued because of what it enjoined the hearer to do and because of the belief that if one did what the text enjoined one would move closer to holiness. The influence of the practical orientation of the monks upon the selection, use, and interpretation of biblical texts is clearly evident here and reveals how a hermeneutical circle of praxis and interpretation operated in the desert. Certain biblical texts served as inspiration for action—for the movement to the desert and for the adoption of particular practices. However, it is also true that certain practices and attitudes were highly valued in the desert and that the value of these practices was then confirmed through reference to Scripture. It is not always easy to distinguish these different aspects of the interpretive process precisely or to say where the hermeneutical circle begins. Rather, both aspects form part of the use of Scripture in the desert and each serves to deepen the other: Scripture was seen as the source of praxis; praxis acted as an organizing principle which sent one to search for particular texts; these texts in turn deepened and purified praxis and clarified its purpose and meaning.[131]

These interpretive approaches suggest some of the strategies employed by the monks for discerning the meaning of Scripture and thereby addressing their own deepest questions. We can learn a great deal about how they understood themselves and their world by exploring the questions that preoccupied the desert fathers, the particular texts which spoke to their concerns, and their manner of interpreting these texts. The following chapters suggest several main "interests" or practices of the monks that drew their inspiration from Scripture and looked to Scripture for confirmation of their validity and importance.

Notes

1. Thomas Merton, *The Wisdom of the Desert* (New York: New Directions, 1960), 12–13.
2. Macarius the Great 39 [*PG* 65:280CD–81A].
3. Poemen 42 [*PG* 65:332C] [RSV].
4. Nau 234 [*ROC* 14:362].
5. Xanthius 1 [*PG* 65:315A].
6. Nau 237 [*ROC* 14:362], [m].
7. Megethius 4 [*PG* 65:301B]; see also Nau 238 [*ROC* 14:362].
8. Nau 359 [*ROC* 18:137]; ὁμιλία, which is ambiguous as it stands in this saying, can refer to an "unprofitable discourse"; see Lampe, *PGL*, 951. The Latin version of this saying provides some help in determining the sense of the word ὁμιλία. It translates ὁμιλία as *locutio saecularis*: [*PL* 73:993B].
9. Sisoes 47 [*PG* 65:405C].
10. Nisterus 3 [*PG* 65:308 AB].
11. Matoes 13 [*PG* 65:293C].
12. Sisoes 5 [*PG* 65:393A], [m]. There may be an echo here of Jas 3:5–6: "So the tongue is a little member and boasts of great things. How great a forest is set ablaze by a small fire."
13. Agathon 1 [*PG* 65:108D–109B]. It is interesting that the key word in this warning is παρρησία, a quality that is extolled elsewhere in the *Sayings*. It is used in the New Testament to refer to the confidence of the saints before God and in the *Sayings* it is normally used in this positive sense (see Evagrius 1; Pambo 14; Hyperchius 8). There appear to be (at least) two distinct meanings of the word in the *Sayings:* (1) Positive: boldness of speech before emperors and princes and before God; (2) Negative: speaking *too freely*, that is, speaking with imprudence. See: Pierre Miquel, O.S.B., *Lexique du désert* (Bégrolles-en-Mauges: Bellefontaine, 1986), 203–16.

14. Hyperchius 3 [*PG* 65:429C], [m].
15. Nau 239 [*ROC* 13:363].
16. Tithoes 2 [*PG* 65:428B], [m]. Tithoes is very likely to be identified with Sisoes. Agathon 1 (see n. 13) advocates that the monks keep this same attitude ("keep the frame of mind of an exile" [φύλοξον τὴν ξενιτείᾳ]) as a way of overcoming carelessness with speech (παρρησιασθῆς). For ξενιτεία, see A. Guillaumont, "Le dépaysement comme forme d'ascèse dans le monachisme ancien," in *École pratique des hautes études, v^e section: Sciences religieuses, Annuaire 1968–69* 76 (1968):31–58.
17. Antony 18 [*PG* 65:81A].
18. Nau 225 [*ROC* 14:360], [m].
19. Or 3 [*PG* 65:437B], [m].
20. John Colobos 10 [*PG* 65:208A].
21. Sisoes 45 [*PG* 65:405B], [m].
22. Poeman 2 [*PG* 65:317B], [m].
23. Ammoes 1 [*PG* 65:125CD].
24. Zeno 8 [*PG* 65:177CD].
25. Hyperchius 4 [PG 65:429C].
26. Achilles 4 [*PG* 65:125A].
27. Hyperchius 5 [*PG* 65:429CD].
28. John Colobos 15 [*PG* 65:208D–209A].
29. Or 15 [*PG* 65:440D]
30. John Colobos 25 [*PG* 65:213A].
31. Peter the Pionite 2 [*PG* 65:376C–377A], [m].
32. Theodora 8 [Guy, *Recherches*, S1:23], [m].
33. Amoun of Nitria 2 [*PG* 65:128C].
34. Gregory the Theologian [*PG* 65:145B].
35. Poemen 63 [*PG* 65:337A]; Poemen 164 [*PG* 65:361B].
36. Poemen 188 [Guy, *Recherches*, S1:29].
37. Tithoes 3 [*PG* 65:428B].
38. Poemen 27 [*PG* 65:329A].
39. John Colobos 45 [Guy, *Recherches*, S5:24].
40. This concern to integrate life and words was not original to the desert fathers. It was a common wisdom found in the New Testament (e.g., Mt 23:3; Rom 2:1, 21–23; 1 Jn 3:18), early patristic writers (e.g., *I Clem* 30:3; Ignatius, *Eph* 15:1), and among pagan philosophers (e.g., Pseudo-Diogenes, *Epistle* 15, Julian *Oration* 7.214BCD; Lucian *Icaromenippus*, 29–31); see A. J. Malherbe, *Moral Exhortation: A Greco-Roman Sourcebook* (Philadelphia: Westminster Press, 1986), 38–40.
41. Poemen 25 [*PG* 65:328D].
42. Moses 17 [*PG* 65:288BC].
43. Silvanus 10 [*PG* 65:412B].
44. Poemen 127 [*PG* 65:353D].
45. Syncletica 12 [*PG* 65:425B].
46. Nau 240 [*ROC* 14:363].
47. Nau 252 [*ROC* 14:365].

48. Cassian 5 [*PG* 65:245A].
49. Pambo 5 [*PG* 65:369C].
50. Anoub 2 [*PG* 65:129D].
51. Or 2 [*PG* 65:437B].
52. Isidore of Pelusia 1 [*PG* 65:221D].
53. Epiphanius 6 [*PG* 65:165A].
54. Moses 3 [*PG* 65:284A].
55. Agathon 15 [*PG* 65:113B].
56. Poemen 205 [Guy, *Recherches*, S18:31].
57. Theodora 4 [*PG* 65:201D].
58. Sisoes 30 [*PG* 65:401BC].
59. Isaac, Priest of the Cells 2 [*PG* 65:224CD].
60. Poemen 45 [*PG* 65:332D–333A].
61. Poemen 37 [*PG* 65:332B].
62. Poemen 84 [*PG* 65:341C].
63. Pambo 2 [*PG* 65:368C].
64. Pambo 5 [*PG* 65:369B].
65. Macarius the Great 33 [*PG* 65:273D–277B].
66. Theodore of Pherme 20 [*PG* 65:192B].
67. Theodore of Pherme 1 [*PG* 65:188A].
68. Poemen 53 [*PG* 65:333D].
69. Romanus 1 [*PG* 65:392B].
70. Nisterius 2 [*PG* 65:305D], [m].
71. Isidore the Priest 6 [*PG* 65:236B].
72. Antony 1 [*PG* 65:76B].
73. Nisterus 5 [*PG* 65:308C].
74. Epiphanius 14 [*PG* 65:165C].
75. Moses 17 [*PG* 65:288BC], [m].
76. Gerontius 1 [*PG* 65:153AB].
77. Isidore the Priest 9 [*PG* 65:221C].
78. Theodore of Pherme 18 [*PG* 65:192AB].
79. Agathon 3 [*PG* 65:109B].
80. Antony 3 [*PG* 65:76C].
81. Benjamin 4 [*PG* 65:145A]; see also N 592/37 [*SPAn*, 223]: "If you question the fathers and hear the Word of God coming from them and from Scripture, hasten to practice what you hear"; XI 50 [*SPTr*, 87]: "If you would be saved, love your God with all your heart and *keep* these commandments: Do not lie, do not speak without purpose,do not grow proud of yourself. . . . Love not only those who love you but also those who do you evil."
82. Pistus 1 [*PG* 65:372C–373B], [m]. Pistus is probably to be identified with Sisoes; see Regnault, *SPAlph*, 265.
83. Daniel 2 [*PG* 65:153BC]; see also Sopatrus 2 [*PG* 65:413A].
84. Anoub 1 [*PG* 65:129AC], [m].
85. Poemen 97 [*PG* 65:345B]; see also Poemen 98 [*PG* 65:345BC].

86. Moses 12 [*PG* 65:285A].
87. Nau 299 [*ROC* 17:204].
88. Abraham 3 [*PG* 65:132B].
89. W. H. C. Frend, *The Rise of Christianity* (Philadelphia: Fortress Press, 1984), 423.
90. Amoun of Nitria 2 [*PG* 65:128C].
91. Arsenius 42 [*PG* 65:105D–108B].
92. Antony 17 [*PG* 65:80D], [m]; see also PA 87,1 [*SPTr*, 126]: "[I]f someone speaks with you of the Scriptures or any subject, do not discuss it with him."
93. Pambo 9 [*PG* 65:372A].
94. Socrates, *Historia Ecclesiastica*, IV, 23, 23.
95. Poemen 8 [*PG* 65:321C–324B]. I. Hausherr, S.J., *Direction spirituelle en orient d'autrefois*, Orientalia Christiana Analecta 144 (Rome: Pontificium Institutum Studiorum Orientalum, 1955), 104, suggests that the elder must show discernment regarding the things that constitute the subjects of conversation, and that the psychology of the passions does not require the same elevation as theological questions. However, Hausherr seems to miss the point of this and other stories like it, that the passions are at the very center of the monastic life and that speculation upon the meaning of Scripture, far from illuminating that work, usually only clouds it. Scripture only makes sense in and through very concrete, practical considerations. See also Zeno 4 [*PG* 65:176D]: Some brothers came to ask Abba Zeno about a particular text from the Book of Job. The old man eventually replied to their question, but not without first calling into question the priorities of the brothers, who, he says "have passed over their sins and inquired about heavenly things"; H 164, 1 [*SPTr*, 109]: A brother questioned an old man on the subject of a word from Scripture and the old man said: "Do not search these; rather chase evil from you and God will reveal to you the things which are above and the things of below."
96. Theodore of Pherme 9 [*PG* 65:189B], [m].
97. Theodore of Pherme 3 [*PG* 65:188C], [m].
98. Ares 1 [*PG* 65:132CD–133A].
99. Joseph of Panephysis 5 [*PG* 65:229BC].
100. Romanus 1 [*PG* 65:392B].
101. Felix 1 [*PG* 65:433CD].
102. Gerontius 1 [*PG* 65:153A]; see also Nau 178 [*ROC* 13:269].
103. Or 11 [*PG* 65:440B].
104. Agathon 18 [*PG* 65:113C].
105. Agathon 13 [*PG* 65:113A].
106. Nau 385 [*ROC* 18:143].
107. Nau 222 [*ROC* 14:359].
108. N 518 [*SPAn*, 189–90].
109. Poemen 204 [Guy, *Recherches*, S17:30–31], [m].
110. Antony 19 [*PG* 65:81BC].
111. Silvanus 5 [*PG* 65:409BCD] [RSV].
112. Lucius 1 [*PG* 65:253BC].

113. Timothy 1 [*PG* 65:429AB].

114. Nilus 4 [*PG* 65:305B]. Nilus is the name given in the *Sayings* to Evagrius. The same saying is found in Evagrius's treatise *Chapters on Prayer*, 17.

115. I. Hausherr, S.J., *Les leçons d'un contemplatif: Le traité de l'oraison d'Evagre le Pontique* (Paris: Beauchesne, 1960), 31.

116. Poemen 64 [*PG* 65:337AB].

117. Pambo 14 [*PG* 65:372B].

118. This text is cited explicitly by Cassian to make just this point. See *Conferences* V:16 (trans. Gibson, 347): "Everything which, as the Apostle says, happened to them 'in a figure' (1 Cor 10:6) we ought to take as written for our correction."

119. On the diverse and often overlapping approaches to Scripture in the early church, see J. L. Kugel and R. A. Greer, *Early Biblical Interpretation* (Philadelphia: Westminster Press, 1986), 155ff.; see also B. Lindars, "The Bible and the Call: The Biblical Roots of the Monastic Life in History and Today," *Bulletin of John Rylands Library* 66 (1983–1984): 239–41.

120. Peter Brown, "The Saint as Exemplar in Late Antiquity," in *Saints and Virtues*, ed. J. Stratton Hawley (Berkeley: University of California Press, 1987), 5.

121. John the Persian 4 [*PG* 65:237D–240A].

122. Nisterus 2 [*PG* 65:305D–308A]; cf. also *Historia Lausiaca* 14:4: Two brothers, Paesius and Isaias, had taken different paths, one devoting himself to ascesis and prayer, and the other to looking after the poor and invalid. After their death an argument broke out about which of them was the greatest. Abba Pambo emphatically stated: "Both were perfect. One showed the work of Abraham; the other that of Elias."

123. Agathon 22 [*PG* 65:116AB].

124. Antony 26 [*PG* 65:84C], [m].

125. Daniel 8 [*PG* 65:160AC]. Melchizedek was, however, esteemed by Epiphanius as "the image of Christ." See Epiphanius 5 [*PG* 65:164D]: εἰχὼν τοῦ Χριστοῦ.

126. N. H. Baynes, *The Thought World of East Rome* (London: Oxford University Press, 1947), 34.

127. Numerous examples of allegorical interpretation are discussed in the following chapters. See, for example, pp. 196–98, 201–3, and 206–7.

128. On Origen's influence on early monasticism, see H. Crouzel, "Origène, précurseur de monachisme," in G. Lemaître, *Théologie de la vie monastique: Études sur la tradition patristique* (Paris: Aubier, 1961), 15–37. On the moral implications of Origen's hermeneutic, see Karen Torjeson, *Hermeneutical Method and Theological Structure in Origen's Exegesis* (Berlin, NY: de Gruyter, 1986).

129. One of the main controversies in fourth-century monasticism had to do with the propriety of using the allegorical method. The Origenist side was eventually discredited, and anti-Origenism is in strong evidence in the *Sayings*. See for example, Lot 1 [*PG* 65:253D–256A]; on the Origenist controversy, see Derwas J. Chitty, *The Desert a City* (Oxford: Blackwell, 1966), 58ff.

130. For examples of ethical interpretation, see pp. 184, 186, 198, 200, 220, 238–39, 242–43, and 265–69.

131. For an illuminating discussion of the relationship between interpretation and experience in terms that are directly relevant to the desert hermeneutic, see Richard R. Niebuhr, ''The Strife of Interpreting: The Moral Burden of Imagination,'' *Parabola* 10 (1985):34–47. Niebuhr suggests that

[t]he art of reading is also an unending conflict between convention and innovation. It is the interpolation of the text or passage into the reader's experience and the reader's experience into the passage, not, to be sure, either haphazardly or according to rigid values but tactfully and experimentally. Earlier generations of readers of Scripture . . . knew this art well. . . . These are the persons who . . . found in the Bible a reflection and adumbration of their own experience. Sometimes they searched in themselves for experiences answering to the examples they encountered in biblical narratives or in the Psalms or in other Wisdom writings; sometimes they were overcome by an unexpected surfacing in their own awareness of an experience that deepened the example set before them on the printed page. (39–40)

III

THE WORD REALIZED

6

Eschatology, *Penthos,* and the Struggle against Evil

How did the desert fathers actually interpret Scripture? In the previous chapters we considered the broad presuppositions which shaped the way in which words—both the words of Scripture and those of the elders—were interpreted in the desert. It is time now to turn from this general consideration of the attitudes and presuppositions that governed the monks' approach to Scripture to a more precise examination of what it meant for the monks to interpret particular texts. In this and the following chapters, I want to articulate the *content* of the "conversation" which occurred between the desert fathers and Scripture. By examining the particular questions which the monks put to Scripture, and the manner and substance of their response to these questions, we can bring into sharper relief the "worlds" of meaning opened up by their encounter with Scripture.

Eschatology

In keeping with the particular logic which governed the thinking of the desert fathers, it is appropriate to begin our consideration of the biblical themes which occupied them with the *end* point—their concern over the eschaton and judgment. The monks' acute awareness of the nearness of death, of the final judgment, and of the age in which they were living as a time of tribulation before the end, shaped their imagination in a profound way. In all of this they were drawing not only on a common theme in Christianity but also a prominent theme in traditional Egyptian religion. "The belief was widely prevalent that after death everyone faced a trial before [Osirus]. . . ." A creed from the fourth century B.C.E. which endured in Egypt until the middle of the sixth century C.E., reveals a completely serious approach to the day of moral reckoning which rich and poor, powerful and puny, alike must face:

> The west is the abode of him who is faultless,
> Praise god for the man who has reached it!
> No man will attain it,
> Unless his heart is exact in doing right.
> The poor is not distinguished there from the rich,
> Only he who is found free of fault,
> By scale and weight before eternity's lord.
> There is none exempt from being reckoned.[1]

It is likely that the importance of the eschaton in the popular imagination of the fourth-century Egyptian was due at least in part to the influence of texts like this. Yet it is clear that the monks' awareness of the "end," of the final judgment, and of the kind of response required of them, was deepened through reference to particular texts and images from Scripture. Certain texts led them to see the apocalyptic character of the age in which they lived and understand the particular struggles and crises they faced in light of this. Remembrance of judgment also engendered an awareness of the need for repentance and for a profound exploration of the self. The fact of an ultimate moral reckoning helped to focus attention on the need to cultivate moral purity—both in the hidden recesses of the heart and in the more visible acts of everyday life.

That the desert fathers considered themselves to be living in the last times—an age of temptation—becomes clear from the kind of questions they asked about the temptations they experienced. A burning question for the monks was whether the frequency and intensity of the attacks of the demons upon them was a particular characteristic of the present time. An old man asked Abba Sisoes: "Did Satan pursue them like this in the early days?" Sisoes responded—in language with echoes of the New Testament—by describing the reasons for the acuity of the temptations during these last days: "He [Satan] does this more at the present because his time is nearly finished and he is enraged [Lk 21:8; Rv 20:10]."[2] Abba Antony expressed a similar thought, echoing the eschatological language of the New Testament in describing the kind of conflicts and disorientation which were soon to arise in the desert. "A time is coming," he said, "when men will go mad, and when they see someone who is not mad, they will rise against him [ἐπαναστήσονται αὐτῷ] [Mt 10:21] saying, 'You are mad, you are not like us.' "[3] Amma Theodora concurred in this assessment, using one of Jesus' most vivid images of the eschatological tribulations to characterize the time in which she is living: "The present age is a storm" [Mt 16:3].[4]

Such images of the tribulations to come impressed themselves deeply upon the minds of the monks. We see this in a story telling of three brothers who came to ask Abba Sisoes about the coming judgment. Each of them was preoccupied, and deeply disturbed by a particular image or allusion from Scripture concerning the coming judgment. The first one asked Sisoes, "How shall I save myself from the river of fire [Dn 7:10]?" The second asked him, "Father, how can I be saved from the gnashing of teeth [Mt 8:12] and the worm which does not die [Mk 9:48; Is 66:24]?" The third pleaded, "Father, what shall I do, for the remembrance of the outer darkness [Mt 8:12] is killing me?"[5] The urgency of these questions reveals how large the threat of judgment loomed in the minds of the desert fathers. Yet their fear of this threat was not always quite so debilitating, nor were their reflections on the coming judgment always so dark. Abba Orsisius had a healthy sense of awe before the prospect of an ultimate moral reckoning. He noted that for all the effort the monk expended upon resisting the temptations of this "end time," "we shall scarcely escape the judgment of God [(Rom 2:3)]." Yet, he also knew that the memory of this sobering reality helped one to cultivate humility.[6] Mindfulness of judgment also meant awareness of the possibility of salvation. In one story we hear how in a spiritual conference some brothers "meditated upon the Holy Scriptures . . . [and] they recalled the kingdom of heaven, the future beatitude, the glory of the just, chastisement of sinners, the rest of all the saints who are rejoicing in happiness in paradise."[7] Whether they were to participate in the "future beatitude" or in the "chastisement of sinners," it is clear that certain vivid biblical images depicting the final reckoning contributed in important ways to the monks' consciousness of the moral exigencies of their life.

As fearful as the prospect of judgment could be, the desert fathers also knew that cultivating an awareness of judgment and of death could help them to come to a deeper knowledge of themselves. We see in numerous stories that such remembrance was more than an occasional thought among the monks; it became for them a discipline, as they sought to keep "that day" always in mind. One elder counseled: "We ought to live as having to give account to God of our way of life every day."[8] Certain monks provided examples of such mindfulness in their own life and practice. Abba Arsenius, at the point of his death, reminded his disciples: "We will be judged before the terrible seat of judgment [2 Cor 5:10; Dt 10:17]. . . ." As his death drew nearer, the brothers saw him weeping and asked him, "Truly, Father, are you also afraid?" He answered them, "Indeed, the fear which is mine at this hour has been with me ever since I became a monk."[9] Arsenius's lifelong example was not lost on others; it helped certain monks as they tried to face their own deaths with courage. Theophilus, at the hour of his death, thanked Arsenius for the encouragement of his example: "You are blessed, Abba Arsenius, because you have always had this hour in mind." [10] The continual awareness of the "end" of one's life, coupled with the knowledge of how easily and often one failed, led the monks to "preempt" the final judgment by "accusing themselves." This form of vigilance helped the monk learn to pay attention to the important things. Abba Ammonas likened this discipline of self-scrutiny to the experience of a person in prison anxiously awaiting the coming of the magistrate. "Even so, the monk ought to give himself up at all times to accusing his own soul, saying, 'Alas for me! How shall I stand before the judgment seat of Christ [2 Cor 5:10]? What shall I say to him in my defense?' If you give yourself continually to this, you may be saved." [11] The monks knew that the road to salvation or condemnation began in the present moment, in the choices one made for or against certain thoughts or actions. Abba Evagrius contended that the continual consciousness of judgment—that of the evil and of the righteous—could have immediate psychological benefits: it could help the monk fight "harmful thoughts." With generous allusions to Scripture, he exhorted his listeners to "remember the day of your death. . . . [R]emember also what happens in hell and think about the state of souls down there. . . . [I]magine the fearful and terrible judgment. Consider the fate kept for sinners, their shame before the face of punishment, the eternal fire, worms that rest not [Mk 9:48], the darkness, gnashing of teeth [Mt 8:12], fear and supplications." He also exhorted them to "keep the day of resurrection and of presentation to God in remembrance. . . . Consider the good things in store for the righteous: confidence in the face of God the Father and His Son . . . the kingdom of heaven, and the gifts of that realm, joy and beatitude." For Evagrius, keeping these thoughts continually in the mind had practical psychological value: "Be careful that the remembrance of these things never leaves you, so that, thanks to their remembrance, you may at least flee wrong and harmful thoughts." [12]

Clearly one of the purposes of calling to mind the coming judgment was to inspire repentance and reformation of lives. Abba Theophilus once presented to the monks an extended meditation, filled with Scriptural allusions, on the final judgment. He concluded these reflections on the inevitability of the judgment with a question, also drawn from Scripture: "*Since this is so, in what manner ought we not to give ourselves to holy and devout works* [2 Pt 3:11]? . . . Let us make every effort to be found blameless and without reproach in peace (I Cor 1:7–8; 2 Pt 3:14). In this way, we shall be worthy to hear it said: 'Come, O blessed of my Father, inherit the kingdom prepared for you from the foundation of the world' (Mt 25:14)." [13] Awareness of judgment, Theophilus implied, should inspire holy lives. Such admonitions to remember the judgment were sometimes used to encourage those who had lost their way to regain their sense of balance and purpose. In one instance, a certain young man who had decided to take up life as a monk was being discouraged from doing so by his mother. However, when he persisted in his resolution, telling her, "I want to save my soul," she finally relented. He then departed for the desert where, instead of seriously pursuing the life of the monk, he negligently frittered his life away. While he was living in the desert, his mother died. Then he himself became seriously ill and had a vision in which he saw the place of judgment and encountered his mother there. She was dumbfounded at seeing him there and exclaimed, "What is this, my child, have you been condemned to this place too? What about the phrase you used to use?—'I want to save my soul'?" The young man was so shaken by this vision, and the encounter with his mother, that he closed himself within a cell and "started to work out his salvation. He repented and wept for what he had done before in negligence." His compunction was so strong that his companions began to worry about him and advised him to relax a little. But he did not want to do this, claiming: "if I could not endure my mother's reproach, how shall I endure shame on the day of judgement before Christ and the holy angels." [14] Awareness of the coming judgment could significantly alter a person's perception of his life and purpose. The sense of urgency which accompanied such awareness was clearly a significant factor in leading the monks to adopt their severe way of life in the desert. Yet it was not only fear which led them to the desert. Consciousness of judgment was also something which helped one in "returning to one's senses" and seeing new possibilities for one's life. The sign of this new awakening was a spontaneous flow of tears.

Compunction

The consciousness of the reality of judgment and of the nearness of the "end time" inspired among the desert fathers a sensitive understanding of the heart's movement toward renewal—which they called *penthos* or compunction. The monks' awareness and sorrow for their faults and the need for and experience of forgiveness sometimes pierced the heart so deeply that tears burst forth. Thus *penthos* was sometimes called "the gift of tears." It involved a "double movement" of the heart: "*penthos* or compunction is the way believers accept both . . . judgement and . . . mercy simultaneously." [15] It was a transforming experience. Through the piercing of the heart, the old experience of the world was washed away and a new one emerged. In this way, one could begin along—or take up again—the path toward God. Scripture was one of the places the monks looked to learn about *penthos*. There they found descriptions and examples of deep repentance which they attempted to emulate in their own lives. Abba Poemen held that both Scripture and tradition pointed to the importance of tears: "Weeping [κλαίειν] is the way that Scripture and our fathers have handed on to us, when they say, 'Weep!' Truly there is no other way than this."[16] Which biblical texts and which of the fathers Poemen was referring to here is not easy to determine. Any number of biblical texts mention the importance of tears as a sign of true repentance and we know that Clement, Origen, and many other patristic writers devoted a good deal of attention to the subject. Whatever his exact sources may have been, Poemen could claim with some justification to be standing in the tradition of Scripture and the fathers in holding tears and compunction to be central to the spiritual life. As Luciana Mortari suggests, "*Penthos* is seen as an essential, not marginal aspect [of the patristic tradition], part of the fulcrum of the spiritual life."[17]

The experience of *penthos* was linked to the monks' acute awareness of the nearness of the end time, and the in-breaking of the kingdom of God. Abba Matoes reminded one of those who came to him—in a phrase reminiscent of Jesus' call to repentance in the Gospels—of the urgency of the moment. He counseled him to "restrain the spirit of controversy in yourself in everything, and weep, have compunction, because the time is drawing near [Mk 1:15]."[18] *Penthos*, like the call to repentance in the Gospels, demanded a fundamental reorientation of one's entire being, so that one would be prepared to enter the world of the kingdom of God. As such, acquiring the spirit of *penthos* involved dying to oneself, at least to those inner habits and addictions which prevented a single-minded devotion to God. We see this in a story Poemen told about a woman he and Abba Anoub encountered in a cemetery, "weeping bitterly" for her dead husband, son, and brother. Observing her, Poemen said to Anoub, "I tell you, if a person does not put to death all the desires of the flesh [Col 3:5; Eph 2:3] and acquire compunction like this, he cannot become a monk. For the whole of this woman's life and spirit are turned to compunction."[19] It is intriguing to note how Poemen reaches this conclusion. His presence with Anoub in the cemetery is itself significant, for it reminds us that the monks were not as isolated from the daily concerns around them as they sometimes appear. And in the present case, Poemen was deeply moved by the woman's grief and drawn into her world of concerns. In a natural and completely convincing way, then, Poemen proceeded to blend the example of the woman's tears with a scriptural allusion to indicate the depth to which *penthos* must reach in the life of the monk. After drawing Anoub's attention to the woman, he makes a comment on the significance of her tears in a statement which apparently conflates phrases from Colossians and Ephesians.[20] Poemen's blending of these two passages allows him to highlight the significance of the woman who is weeping for her family: she exemplifies that single-minded devotion for which the Scriptures call. Her "whole life [ὅλος . . . ὁ βίος]" is characterized by the spirit of *penthos,* and she serves as a reminder to aspirants in the desert of the depth to which their own commitment must reach if they are to realize this call within themselves.

Cultivating the spirit of *penthos* involved more than a remembrance of one's sin or the transitory nature of life. Remembrance of God's mercy was also vital, and Scripture was seen as the source par excellence of God's merciful deeds. Abba Poemen knew this, and when a brother filled with turmoil approached him to talk about all the things that were troubling him, Poemen responded with a brief invitation: "Let us weep before the goodness of God in all our afflictions, until he shows mercy on us."[21] This deceptively simple saying is what Lemaire calls a "pensée imprégnée de la Sainte Écriture."[22] Poemen's invitation to weep in God's presence echoes a number of biblical passages. It is reminiscent of Ps 94:6, which says, "Let us weep before the Lord who made us." The expression "until he shows mercy on us" is recounted frequently in the prayers of the Old Testament (for example, 1 Sm 20:14), and is used elsewhere by Poemen as a form of intercessory prayer.[23] Poemen's attribution to God of the word "goodness" (ἀγαθότητος) also recalls certain biblical passages. It is found several times in the Wisdom literature and twice with particular reference to God (Wis 7:26; 12:22). In Wis 12:22, goodness is used parallel to mercy, as it is in Poemen's saying.[24] Poemen's brief comment to the troubled brother appears to be sprinkled with biblical reminiscences, rather than quotations as such. These reminiscences enable Poemen to convey to the brother the sense that one weeps, not from fear or despair, but as an expression of one's utter dependence upon God and in the firm hope that God's mercy will soon be made manifest.

Poemen confirms the connection between *penthos* and dependence upon God's mercy in two different comments on the episode in the Gospels concerning Jesus and the Canaanite woman (Mt 15; Mk 7). His use of this particular episode to comment on the meaning of *penthos* reveals both the attitude of humility which he understood must precede genuine *penthos* and the deep peace which flows from it. In one saying, Poemen tells the brothers that one of the reasons they have had so many "difficult labors" is that "we do not *see* the woman of Canaan who followed the Savior crying [κράζουσα] and begging for her daughter to be cured. The Savior heard her and gave her peace [ὁ Σωτὴρ . . . ἀνέπαυεν]."[25] Elsewhere, Poemen again alludes to the woman from Canaan, this time as a means of commenting on why monks find themselves caught up "in such great temptations." Poemen asks them, "Do we not *see* the Canaanite woman, who has accepted the name which she was given? Because of this the Savior gave her peace [ἀνέπαυσεν αὐτὴν ὁ Σωτήρ]."[26] Taken together, the two sayings show Poemen using Scripture to address genuine problems raised by the monks—in this case "difficult labors" and "great temptations." In particular, he draws upon a memorable and poignant story from the New Testament to show his listeners the way they must travel if they are to find peace.

It is significant that Poemen begins both comments by simply asking those listening to him why they do not "see" the woman of Canaan. He implies that they knew the story well, but had neglected to look there for help. He also indicates in this way that he wants them to pay attention to the example of this woman; that if they do, they may begin to understand something of the spirit of *penthos*. In the first saying, Poemen emphasizes, in language dependent upon Mt 15:22, how the woman "cried [ἔκραξεν]" to Jesus for help. Part of what gives this brief allusion to the woman's exclamation its poignancy and power comes from what is left unsaid. Although Poemen does not elaborate on her words and actions in the remainder of this Gospel story, anyone hearing him retell the story would have recalled the woman's desperate cry to Jesus concerning her demon-possessed daughter: "Have mercy on me, O Lord, Son of David." Her cry, as Poemen wants to underline in telling the story, is a plea for mercy. The second saying of Poemen's emphasizes that the woman "accepted the name which she was given." Again, it is a comment from the Gospel story not explicitly mentioned by Poemen which provides the clue to the meaning of this curious comment. In the Gospel story, the woman continued to plead with Jesus for help, but he dismissed her plea, saying, "It is not fair to take the children's bread and throw it to the dogs [κυναρίοις]" (v. 26). The "name" Jesus gave to the woman was "dog." In a response which clearly surprised and astonished Jesus, she accepted this name: "Yes, Lord, but even the dogs . . . [ναί, κύριε. καὶ γὰρ τὰ κυνάρια]" (v. 27). The woman's response was an expression of deep humility and—as Jesus himself acknowledged—"great faith." Poemen's use of these biblical stories had a practical and particular aim. He wanted to show those who were suffering from "labors" and "temptations" the kind of outlook which they needed to cultivate to become free from these torments. In the weeping Canaanite woman, a picture emerges of one who is utterly dependent upon God's mercy for help in her distress and who expresses a deep level of humility and an audacious faith in seeking that help. These qualities led Poemen to add a comment of his own to the story regarding the effects of the practice of *penthos*, expressing in his own language what he no doubt knew from experience. He contended that if the monks gave themselves over to *penthos* as intensely as the Canaanite woman gave herself to seeking a cure for her daughter, they would experience, just as she did, "a deep peace."

Weeping was an expression of a deep change of heart necessary for seeking salvation. Once when a brother came to Poeman asking, "What should I do?" he told him the story of Abraham's purchase of his tomb: "When Abraham entered the promised land, he bought a sepulchre for himself [Gn 23] and by means of this tomb, he inherited the land." The brother's interest was piqued by this response, and he asked Poemen, "What is the tomb?" Poemen explained that "the tomb is the place of tears and compunction."²⁷

Poemen shows, as Lemaire suggests, "a refined pedagogical sense" in his use of this particular text about Abraham to make his point about compunction and salvation. The context for Poemen's moral lesson connecting Abraham's purchase of the tomb with "weeping and compunction [κλαυθμοῦ καὶ πένθους]" is provided by the story of the death of Sara and the mourning and tears of Abraham (LXX Gn 23:2: πενθῆσαι) that introduces the episode of the purchase of the tomb in Genesis 23. Poemen draws on the mention of tears in the Genesis story to engage in a piece of ambitious and inventive interpretation: he blends an allegorical interpretation of Abraham's action of purchasing the tomb—seen as symbolizing weeping and compunction—with a more subtle interpretation based on the significance of Abraham's action in the history of salvation. He begins by noting that it was through Abraham's act of faith in purchasing the tomb that he came to "inherit the land." Poemen then makes a connection between tears and inheritance, using the example of Abraham to suggest to the brother who had come to ask him for a word, that tears and compunction are vitally important to salvation. If the brother will imitate Abraham and "purchase the tomb" ('the place of tears and compunction') he too can "inherit the land."²⁸

Another story of Abba Poemen shows how much he admired and sought to imitate Mary for the tears she wept at the foot of the cross. Once, Abba Isaac came upon Poemen while he was caught up "in ecstasy." He was so struck by what he saw, that he threw himself before Poemen, and begged him, "Tell me where you were." Poemen said, "My thought was there, where holy Mary, the Mother of God stood and wept near the cross of the Savior [Jn 19:25]." Poemen acknowledged that it was the example of her tears which stood out for him above all else: "I wish I could always weep like that [καὶ ἐγὼ ἤθελον πάντοτε οὕτως κλαίειν]."²⁹ This episode reveals again the intimacy and familiarity which the monks sometimes experienced with their predecessors in the faith. Poemen's language suggests that he was taken out of himself in a powerful experience of ecstasy and found himself standing with Mary at the foot of the cross. Such an account illustrates how the monks' experience of the biblical exemplars, while strongly influenced by their reading or hearing of the texts, was also affected to some extent by the piety of the desert. While Poemen clearly had in mind the scene from the Gospel where Mary is at the foot of the cross he also added something to the picture from his own personal piety. The verb "to weep" [κλαίειν] is not found applied to Mary in any Gospel, whether canonical or apocryphal.[30] The trait of tears, which Poemen so admired in Mary, was probably attributed to her at least in part by Poemen's own piety—the sense of intimacy he had cultivated with this woman through years spent in her company. His reflection on the biblical story and his use of the example of Mary as one who was full of *penthos* was to some extent the fruit of his own contemplation.[31]

Another, very brief saying by Abba Poemen, brings us full circle in our reflections on the meaning and effects of *penthos*. Just as the cultivation of *penthos* was associated with an awareness of the nearness of the end time, so it was thought to help bring about a return to paradise. Poemen said that *penthos* does two things: "it works and it guards [ἐργάζεται καὶ φυλάσσει]."[32] This saying, through an allusion to a text from Genesis, reveals the practical effects of *penthos* and the world into which one was called to dwell through its practice. The phrase is borrowed from Gn 2:15, which describes how, in the time before woman was created, man was given the garden to "work it and guard over it [ἐργάζεσθαι αὐτὸν καὶ φυλάσσειν]." *Penthos*, in this sense, recalls human beings to the conditions of life which Scripture attributes to the inhabitants of paradise—what Hausherr calls the "recovery of divine familiarity." There is a profound intuition of the value of *penthos* in this reference to the state of innocence preceding the first sin, implying that through the cultivation of *penthos*, the ancient order of paradise can be restored to the present moment. *Penthos*, as this recollection of the text from Genesis suggests, implies both an ongoing awareness of the grace of redemption and a responsibility to cultivate and care for it. A saying from Evagrius's treatise *On Prayer* provides a hint for solving the riddle of these two words "work and keep": "What you have been destined for from the beginning is to work and to keep." In other words, as Hausherr notes: "In this new paradise, we find once again, closeness to God."[33]

What did this mean in practice? And what did *penthos* look like? We can catch a glimpse of the fulfillment of the biblical call to weep and realize intimacy with God in two stories of conversion contained in the *Sayings*. One of the ways Scripture was fulfilled in the desert was through effecting conversion, by bursting forth in a "word event" of great power and transforming the life of the one who heard the text. There is a real drama to such stories, for they raise the question of what it means to enter into conversation with the world of the sacred texts and to take the risk of believing that what they say might be true. We see that to open oneself to the message of the sacred texts means to allow one's inner depths to be pierced, to allow oneself to be transformed into a new being.

A saying of Abba Paul the Simple shows how powerful an experience repentance and conversion could be for a person who had lost his way, and how the Word could help to bring about that repentance. The story begins with the acknowledgement that Abba Paul possessed a special gift: "[H]e had received the grace from the Lord of seeing the state of each one's soul just as we see their faces." One day, while observing the brothers in the church during the *synaxis,* Paul noticed that one of the brothers was dark inside and was being dominated by demons. At this sight, Abba Paul "beat his breast and sat down in front of the church, weeping bitterly . . . [with] tears and compunction." After the *synaxis,* as everyone was coming out of the church, he saw that the man, who had been previously dark and gloomy, now had a shining face and a radiant body. At this dramatic turn of events, Paul leapt for joy, began to cry out and bless God, citing a number of biblical texts, and then beseeched the brother to tell him what had happened to him. Before all the others, the brother said:

> I am a sinful man; I have lived in fornication for a long time, right up to the present moment; when I went into the holy church of God, I heard the holy prophet Isaiah being read, or rather God speaking through him: "Wash you, make you clean, take away the evil from your hearts, learn to do good before my eyes. Even though your sins are like scarlet I will make them white like snow" (Is 1:16–18). And I . . . the fornicator, am filled with compunction in my heart because of the word of the prophet and I groan within myself, saying to God, "God, who came into the world to save sinners, that which you now proclaim by the mouth of Your prophet, fulfill in me who am a sinner and an unworthy man. . . . Master, from this time forward, receive me, as I repent and throw myself at your feet. . . ." [34]

The story illustrates several important aspects of the power of Scripture to effect conversion and be fulfilled in a new life. In the first place the brother indicates that what happened to him in the church was not simply that he heard the prophet Isaiah being read but that he heard "God speaking through him." The living power of the word is acknowledged here in the strongest possible terms. Secondly, the effect of the word: "filled [him] with compunction in his heart." The experience of compunction, of being pierced to the depths of one's being, was seen as being a direct effect of the Word of God. Finally, although the man had already begun to realize within himself the renewal of which the text from Isaiah speaks, he asked God to fulfill the text in him, to bring to completion the good work that had been set in motion by the sacred text.

The effect of *penthos* and the power of the sacred texts to effect transformation can also be seen in a story told about Abba Serapion and a prostitute. In the story, we hear that Serapion encountered a "courtesan" as he was passing through a village and told the woman, "[E]xpect me this evening for I should like to come and spend the night with you." The courtesan, not wanting to bypass an opportunity, agreed to meet him and returned to her dwelling to prepare the bed. Upon arriving, Serapion asked her if the bed was ready, and being told that everything had been prepared, said to her that he must first fulfill his "rule of prayer." He then "took out the Psalter, and at each psalm he said a prayer for the prostitute, begging God that she might be converted and saved, and God heard him. The woman stood trembling and praying beside the old man. When he had completed the whole Psalter, the woman fell to the ground. Then the old man, beginning the Epistle, read a great deal from the apostle and completed his prayers. The woman was filled with compunction. . . ."[35] The power of the sacred texts to bring about conversion is clear from this story. Serapion makes no attempt to say any words of his own to the woman. Rather, he recited the Psalter and the Epistles and let them do their own work. He "helped the word event to happen," which in this case meant enabling the words to pierce the woman's heart and initiate the process of transformation.

Asceticism and the Struggle against Evil

To cultivate the intimacy with God initiated by *penthos,* the monks had to face on a daily basis that most perplexing of challenges: rooting out the sources of evil within themselves. An ability to discern the different ways in which demons, thoughts or passions attacked them was one of the most crucial necessities for those living in the desert. Many of the desert fathers' stories present us with what appears a crude and naive depiction of demons, swarming through the skies above the desert, or tempting and testing the monks in endless guises in every possible circumstance. Yet their tendency to personify evil in this way should not lead one to think that the monks were unaware of the more subtle realities to which these personifications pointed. They were part of a culture which took the demonic world—everything that is intermediate between God and mortal—seriously: "Virtually every one, pagan, Jewish, Christian, or Gnostic, believed in the existence of these beings and in their function as mediators, whether he called them daemons or angels or aions or simply 'spirits' (pneumata). . . . And the 'daemonic man,' who knew how to establish contact with them, was corre-spondingly esteemed.''[36] The monks took their own role as "daemonic men" seriously and gained esteem through their capacity to exorcise the demons from themselves and others. The often graphic and cartoonlike imagery of these demons in the *Saying* belies the clear sense among the monks that the real drama of the demonic was psychological. The demonic "was sensed as an extension of the self. A relationship with the demons involved something more intimate than attack from the outside: to 'be tried by demons' meant passing through a stage in the growth of awareness of the lower frontiers of the personality. The demonic stood not merely for all that was hostile *to* man; the demons summed up all that was anomalous and incomplete *in* man.''[37] The monks showed themselves to be fully aware that the source of their most trenchant and problematic impulses and actions arose from within themselves. As Syncletica noted, "They attack us from outside, and they also stir us up from within.''[38] Poemen put this in even starker terms, say-ing, "Our own wills become demons.''[39] To a brother who asked about the passions, Sisoes recalled the words of James, " 'Each person is tempted when he is lured and enticed by his own desire (Jas 1:14).' ''[40] The ascet-ical life, then, sought to free the monk from the domination by the demons that beset him. This helps to explain the urgency with which questions about demons, thoughts, and passions were put to the elders; it was only by root-ing out the sources of these impulses that the monk could become free to love. Questions about the meaning and purpose of this struggle against evil and of the different ascetical practices which were meant to aid battling the demons thus comprised an important part of the dialogue between master and disciple. To address these concerns regarding the appropriate use of fasting and vigils and the complex psychological issues associated with the struggle with thoughts and passions, the elders found Scripture an invaluable source of illumination and insight. It provided guidance, understanding, and wisdom as well as strength and protection in the midst of this struggle.

Asceticism

Physical asceticism was one of the means by which the monks sought to gain freedom from the domination of the demons. By asceticism, however, one is not necessarily talking about the most excessive displays of rigor for which the desert fathers are often known. Attitudes toward physical asceti-cism among the desert monks were more complex than often appears from a cursory glance at the literature.[41] Notwithstanding occasional instances of extreme behavior, which reveal a desire to reduce the body to submission in the most brutal fashion, the general tone of the *Sayings* on the subject of asceticism is moderate. The monks were aware of the complex relationship between the body and the mind and knew better than to attribute the source of all their problems to their bodies. Yet they also knew that they were limited by their physical bodies and that ignoring those limitations would only lead to disaster. They sought therefore to dominate their bodies, that is, not to submit to all physical urges if they violated the monk's desires and goals. At the same time, they knew enough to care for the body, to treat it as the fragile vessel that it was. In their quest to find a balance in the practice of asceticism, and to help them keep a close watch on their attitudes toward such practical matters as eating, sleeping, and sexuality, the monks drew upon the guidance of Scripture. In these reflections, Scripture served sometimes as a foil to help the monks overcome the most obvious forms of self-deception, sometimes as a mirror in which they could examine their motives and actions clearly, and other times as a guide to be followed with care.

Asceticism was a way of guarding against one's own worst impulses and tendencies. In their prolonged struggle against the various demons and temptations that beset them, the desert fathers looked to the experiences of certain biblical predecessors who had endured temptations of their own. Adam, who was revered by the monks as the original patriarch,[42] and as the representative of the time of paradise before the fall, was also remembered as the first one to be deceived by the devil. Abba Isidore held Adam up as a warning to those in the desert who were beset by temptations, that they should *not* do as Adam did and give in to them.[43] Clearly such counsel was not easy to adopt, and other exemplars were seen as providing positive models for how the monks should behave in the midst of their struggles. The patriarch Abraham, honored by the monks as the "father of the Jews,"[44] was seen as exemplifying the kind of commitment required to endure the trials of monastic asceticism. In one instance, some brothers urged one of the elders to lessen his ascetic efforts. But the elder demurred, citing the example of Abraham: "I tell you, my children, that Abraham, when he saw the great gifts of God, had to repent for not having striven beforehand."[45] This saying is significant for it reveals that asceticism was more than a matter of naked effort on the part of the monk. It was, like Abraham's response to the covenant, a heartfelt act of thanksgiving for the touch of grace. The monks were capable of resorting to ingenious interpretations to connect their own struggles with those of their biblical predecessors. We see an example of this in Poemen's reference to David as a champion of the ascetical struggle. In this particular case Poemen takes the interpretation in a distinctly allegorical direction, recalling the time "when [David] was fighting with the lion, seized it by the throat, and killed it immediately [1 Sm 17:35]."

Poemen goes on to compare this struggle to the battle the monks face, and the means they must be prepared to use if they hope to triumph: "If we take ourselves by the throat, and by the belly, with the help of God, we shall overcome the invisible lion." [46] David was presented as "the fighter." Even though the monks faced a very different kind of fight, they could still look to David as one who showed courage in the face of adversity.

The ascetical exercises carried out by the monks could be difficult and questions sometimes arose about the proper limits of such exercises. In one instance Abba Abraham questioned Abba Ares about a task which he had ordered a brother to carry out, wondering whether it was not too "heavy [of a] burden [φορτία βαρέα]" for the young man. This is the same expression Jesus used in the Gospel to condemn the practice of the pharisees (Mt 23:4), and Abba Abraham expressed similar doubts about the usefulness of such heavy ascetical burdens. Unlike the situation which called forth Jesus' condemnation in the Gospel, however, Abba Ares noted that he had carefully weighed this burden, which was designed to meet the needs of the particular brother. Not only was Abba Ares careful not to give the brother anything heavier than he could carry; he was attentive to provide the brother with precisely the stimulus he needed to penetrate more deeply within himself. [47] On another occasion, Abba Joseph asked Abba Poemen how he should fast. Poemen responded that it was better to eat a little every day than to extend a fast inordinately. But Joseph pressed him on this, for he knew that in his younger days Poemen had fasted for long periods of time. Poemen admitted that he had done this at one time, but that he had changed his practice in favor of the general consensus established by the elders: "The fathers tried all this out as they were able and found it preferable to eat every day, but just a small amount. They have left us this 'Royal Way' [βασιλιχὴν ὁδὸν] [Nm 20:17] which is light." [48] Poemen's use of this biblical expression, "Royal Way," to describe a moderate approach to fasting illustrates how a certain monastic practice could sometimes be "explained" in light of a prominent biblical figure or idea. It also indicates the recurring tendency to transpose diverse biblical themes to the psychological or ascetical realm. However, the use of the expression Royal Way to describe the way of moderation in fasting is not altogether arbitrary. The Royal Way in the Old Testament refers to the route by which Moses sought to lead the Hebrews through Edom and Moab. It was the major international route that transversed the entire length of the Transjordan plateau, and was used by all kinds of travelers. The Royal Way of asceticism, which was developed through long experience in the desert, had a similarly wide appeal. It was moderate enough to be used, not simply by an elite band of ascetical warriors, but by the entire range of people who took up life in the desert.

Poemen's moderate approach to asceticism did not mean that he underestimated its importance. He clearly believed that the detachment wrought
by asceticism could help to curb certain abuses of freedom. Citing a simple
moral injunction from Ps 118:37: "Turn away your eyes lest they behold
vanity," Poemen commented, "Freedom destroys souls [ἐλευθερία ψυχὰς
ἀναιρεῖ]."[49] Poemen's critique of freedom reflects an insightful psychological interpretation of the concrete language of the psalm. In the psalm, the
"eyes" suggest all sensible and imaginative knowledge and even the seat of
knowledge, the heart. Poemen takes the word "eyes" in this rich sense to
urge his listeners to refrain from the kind of indiscriminate lusting after
knowledge which poses as freedom and which can destroy the soul. He
invites them instead to discipline the eyes of the body and to be discriminating about what they take into their inner world.[50] Abba Cronius elsewhere interpreted Scripture allegorically in order to emphasize the importance of asceticism in the life of the monk. He said, "If Moses had not led
his sheep to Mount Sinai, he would not have seen the fire in the bush [Ex
3:1–17]." When a brother asked him what the burning bush symbolized,
Cronius told him "the bush signifies bodily action"—or asceticism. He amplified the meaning of this by citing a text from the Gospel of Matthew
(13:44): "The kingdom of heaven is like a treasure hid in a field." This
prompted another question from the brother: "So a person does not advance
toward any reward without bodily affliction?" Cronius responded with two
more biblical texts to affirm the truth of this: "Truly it is written, 'Looking
to Jesus, the pioneer of and perfecter of our faith who for the joy which was
set before him, endured the cross (Heb 12:2).' David also said, 'I will not
give sleep to mine eyes nor slumber to my eyelids, until I find a place for
the Lord (Ps 132:4).' "[51] There is something fairly arbitrary in Cronius's
allegorical interpretation of this Old Testament passage, especially considering that he is referring to a matter of great significance in the spiritual life
in the desert. The arbitrariness of the correspondence between "the bush"
and "bodily affliction" says something about how presuppositions influenced interpretation in this approach. The issue in question is clear: asceticism occupied a central part of the desert life. Cronius chose the original
text from Exodus as a result of this assumption and his interpretation of the
text follows naturally from it. There is very little in the text from Exodus to
support his claim that Moses' journey to the bush represented "bodily action" or asceticism. The additional texts cited actually come closer to sup-
porting the claim being made about the need for asceticism, and they are
used to broaden and deepen the interpretation of the first text. In spite of the
arbitrary character of the allegory, there is something carefully considered
in Cronius's approach to interpretation in this saying. It has to do with what

he sees as the aim of the monastic life: finding God. Moses, David, and Jesus are all portrayed as having been steadfast and courageous in their faith. All of them had come to know the presence of God. The image of the fire in the bush becomes a lively image of the possibility of this presence in the life of the monk.

A saying of Abba Poemen also combines allegorical and exemplary interpretation to emphasize the importance of asceticism in pursuit of the monks' deepest goals. And again, we see the effect of the monks' interests on the interpretation of Scripture. The saying begins by stating clearly the central point that Poemen wishes to make: "Poverty, hardship, austerity and fasting, such are the instruments of the solitary life." This *truth* is then confirmed by a citation from Scripture, which has been reworked to fit the context: "It is written, 'When these three men are together, Noah, Job, and Daniel, there am I, says the Lord.'(Ez 14:14)." Poemen then makes the correspondence clear: "Noah represents poverty, Job suffering, and Daniel discernment. So if these three works are found in a man, the Lord dwells in him."[52] In this saying, Poemen attempts to show that the four principal points of monastic asceticism are represented by three figures of the Old Testament. He cites Ez 14:14 (following the LXX which has read Daniel for Danel, a legendary figure less well known than the prophet Daniel), but only briefly, as an allusion. This in itself is significant, for Poemen simply assumes that the context of his allusion is well known to his hearers, an indirect indication of the extent of their biblical culture. Poemen modifies the order of the appearance of the biblical figures, so that Noah who represents poverty is now followed by Job who represents suffering, reflecting no doubt the experience of the monks themselves, for whom material poverty often represented a real source of suffering. The correspondence of the text in Ezekiel with the list of principles Poemen cites at the beginning of the saying is less than exact, as is the correspondence between the original setting of the text and the meaning Poemen construes from it. Of the four virtues mentioned at the beginning, two appear in the interpretation of the biblical passage, and a fifth, discernment, is added to the list as that virtue exemplified by Daniel. Similarly, the original setting of the passage has to do with the power of these saints as intercessors. But Poemen's interpretation reveals that for him the most important aspect of the text was the heroic practice of virtue of these saints, which made such prayer possible. The saying as a whole and the allegorical interpretation in particular serve to illustrate how the desert fathers conceived of the monastic life and how important Scripture was as a formative influence in that life. The practical works of asceticism are shown to be important, but only as a means to an end. Furthermore, these practices are seen, not as inventions of the desert

monks or a departure from the way of Scripture, but as derived from the
practice of the great biblical exemplars.

Enduring Temptation

The reality of temptation and of the struggle against evil leaps from nearly
every page of the *Sayings*. If asceticism helped to clear the ground, resistance to the demons was necessary for "uprooting" the most tenacious passions and thoughts from within. Although on one level, the monks certainly
did not welcome the struggle, they recognized that such testing was a necessary part of the process of purification which would enable them to participate in the kingdom of God.

In this conviction, they felt themselves to be recapitulating the experience
of Jesus in the New Testament. As one would expect, the example of Jesus'
fasting and enduring temptation in the desert was of special importance to
the desert fathers. There are numerous references in the *Sayings* to the idea
of monks spending forty days in the wilderness. The way the monks thought
about the desert and about spending time in solitude owed a great deal,
either explicitly or implicitly, to the example of Jesus. It was said of Abba
Sarmatus for instance, that, on Abba Poemen's advice, he was "often alone
for forty days."[53] Abba James once spent forty days alone in the wilderness
trying to discern the meaning of a particularly difficult doctrinal idea; on
another occasion passing forty days in the wilderness helped him to overcome a fierce and persistent demon.[54] We hear elsewhere of one who was
afflicted with "battles" with the demons, and who didn't know how he
could overcome them. An elder told him: "Take forty measures of bread
and palm leaves for forty days' work with you, and go to the interior desert,
and stay there for forty days; and may the Lord's will be done."[55] The
desert fathers were not explicit about their reasons for spending this specific
amount of time in solitude. However, the recurring mention of spending
forty days alone in the wilderness is a reminder of the symbolic importance
of Jesus' example. In fleeing into solitude and doing battle with the demons
there, they were imitating the one who had gone before them and van-
quished the evil powers in the desert.

The monks also drew upon other biblical images to help them understand
and endure their trials. Amma Theodora, for instance, used allusions from
Scripture to characterize the harshness of the age in which she and the monks
were living and to suggest the qualities needed to endure it. "Just as the
trees, if they have not stood before the winter's storms cannot bear fruit, so
it is with us; this present age is a storm and without many trials and temptations we cannot obtain an inheritance in the kingdom of heaven [Acts

14:22; Jas 2:5].''[56] Theodora apparently conflates phrases from Acts and James to drive home her message that entering the kingdom in such a stormy age will require one to either skillfully negotiate or simply endure the buffeting winds of trials and temptations. Temptations were valued in the desert not simply for their own sake but because they comprised a testing fire through which one gained *experience.* Poemen commented, in language echoing the letter of James: "Experience is a good thing; it is that which teaches a person to be tested [Jas 1:12].''[57] This experience [πεῖρα] of which Poemen speaks—linguistically related to temptation [πειρασμός]— was valued because it gave one the practical knowledge necessary for ''discernment of spirits.'' And such discernment had important implications for the monk—in his solitude and in his relations with others. The ability to distinguish between different spirits was quite simply a matter of survival for the monk living in the lonely solitude of the desert. Because he often went for days, weeks, or even months without anyone to advise him, it was essential that he learned to evaluate the shifting winds of the spirits. Possessing genuine experience in such matters could also have an effect on one's relations to others; it could mean the difference between helping and harming another person. We hear of one anchorite, esteemed and admired by many, but who was ''without experience [ἄρειρος] of the great astuteness of the demon who was setting snares for him.'' As a result, he caused himself and others great harm.[58]

One of the most basic strategies for resisting the demons was to rebuke them, not allowing them any stature or authority. Examples from Scripture taught the monks this and reminded them of their authority over demons. And, as we noted earlier, the words of Scripture themselves were thought to be particularly effective in issuing rebukes. In one saying, we hear that some demons asked one of the old men, ''Do you want to see Christ?'' The old man answered them sharply, citing a passage from the Gospels: ''A curse on you and on whatever you say! In truth, I believe in my Christ who has said, 'If someone says to you, here is Christ, or there he is, do not believe him [Mk 13:21].' And immediately, they vanished.''[59] To a monk who was constantly plagued by a particular sin, Poemen suggested that he use a phrase from the Psalms to deflect the poison of Satan's arrow: ''[E]very time this thought comes to you say, 'It is no affair of mine, may your blasphemy remain upon you Satan [Ps 7:17], for my soul does not want it.' ''[60]

The desert fathers were convinced that the words of Scripture possessed the power to deliver them from evil, and during moments of intense temptation they acted upon this conviction. In one instance, a certain monk who was troubled by sexual temptations asked Abba Amoun what he should do when he had to go out on errands and was exposed to this temptation. The old man answered, with language echoing Scripture, "Whatever the hour when the temptation comes upon you, say, 'God of all virtue [Ps 58:6], by the prayers of my father [Ex 15:2], save me from it.' " One day, when a young woman entered his cell and closed the door behind her, he found himself weakening, and "he began to cry out with all his might [Mt 27:46], 'God of my father, save me,' and immediately he found himself on the road to Scetis." [61] The pedagogical point of the story, in spite of the implausibility of the monk's manner of escape, would have been clear to those facing similar temptations: the Word of God has the power to effect what it says, and to deliver those who speak this language in beseeching God for help. Sometimes the intensity of the struggle was such that one would be hard pressed to utter any words at all. Abba Moses recognized that although there were times when one might be reduced to throwing oneself before the mercy of God without any words, even here Scripture provided a model for the monks to emulate. Someone asked him, "What should a person do in all the temptations that come upon him and in every thought of the enemy [λογισμῷ τοῦ ἐχθροῦ]?" Moses responded, "He should weep before the goodness of God in order that God might come to help him. He will have peace immediately if he prays with knowledge [ἀναπαύεται ταχέως, ἐὰν παρακαλῇ ἐν γνώσει]. For it is written, 'With the Lord on my side I do not fear. What can man do to me' (Ps 118:6)?" [62] It is interesting that Moses does not advise his questioner to recite the text from the Psalms when he feels himself being overwhelmed by temptation. Rather, he uses the text as a reminder of the power of God and as a means of encouraging the monk to have confidence to cry out to God in a moment of crisis. This story suggests that the work of resisting attacks of the demons had less to do with a strenuous ascetical effort or even with recitation of particular texts from Scripture than with a total release into the arms of God. [63]

The innumerable ways in which demons worked to overwhelm those who had taken up life in the desert led the elders to scour Scripture for help, seeking not only words of power but also words of encouragement. Amma Syncletica suggested a whole catalogue of biblical texts to be used in time of trial. To those who are severely tried, she says:

> Rejoice that God visits you and keep this sweet-sounding word on your lips, "The Lord has chastened me sorely but he has not given me over unto death" (Ps 117:18) . . . Have you been given a thorn in the flesh [2 Cor 12:7]? Exult, and see who else was treated like that: it is an honor to have the same sufferings as Paul. Are you being tried by fever? Are you being taught by cold? Indeed Scripture says, "We went through fire and water; yet you have brought us forth to a spacious place" (Ps 65:12). . . . By this share of

wretchedness you will be made perfect. For he said: "The Lord hears when I call him" (Ps 4:3). It is with these exercises that we train our soul, seeing that we are under the eyes of our enemy.[64]

Syncletica's words remind us again that these exercises were an oral phenomenon, that much of their value came from keeping these "sweet-sounding words" on the lips. Her choice of texts also suggests that an awareness of the *content* of the biblical passages recited was as important to the work of resisting the demons as a consciousness of their inherent power. Here, the scriptural passages recited served to remind the one who was beset by attacks that others who had gone before had also endured, and that God was not removed from the struggle.

The eucharist was a source of deep solace to the monks in the midst of their struggles, and Abba Poemen reminded his listeners of this with a colorful interpretation of one of the Psalms. Poemen cites Ps 42:1, "As the hart longs for flowing streams, so my soul longs for You, my God," and engages in an explicitly allegorical interpretation of the text. He first illuminates the text by drawing on an animal legend concerning harts in the desert who devour venomous reptiles and then must drink from the springs to assuage the venom's burning. He then suggests that the monks are like those harts in that they "are burned by the venom of evil demons, and they long for Saturday and Sunday to come to be able to go to the springs of water, that is to say, the body and blood of the Lord, so as to be purified from the bitterness of the evil one."[65] This saying shows the blending of allegory and typology. In a sense, the spring of the Psalms is a type of the true spring to come in Christ, and a type of the eucharist; there is a historical progression. At the same time, the action of the hart drinking at the spring is made to *stand for* the spiritual struggle of the monks against the demons. A further point of interest in this passage is the explicitly christological reading of the Psalm. The naturalness of Poemen's interpretation indicates how readily this christological hermeneutical principle, which was so important in patristic exegesis, was accepted in the desert.

Simply *enduring* long stretches of temptation and struggle was a profound challenge for many in the desert. Certain biblical figures were seen as providing evidence that it was indeed possible to persevere through such difficulties. A young brother complained to Abba Poemen that his heart tended to waver and become lukewarm whenever a little suffering came his way. Poemen responded by citing the example of endurance provided by two biblical heroes: "Do we not admire Joseph, a young man of seventeen, for enduring temptation to the end? And God glorified him. Do we not also see Job, how he suffered to the end, and lived in endurance?" These two figures are clearly part of Poemen's own experience. It is their proximity to his own life and his sense of the reality of their triumph over adversity which enables him to declare to the brother with confidence and authority: "Temptations cannot destroy hope in God."[66] Abba Orsisius also refers to the example of Joseph's endurance, although for him, Joseph is seen as a model for those who would hold positions of leadership in the monastic community. He notes a specific quality in Joseph's outlook which helped to produce his endurance and which should be imitated by the monks: fear of God. Using an image which would have been familiar to those living in the desert, Orsisius said: "If an unbaked brick is put in the foundation near to the river, it does not last for a single day, but baked it lasts like stone. So the man with the carnal disposition of soul who has not been in the fire through fear of God like Joseph [Gn 39:7ff; Ps 104:19] utterly disintegrates when he accepts a position of authority."[67] Looking toward the example of Joseph, Orsisius implied, could help the monk to accept the testing fire as a necessary part of his growth.

Sometimes more than endurance was necessary for overcoming the demons. The monk had to cultivate a discerning eye, to know how to respond to the shifting winds of the inner world. Abba Poemen recognized that the most devastating kind of self-delusion could be avoided if one learned to keep from giving way to certain thoughts. On the question of impure thoughts, Abba Poemen cited Is 10:15, "Is the axe any use without someone to cut with it?" He commented on this text: "If you do not make use of these thoughts, they will be ineffectual too."[68] The quotation from Isaiah is rendered fairly loosely and is given a different sense from the original context. In Isaiah, it marked a contrast between human beings and God. Poemen uses it to suggest that if one is wise enough not to give certain thoughts a foothold, they will not be able to do any damage. The text is quoted for a very practical purpose: to show those who are plagued by thoughts how to begin the process of turning back the tide.

Another story dealing with discernment tells of a brother who asked Cronius what to do about his problem with forgetfulness. "What should I do to correct the forgetfulness which captures my spirit, and prevents me from perceiving anything until I am led into sin?"[69] Cronius responded by recounting the story in which the Philistines captured the ark of the covenant and drew it to the temple of Dagon their god, who then fell to the ground dead (1 Sm 5:1–5). What this *means,* he said, is that "if the demons attempt to capture a person's spirit through his own impetus, they draw him in this manner until they lead him to an invisible passion. But if, at that point, the spirit returns, seeks after God and remembers the eternal judgment, immediately the passion falls away and disappears. It is written, 'In returning and rest you shall be saved' (Is 30;15).''

This is clearly an allegorical interpretation of an Old Testament text, in that the meaning of the text is said to be found in the spiritual drama of salvation being worked out in the soul of the one who posed the question. At the same time the story is meant to act as a model of how not to respond to a particular form of temptation. Although it would seem at first sight that the relationship between the question posed and the answer given from Scripture is remote and arbitrary, there are several hints in the text which reveal the kind of logic at work here. It is likely that a word in the brother's original question—the one rendered as "captured"—helped to link the question with the text from Samuel. The questioner asked about the problem of forgetfulness (λήθη) which "captures [αἰχμαλωτιζούσῃ]" his spirit. Apparently this recalled to Cronius's mind the episode in 1 Samuel in which the ark of the covenant was captured by the Philistines. Having settled on the passage in this almost arbitrary way, Cronius proceeded to draw further and more significant parallels. He pointed out that just as the questioner was seeking to understand how he was led (ἐνέγκῃ) into sin, so the text of Samuel considers how the ark was led (ἤνεγκαν) into the house of Dagon. Similarly, as the Philistines drew (ἔσυρον) the ark into their temple, so the demons attempted to draw (ὑποσύρωσιν) a person and "lead" (ἐνέγκωσιν) him to "invisible passions." Finally, as a way of bringing the discussion full circle, Cronius suggested a solution to the problem of forgetting, which was at its root a matter of forgetting the meaning of salvation. Since part of the cause of such forgetfulness was being too passive and allowing oneself to be led into sin, Cronius suggested that the brother should turn, seek after God, and remember the eternal judgment. Like the power of the ark of the covenant which overcame Dagon, so also through this act of turning and remembering, "immediately the passion falls away and disappears." Cronius concludes by quoting Isaiah: "In returning and rest, you shall be saved (Is 30:15)." This final quotation of Isaiah acts as a kind of interpretive key, helping to shed light on both the original question and on the text from 1 Samuel. It is by returning that one is able to keep from being led away by the invisible passions; and in returning, one finds salvation.

Vigilance

An important part of the ascetical practice in the desert was vigilance, or watchfulness. The monks kept vigil not only by remaining awake deep into the night reciting their *synaxis,* but also strove to cultivate a continual interior vigilance. Abba Poemen emphasized to the desert monks the importance of vigilance as well as the accompanying gifts, saying, "[V]igilance, self-knowledge, and discernment . . . are the guides of the soul."[70] By keeping watch the monks hoped to protect themselves from the assaults of the evil one and to develop a heightened sensitivity to the presence of God. The use of "vigilance [νῆψις]" as a moral term occurs frequently in the *Sayings* and follows a similar usage of the term in the New Testament.[71] Vigilance is associated with the verb "to watch [γρηγορεῖν]" in 1 Thes 5:6 ("let us watch and be sober"—γρηγορῶμεν καὶ νήψωμεν) and 1 Pt 5:8 ("Be sober, be watchful"—νήψατε, γρηγορήσατε). In these New Testament passages, the word is connected closely with its root meaning, "to be sober." This moral connotation can be seen in a saying of Abba Poemen concerning purity. When he was asked about impurities, he replied, "If we pay careful attention to our practice and are very watchful [νήψωμεν], we shall not find impurities within ourselves."[72]

The need for vigilance was often expressed in terms of the exhortation to "watch yourself [πρόσεχε σεαυτῷ]." This phrase may have derived partly from biblical use (Gn 24:6; Ex 23:21), but it also had a long history of usage in ancient philosophy and the church.[73] In the desert the expression referred in general terms to the need to be attentive to all the inner motivations and desires which drive a person. Sometimes it was the only thing that needed to be said. Once, when a brother came seeking a word from him, Abba Ammoes remained silent for seven days. Finally he sent the brother away, saying simply, "Go, watch yourself."[74] Nor was this "watching of oneself" understood as a purely interior activity; it extended to the practical sphere as well. To a brother caught with a woman in his cell, Abba Ammonas, after forgiving him, warned him of the danger of his situation, saying: "[W]atch yourself, brother!"[75] In other words, watch what you do.

Vigilance meant learning to be mindful of God's presence. Sometimes this learning process led to some unlikely readings of Scripture. For Abba John Colobos, "[w]atching [φυλακή] means to sit in the cell and always be mindful of God." He elaborated on this, pointing out: "This is what is meant by, 'I was in prison [φυλακῇ] and you came to me' (Mt 25:36)."[76] John's interpretation of this text is, as Mortari notes, truly singular.[77] It is also quite revealing. The Greek word in Matthew's gospel, φυλακῇ, refers to the "prison" or "prison cell" in which the hidden Christ dwells and to which the true disciple, moved by love for the "least of Christ's brothers and sisters," makes a visit. John Colobos takes this word in a different sense and uses it to refer to the "watchfulness" or vigilance (φυλακή) that the monk should keep in his monastic cell. In spite of the unusual logic John uses here, his interpretation of the text makes a certain amount of sense. The encounter with the hidden Christ in the prison cell is a useful image for reminding the monk of the purpose of his practice of vigilance. The object of this vigilance is after all, says John, to be "always mindful of [the presence] of God [μνημονεύειν τοῦ θεοῦ πάντοτε]." The monk, keeping watch in his cell, remains always mindful of the presence of the hidden Christ there.[78]

An anonymous saying emphasizes the need for vigilance by glossing a text on prayer from the Gospel of Matthew: "Do you wish to be saved after death?" an old man asked one of the brothers. "Go, seek and you shall find; watch and knock and it will be opened to you [Mt 7:7 ff]."[79] The old man either inadvertently or purposely added a word—"watch" (γρηγόρησον)—not found in the text from Matthew, to his comment. This one word significantly alters the meaning of the biblical text and reveals how the desert fathers could reread a text in light of their own interests and concerns. An important element of prayer, for this elder, and for the desert fathers as a whole, was vigilance, and he was quite willing to gloss the text from Matthew to make this clear.

For Orsisius, vigilance was associated explicitly with "guarding the heart." He explains the consequences of failing to guard the heart with the help of images from two different Gospel passages: "[I]f a man does not guard his heart well [φυλάξῃ τὴν ἑαυτοῦ καρδίαν καλῶς], he will forget and neglect everything he has heard, and thus the enemy, finding room in him [Mt 12:44] will overthrow him. It is like a lamp filled with oil and lit; if you forget to replenish the oil [Mt 25:3ff], gradually it goes out and eventually darkness will prevail." To this biblical image of the lamp and the oil, Orsisius adds another twist, possibly drawn from his own experience. "It is still worse," he says, "if a rat happens to get near the lamp and tries to eat the wick; it cannot do so before the oil is exhausted, but when it sees the lamp not only without light, but also without heat, it tries to pull out the wick and brings the lamp down." Orsisius then offers his own comments on the meaning of these images and the consequences of not keeping vigilance: "[T]he Holy Spirit gradually withdraws until his warmth is completely extinguished. Finally, the enemy devours the ardor of the soul, and wickedness spoils the body too."[80] Guarding the heart, or vigilance, is linked here, as it is elsewhere in the *Sayings,* with memory. Failure to guard the heart is said to result in one forgetting everything he has heard, either particular biblical texts or words of salvation uttered by the elders or, in a more general sense, all that one has heard regarding the meaning of salvation. Vigilance, here meaning remembrance of the story of salvation, is a key to the salvation of one's soul. Orsisius drives the point home in an effective fashion through his use of the two scriptural texts. The first, concerning the enemy finding room in an empty house, is interpreted in psychological terms to indicate the dangers of a vacant mind. The second text, an allusion from the parable of the wise and foolish virgins, uses the vivid image of the fading lamp to express the terrible consequences of allowing the heat and light from the lamp to fade. As if that were not enough to drive the point home, Orsisius offers his own image—probably not unfamiliar to those living in the desert—of a rat chewing on the wick of a lamp without oil. Conversely, remembrance and a return to guarding one's heart would bring with it the inner climate in which the Spirit might dwell.

A saying recorded under Abba Cronius's name blends an allegorical interpretation of a biblical text with a moral application to express the complex psychological processes involved in the practice of vigilance. And it reveals, as we have seen elsewhere, how the desert fathers' predispositions could affect the choice and interpretation of a biblical text. A brother asked Abba Cronius for a word, to which the old man responded by telling part of the story of Elisha and the Shunamite woman (2 Kings 4:8–17): "When Elisha came to the Shunamite, he found her not having relations with anyone. So she conceived and bore a child through the coming of Elisha." The brother asked Cronius the meaning of this word, and he responded: "If a soul is vigilant and withdraws from all distraction and abandons its own will, then the spirit of God enters into it and, though it was barren, it can henceforth conceive."[81] Although Cronius is not explicit here about the manner in which he moves from the biblical text to his interpretation, its allegorical character is clear: the Shunamite woman represents the soul and Elisha represents the Holy Spirit acting on the soul.[82] We can see in Cronius's interpretation of this text, how his prejudice—in this case his awareness of a question with real currency in the desert—influenced his choice and rendering of the text as well as his particular way of interpreting it. The question which the brother posed to him was of the most general kind, but Cronius perceived that behind the question was a more particular concern: how to overcome inner dryness in order to begin living a more fruitful life. Cronius's choice of text and his interpretation are therefore guided by a concern to shed light on this problem and to present an example of how one can overcome distractions and willfulness and experience the presence of the Holy Spirit. He makes a special point of noting that the Shunamite woman "did not have relations with anyone" and that the subsequent conception and birth of a son occurred in a miraculous way through the coming of Elisha.[83] Yet, nowhere does the text of 2 Kings mention any connection between the Shunamite woman's lack of relations with others—including her husband—and her conception of a son through Elisha's blessing. The text only says that she had not been able to bear any children. Cronius, in emphasizing her "lack of relations" with others, apparently wanted to show both the miraculous character of the birth and the contribution the Shunamite woman made—through her restraint—to this miracle. While the woman's restraint is not specifically mentioned in the biblical text, it is easy to see how Cronius could have arrived at such a picture. For the biblical text *does* speak of the woman's single-minded devotion to Elisha, a quality which apparently greatly impressed Elisha. The woman's lack of relations is, in fact, another way of talking about her singlemindedness toward the things of God. Having established the importance of the Shunamite woman's lack of relations as one of the conditions which allowed her to overcome her barrenness, Cronius easily shows how this applies to the brother who put the question to him, who was longing for his own barren soul to bear fruit. Cronius suggests that, like the Shunamite woman, the brother's soul must be characterized by lack of relations—by vigilance, singlemindedness, and abandonment to God's will. These attitudes will provide the conditions under which the blessing of Elisha—the birth of the Holy Spirit in his soul— can become a reality.

Scripture was immensely helpful to the monks in their attempt to illuminate the challenges and possibilities of the life they had taken up in the desert. Their recollection of the immanent judgment to come, while it may well have owed something to popular beliefs within the contemporary Egyptian world, also drew heavily on images from Scripture. These images of the end served as a vivid reminder to the monks of their mortality; they also filled the world of the monks with a sense of moral urgency and purpose. The same urgency characterized the monks experience of repentance, and its characteristic expression in the desert tears. The biblical texts witnessing to the need for true repentance struck a deep chord within the monks. They sought to rekindle in their own lives the spirit of repentance found in the Gospels and exemplified by some of the great figures of Scripture. Through empathy and imitation, the monks opened themselves to be pierced by the unpredictable spirit of *penthos*. Only in so doing did they feel they would be open to the movement of the Holy Spirit in their lives. In this spirit of openness, the monks embarked upon the hard work of purifying themselves, of stripping away all that prevented them from knowing themselves and experiencing the presence of God. In their physical asceticism, their battles with demons, thoughts, and passions, and their "watchfulness," the monks looked to Scripture. Sometimes supplying them the power to rebuke evil, sometimes providing examples of encouragement or endurance, and still other times giving them hints at how to duck a particular demonic blow, Scripture was a constant source of help to the monks in their pursuit of freedom.

Scripture helped the monks to free themselves gradually from the tenacious grip of the demonic forces which threatened to enslave them. This is perhaps the reason that the monks' discussion of the meaning of freedom—expressed in the biblical language of "freedom from care"—occupies so much of the *Sayings*. It is to this discussion that we now turn.

Notes

1. See J. Gwyn Griffiths, "The Faith of the Pharaonic Period," in *Classical Mediterranean Spirituality*, ed. A. H. Armstrong (New York: Crossroad, 1986), 33–34.

2. Sisoes 11 [*PG* 65:396A].

3. Antony 25 [*PG* 65:84C], [m]; there is a verbal similarity between Antony's expression and that of Mt 10:21: In Matthew the expression is "children will rise up [ἐπαναστήσονται] against parents and have them put to death."

4. Theodora 2 [*PG* 65:201B].

5. Sisoes 19 [*PG* 65:397D–400A].

6. Orsisius 1 [*PG* 65:316B].

7. PA App 8 [*SPTr*, 127].

8. Nau 136 [*ROC* 13:48]. Remembrance of death is closely related to the memory of judgment. John Colobos, 34 [*PG* 65:216AC], counseled: "Shut yourself in a tomb as though you were already dead, so that all times you will think that death is near."

9. Arsenius 40 [*PG* 65:105BC].

10. Theophilus 5 [*PG* 65:201A].

11. Ammonas 1 [*PG* 65:120A], [m].

12. Evagrius 1 [*PG* 65:173AC]; see also Evagrius 4 [*PG* 65:173D]: "Always keep your death in mind and do not forget the eternal judgement; then there will be no fault in your soul."

13. Theophilus 4 [PG 65:200A–201A] (emphasis mine).

14. NAU 135 [ROC 13:48–49].

15. A. Jones, *Soul Making: The Desert Way of Spirituality* (San Francisco: Harper and Row), 95.

16. Poemen 119 [*PG* 353A]; see also Poemen 209 [Guy, *Recherches*, S22:31].

17. Luciana Mortari, *Vita e Detti dei padri del deserto*, vol. 2 (Rome: Città Nuova, 1971), 113–14, n. 96. For biblical allusions to weeping, see: Jl 1:13: "Put on sackcloth and lament [κόπτεσφε], you priests! Wail [θρηνεῖτε], you ministers of the altar!"; Jl 2:12–13: "Return to me with your whole heart, with fasting and weeping and mourning [κλαυθμῷ καὶ ἐν κοπετῷ]"; Jas 4:9: "Lament and mourn and weep [πενθήσατε καὶ κλαύσατε]"; Mt 5:4: "Blessed are those who mourn [πενθοῦντες]." On the sources of *penthos* within the patristic tradition, see I. Hausherr, S. J., *Penthos: The Doctrine of Compunction in the Christian East*, trans. Anselm Hufstader, O.S.B. (Kalamazoo, MI: Cistercian Publications, 1982), 11–16. For a perceptive discussion of the influence of Mt 5:4 on desert spirituality, see L. Regnault, "Les béatitudes évangéliques dans les Apophtegmes," in L. Regnault, *Les pères du désert*

à travers leurs Apophtegmes (Sablé-sur-Sarthe: Solesmes, 1987), 163–68. For other references in the *Sayings* to *penthos* and its effects, see Arsenius 41 and 42; Dioscorus 2; Poemen 208 and 209.

18. Matoes 12 [*PG* 65:293B]; Matoes's words, "weep, have compunction, because the time is drawing near [κλαῦσον δὲ καὶ πένθησον ὅτι ὁ καιρὸς ἤγγισεν]" are similar to those used by Jesus to proclaim the breaking in of the kingdom of God (Mk 1:15): "The time is fulfilled, and the kingdom of God is at hand; repent . . . [πεπλήρωται ὁ καιρὸς καὶ ἤγγικεν ἡ βασιλεία τοῦ θεοῦ μετανοῖτε]." See also Lk 21:8.

19. Poemen 72 [*PG* 65:340BC].

20. Col 3:5 reads: "Put to death [νεκρώσατε] therefore what is earthly in you." Eph 2:3 reads: "We all once lived in the passions of the flesh [τὰ θελήματα τῆς σαρκὸς]."

21. Poemen 122 [*PG* 65:353B], [m].

22. See J. P. Lemaire, "L'abbé Poemen et la Sainte Écriture" (licentiate thesis, University of Freiburg, 1971), 53.

23. Ps. 94:6 (*LXX*): καὶ κλαύσωμεν ἐναντίον κυρίου τοῦ ποιήσαντος ἡμᾶς. 1 Sm 20:14: "If I am still alive, show me [Yawheh's] own mercy. [καὶ μὲν ἔτι μου ζῶντος καὶ ποιήσεις ἔλεος μετ᾽ἐμοῦ]"; see also Poemen 94 [*PG* 65:345A]: "If we are courageous, he will have mercy on us [ποιεῖ μεθ᾽ ἡμῶν τὸ ἔλεος αὐτοῦ]."

24. Wis 12:22: "that we may think earnestly of your goodness when we judge, and, when being judged, may look for mercy."

25. Poemen 204 [Guy, *Recherches,* S17:30–31], [m] (emphasis mine).

26. Poemen 71 [*PG* 65:340B], [m] (emphasis mine).

27. Poemen 50 [*PG* 65:333B].

28. See Lemaire, "L'abbé Poemen," 19; Lemaire concludes his analysis of this saying by noting the way different styles of interpretation are blended together. Not only is Abraham used an an exemplar, but we also have here "an example of allegorical exegesis founded on a profound intuition of the literal sense of the sacred text and its place in the economy of salvation."

29. Poemen 144 [*PG* 65:357B].

30. Luke mentions only the tears of the daughters of Jerusalem during the ascent to Calvary (Lk 23:27). In John's Gospel, Mary Magdalene is said to have "stayed outside near the tomb, weeping" (Jn 20:11).

31. See Lemaire, "L'abbé Poemen," 57–58: "This saying . . . suggests the part which Scripture played in the contemplation of the fathers; their mystical life is neither the fruit of an ascetic tension toward an absolute to be conquered, nor a search for God without any created intermediary. It is drawn from the Revelation God makes of himself in the Bible, and from an intimate participation in the redemptive work of the Savior."

32. Poemen 39 [*PG* 65:332B].

33. Evagrius *On Prayer,* 48; cited in Hausherr, *Penthos,* 123. On this whole passage, see Lemaire, "L'abbé Poemen," 18.

34. Paul the Simple 1 [*PG* 65:381CD–384D].

35. Serapion 1 [*PG* 65:413–416A].

36. E. R. Dodds, *Pagan and Christian in an Age of Anxiety* (New York: W. W. Norton, 1970), 38. For one source of this thinking, see Plato, *The Symposium* 202D13–203A6:

> Everything that is daemonic is intermediate between God and mortal. Interpreting and conveying the wishes of men to gods and the will of gods to men, it stands between the two and fills the gap. . . . God has no contact with man; only through the daemonic is there intercourse and conversation between men and gods, whether in the waking state or during sleep. And the man who is expert in such discourse is a daemonic man, compared to whom the experts in arts or handicrafts are but journeymen. (Dodds, 37)

37. Peter Brown, *The Making of Late Antiquity* (Cambridge: Harvard University Press, 1978), 90.

38. Syncletica 24 [Guy, *Recherches*, S6:34].

39. Poemen 67 [*PG* 65:337B].

40. Sisoes 44 [*PG* 65:405B].

41. Cf. Peter Brown, *The Body and Society: Men, Women and Sexual Renunciation in Early Christianity* (New York: Columbia University Press, 1988), 213–35; R. Bondi, *To Love as God Loves: Conversations with the Early Church* (Philadelphia: Fortress Press, 1987), 62–65.

42. Daniel 8 [*PG* 65:160ABC].

43. Isidore the Priest 1 [*PG* 65:220BC]. In the same saying, Lot is also seen as a negative example. For another example of Adam as a model of disobedience, see Nau 378 [*ROC* 18:142]: "Adam, while he was in paradise, disobeyed the commandment of God."

44. Epiphanius 5 [*PG* 65:164D].

45. Nau 197 [*PG* 13:277].

46. Poemen 178 [*PG* 65:365A].

47. Ares 1 [*PG* 65:132 C–133A].

48. Poemen 31 [*PG* 65:329C]. Similar expressions appear in Mt 22:16: ὁδὸν τοῦ θεοῦ; Jas 2:8: νόμον . . . βασιλικὸν, referring to the command to "love your neighbor as yourself." On the interpretation of the expression "Royal Road" in the early Church, see Jean Leclercq, O.S.B., *The Love of Learning and the Desire for God* (New York: Fordham University Press, 1961), 130–35.

49. Poemen 172 [*PG* 65:364B], [m].

50. See Lemaire, "L'abbé Poemen," 65.

51. Cronius 4 [*PG* 65:248C–249A].

52. Poemen 60 [*PG* 65:336C].

53. Sarmatus 2 [*PG* 65:413B].

54. Phocas 1, 2 [*PG* 65:432A–433C].

55. Nau 173 [*ROC* 13:56].

56. Theodora 2 [*PG* 65:201B], [m]: "[W]ithout many trials and temptations we cannot obtain an inheritance in the kingdom of heaven [ἐὰν μὴ διὰ πολλῶν θλίψεων καὶ πειρασμῶν, οὐ δυνησόμεθα τῆς βασιλείας τῶν οὐρανῶν γενέσθαι κληρονόμοι]." Acts 14:22: "Strengthening the souls of the disciples, exhorting them to continue in the faith, and saying that through many tribulations we must enter the

kingdom of God [διὰ πολλῶν θλίψεων δεῖ ἡμᾶς εἰσελθεῖν εἰς τὴν βασιλείαν τοῦ θεοῦ].'' Jas 2:5: "Has not God chosen those who are poor in the world to be rich in faith and heirs of the kingdom [κληρονόμους τῆς βασιλείας] which he has promised to those who love him?"

57. Poemen 24 [*PG* 65:328C], [m]; Jas 1:12: "Blessed is the man who endures trial, for when he has stood the test he will receive the crown of life which God has promised to those who love him."

58. Nau 175 [*ROC* 13:266].

59. Nau 313 [*ROC* 17:206].

60. Poemen 93 [*PG* 65:344C–345A]: ἡ βλασφημία σου ἐπάνω σου, Σατανᾶ. Ps 7:17: "His mischief shall recoil upon his own head [ἐπιστρέψει ὁ πόνος αὐτοῦ εἰς κεφαλὴν αὐτοῦ]."

61. Amoun of Nitria 3 [*PG* 65:128D].

62. Moses 18C [*PG* 65:288D–289A], [m].

63. Mortari, *Vita e detti,* 2:37, n. 55, suggests that the confidence to cry out and to "pray with knowledge" recalls the kind of prayer St. Paul speaks about in Rom 8:26 ff., where, with the Holy Spirit interceding for us, we pray with knowledge of the deep things of God.

64. Syncletica 7[*PG* 65:424ABC], [m].

65. Poemen 30 [*PG* 65:329BC]. The source of the animal legend referred to here is probably the *Physiologus,* a work composed in Greek in Alexandria, probably before 140 C.E. Lemaire, in "L'abbé Poemen," comments: "[I]l dut avoir une bonne diffusion en Egypte et plus au sud, puisque la version éthiopienne semble être la plus proche de l'original" (13).

66. Poemen 102 [*PG* 65:348A].

67. Orsisius 1 [*PG* 65:316AB].

68. Poemen 15 [*PG* 65:3225C].

69. Cronius 2 [*PG* 65:248B] (RSV). The word αἰχμαλωτίζω, "capture," has rich connotations in the New Testament: on becoming captive to the law of sin, see Rom 7:23; on taking thoughts captive and making them obey Christ, see 2 Cor 10:5.

70. Poemen 35 [*PG* 65:332B].

71. On the rich meaning of νῆψις in early Christian spirituality, see I. Hausherr, S. J., "L'hésychasme: Étude de spiritualité," *OCP* 22 (1956): 273–85.

72. Poemen 165 [*PG* 65:361BC].

73. See Pierre Hadot, "Exercices spirituels antiques et «philosophie chrétienne»," in *Exercices spirituels et philosophie antique* (Paris: Études Augustiniennes, 1981): "This *prosoché,* this attention to oneself, which was the fundamental attitude of the philosopher, became the fundamental attitude of the monk" (64).

74. Ammoes 4 [*PG* 65:128A].

75. Ammonas 10 [*PG* 65:121D–124A].

76. John Colobos 27 [*PG* 65:213B].

77. Mortari, *Vita e detti,* 1. 252–3, n. 12.

78. The prison metaphor is also taken up by Syncletica, 20 [Guy, *Recherches,* S2:34], who says, "in the world, if we commit an offence, even an involuntary one, we are thrown into prison; let us likewise cast ourselves into prison because of

our sins, so that voluntary remembrance may anticipate the punishment that is to
come.''

79. Nau 166 [*ROC* 13:54].

80. Orsisius 2 [*PG* 65:316C].

81. Cronius 1 [*PG* 65:248A], [m].

82. The comparison is made explicit in another version or variation of this saying,
Nau 363 [*ROC* 18:138], which states: ''The Shunamite represents the soul and Elias
the Holy Spirit.''

83. Nau 363 [*ROC* 18:138] states this even more explicitly: ''The Shunamite received Elisha because she had no relations with a man.''

7

Renunciation, Freedom from Care, and the Recovery of Paradise

"Renounce this life, so that you may be alive to God."[1] These words of Abba Antony capture one of the fundamental impulses of desert monasticism: to renounce everything in order to come to an intimate and abiding knowledge of God. There are indications that certain key gospel texts (for example, Mt 19:21) played an important role in shaping the ideal of renunciation.[2] In the Sayings we see Scripture used in a variety of ways to explore the different dimensions of this ideal and to exhort those who had taken up the monastic life to persevere in it.

Renunciation and detachment involved, in the most basic sense, cutting one's ties to certain habitual ways of living, including certain places, and withdrawing to a marginal existence in the desert. To some extent, the desert monks were simply responding to certain gospel texts in that peculiarly literal fashion which had marked the Christian ascetical tradition from its earliest moments; it was necessary to clear away all the bonds to the world that prevented one from following the Gospel with total devotion. The monks also recognized that there was more to renunciation than this physical and social dislocation; learning to be free from the ties that bound one was a painful, lifelong process. Therefore they gave considerable attention to cultivating the spirit of detachment. This included not only learning to free themselves from dependence on certain habits of living but also rooting out the inner sources of of all kinds of false dependence. The ultimate goal of this process of detachment was freedom. And the monks thought and spoke of this freedom in terms directly dependent on the Gospels: they sought to realize in their own lives that elusive "freedom from care" which Jesus spoke of in the Sermon on the Mount. We see in the *Sayings* both their struggle to know what this might mean, as well as glimpses and hints that some of the desert fathers indeed realized such freedom in their lives.

The monks did not view the call to renounce all for the sake of the Gospel, to follow Christ, and to become free from care merely as a remote, unattainable ideal but as a call which could be realized in their lives. The realization of this call to renunciation occurred on many different levels, from the practice of poverty and detachment from material things to the deeper levels of detachment from all misguided, egocentric desires and thoughts. Nor was the fulfillment of the ideals of renunciation and freedom from care isolated from the other concerns of the monastic life. It was part of a larger project of holiness. Renunciation was a means of pursuing the freedom from care so cherished in the desert and detachment was the sign of that freedom. Moreover, detachment and freedom from care were not ends in themselves; detachment from things and from concern for oneself bore fruit in compassion toward others. Stories conveying the fulfillment of the ideal of renunciation revealed to the desert monks and to their contemporaries the power of Scripture to bring about in living beings the reality of which it spoke. This was proof that human beings could overcome the various levels of attachment and addiction that enslaved them and enjoy intimacy with God. Such people had power.

Renunciation

The Call to Renunciation

The *Life of Antony* begins with a dramatic rendering of Antony's act of renunciation. It is a highly stylized account, perhaps more valuable as a depiction of the mythic beginnings of monasticism in Egypt than as an accurate historical record. Nevertheless, its portrayal of Antony's encounter with certain biblical texts, and his subsequent response to those texts is, as we noted, entirely plausible given what we know of historical circumstances. In any case, it is the *locus classicus* of the monastic call to renunciation and sheds light on how the desert fathers understood that call. In the narrative, we are told that Antony had been pondering how "the apostles, forsaking everything, followed the Savior (Mt 4:20), and how in Acts some sold what they possessed and took the proceeds and placed them at the feet of the apostles for distribution among those in need (Acts 4:34–35). . . ." The turning point in Antony's life came when he wandered into a nearby church: "just then it happened that the Gospel was being read, and he heard the Lord saying to the rich man, 'If you would be perfect, go, sell what you possess and give it to the poor, and you will have treasure in heaven (Mt 19:21)."[3] Antony owned some land, so his response to the call was not academic; it required him to divest himself of a not inconsiderable sum of money. He did so, at first keeping some back for the care of his sister, and finally giving the rest away and renouncing his old life completely. The *Sayings* provides further evidence that the particular biblical text which inspired Antony's *anachōrēsis* and other similar texts played a significant role in shaping desert spirituality. The challenge of fulfilling these texts came not only in the beginning of the monastic life but all through the long process of purification. Thus, we find a variety of responses to the ideal of renunciation among the monks, from the literal fulfillment of the ideal in the form of a simple, materially poor existence, to the more complex and probing questions of inward appropriation of the ideal.

Why did the monks value renunciation so highly? It was at least in part because they recognized that attachment to things could compromise the freedom from care which the solitary life promised them; that possessions could inflame desires to the point where they became all-consuming. Abba Isidore of Pelusia expressed this tendency in stark terms, "The desire for possessions is dangerous and terrible, knowing no satiety; it drives the soul which it controls to the heights of evil. Therefore, let us drive it away vigorously from the beginning."[4] Possessions, or more precisely the desire for possessions, could obtain a tenacious grip on the soul. Thus in the desert, renunciation of goods was based not only on the desire to follow the Gospel but also on the practical realization, based on experience, that immoderate concern for possessions could ultimately consume the soul.

While this realization often prompted dramatic, even heroic acts of renunciation among the monks, there is evidence that the prospect of undertaking such a deed clearly presented real difficulties for many. There are numerous instances of "false starts" or partial acts of renunciation that turned out badly. Such stories are sometimes thought to reflect a narrow, rigorist mentality—all or nothing. However, the truth is somewhat more complex than this. After all, even Antony had undergone the process of renunciation gradually. Rather, what lies behind these stories and what drove the monks was a profound need to give themselves completely—to the solitary life, to the process of purification, and ultimately to God. There were any number of reasons why one might fail to make a complete break. The precipitous drop in social status that could result from such an act certainly caused hesitation for some. A story tells of "a distinguished official who had renounced everything and distributed his goods to the poor. He kept a little bit for his personal use because he did not want to accept the humiliation that comes from total renunciation [τελείας ἀποταγῆς]. . . ."[5] Such fears were understandable. It was a long way down for some and this practice of "hedging one's bets" was not uncommon in the desert. And while the elders rarely chastised those who, through either fear or weakness, found themselves unable to make a complete renunciation, they made it clear that such hesitation could be costly.

The monks were not afraid of using vivid symbolic imagery to drive home this point. Abba Antony illustrated this graphically for a certain brother who

> renounced [ἀποταξάμενος] the world and gave his goods to the poor, but kept back a little for personal expenses. He went to see Abba Antony. When he told him this, the old man said to him, "If you want to be a monk, go into the village, buy some meat, cover your naked body with it and come here like that." The brother did so, and the dogs and birds tore at his body. When he came back, the old man asked him whether he had followed his advice. He showed him his wounded body, and Saint Antony said, "Those who renounce the world but want to keep something for themselves are torn in this way by the demons who make war on them." [6]

This startling and disturbing image sent an unmistakable message: the desire for possessions if left unchecked would eventually provide an easy and attractive target which other ferocious and even more intractable desires would attack mercilessly.[7]

Such concerns did not arise out of the pure air of solitude. They reflect the monks' personal experience of the tenacious power and debilitating effects of their own attachments to family and village concerns. In one instance, a brother who was left an inheritance asked Abba Poemen what he should do. Poemen indicated the various possibilities that lay before the brother and hazarded a guess at the probable consequences of each action. "If I tell you to give it to the church, they will make banquets with it; if I tell you to give it to your relations, you will not receive any profit from it. . . ." Then he suggested to the brother a very different possibility: "[I]f I tell you 'give it to the poor'[Δὸς αὐτὰ πτωχοῖς]' [Mt 19:21], you will be free from care [ἀμεριμνεῖς] [Mt 6:25]. If you want to, do it." [8] Poemen's final comment—especially his conflation of phrases from two different texts of Matthew's Gospel—reveals his understanding of the positive effects of renunciation. Selling one's possessions and giving to the poor, apart from its merits as an act of charity, had a profound effect on the one who carried out the act: it helped one taste that freedom from care promised in the Sermon on the Mount.

The severe demands of renunciation were sometimes expressed in terms which drew on images of sacrifice from Scripture. Abraham's willingness to sacrifice his son Isaac also served as a model for those who wanted to know the level of commitment required of them in their monastic life. This can be seen in a story, noted in chapter 4, in which an elder tested one of his disciples by demanding that he throw his son into a burning furnace. The father took his own child and threw him into the furnace which immediately became like dew, full of freshness. Through this act, he received glory like the Patriarch Abraham.[9] The message was clear: anyone who would embark upon the struggle of life in the desert must be prepared, as Abraham was, to sacrifice everything. The story also provides some insight into how the monks saw themselves in relation to the biblical exemplars: they were not merely imitating the way of the biblical heroes, but were, in a sense recapitulating the wonders of those earlier times in the present day.

Poverty

On one level, renunciation meant simply learning to live in simplicity and poverty. These were relative terms in the desert, not only because monks lived with varying degrees of privation but because the differing social backgrounds of the monks meant that what appeared as poverty to one could seem like luxury to another.[10] Nevertheless, the monks cherished poverty, both as an interior disposition or virtue, sometimes referred to as "poverty of spirit," and as a way of life marked by material simplicity. This was the climate, the setting, most conducive to approaching God.

The value of poverty to the monks can be seen in its frequent inclusion in lists of the virtues considered necessary for living the monastic life. For Abba Andrew, "exile, poverty and endurance in silence" were "the three things appropriate for a monk."[11] Abba Euprepius claimed that "if a person is possessed of humility and poverty, and if he does not judge others, the fear of God will come to him."[12] Poemen's list included "poverty, hardship, austerity and fasting." These, he said, "are the instruments of the solitary life."[13] The three things Abba Theodore of Pherme held to be fundamental were "poverty, asceticism, and flight from men."[14] Abba Elias claimed that in his time, such virtues had disappeared. During the days of his predecessors, however, "they took great care about these three virtues: poverty, obedience and fasting."[15] We hear echoes from Scripture in some of the monks' references to poverty. Abba Hyperchius claimed: "A monk's treasure is voluntary poverty. Lay up your treasures in heaven, brother [Mt 6:20] for there are the ages of quiet and bliss without end."[16] Abba John Colobos echoed St. Paul's description of all he had endured for the sake of the Gospel in exhorting the brothers to "persevere in hunger and thirst, in cold and nakedness [2 Cor 11:27], and in sufferings."[17] These lists are instructive. They reveal poverty neither as a practice isolated from other concerns of monastic life nor as a matter having to do with renunciation of material goods. Simplicity of living had one primary purpose: to help the

monks cultivate that interior detachment which could lead them toward freedom from care.

The actual practice of poverty was considered an important part of fulfilling the call to renunciation, and the desert fathers made note of examples of
this poverty among the elders. Abba Megethius, we are told, "owned nothing in this world except a knife with which he cut reeds. . . ."[18] To a
brother who asked him how he could be saved, an old man, "took off his
habit, girded his loins and raised his hands to heaven, saying, 'so should
the monk be: denuded of all things of this life [γυμνὸς ἀπὸτης ὕλης τοῦ
βίου].' "[19] We have already noted certain stories indicating a reluctance
on the part of some of the monks to possess books. However, the practice
of poverty went beyond this to include the renunciation of possessions of
any kind. A story concerning Theodore of Pherme, who at Abba Macarius's
suggestion sold his books and gave the money to the poor, shows him to be
one who took the practice of poverty very seriously. Theodore is quite clear
about why he values poverty: he practices it not for its own sake but in
order to become detached from the requirements of appearance and propriety. He is described as "wearing a torn habit, his chest bare and his cowl
hanging in front of it." We are told that a great man came to see Theodore,
and that his disciple, presumably out of embarrassment, covered Theodore's
shoulder with the cloak to make him appear more presentable. Theodore,
however, snatched it off. When the visitor had gone, Theodore's disciple
asked him why he acted in that way, saying, "[T]his man came to be edified; perhaps he will be scandalized." Then the old man said, "What do
you mean Abba? Are we still the slaves of men [Gal 1:10]? We did what
was necessary, the rest is superfluous."[20] The allusion to Galatians provides
a hint regarding how Theodore understood the value of poverty: he saw it
as an aid in developing a detachment from the concern for appearance or
propriety which could compromise the monk's total devotion to God.

The attitude of indifference cultivated through the practice of poverty was
seen as a key to bringing forth the new life of the resurrection. Macarius
said, "If slander has become the same as praise, poverty as riches, depri-
vation as abundance, you will not die."[21] The same sentiment was expressed by Amma Syncletica, who was once asked if poverty was a perfect
good. She said that it was and used a biblical allusion to describe its benefits
to the soul: "For those who are capable of it, it is a perfect good. Those
who can sustain it receive suffering in the body [θλίψιν . . . σαρκὶ] [1
Cor 7:28], but rest in the soul [ψυχῇ ἀνάπαυσιν], for just as one washes
coarse clothes by trampling them underfoot and turning them about in all
directions, even so, the strong soul become much more stable thanks to
voluntary poverty."[22] Syncletica's use of the phrase θλίψιν . . . σαρκὶ is
interesting, for she takes it to mean something quite different from what St.

Paul understands it to mean in 1 Corinthians. In 1 Corinthians 7, Paul uses the expression to refer to the worldly troubles associated with marriage which, due to the "shortness of time," he would like all those who are unmarried to avoid. He urges them to avoid the "suffering in the body" precisely so that they may be "free from care [ἀμερίμνους] (1 Cor 7:32)." Syncletica, on the other hand, takes θλῖψιν . . . σαρκὶ in a very positive sense. She takes it to refer to voluntary poverty which, while undeniably difficult, leads to something of great value, "rest in the soul," something closely related to the "freedom from anxiety" of which Paul speaks. Abba Evagrius understood the classic text about renunciation as providing a clue regarding how to reach a deep level of prayer: "Go, sell all that belongs to you and give it to the poor (Mt 19:21) and taking up the cross, deny yourself (Mt 16:24); in this way, you will be able to pray without distraction." [23] Only by clearing away all that stands between oneself and God could one realize the silent clarity from which prayer emerges.

"Deny yourself." The monks took this task seriously. They knew from experience that the freedom and intimacy with God which they sought could come about only through renunciation of one's very self—that is the will. Abba Poemen believed that such renunciation was the only way to reach God: "The will of man is a brass wall [Jer 1:18] between him and God and a stone of stumbling. When a man renounces it, he is also saying to himself, 'By my God, I can leap over the wall' (Ps 18:29)." [24] What this meant in practice for most monks was putting themselves under the direction of an elder and learning the exacting way of obedience. Abba Joseph of Thebes related that of the three works "approved in the eyes of the Lord," the most exalted was "when someone remains in submission to a spiritual father in complete renunciation of his own will." [25] Abba Pambo confirmed this, indicating that poverty, in the sense of renunciation of material goods, was in fact a relative term. Renunciation of the will, on the other hand, brought one into the company of the martyrs. Four monks came one day to see him, and each revealed the virtue of his neighbor. One fasted a great deal, the other was poor, and the third had acquired great charity. The fourth "had lived for twenty-two years in obedience to an old man." Abba Pambo then said: "I tell you, the virtue of this last one is the greatest. Each of the others has obtained the virtue he wished to acquire; but the last one, restraining his own will, does the will of another. Now it is of such men that martyrs are made. . . ." [26]

The Narrow Gate

Throughout the *Sayings*, we see the monks wrestling with what it meant to realize the ideal of renunciation in the day-to-day events of their lives. Learning

the way of detachment involved ever deepening levels of self-scrutiny as
they sought to free themselves from the tenacious grip of their cares. The
monks were helped in this by various biblical images, which served sometimes as models of how to behave, other times as mirrors in light of which
they could see themselves and their aspirations more clearly. One biblical
image that played a particularly prominent role was the "narrow gate" or
"narrow way" (Mt 7:13–14). The exploration of this image led the monks
to ever deeper levels of detachment and helped bring them closer to their
cherished ideal of "freedom from care."

The "narrow gate" or "narrow way" referred to in Matthew's Gospel
(Mt 7:13–14) was a rich and lively biblical symbol for the desert fathers. In
general terms, it was a metaphor for the "way of renunciation" chosen by
those living in the desert. Yet it was an expression with real elasticity and
for the monks it contained a multitude of possible meanings. Amma Theodora recalled the text from Matthew—"strive to enter by the narrow gate
[στενῆς πύλης] (Mt 7:13)"—to highlight the severe challenge of the life
in the desert and the depth of the commitment required to persevere in it.[27]
Abba Poemen referred to this same image to emphasize the single-minded
devotion necessary for following the way of the Gospel. Specifically, he
uses the text from Matthew to help him interpret a difficult and ambiguous
passage from the Gospel of Luke: "This saying which is written in the
Gospel: 'Let him who has no sword, sell his cloak and buy one (Lk 22:36),'
means this: let him who is at ease give it up and take the narrow way
[στενὴν ὁδόν] [Mt 7:14]."[28] The passage in Luke refers to a change in the
times in which the disciples were living. Until that time the disciples had
needed nothing, but from that point on, they would be entering a world
hostile to them and would need a sword. It is a metaphorical way of expressing the insecurity which characterized their new situation. In Poemen's
interpretation of the Lucan text, "sword" and "mantle" keep their same
fundamental signification—the movement from a time of security to insecurity. However Poemen transposes this tension into the inner world of the
monk. The parallels Poemen draws between the two passages reveal the
particular monastic concerns which influence his interpretation: having a "cloak
[ἱμάτιον]" is taken as the equivalent of being "at ease" or "at rest
[ἀνάπαυσις]," taken here in the pejorative sense of "living carelessly."
"Buying a sword [μάχαιραν]" is taken as the equivalent of entering upon
the "narrow way [στενὴν ὁδόν]," an expression borrowed from Mt 7:14.[29]
In making these comparisons, Poemen wants to impress upon his listeners
the urgency of the moment and the need be mindful of the insecurity of the
times in which they are living. While "rest [ἀνάπαυσις]" in the positive
sense of deep peace and security may indeed come to them during the course

of their life in the desert, they must not presume to rest now in these uncertain times. Entering the "narrow gate," then, means to remain attentive to the task at hand, which is to purify the heart.

Abba Ammonas addressed this issue specifically, taking the "narrow way" to refer to the hard work of psychological purification required in the desert. When someone asked him, "What is the narrow and hard way (Mt 7:14)?" he replied, "The narrow and hard way is this, to do violence to your thoughts, and to strip yourself of your own will, for the sake of God." He amplified this interpretation with reference to another text from Matthew, saying, "This is also the meaning of the sentence, 'Lo, we have left everything and followed you (Mt 19:27).' "[30] The practical character of this interpretation is notable. Ammonas tells the one who asked him about this text that its meaning is to be discovered through a particular praxis: through the work of putting one's inner world in order, through doing violence to one's thoughts, and through denying one's own will for the sake of God. Entering through the narrow gate thus involves an uncompromising commitment to inward purification.

An illustration of what this might mean in practical terms can be seen in a story which takes the "narrow gate" to refer to the purification learned through "bearing insults." John Colobos tells a story concerning a young man whose father died and who afterwards went to live with one of his father's close friends. He betrayed his guardian's trust however, when he slept with his wife. The guardian at first turned the boy out of the house, but after the boy pleaded with him for forgiveness, he agreed to accept him back. Before doing so, he required the young man to carry out a strict penance. He was required first to work as a ferryman for several years, with the stipulation being that he "give away all his wages, and bear all insults [ὑβριζόμενος]." Having done this, the young man was then instructed by his guardian to go to Athens to learn philosophy (his father had been a philosopher, as was his guardian). Arriving there, he was greeted with ridicule and insults from the other philosophers. However, he responded to this abuse with laughter, telling those who mocked him, "For three years I have paid to be insulted and now I am insulted free of charge." Commenting on this story, John Colobos said, "The gate of God [ἡ πύλη τοῦ θεοῦ] [Mt 7:13] is like that, and we fathers go through many insults [πολλῶν ὕβρεων] in order to enter joyfully into the city of God." By linking the image of the narrow gate with the important New Testament idea of bearing insults, this story illustrates the practical dimensions of the process of purification required by anyone who would enter through the "gate of God." Entering through the narrow gate implied a willingness to accept and participate in the abuse and insults which Jesus bore for the sake of humanity and which

St. Paul exhorted the Corinthians to accept for Christ's sake.[31] It suggested
a life marked by increasing detachment from artificial images of oneself, by
a willingness to have the rough edges of oneself worn down, and by a
gradual emergence as a free person.

Freedom From Care

The *telos* of the monks' life in the desert was freedom: freedom from anxiety about the future; freedom from the tyranny of haunting memories of the
past; freedom from an attachment to the ego which precluded intimacy with
others and with God. They hoped also that this freedom would express itself
in a positive sense: freedom to love others; freedom to enjoy the presence
of God; freedom to live in the innocence of a new paradise. The desert
fathers' aspiration toward freedom expressed itself in many different guises
and touched upon various levels of their lives. They drew heavily upon
biblical images to articulate their hopes, focusing on such New Testament
ideas as "not being anxious about anything (Mt 6:25)," "not worrying about
tomorrow (Mt 6:34)," "seeking first God's kingdom (Mt 6:33)", believing
in the limitless goodness of God (Mk 9:23), and on what the Psalms call
"casting one's cares upon the Lord (Ps 54:23)." [32] Taken altogether, these
images comprise a montage expressing the ultimate goal of renunciation and
detachment for the desert fathers: freedom from worry, anxiety, and care,
born of a sense of total dependence upon and confidence in God.

Learning the Way of Freedom

The struggles against temptations of all kinds fill the *Sayings* and represent
the most persistent, enduring challenge to the monks' freedom. These temptations run the gamut, from the baser enticements of gluttony and impurity
to the subtler though ultimately more dangerous traps posed by anger and
pride.[33] At root, all of these temptations created the same problem: they
drove a rift between the monk and God, leaving the monk feeling isolated
and powerless. In these circumstances, it became increasingly difficult for
the monk to believe that help was near at hand and led to the common but
deeply troubling anxiety that he would likely be overwhelmed by his temptation. The Gospel text calling for refraining from anxiety served as an important reminder for those beset with this particular worry that they were
indeed *not* cut off from help. Abba Poemen was asked for whom this saying—"Do not be anxious about tomorrow (Mt 6:34)" was suitable. The old
man replied, "It is said for the man who is tempted and has not much

strength, so that he should not be worried, saying to himself, 'How long must I suffer this temptation?' He should rather say every day to himself, 'Today.' "[34] Freedom from care in this sense meant taking to heart God's presence and care each day.

Being able to "cast one's cares upon the Lord (Ps 54:23)" was a fundamental expression of the freedom from care so cherished by the desert fathers, and several sayings use this language to describe the attitude one should have in the desert. One monk had been severely plagued by memories and temptations arising from his former life in the world. He told some of the elders about this and to help him they gave him a strict ascetical regime to follow. However, it turned out to be too severe for him and "his body became so weak that he could not longer stand up." An elder who was visiting from another place came upon the monk in his cell and seeing that he was ill, inquired about the reason for his condition. When he discovered what had happened, he immediately counseled the brother to follow a different course: "Give all this up, and take a little food at the proper time, say a few prayers, and 'throw your care upon the Lord' [ἐπίρριψον ἐπὶ κύριον τὴν μέριμνάν σου] (Ps 54:23)." The brother did so and in a few days "the warfare ceased."[35] Not in ascetical rigor, that is, but in abandonment of one's cares to God, would one be able to find peace. An interesting variation of this ideal, revealing the importance of recognizing one's dependence upon God, was expressed by Abba Agathon. To one who was being tempted by sexual desire, Agathon said: "Go, cast your powerlessness [τὴν ἀδυναμιαν σου] before God and you shall find rest [Ps 54:23]."[36] A frank admission of one's weakness was the first step toward finding one's way out of the labyrinth of cares and anxieties brought on by temptations.

Abba Poemen's comments upon this text from the Psalms takes the issue a step further, suggesting that one's trust in God must run as deep as the roots of the self. He said, "The instruments for the work of the soul are: to 'throw yourself before God' [Ps 54:23], not to measure your progress, to leave behind all self-will."[37] Poemen departs in a significant way from the language of the Psalm to show just how deeply such trust must take root in the soul. While Psalm 54 says "cast your care upon the Lord [ἐπίρριψον ἐπὶ κύριον τὴν μέριμνάν σου], and he will support you," Poemen exhorts the monk, "cast *yourself* before God [τὸ ρίψαι ἑαυτὸν ἐνώπιον τοῦ θεοῦ]." Nothing less than utter dependence upon God would bring the monk to the freedom from care that he sought. The other two instruments included in this saying provide further insight into what it means to cast oneself before God. First, there can be no measuring of one's progress. To do so would show a fundamental lack of trust. Secondly, one must genuinely and with a sense of openness seek the will of God. The cultivation of such an attitude could have direct practical benefits in one's struggles against "thoughts." Abba Poemen likened this struggle to a man who has a fire on his left and a cup of water on his right. If the fire kindles, he must take the water from the cup and extinguish it. "The fire," he says, "is the enemy's seed, and the water is the act of throwing oneself before God [τὸ ῥίψαι ἑαυτὸν ἐνώπιον τοῦ θεοῦ] [Ps 54:23]."[38] Poemen suggests that the single most important act for surviving in the desert is the act of trust—to place oneself completely in the hands of God. No amount of ascetical practice could protect one as surely as the act of presenting oneself before God in an attitude of complete trust.

This same message is conveyed in a slightly different way in a saying which contrasts the "work of God"—seeking God's kingdom—with "bodily needs"—physical asceticism. Abba John the Eunuch questioned an old man about how he had managed to "carry out the 'work of God' in peace." John confessed his own difficulties with this to the old man, saying, "[W]e cannot do it, not even with labor." The old man responded that he and his companions had been able to do the work of God because they considered "the work of God as primary, and bodily needs as secondary." The younger monks, he said, had placed far too much emphasis on the bodily needs and had held the work of God to be secondary. That is why they had to labor so much and had so little peace from their efforts. To understand what was meant by the "work of God," the old man suggested that they listen to what "the Savior said to the disciples, 'Seek first his kingdom and his righteousness, and all these things shall be yours as well (Mt 6:33).' "[39] The purpose of such advice was primarily to encourage those dwelling in the desert to have confidence in the sustaining force in their life. It is precisely this sentiment which lies behind the words of Abba Biare to a brother who asked what he should do to be saved. Abba Biare told him that in addition to manual labor and moderating his appetite, "[you should] dwell without care [μὴ ταράσσου] in your cell, and you will be saved."[40]

Sickness and depression often tested the monks' resolve and even their faith as they sought to persevere in their monastic life. For these, the call to be free from care presented a particular challenge as well as the possibility of new hope. To some monks mired in the physical and psychological pains of illness, an elder recalled Jesus' haunting words in the Sermon on the Mount: "Will [God] not himself care for you in all things [οὐκ αὐτός σου φροντίζει ἐν πᾶσιν]? Can you live without him? Be patient then, and beg him to supply you will all that is necessary. That is what his will is, that you should remain in patience, eating the charity which is brought you."[41] This was no cavalier statement, enabling other monks to escape the responsibility to care for those who were sick. As we shall see later, they took such responsibilities quite seriously. Rather, it is a reminder that even in circumstances of illness, a monk should remember the ultimate source of his life and hope. Even apart from illness, the struggle of life in the desert, or simply the mundane challenges of day to day existence could lead to depression. Abba Euprepius encouraged some who felt this way by reminding them of something they already knew but had forgotten: "Knowing that God is faithful and almighty, have faith in him, and you will share what is his. If you are depressed, you do not believe. We all believe that he is mighty and we believe all is possible to him [Mk 9:23]."[42] The cultivation of this supreme confidence in the sustaining and loving power of God was, for the desert fathers, one of the keys in their quest for holiness.

Realization of Freedom

The *Sayings* presents numerous stories that reflect the realization of freedom in the lives of the desert fathers. We see the realization of such freedom in the desert through sayings and images which hold up the free person as an exemplar, showing that freedom from the bonds and cares of life was indeed possible. While no one biblical text stands as the primary model or example, the spirit of the Gospels breathes through this realization of freedom in the desert.

One expression of freedom from care in the desert was a willingness to move, to leave behind the known and certain for unknown territory. A story tells how Abba Agathon spent a long time building a cell with his disciples, after which he settled there with them. However, during their first week there, Agathon saw something unedifying and said to his disciples, "Arise, let us leave this place [ἐγείρεσθε, ἄγωμεν ἐντεῦθεν]." But his disciples were dismayed at this and asked Agathon why they had spent all that time building the cell only to abandon it after a week. They pointed out that people would be scandalized at this, saying, "Look, these unstable ones are moving again [μετέβησαν πάλιν]." Agathon, seeing their faintheartedness, said to them, "If some are scandalized [by our moving], others, on the contrary, will be much edified and will say, 'How blessed are they, who go away for God's sake, and despise everything [διὰ τὸν θεὸν μετέβησαν, καὶ πάντων κατεφρόνησαν].' Those of you wishing to come, come. As for me, I am going."[43]

This story, with its echoes of biblical language, conveys well the importance of being willing to leave everything for the sake of the Gospel and how this was related to freedom from care. Although Agathon does not say why he felt compelled to leave the place in which he had recently settled with his disciples, it clearly had something to do with his sense that they could not live the monastic life with integrity and freedom in that particular place. The story is thus about the importance of leaving or moving, leaving behind that which is problematic and moving toward that which is life-giving. The implication of the story, both from the language used and the content of the dialogue, is that leaving under these circumstances, far from being a cause for scandal, is in harmony with the example of Jesus in the Gospels. The language Agathon used to beckon his disciples to join him in leaving that place, "Arise, let us leave this place," is exactly the same phrase Jesus used with his disciples at the end of an important juncture in the last discourse in John's Gospel (Jn 14:31). In John's Gospel, the words follow immediately upon Jesus' statements about his imminent departure to the Father and about his desire to "do as the Father has commanded." Agathon's words convey this same sense of singlemindedness and commitment to the life upon which he has embarked. His resolve to "leave that place" is tested, however, when his disciples protest that they will create a scandal and will all be mocked if they move again. His rejoinder to their protest, which he perceives to be motivated more by faintheartedness than commitment to the ideal of stability, turns their objection on its head. He claims that those who witness their action will "bless them" for "going away [μετέβησαν] for God's sake." Although there is no exact biblical equivalent for Agathon's phrase, it is interesting to note that "going away," the phrase over which Agathon and his disciples contend, is used on numerous occasions in the Gospels to describe Jesus' departure from one place to another at important junctures in his ministry, and even to describe Jesus' imminent departure from the world.[44] These connections with the language of the Gospels help to shed light on the central point of this story: to "go away for God's sake" is indeed blessed because it is the way of Jesus himself. The fact that their departure took place in the middle rather than the beginning of the monastic journey indicates the extent to which renunciation was understood to be a lifelong challenge. Agathon's action suggests that those who came to live in the desert must be prepared to start from the beginning again and again and to "go away for God's sake." The peculiar language used to describe the motive for such action—the need to "despise all" for the sake of God— was yet another way of expressing the kind of freedom from care which characterized those prepared to make this break.[45]

This freedom also expressed itself in another kind of break, symbolized by the willingness of the desert fathers to relinquish even what little they had when it was demanded of them. The elders were keenly aware that if the long, interior process of detachment was to have any real meaning, it had to bear fruit in their lives. Because of this, they cherished stories and sayings that provided evidence of such realization in the lives of their fellow monks. In a striking commentary on what qualifies as true asceticism, Abba Gelasius tells of an old man he knew whose "particular acts of asceticism had been to guard against having two tunics [Lk 3:10; Mt 5:40] and till the day of his death not to think of the morrow while he was with his companions [Mt 6:34]."[46] The aim of the old man's *ascesis,* or discipline, an aim which we are told that he fulfilled, was to realize within himself the meaning of these two texts from the Gospel. One of the texts refers to something very concrete, the need to "guard against having two tunics," and the old man strove to keep this commandment as literally as possible. However, it is the second text that reveals his true intention. He wanted to "guard against having two tunics" so that he would be able to fulfill the command from Matthew's Gospel, "do not worry about tomorrow." The concrete act of physical privation was a means of fulfilling the true meaning of asceticism: to be free from care.

A story about Abba Nisterus illustrates a similar willingness to be without anything in the world. A brother asked Nisterus, "If a poor man came to ask you for a tunic, which would you give him?" He replied, "The better one." "And if someone else asked you for one, what would you give him?" The old man said half of the other one. The brother said, "And if someone else asked for one, what would you give him?" He said, "I should cut the rest, give him half, and gird myself with whatever was left." So the brother said, "And if someone came and asked you for that, what would you do?" The old man said, "I would give him the rest and go and sit down somewhere, until God sent me something to cover myself with, for I would not ask anyone for anything."[47] This exchange illustrates the extent to which the practice of detachment from material goods derived from and led to freedom from care and compassion for others. Here, the fruit of renunciation is a detachment which expresses itself as compassion for one who has nothing. Moreover in his expression of need, the old man showed himself to have interiorized the Gospel call to be dependent upon God for everything.

Freedom from care often engendered spontaneous acts of compassion. We are told of a brother who approached Theodore of Pherme, saying "I wish to fulfill the commandments." In response, Theodore told him a story concerning Abba Theonas who, "wanting to fill his spirit with God, took some flour to the bakery, and made some loaves which he gave to the poor who asked him for them; others asked for more, and he gave them the baskets, then the cloak he was wearing, and he came back to his cell with his loins girded with his cape. Afterwards he took himself to task telling himself that he had still not fulfilled the commandment of God."[48] The commandment here is shorthand for the commandment to love. Here, as in the story of Nisterus, detachment naturally expressed itself in a practical act of kindness.

Freedom from care meant being able to respond compassionately to the needs of the other.

One of the most vivid and memorable signs of the desert fathers' realization of freedom from care can be seen in their response to being robbed by thieves. The frequency with which stories of robberies are reported in the *Sayings* may or may not accurately reflect the actual frequency of such incidents in the desert. What they clearly indicate is the importance the monks attached to these stories, and how much they cherished the example of those who chose not to resist those who stole from them. The stories reveal a profound level of detachment on the part of those who were robbed and in some cases a self-conscious reference to Scripture as a way of explaining their action. Here again, true detachment was expressed as kindness and compassion. In one such episode, Abba Macarius was said to have returned to his cell and encountered a man who was engaged in plundering his goods. Without any hesitation, "he came up to the thief as if he were a stranger and he helped him to load the animal. He saw him off in complete tranquility [ἡσυχίας], saying, 'We have brought nothing into this world, and we cannot take anything out of the world' (1 Tm 6:7). 'The Lord gave and the Lord has taken away; blessed be the name of the Lord' (Jb 1:21)."[49] The texts cited indicate the extent to which Scripture may have influenced the monks' behavior in such instances and suggest that Macarius's action is to be understood as a fulfillment of the biblical texts which call for detachment in relation to material things. The *manner* of Macarius's behavior is also significant. He sees the thief off "in complete tranquility," a sign that his actions flow from a pure heart and a deep appropriation of the meaning of renunciation. It is this freedom from concern for goods that Abba Euprepius refers to when he says that "if we happen to lose something, we must accept this with joy and gratitude, realizing that we have been released from care [φροντίδων ἀπαλλαγέντας]."[50] Euprepius himself practiced a remarkable degree of detachment in response to being robbed, displaying a positive eagerness to be freed from concern for things. Whereas Macarius merely aided the thieves in taking what they were in the process of stealing, Euprepius, upon discovering that those who had robbed him had left something behind, ran after them to make sure they had taken everything they had come for.[51]

An encounter that Abba Gelasius had with a thief reveals in a more personal way a dimension of detachment that is only implicit in the other stories: freedom from care flows from and expresses itself in love. As we noted earlier, Abba Gelasius possessed a Bible of great value. It was in fact the community's book, placed in the church, "so that any of the brothers who wished could read it." We are told that a "brother from another place" [ἀδελφῶν ξένος] came to see Abba Gelasius, and seeing the Bible, wished to have it for himself and stole it as he was leaving. He took it to the city to try to sell it, but the prospective buyer, being uncertain of its worth, wanted first to have it appraised. The dealer, knowing of Gelasius's authority in such matters, brought it to him to have it appraised and Gelasius advised him (even though the price the brother was asking for it was far less than what it was worth), "Buy it, for it is beautiful and worth the price you tell me." When the buyer related to the brother what Gelasius had said, he was incredulous: "Didn't the old man say anything else?" he asked. But the dealer told him that was all Gelasius had said to him. Hearing this, the brother decided he no longer wished to sell the Bible. He was "filled with compunction [κατανυγεὶς], and went to find the old man, to repent and ask him to take the book back." But Gelasius told the brother he didn't want it back. Finally, in desperation, the brother told him, "[I]f you do not take it back, I shall have no rest [ἀνάπαυσιν]." For the sake of the brother's peace of mind, Gelasius relented and agreed to take the book back. We are told that the brother remained with Gelasius until his death.[52]

This story illustrates well the transforming effects that the realization of freedom from care in a life could have on another. For Gelasius, mercy was clearly more important than justice and his compassion and lack of judgment toward the one who had committed the crime confirmed this. Although he had the opportunity to achieve justice, or at the very least retrieve the precious Bible, he instead refrained from even acknowledging that the book belonged to him. It is this pure and spontaneous expression of detachment which produces the shock of recognition in the brother. When he realized he had not been judged, he was "pierced to the depths" and repented of what he had done. It is a good example of how a person could be brought to the light of truth by another person's purity of heart and purity of action.

Freedom from care was not only an ideal to be realized in dramatic gestures but was meant to permeate the most mundane routines of daily life. Freedom from the tyranny of time was one manifestation of this. We see an illustration of this in a story of Abba Ammonas's attempt to find a means of getting across the river one day. He sat down waiting for the ferry to embark, while in the meantime, another boat—a private one—arrived to transport those who were waiting across the river. Ammonas's companions said to him, "Come here, Father, and cross the river with us." But he replied: "I will not embark except in the public vessel." And he sat down and began to weave and undo his palm branches until the public boat came along. Thus, he made his crossing. The brothers, puzzled by his action, asked him why he did this. He answered them, "So as not always to walk around in anxiety of spirit . . . we must walk with calm in the way of God."[53] Am-

monas's obstinacy here seems at first to have no purpose. Yet his unhurried
contentment communicates to the brothers how unnecessary their haste was
and the high price it could exact on their lives. Freedom here meant recognizing the fullness present in every moment.

The desire to have a little something extra just in case—money, water,
food—was another persistent challenge to the monks' commitment to freedom from care. In one instance, a person brought some money to an old
man, saying, "[K]eep it for your expenses, for you are getting old and you
are ill." The old man was indeed ill, and while he appreciated the other's
consideration for him, he resented what the gift suggested: that he could not
receive all he needed from God. He asked the one bringing the money,
"Are you really going to take my prize from me after sixty years, for I have
been ill as long as that? I need nothing. God supplies what I need and feeds
me." [54] A similar attitude of utter dependence upon God can be seen in
Abba Bessarion's response to Abba Doulos's desire to "hedge his bets" and
carry a little extra water in the desert. Even apparently "sensible" behavior
like this was seen as problematic when viewed in light of the aspiration to
become free from care. Abba Bessarion asked Abba Doulos why he insisted
on carrying water with him wherever he went. Doulos replied, somewhat
sheepishly, but with a certain amount of common sense: "Forgive me, it is
for fear of being thirsty later on." But the old man said, "God is here, God
is everywhere." [55] This level of trust appears foolhardy from a practical
point of view, yet it reveals the seriousness with which the monks took the
Gospel call to be "free from care." In another story, Abba Moses is said to
have gone on a journey to Petra, but on the way he grew tired and began to
wonder where he would get water there. But a voice said to him, "Go and
do not be anxious about anything [μηδὲν φροντίσῃς] [Mt. 6:25]." So he
continued and when he arrived, he cooked beans for some of the brothers
with what little water he had left. Only then did a cloud of rain come to
Petra and fill the cisterns. [56]

The desert fathers recognized the need to maintain a balance between
working for their food and cultivating an awareness of their utter dependence upon God. Still, even while maintaining this tension, the most important thing to remember, Abba Silvanus said, was one's utter dependence on
God. He described his own attitude thus: "I am a slave, and my master says
to me: 'Do your work and I will feed you; but do not try to find out whence
I shall feed you. Do not try to find out whether I have it, or whether I steal
it, or whether I borrow it; simply work, and I will feed you.' Therefore,
when I work, I eat the fruit of my wages; but if I do not work, I eat charity." [57] For the monks, learning to cast their cares upon God, to live free
from all anxiety was an expression of faith. They knew well enough that

lack of faith was the root cause of their hesitation to give themselves completely to God: "If a monk knows a place where he can make progress, but where he can get the necessities of life only with difficulty, and for that reason he does not go there, such a monk does not believe God exists." [58] The stories testifying to those who had learned to overcome their fears and anxieties about the future thus carried real weight for the monks. They served to remind those struggling with their own attachments—to things, to reputation, to security—that freedom was indeed possible.

Recovery of Paradise

The monks' belief in the possibility of realizing a life free from care is symbolized most vividly in the numerous sayings and stories alluding to the recovery of paradise. There is a sense of longing present in these sayings— a desire to recapture in the present moment a taste of innocence and intimacy with God which Adam knew in paradise. The stories likening the elders to Adam recall the simplicity of paradise which the monks were now seeing rekindled in the desert. We see this in the power certain monks were said to possess over animals and the capacity some of them had to live as Adam did, in innocence and without care.

Abba Paul, who was said to have had a mastery over snakes, explained his own authority and its source by referring to Adam: "If someone has obtained purity, everything is in submission to him, as it was to Adam, when he was in Paradise before he transgressed the commandment." [59] Numerous other stories allude to the power which the monks had over animals. While there is no direct mention of Adam in these stories, the echoes of paradise reverberate through them. Abba Theodore of Pherme was said to enjoy such power over animals. One day he went to draw water with a brother. "The brother going ahead, saw a dragon in the lake. The old man said to him, 'Go and walk on his head.' But he was afraid and did not go. So the old man went. The beast saw him and fled away into the desert as if it was ashamed." [60]

Such power was not inherent in the monks but was at least in part a product of their long struggle in the desert. Antony noted that "obedience with abstinence gives men power over wild beasts." [61] We see evidence of this in a story about Abba John and a wild hyena. John was instructed by Abba Paul to go to some nearby tombs to collect dung for fuel. However, John was frightened by a hyena that lived there and asked his abba what he should do if he encountered it. The old man told John jokingly that he should "tie it up" and bring it back to him. Later, when John went to collect the dung, the hyena attacked him. Following the old man's instructions to the letter, he pursued her, saying "My abba says I am to tie you up." He did eventually manage to seize her, tie her up, and bring her back to Abba Paul as he had been instructed. The old man, for his part, was astonished by this act of obedience.[62] The main point of the story is clearly the extraordinary obedience shown by Abba John. Yet here obedience is an expression of the innocence and purity of heart which lead John to pursue the hyena with total abandon and to attempt to communicate with her somehow. These qualities, as much as John's power over the hyena, suggest the recovery of a primal innocence which marks the return to paradise.

It was not only Adam's power over animals which the monks were said to have recovered but also his sense of intimacy with them. Abba James recalls a story one of the elders told him about an extraordinary sight he had witnessed: "One of the elders had said: 'When I lived in the desert, I had as a neighbor a child who lived all alone. In observing him, I saw him pray and ask God to let him live in peace with the wild beasts. After the prayer, a hyena was found there nursing its young, and the child slipped himself under and began nursing with them.' "[63] Who this mysterious child was we are not told. But a story contained in the *Historia Monachorum* provides an interesting parallel which suggests that the monks themselves sometimes enjoyed such intimacy with animals: "Macarius was praying in his cave in the desert. There happened to be another cave nearby which was the den of a hyena. While he was at prayer, the hyena suddenly appeared and began to lick his feet. And taking him by the hem of his tunic, she drew him towards her own cave. . . . [S]he went in and brought out to him her own cubs, which had been born blind. He prayed over them and returned them to the hyena with their sight healed. She in turn, by way of thank-offering, brought the man the huge skin of a large ram and laid it at his feet. He smiled at her as if at a kind and sensitive person, and taking the skin, spread it under him."[64] Such intimacy with animals expressed in symbolic terms a conviction which the desert fathers cherished: that they were recovering in their life in the desert a small taste of paradise.

A haunting, miragelike picture of this paradise and the quality of freedom enjoyed by the monks who inhabited it is conveyed in a story told by Abba Macarius. He had been prompted by the spirit to go out into the remotest part of the desert. "There I found a sheet of water and an island in the midst, and the animals of the desert came to drink there. In the midst of these animals I saw two naked men. . . . They said, 'It is God who has made this way of life for us. We do not freeze in the winter, and the summer does us no harm.' "[65] This extraordinary sight sent a chill through Macarius. Yet it also spoke to his deepest aspirations and to those of all the monks—

to live an unfettered, graced existence, as their ancestors in paradise had done before them. And Macarius's encounter with these ghostly figures in the remotest regions of the desert served as a reminder that the recovery of paradise was not merely a dream: "The monk['s] . . . decision to 'sit alone' in the desert gave reality to a long tradition of speculation on the lost simplicity of Adam: the 'glory of Adam' was summed up in his person."[66] This glory was freedom.

Notes

1. Antony 3 [*PG* 65:76C].
2. See Jacques Fontaine and Charles Pietri, eds., *Le monde latin antique et la Bible* (Paris: Beauchesne, 1985), 410–11.
3. *VA* 1–2. R. C. Gregg, *The Life of Antony and the Letter to Marcellinus* (New York: Paulist Press, 1980), 30–31.
4. Isidore of Pelusia 6 [*PG* 65:224].
5. Cassian 7 [*PG* 65:245C].
6. Antony 20 [*PG* 65:81CD].
7. See also J 721 [*SPAn*, 303]. There, some brothers who had renounced all became the "joy of the demons" when they began to give themselves to "making bags and chests containing fruits and delicacies, needles and scissors and sashes." The saying makes explicit connection between the failure of nerve of these monks and that of Ananias and Saphirus in Acts 5.
8. Poemen 33 [*PG* 65:329D–332A]: ἐὰν δὲ εἴπω σοι, Δὸς αὐτὰ πτωχοῖς, ἀμερμινεῖς); Mt. 19:21: δὸς πτωχοῖς; Mt. 6:26: μὴ μεριμνᾶτε.
9. Nau 295 [*ROC* 14:378].
10. See, for example, Arsenius 36 [*PG* 65:101C–104A] and Abba of Rome [*PG* 65:389A].
11. Andrew 1 [*PG* 65:136B].
12. Euprepius 5 [*PG* 65:172C].
13. Poemen 60 [*PG* 65:336C].
14. Theodore of Pherme 5 [*PG* 65:183D].
15. Elias 8 [*PG* 65:185AB].
16. Hyperchius 6 [*PG* 65:429D].
17. John Colobos 34 [*PG* 65:216AC].
18. Megethius 1 [*PG* 65:300D].
19. Nau 143 [*ROC* 13:49], [m].
20. Theodore of Pherme 28 [*PG* 65:193D–196A], [m].
21. Macarius 20 [*PG* 65:269D].
22. Syncletica 5 [*PG* 65:421D]. For another example of a "reversal" of a biblical text, based on the experience of the monastic community, see Poemen 88 [*PG* 65:344AB]: " 'Can a man keep all his thoughts in control and not surrender one to

the enemy?' An old man said to him, 'There are some who receive ten and give one' " (Lk 19:16: "Lord, the sum you have given me has earned you another ten. . . ."). See Luciana Mortari, *Vita e detti dei padre del deserta*, vol. 2 (Rome: Città Nuova, 1971), 37.

23. Nilus 4 [*PG* 65:305B].

24. Poemen 54 [*PG* 65:333D–336A].

25. Joseph of Thebes [*PG* 65:241C].

26. Pambo 3 [*PG* 65:369AB].

27. Theodora 2 [*PG* 65:201B].

28. Poemen 112 [*PG* 65:349C–352A].

29. See J. P. Lemaire, "L'abbé Poemen et la Sainte Écriture" (licentiate thesis, University of Freiburg, 1971), 38–39.

30. Ammonas 11 [*PG* 65:124A], [m] [RSV]; see also Nau 249 [*ROC* 14:365].

31. John Colobos 41 [Guy, *Recherches,* S1:23]; on bearing insults see Mt. 22:6: "seized his servants, insulted [ὕβρισαν] them, and killed them. . . ."; Lk 18:32: "He [the Son of Man] will be delivered to the gentiles, and will be mocked, insulted [ὑβρισθήσεται] and spat upon"; 2 Cor 12:10: "For the sake of Christ, I am content with weaknesses, insults [ὕβρεσιν]."

32. See I. Hausherr, S. J., "L'hésychasme: Étude de spiritualité," *OCP* 22 (1956): 268, who, speaking of the freedom from care found among the desert fathers, asserts: "[T]heir *"amerimnia* (freedom from care) comes straight from the Gospel."

33. On the "Eight Capital Vices," see Evagrius, *Praktikos,* 6–14.

34. Poemen 126 [*PG* 65:353C].

35. Nau 174 [*ROC* 13:57], [m].

36. Agathon 21 [*PG* 65:116A], [m].

37. Poemen 36 [*PG* 65:332B]. Antony echoed this same conviction, saying, "The greatest thing a man can do is throw his faults before the Lord. . . ."; Poemen 125 [*PG* 65:333C]; see also Antony 4 [*PG* 65:77A].

38. Poemen 146 [*PG* 65:357C].

39. John the Eunuch 1 [*PG* 65:223A] [RSV].

40. Biare 1 [*PG* 65:145A]. The word ταράσσω, meaning to stir up, disturb, unsettle, or throw into confusion, is found in several biblical texts, usually in a negative sense; see Ps 48:5 *(LXX);* Acts 15:24; Jn 11:33; Mk 6:50.

41. Nau 213 [*ROC* 13:282].

42. Euprepius 1 [*PG* 65:172B]; Mk 9:23: "And Jesus said to him, 'If you can! All things are possible to him who believes.' "

43. Agathon 6 [*PG* 65:112A], [m].

44. On Jesus' departures during his ministry, see Mt. 8:34; 11:1; Jn 7:3; Mt 12:19; 15:29; on Paul's departure from the abuse he was receiving at the hands of certain Corinthians, see Acts 18:7; on Jesus' departure from the world, see Jn 13:1: "Jesus knew that his hour had come to depart out of this world to the Father."

45. This too may echo certain biblical texts; see Mt 6:24: "No one can serve two masters . . . he will hate one and despise [καταφρονήσει] the other"; Heb 12:2: "Jesus . . . who for the joy that was set before him endured the cross, despising [καταφρονήσας] the shame."

46. Gelasius 5 [*PG* 65:152ABC].

47. Nisterius 4 [*PG* 65:308BC].

48. Theodore of Pherme 18 [*PG* 65:192AB].

49. Macarius the Great 18 [*PG* 65:269BC] [RSV]; see also Macarius the Great 40 [*PG* 65:281AB].

50. Euprepius 3 [*PG* 65:172C].

51. Euprepius 2 [*PG* 65:172B]; see also Nau 337 [*ROC* 17:294], which relates a similar story with the difference that the thieves eventually return everything.

52. Gelasius 1 [*PG* 65:145CD–148A], [m].

53. Ammonas 6 [*PG* 65:120D–121A], [m].

54. Nau 260 [*ROC* 14:368].

55. Bessarion 1 [*PG* 65:137C–140A].

56. Moses 13 [*PG* 65:285D–228A], [m].

57. Silvanus 9 [*PG* 65:412B].

58. Nau 236 [*ROC* 14:362].

59. Paul 1 [*PG* 65:380D].

60. Theodore of Pherme 23 [*PG* 65:192D–193A].

61. Antony 36 [*PG* 65:88B].

62. John the disciple of Abba Paul [*PG* 65:240BC].

63. James 5 [Guy, *Recherches,* S1:25]. Cf. also James 6 [Guy, *Recherches,* S2:25]: "Another time, I saw him pray and ask the Lord 'give me the grace to be friends with the fire.' Having made a fire, he knelt down in the middle of it, praying to the master."

64. Macarius 15–16 [*Historia Monachorum* 21:15–16; *The Lives of the Desert Fathers*. introd. Benedicta Ward, trans. Norman Russell (London: Mowbray, 1980), 110]; see also *Historia Lausiaca* 18:27; *Palladius: The Lausiac History*, trans. Robert T. Meyer (Westminster, MD: Newman Press, 1965), 66.

65. Macarius 2 [*PG* 65:260B–261A].

66. Peter Brown, *The Making of Late Antiquity* (Cambridge: Harvard University Press, 1978), 86.

8

The Humble Way of Christ

"First of all, the monk must gain humility; for it is the first commandment of the Lord who said: 'Blessed are the poor in spirit, for theirs is the kingdom of heaven (Mt 5:3).' "[1] This saying of Abba John of Thebes expresses well the significance this beatitude had in the imagination of the desert fathers. Humility was the starting point for the desert monks, both because it was the first commandment and because they knew that without the self-emptying which humility implied, the treasures for which they had come to the desert would forever elude them. The *Sayings* is filled with questions about the meaning of humility and about how to acquire and cultivate it: its importance was equalled only by its elusiveness. The monks' questions about humility focused on and drew upon various words of Scripture and in particular the witness of Christ. In pursuing humility, they were attempting to realize in their own lives the call to self-emptying exemplified in the words and witness of Jesus.

In their quest for this virtue of lowliness, then, the desert fathers showed themselves to be deeply influenced by the Christian ethos. Humility was in fact a characteristically Christian virtue and its pursuit by the monks distinguished their quest for holiness in important ways from that found among contemporary pagans.

> Among pagan authors humility had almost never been a term of commendation. It belonged with ignoble and abject characters. Men were born "sons of God," said the Stoics, and thus they should cherish no "humble or ignoble" thoughts about their nature. The humble belonged with the abject, the mean, the unworthy. Christianity, however, ascribed humility to God's own Son and exalted it as a virtue of man, his creature whom he had redeemed.[2]

The desert fathers strove to incorporate the humility of Christ and the Gospels into their lives, to become bearers of this humility. In their sayings and stories, we see them struggling to learn the ways of humility and, in rare cases, realizing its meaning in their lives.

236

Learning the Way of Humility

Numerous sayings testify to the necessity of humility in the life of the monk. In fact, they suggest that humility was the one thing necessary. For Abba Poemen humility was as vital as the breath of life itself: "As the breath which comes out of his nostrils, so does a man need humility and the fear of God."[3] Syncletica noted that it was humility which held the monk's life together and made salvation possible: "[J]ust as one cannot build a ship unless one has some nails, so it is impossible to be saved without humility."[4] Humility was given a special place in relation to all the other virtues which the monks sought to cultivate in their lives. Abba John Colobos contended, "Humility and the fear of God are above all virtues."[5] Amma Theodora spelled this out in greater detail, placing the relative power of the other monastic virtues in a distinctly inferior position to that of humility: "[N]either asceticism, nor vigils, nor any kind of suffering are able to save, only genuine humility can do that."[6]

None of the other virtues could save a monk, because none of them could so effectively overcome the natural human tendency to rely on oneself, to look to one's own achievements as the reason for one's happiness and well-being. The elders were well aware of the treachery of this kind of thinking and warned against it. They were especially concerned that no one should imagine that the work of asceticism alone could bring one closer to God. The martyrdom of obedience for instance—suspending one's own wishes and desires by placing oneself under the authority of another—would do more to loosen the tenacious grip of one's ego than any amount of fasting. It is for this reason that Amma Syncletica said, "[O]bedience is preferable to asceticism. The one teaches pride, the other humility."[7] The pride and lack of discernment bred by false dependence on one's ascetical achievements could bankrupt the whole monastic endeavor. Isidore of Pelusia emphasized just what was at stake in this struggle to maintain humility through an ironic use of spatial imagery: "The heights of humility are great and so are the depths of boasting; I advise you to attend to the first and not to fall into the second."[8] We hear one elder reflect sadly at how easy it was to fall into an attitude of misplaced pride: "Many have injured their bodies without discernment and have gone away from us having achieved nothing. Our mouths smell bad through fasting . . . but we do not have that which God seeks: charity and humility."[9] The cultivation of humility was the only way of avoiding such deception and the disappointment that would ultimately follow.

Humility was perceived to be especially effective in helping one to resist and overcome the myriad attacks from the demons. Abba Antony related a vision that he had: "I saw the snares that the enemy spreads out over the world and I said groaning, 'What can get through this?' Then I heard a voice say to me, 'Humility.' " [10] The monks knew from bitter experience the demonic force that pride, especially pride in their achievements, could wreak on their souls. Once, when Abba Zeno encountered a brother who had been excessive and ostentatious regarding his ascetical feats, he rebuked him, echoing Jesus' words in the Gospel: "Whatever you do, do it secretly [Mt 6:4–5]." [11] Acting in secret, with genuine humility, was the one thing necessary for overcoming the attacks of the evil one in general and the power of pride in particular. Humility in this sense meant recognizing that one was just like everyone else. It was a means of disappearing into the crowd. Abba Motius once said: "If you live somewhere, do not seek to be known for anything special . . . for this is humility: to see yourself to be the same as the rest." [12] To enter into this kind of obscurity was not a casual undertaking. It required careful self-scrutiny.

Humility: Consciousness of Sin and Dependence upon God

For the monks, cultivating a spirit of humility meant moving in two opposite directions at once: fostering both a sense of one's sinfulness and a sense of one's utter dependence upon the mercy of God. The self-abnegation which the monks so often expressed should not be mistaken for self-hatred. It reflected rather an honest assessment of their endless capacity for guile and self-deceit. On the other hand, by cultivating this sense of themselves as sinners, as people incapable of doing anything good, they found they were able to open themselves to receive the mercy of God—and of others. In so doing, they discovered unexpected resources of power and goodness in their lives. To describe this experience of humility for themselves and others, the monks looked both to Scripture and to their own experience.

One elder alluded to this "double movement" of humility by pointing out how one should see oneself in relation to others: "The divine work of humility [is] considering oneself a sinner, inferior to all . . . not paying attention to other's sins but always to one's own, praying to God ceaselessly." [13] A similar sensibility also pertained to religious experiences. For the desert fathers, a humble consciousness of one's sins was far more important than any special religious experiences. One elder used a play on words to illustrate this for a brother whose imagination had been captivated by talk of extraordinary visions. He asked the elder, "How is it that some say, 'we have seen [βλέπομεν] visions of angels'?" The old man replied in language which echoes the Beatitudes, shifting the brother's attention to another kind of vision, "Happy [Μακάριός] is he who always sees [βλέπων] his sins." [14] This awareness of one's weakness and sin was shown to be part of the virtue of ascetical practices. In response to someone who wanted to know the good of fasting and vigils, Abba Moses said, "They make the soul humble." In support of this, he cited Ps 25:18, "Consider my affliction and my trouble, and forgive all my sins." He comments further, "If the soul gives itself all this hardship, God will have mercy on it," suggesting that, like the psalmist, the soul will be more open to the grace and protection of God from the lowly place of humility. [15] Abba Sisoes emphasized the connection between humility and the cultivation of a silent confidence in God through an allusion to a text from Isaiah. He told a brother who came to ask him for help: "The thing which you seek is great silence and humility. For it is written, 'Blessed are those who abide in him (Is 30:18)' for thus they are able to stand." [16] Humility in this instance refers to a deep confidence in the goodness of God which is symbolized by a silent, abiding trust. Nor was such confidence misplaced. Abba Poemen claimed that humble attentiveness to one's own sins carried with it its own rewards, namely a deep peace or rest for the soul. Poemen held that, "If you take little account of yourself, you will have rest [ἀνάπαυσιν] wherever you live." [17] Elsewhere he said, "Let go of a small part of your righteousness [δικαιοσύνης], and in a few days you will be at rest [ἀνάπαυσιν]." [18] All of this suggests that the monks took seriously the exhortation of the beatitude calling them to be "poor in spirit." By cultivating an honest sense of their own lowliness, sinfulness, or poverty of spirit, they could keep at bay the treacheries of self-deception to which their pride always led them. From this deepened awareness of their capacity for sin, they developed the capacity to give themselves over in a spirit of trust to the source of their life and salvation.

While the practice of humility indeed brought with it certain undeniable benefits, the monks were only too aware of how easily these could be lost through complacency. Humility meant therefore that cultivating a sense of one's sinfulness must be an ongoing task, an unfolding process which required vigilance at each step of the way. Two texts from 1 Corinthians 10, both warning against complacency, figured in the thinking of the desert fathers on this subject. To warn those who thought that merely by becoming monks and engaging in ascetical practices they would be protected from temptation, Syncletica cited Paul, who said, "Let him who thinks that he stands take heed lest he fall (1 Cor 10:12)." Standing—assuming that one was in control or that one had reached a necessary level of holiness—was dangerous and foolish, for such presumptions simply prepared one for a precipitous fall. As Syncletica reminded them, "taking heed" or having humility, was crucial because there was so much that was beyond their con-

trol or understanding: "we sail on in darkness." [19] Another elder alluded to
the same text to warn the monks not to measure themselves against one
another, trying to outdo one another in ascetical endurance. Rather, he said
"By the grace of Christ, submit yourself in a spirit of poverty and sincere
charity so that you may not lose your labor through the spirit of vainglory.
Indeed, it is written, 'Let him who thinks he is standing take heed, lest he
fall' (1 Cor 10:12)." [20]

Constant attentiveness to humility was felt to be especially important during times of relative calm, for it was precisely in such moments that one
could be lured into a false and superficial sense of security. Thus one elder
recommended that, "When we do not experience warfare, we ought so much
the more to humiliate ourselves. For God, seeing our weakness, protects us;
when we glorify ourselves, he withdraws his protection and we are lost." [21]
A similar saying from Abba Bessarion emphasizes more strongly the scriptural basis of the exhortation to embrace weakness in order to overcome
pride. "When you are at peace," Abba Bessarion said, "and are not at-
tacked, humiliate yourself even more [$\mu\tilde{\alpha}\lambda\lambda o\nu\ \tau\alpha\pi\epsilon\iota\nuo\tilde{\upsilon}$] for fear that if an
alien joy arises, you will be led into glorifying yourselves and be delivered
to warfare. For often, because of our weakness, God does not allow us to
be tempted, in order that we might not perish [1 Cor 10:13]." [22] Such psychological acuity regarding the inner machinations of pride could only come
from experience. And this provides a clue regarding how the monks' own
interests and keen psychological insight could influence their reading of the
texts. In this instance, the text to which Bessarion makes reference nowhere
actually mentions humility. However, Bessarion interprets the phrase, "God
does not allow us to be tempted" as a source of encouragement, leading the
monks to "humiliate themselves" as a constant protection against "alien
joy" or pride. It is precisely by recognizing, even cultivating "our weakness
[$\dot{\alpha}\sigma\theta\epsilon\nu\epsilon\dot{\iota}\alpha\varsigma\ \dot{\eta}\mu\tilde{\omega}\nu$]," he suggests, that those who are tempted by this "alien
joy" can overcome it and remain "in peace."

Humility: Sharing in Christ's Sufferings

Jesus Christ himself was the model of humility *par excellence* for the monks.
The endurance of afflictions, insults, trials, and dishonor for the sake of
Christ, one of the signs of blessedness in the Beatitudes (Mt 5:10–12), was
an important ideal for those living in the desert, and an expression of humility. However, it is Christ's own example of humility—his *kenosis* or
self-emptying (Phil 2)—whose shadow falls most dramatically across the
Sayings. The desert fathers sought to follow Christ by walking in the way
of his humility, by sharing in his sufferings, and by repaying a debt of love

to the one who had suffered for them. They were clearly moved by this aspect of Christ's life, and the *Sayings* reflect how much they struggled to realize its meaning in their own lives. By doing so, they hoped to bring Christ to life in the desert.

For Abba Poemen, the whole purpose of the monk's life in the desert could only be understood in reference to the Beatitudes. He asked, "Is it not in order to endure affliction [κόπου] [Mt 5:10ff] that we have come to this place?" [23] Similarly, Abba Paphnutius exhorted a brother who asked him for a word to seek the way of lowliness portrayed in the Beatitudes: "Go and choose trials rather than rest, dishonor rather than glory, and seek to give rather than to receive." [24] Abba Evagrius compared the ideal attitude of the monk to the sorry state of the early Christians: "Happy [μακάριός] is the monk who thinks he is the offscouring [περίψημα] of all [1 Cor 4:13]." [25] In words which echo the gospel language regarding the harsh treatment Jesus endured, one of the elders declared, "If you can bear to be despised [ὑβισθῆναι] [Lk 18:32], that is the great thing, more than all the other virtues." [26]

It was all too easy to mistake false humility for the genuine humility of Christ. Because of this, the elders recognized the need for careful discernment in navigating their way around the shoals of self-deception. We see an example of this in a story concerning a brother who came to see Abba Serapion for help in overcoming his sinfulness. Having arrived at the elder's cell, the brother refused to join Serapion in prayer or to allow the old man to wash his feet, all the while protesting loudly that he was a "sinner and unworthy of the monastic habit." Serapion quickly perceived that the brother was agitated and was behaving disingenuously; he therefore admonished him to stay in his cell, pay attention to himself, and do some manual work. The brother took great offense at this, and vividly displayed this in his annoyed expression. Noticing this, Serapion then confronted the brother, "Up to now you have called yourself a sinner and accused yourself of being unworthy to live, but when I admonished you lovingly, you were extremely put out. If you want to be humble, learn to bear generously what others inflict upon you." [27] A similar warning was issued by Antony when some brothers praised a certain monk before him. "When the monk came to see him, Antony wanted to know how he would bear dishonor [φέρει ἀτιμίαν] [2 Cor 6:8]; and seeing that he could not bear it at all, he said to him, 'You are like a village magnificently decorated on the outside, but destroyed from within by robbers.' " [28] Genuine humility had to penetrate beyond the level of appearances and words to reach the core of the person. Sometimes only a certain amount of testing and probing could lead the monk to enter into that deeper level of humility.

For Abba Arsenius, this meant thinking more carefully about what it meant for him to take upon himself the *yoke* of Christ's humility. He was prompted to do this after observing several different people working at their various tasks in utter futility. One person had cut some wood and was struggling unsuccessfully to carry the pile he had already cut. But instead of taking some wood off of the pile, he continued to add more to it. Another was trying to draw some water from a lake but poured it into a broken receptacle so that the water ran back into the lake. Finally, he saw a pair of men on horseback trying to carry a large beam of wood through a doorway. Because they insisted on staying on their horses and carrying the wood crosswise, they remained outside the door, unable to enter. Then a voice spoke to Arsenius, explaining to him the significance of what he had seen: "These men carry the yoke of righteousness with pride, and do not humble themselves [οὐκ ἐταπεινώθησαν . . . ἑαυτοὺς] so as to correct themselves and walk in the humble way of Christ [πορευθῆναι τῇ ταπεινῇ ὁδῷ τοῦ Χριστοῦ] [Mt 11:29; Phil 2:5ff]. So they remain outside the Kingdom of God . . . [E]veryone must be watchful of his actions, lest he labor in vain" [Phil 2:16].[29]

There are echoes of a cluster of New Testament passages in this saying, which suggest the influence of Christ's example of humility on the need for vigilance in the monastic life. The people Arsenius observes, who are in fact reflections of himself, are shown to be working at different tasks. Still, they share one thing in common: none of their work is bearing fruit. Their mistake, as Arsenius sees it, is in the insistence with which they "carry the yoke of righteousness with pride, and do not humble themselves and . . . walk in the humble way of Christ." This expression calls to mind both Jesus' exhortation to his disciples to practice a "righteousness [that] exceeds that of the scribes and pharisees" (Mt 5:20) as well as his invitation to "take my yoke upon you . . . for I am gentle and lowly [ταπεινὸς] in heart. . . ." (Mt 11:29). However, there is another, even more central image at work here, which explains the meaning and significance of watchfulness as it is understood in this context: it is the image of Christ found in the great hymn in the second chapter of Philippians. There, in contrast to the example of the workers in Arsenius's vision who "do not humble themselves," we see one who "humbled himself [ἐταπείνωσεν ἑαυτὸν] and became obedient unto death (Phil 2:8)." In light of this unparalleled example of humility, Paul calls the Philippians to a very practical response, to live lives of holiness, "blameless and innocent," so that he will know that he did not "labor in vain (Phil 2:16)." Arsenius recalls the same example to encourage each of his disciples to "be watchful in his actions [νήφειν . . . εἰς τὰ ἔργα αὐτοῦ], lest he labor in vain." Thus, vigilance is understood here to imply an attentiveness toward all of one's actions, a singleness of purpose informed in a particular way by the spirit of humility exemplified by Christ.

These same texts were drawn upon by Abba John Colobos to emphasize the importance of self-accusation in the cultivation of humility. As exacting as such self-accusation could be, John recognized that it was in reality a light burden when seen in comparison with the habit of pride. "We have put the light burden [ἐλαφρὸν φορτίον] on one side, that is to say, self-accusation, and we have loaded ourselves with a heavy one [τὸ βαρὺ], that is to say, self-justification [Mt 11:30; Mt 23:4]."[30] Cultivating humility was meant to lead to a spiritual transformation, characterized by an unlikely reversal: that which was previously seen to be easy to bear, namely self-justification, was to be exchanged for that which had previously been experienced as impossibly heavy, namely self-accusation.

Following Christ's way of humility also meant cultivating within oneself the attitudes and disposition which led Christ to his death. For Abba Hyperchius, the need for obedience in the monastic life derived from Christ's example of self-emptying. For this reason, he claimed: "Obedience is the best ornament of the monk. He who has acquired it will be heard by God, and he will stand beside the crucified with confidence [μετὰ παρρησίας τῷ σταυρωθέντι παραστήσεται], for the crucified became obedient unto death (Phil 2:8)."[31] Obedience in the life of the monk was a kind of crucifixion, a death to self which, if undertaken freely, could produce abundant fruit. To another elder, imitating the crucified one meant being like Christ in his total dependence upon God in the midst of his sufferings. When a brother asked the old man how to be saved, he answered him with a dramatic gesture: "[He] took off his habit, girded his loins and raised his hands to heaven, saying, 'So should the monk be . . . crucified. . . . [I]n his thoughts the monk stands, his arms stretched out in the form of a cross to heaven, calling on God. . . .'"[32] For another, following the crucified one was synonymous with single-minded resolve to resist all other distractions and enticements: "Only the one who has seen the hare follows it till he catches it, not letting himself be turned from his course by those who go back, and not caring about the ravines, rocks and undergrowth. So it is with him who seeks Christ as master: always devoting himself to the cross, he cares for none of the scandals that occur, till he reaches the crucified."[33] This saying echoes an attitude we saw earlier referring to the monk's approach to Scripture: just as one was not to be satisfied until he had "attained" the words of Scripture, so too the monk was not to rest until he had "reached" or "attained" the place where the crucified one dwells.

To attain the place of the crucified one in this way meant participating deeply in the paschal mystery itself. The monk had to die to all that within

himself which separated him from God and to come to live completely in
Christ. We can see this aspiration expressed in some questions which were
put to Abba Moses. A brother came to him saying, "I see something in
front of me and I am not able to grasp it." The old man said to him, "If
you do not become dead like those who are in the tomb, you will not be
able to grasp [κατασχεῖν] it."[34] Another time, a brother asked Abba Moses
how someone could consider himself to be "dead toward his neighbor."
Moses responded: "Unless a person considers in his heart that he is already
three days in the tomb, he cannot attain [φθάνει] this saying."[35] The question of how to "die toward one's neighbor" apparently preoccupied Abba
Moses, for it figures in several of his sayings.[36] Taken altogether, they express an attitude toward humility which draws inspiration from several biblical images and which is based on a profound appropriation of the paschal
mystery. The allusion to Christ's burial is clear; the monk is called to participate in this burial. To "become dead" in this way is an expression of
one's allegiance, of where one's life is rooted. The biblical impulse for this
idea can be found at least in part in Romans (6:10ff). Speaking of Christ,
Paul said: "The death he died he died to sin, once for all, but the life he
lives he lives to God. So you must also consider yourself dead to sin and
alive to God in Christ Jesus." There may also be echoes of Colossians (3:3–
5) here: "For you have died and your life is hid with Christ in God . . .
put to death therefore what is earthly in you. . . ." As Abba Moses understood it, the expression of such an attitude should be practical, and ought to
manifest itself in one's relationships with others. Humility in this sense means
cultivating a genuine indifference toward both the praise and criticism of
others, based on the knowledge that the source and center of life lie elsewhere, hidden in Christ. This aspiration to follow Christ in his path of self-
emptying, to live completely in the mystery of Christ's suffering, is aptly
expressed by Abba John Colobos. He counseled the brothers simply to live
"in the cross [ἐν σταυρῷ]."[37]

The desert fathers were conscious that their own sufferings were to be
embraced because of the sufferings endured by Christ for their sakes. An
episode related by Abba Elias indicates an awareness of Christ's presence in
the midst of the struggles of the monks and the Christ-centered character of
their labors. He tells of an elder who occupied a pagan temple and was
attacked by demons who commanded him to depart from "their domain."
When the old man refused to leave the place, the demons increased their
attacks. One of them even dragged him bodily to the door of the temple to
throw him out. In desperation, the elder cried out, "Jesus, save me," and
immediately the demons left him. Finally, overwhelmed by the level and
intensity of the violence that had been inflicted upon him, the elder broke

down and wept. Then the Lord appeared to him, and said: "Why are you weeping?" and the old man said: "Because the devils have dared to seize a man and treat him like this." The Lord said to him: "You had been careless. As soon as you turned to me again, you see I was beside you." Elias comments on the significance of this story: "I say this, because it is necessary to take great pains, and anyone who does not do so, cannot come to his God. For he himself was crucified for our sake." [38] Expressing a similar sentiment, Abba Isidore said: "Even if Isidore were burned, and his ashes thrown to the winds, I would not allow myself any relaxation, because the Son of God came here for our sake." [39] The humility Christ showed in embracing the full range of human experience provided the model and the inspiration for the monks' unrelenting quest for lowliness. The monks' "hard work," in fact the whole monastic endeavor, only makes sense as a response of love for what God had done for them in Christ. The movement toward humility, then, was rooted in love.

Realization of Humility

Because fulfilling the commandment to be humble required one to move ever deeper into obscurity, to consciously acquire a lowly place, it would be surprising if we were to find many places in the *Sayings* celebrating the monks' fulfillment of this virtue. Acts of humility are, by their very nature, difficult to see. Even here, however, the desert fathers had an eye for the significant gesture, the act which expressed an inner grasp of the virtue of humility. Their attention to these acts reflects the monks' conviction that the commandment to take on the humility of the cross, to become poor in spirit, had been fulfilled by some in their midst. Words and stories of those who had realized this humility were thus cherished and passed on, so that others could absorb something of this spirit in their own lives.

Moving Toward Obscurity

A conscious movement toward obscurity, a social, material, and spiritual "downward mobility," was startling to encounter in the flesh. Therefore it is not surprising to find stories which narrate the meaning of this movement toward humility in considerable detail. What did such movement look like? As we noted earlier, poverty and social status were relative and subjective matters. The monastic life might well represent a way up in the world for certain poor villagers. The important thing was to begin from where one was and make one's whole life a movement toward humility. This could mean completely different things for different monks. We see a striking illustration of this in a story concerning an encounter between Abba Arsenius, a well-educated man of senatorial rank who had taken up life in the desert, and "one of the great Egyptian [monks]." The story reveals how different the attitudes toward humility could be for people from different cultural and social backgrounds and how, where humility was concerned, appearances could be deceiving. The Egyptian monk had heard about Abba Arsenius and had come to visit him. When he arrived at Arsenius's place, he noticed that he was wearing fine clothing, that he possessed a bed with a cover and a pillow, and that his feet were clean and shod in sandals. "Noticing all this, he was shocked, because such a way of life is not usual in that district; much greater austerity is required." Now Arsenius recognized that his visitor was shocked and proposed that they celebrate a feast together on account of the elder's visit. The elder left the next morning "without being edified." But Arsenius, unhappy with the turn of events and wanting to edify the old man, sent someone to bring him back. Arsenius then proceeded to put some questions to him:

> "[O]f what country are you?" He said, "Egypt." "And of what city?" "I am not a citizen at all." "And what was your work in the village?" "I was a herdsman." "Where did you sleep?" He replied, "In the field." "Did you have anything to lie upon?" He said, "Would I go and put a bed under myself in a field?" "But how did you sleep?" He said, "On the bare ground." [Arsenius] said next, "What was your food in the fields and what did you drink?" He replied, "Is there food and drink in the fields?" "But how did you live?" "I ate dry bread, and, if I found any, green herbs and water." [Arsenius] replied, "Great hardship! Was there a bath-house for washing in the village?" He replied, "No, only the river, when we wanted it."

After Arsenius heard all this and saw how hard the man's former life had been, he told him of his own former way of life when he was in the world, "with the intention of helping him."

> "I, the poor man whom you see, am of the great city of Rome and I was a great man in the palace of the emperor. . . . [T]hen I left the city and came to this desert. I whom you see had great houses and many riches and having despised them I have come to this little cell. I whom you see had beds all of gold with coverings of great value, and in exchange for that, God has given me this little bed and this skin. Moreover, my clothes were the most expensive kind and in their stead I wear these garments of no value. Again, at my table there was much gold and instead of that God has given me this little dish of vegetables and a cup of wine. There were many slaves to serve me and see how in exchange for that, God troubles this old man to serve me. Instead of the bath-house, I throw a little water over my feet and wear sandals because

of my weakness. Instead of music and lyres, I say the twelve psalms and the same at night. Instead of the sins I used to commit, I now say my rule of prayer. So then, I beg you, abba, do not be shocked at my weakness.'' Hearing this, the Egyptian came to his senses and said, ''Woe to me, for after so much hardship in the world, I have found ease; and what I did not have before, that I now possess. While after such great ease, you have come to hardship; from great glory and riches, you have come to humility and poverty.''[40]

This story presents a startling and memorable image of what it meant to embrace a life of humility. It surprises in part because Arsenius's way of life has so little to commend it when measured against the accepted ascetical standards of the desert. By those standards, he has adopted not a life of humility, but a life of ease. Nor does Arsenius's lengthy explanation and defense of his way of life seem to present a sterling example of humility. Still, the contrast between the two men's lives, and in particular the contrast in the *directions* of their lives, was clearly a memorable and poignant reminder for the monks of how personal and subjective the experience of humility was. Arsenius, in spite of the relative ease of his life, had clearly ''come down in the world.'' He had learned to ''despise'' the riches and wealth of his life, taking up instead life of hardship, humility, and poverty in a tiny cell in the desert. The Egyptian monk had moved in precisely the opposite direction—from a life of great hardship and vulnerability in the open fields to the relative security and ease of the monastic life. Although the Egyptian's life was still, by any objective standards, much harder and lowlier than Arsenius's, the consistent downward trajectory of Arsenius's life revealed an experience of humility which the Egyptian did not have. Even Arsenius's defense and explanation of his way of life reveals this humility: having drawn out the contrasts between their two lives, he begs the Egyptian ''not to be shocked at my weakness.'' After his long years in the desert, even after his great descent, it is not the virtue of his life, but his ''weakness'' which is most painfully apparent to Arsenius.

This acute sense of weakness, or sinfulness—even after years of striving in the desert—was a quality which often marked the end of the lives of the holy ones in the desert and was seen as one of the clearest signs of humility. It was often expressed in terms of ''not having yet begun'' along the way. This unselfconscious acknowledgement of one's status as a beginner was seen as an indication of deep self-knowledge and as an expression of how much space one had allowed within oneself for God. Ironically, this sense of being at the beginning was almost never expressed by beginners, but rather by those who had lived many long years in the desert, and who were most highly esteemed. Because of this, such a declaration on the part of a revered elder often shocked and scandalized those who heard it. At the same time, these words conveyed the actual "presence" of humility in the one who uttered them. As Pambo neared death, he reflected on his life and all that he had accomplished: "I do not remember having eaten bread which was not the fruit of my hands and I have not repented of a word I have said up to the present time . . . yet I am going to God as one who has not yet begun to serve God."[41] When Sisoes was nearing death, he told those gathered around him that he wished to "do a little penance" before he died. His disciples protested, insisting that surely *he* no longer had the need to do any penance. But Sisoes only responded, "Truly, I am not aware of having made a beginning yet."[42]

Such consciousness of one's status as a beginner also had a sobering influence upon anyone who might wish to exaggerate the importance of extraordinary religious experiences. Abba John Colobos was sitting in church on one occasion and "gave out a sigh, unaware that there was someone behind him. When he noticed the other one, he prostrated himself before him, saying, 'Forgive me, Abba, for I have not yet made a beginning.' " This is a telling response. We know from other instances in the *Sayings* that such a sigh or groan was sometimes associated with an ecstasy or some kind of extraordinary experience. Abba John's insistence on being treated as a beginner served to deflect attention from his experience and focus it on his palpable sense of being utterly dependent upon God for everything. The immediacy of John's response illustrates how deeply this sensitivity had penetrated his heart. Even though he was gifted with an intimate and profound experience of God, or perhaps *because* of this very experience, he remained firmly convinced of his own obscurity before God. It was, however, a fruitful obscurity.[43] Abba Arsenius shows that a consciousness of being "at the beginning" was one of the most powerful weapons in the fight against the demons. One day, as he was being harassed by demons, he was overheard to pray to God in language soaked in humility, "O God, do not leave me. I have done nothing good in your sight, but according to your goodness, let me now make a beginning of good."[44]

A saying from Abba Matoes suggests the importance of humility even in the face of great spiritual accomplishments. It concerns some monks who were said to have fulfilled and even surpassed the command to "Love your enemies [Mt 5:44]." Hearing of this, a brother asked Matoes: "How is it that the monks did *more* than the Scriptures required in loving their enemies more than themselves?" Matoes responded by agreeing with the brother that it was a great thing to have surpassed the teaching of Scripture in this way. But he also reminded him that it was always necessary to remember one's status as a beginner. Speaking of his own experience, Matoes says: "As for me, I have not yet managed to love those who love me as I love myself [Mt 22:39; Lv 19:18]."[45] Matoes's honesty is disarming. His comments reveal him to be a person who has realized within himself what it means to be always at the beginning. His brief understated reference to his own limitations provides a glimpse of someone who *knows* the meaning of humility. Moreover, he shows that the sense of one's limitations and dependence upon the grace of God which characterizes true humility could give one real insight into the meaning of the Gospel.

Humility in Relationships

The monks sought to cultivate an attitude of humility not only in relationship with God, but also in relationship with their fellow human beings. Practicing humility in relationships was one of the most demanding and personally costly dimensions of monastic life. It was the "acid test" for deciding whether humility was to remain on the level of ideas or was to become a living reality. Every day there were endless opportunities to assert oneself and one's opinions at the expense of others, to insist on one's status, to engage in petty disputes, to hold grudges, to respond to perceived injustices against oneself with righteous indignation. And such responses were often natural and understandable. However, the monks sought to overcome their natural tendency to grasp at their own rights and privileges through the practice of humility. They wanted to place human relationships on a different footing, to undermine the impulses which perpetuated discord and factionalism. In short, they sought to create an atmosphere in which it would be easier to love. Consciously taking the lowest place was a first step in this process. In this sense, humility became an expression of love.

The humility of the biblical heroes could be useful in shedding light on what it meant to practice such humility in everyday life. One issue that caused some confusion for the monks was their practice of making prostrations before one another. Although this gesture was grounded in a sense of respect for the other person, it was apparently unclear to some how far these acts should be taken. Once a brother asked an elder whether or not it was correct to "make many prostrations [μετανοίας πολλάς]." The elder responded with a telling reference to the example of Joshua: "We see that God appeared to Joshua, son of Nun, when he was prostrate [ἐπι πρόσωπον] [Jos 5:14]."[46] The passage from the book of Joshua tells how Joshua, realizing that he was standing on holy ground in the presence of an angel of the Lord "fell prostrate [ἔπεσεν ἐπὶ πρόσωπον] to the ground in worship." The elder's reference to the example of Joshua's humility before God indicates the reverence with which the monks approached the question of prostrations and the significance they attached to the practice. Without answering the question about prostrations directly, the elder nevertheless hints that such an act of humility and respect toward others is entirely appropriate. Every human encounter, he suggests, represents a potential experience of God's intimate presence. A similar sensibility is reflected in a saying which uses the example of Abraham's hospitality to his angelic visitors (Gn 18) as a model for the respect and hospitality that the monks were to show one another. Abba Apollo told the brothers that they should "bow before the brothers who come, because it is not before them, but before God that we prostrate ourselves. . . ." On what authority does he say this? Apollo noted simply, "[W]e have received that from Abraham." [47] This concrete act of prostration before others, a small act in itself, captures well the motivation behind the monks' practice of humility in relationships: the "other" is God.

Silence could also be a profound expression of humility. As we saw earlier, the monks were painfully aware of the damage which words could inflict on others, and for this reason they sought to practice silence as much as possible. In the heat of an argument however, it was completely natural to want to defend oneself or defend another. To refrain from doing so was an expression of humility. Abba Matoes said, "If someone speaks to you about some topic, do not argue with him, but if he is right, say, 'Yes'; if he is wrong, say, 'You know what you are saying' and do not argue with him about what he has said. That is humility." [48] Abba Poemen looked directly to Scripture for help in this matter, citing the example of the psalmist as one who taught him the importance of maintaining silence whenever a troublesome matter came up at the monastery. Abba Nisterus once asked Poemen how he had learned to restrain himself in this way. Poemen said he had been influenced by the example of the psalmist: "When I first came to the monastery, I said to myself, 'You and the donkey are the same. The donkey is beaten but he does not speak, and when ill treated he does not reply: now you must do the same, as the psalmist says [to God]: 'I have become like a beast in your sight; nevertheless, I am continually with you' (Ps 72:22–23)." [49] The sentiment of the Psalm reveals a curious mixture of severe humility and serene confidence. In imitating the humility of the psalmist, Poemen seems to suggest, one could learn to be free from the need to throw oneself into every fray that arises. Furthermore, the practice of this silent humility would bring one close to God.

For Abba John Colobos, the relationship between silence and humility was revealed through the example of the patriarch Joseph. John asked some brothers who were with him: "Who sold Joseph [into slavery] [Gn 37:27–36]?" One brother replied, with what must have seemed to him like a safe answer: "It was his brothers." But Abba John said to him, "No, his humility sold him [τατείνωσις αὐτοῦ πέπρακεν αὐτόν]. He could have objected and said, 'I am their brother' but because he kept silence, he sold himself by his humility."[50] We see here an interesting example of how the interests and imagination of the monks could influence their interpretation of certain biblical texts. In this case, Abba John's interest in the virtue of humility led him to search for it in the biblical story, even when there was no evidence that it was mentioned anywhere in the text. He engages in a piece of imaginative exegesis, drawing from his own experience of how silence is often linked to humility to show Joseph as a model of silent humility. Though he clearly reads into the text from from his own experience, he nevertheless makes legitimate use of a particular element of the text— Joseph's silence—to suggest another possible meaning for this biblical story. The pedagogical significance of his interpretation of Joseph's example is plain: Joseph's humility was not merely a virtue he occasionally practiced but was intrinsic to him. His refusal to be drawn into defending himself in any way was an expression of who he was. So, too, all of those living in the desert should be willing to embrace humility and realize it completely within themselves.

Concern for status sometimes caused conflict within the early monastic communities and it could severely test one's commitment to humility. The tension which the issue of status produced manifested itself sometimes in relationships between the ordained and the unordained monks, and other times between elders with varying amounts of personal and spiritual authority. Those who showed themselves uninterested in either seeking or preserving such status provided living examples of the practice of humility. For many of the elders, ordination was something to be avoided at all cost. For one thing, it was felt to be only for those who were "without reproach," and rarely did the monks see themselves as worthy. Also, the status and honor which accompanied ordination were seen as nuisances, or even worse, impediments to salvation. We can well understand then, Abba Matoes's consternation when, during a journey with a companion to the desert near Mt. Sinai, he was seized by the local bishop and ordained a priest. Matoes expressed his reservations this way: "I did not wish it to be sure; but what really troubles me is that I must be separated from the brother who is with me and I am not able to keep on saying the prayers quite alone." The bishop, wishing to accommodate Matoes, asked him whether his brother was worthy of ordination. Matoes said, "I do not know if he is worthy of it; I only know one thing, that he is better than I." So the bishop ordained the brother also. But in spite of their ordinations, neither of them ever approached the sanctuary to celebrate the eucharist. Their sense of unworthiness kept them away.[51] Others who had been ordained were similarly reserved about their status and showed real sensitivity for the feelings of others. Thus we hear that, "Peter, priest of Dios, when he prayed with others, ought to have stood in front, because he was a priest. But because of his humility, he stood behind. . . ." Nor did he make a show of this humility. Rather "he did this without annoying anyone."[52]

Status differences existed not only between the ordained and unordained but also between unordained elders. A certain elder who lived at Scetis enjoyed considerable fame and repute. But when Abba Poemen's group came to Scetis, some of the elders' followers left him and came to seek the counsel of Abba Poemen. Poemen was grieved by this and said to his followers, "What is to be done about this great old man, for men grieve him by leaving him and coming to us who are nothing? What shall we do, then, to comfort this old man?" Then they prepared some food and went off to visit the old man, hoping to share a meal with him and so bring some comfort to him. When they arrived, they knocked on the door and told the old man's disciple, "Tell the abba it is Poemen who desires to be blessed by him." The old man would not let them in, but in spite of the heat, Poemen and his disciples refused to depart but waited outside his door. Finally, "seeing their humility and patience, the old man was filled with compunction and opened the door to them. They they went in and ate with him. During the meal he said, 'Truly, not only what I have heard about you is true, but I see that your works are a hundred-fold greater,' and from that day, he became their friend."[53] The humility exemplified by Poemen in this story shows how this quality could help to break down the animosity and jealousy which could build up between "rival" elders and their disciples. He refused to be drawn into such a dispute and initiated action which he hoped would diffuse tensions and ease the feelings of the old man. It is Poemen's humility *in action*—his decision to seek the old man's blessing and his willingness to sit outside the old man's door—which resolves the tension and eases the feelings of the old man. It is only when the old man *"sees* their humility"— Poemen and his disciples crouching outside his door waiting for his blessing—that his heart is pierced. He had "heard of" Poemen and of his reputation for humility but had remained skeptical about it. Now, witnessing Poemen's humility—his "works"—before him, he was moved beyond words.

It was not uncommon for such misunderstandings between the monks to become hardened, leading to deep, unresolved tensions. When one or both of the persons involved insisted on justifying themselves, it could make reconciliation appear almost impossible. In such circumstances, the elders recognized that nothing short of an *act* of genuine humility would allow the knot to be unraveled. In the context of such a deep misunderstanding, the question, "What is humility?" had a simple but penetrating answer: "It is when your brother sins against you and you forgive him *before* he comes to ask for forgiveness."[54] One story, which illustrates this, suggests that it was only through realizing this kind of humility in practice that one could become reconciled to another with whom one had a disagreement. A brother was angry with another brother for something he had done. As soon as the second one learned of this, he came to ask the brother to forgive him. But the first brother would not open the door to him. So the one who had come to ask for forgiveness went to ask an old man the reason for this and what he should do. The old man told him,

"See if there is not a motive in your heart such as blaming your brother or thinking that it is he who is responsible. You justify yourself, and that is why he is not moved to open the door to you. In addition, I tell you this: even if it is he who has sinned against you, settle it in your heart that it is *you* who have sinned against him and justify your brother. Then God will move him to reconcile himself with you." Convinced, the brother did this; then he went to knock at the brother's door and almost before he heard the sound, the other was first to ask pardon from the inside. Then he opened the door and embraced him with all his heart.[55]

This story reveals the kind of psychological honesty and moral courage which was required if one was to realize the meaning of humility in one's actions. The second brother's apparently virtuous action of going to ask his brother's forgiveness was shown by the elder to have been compromised by the real motives of his heart: a desire to blame the other and justify himself. Another version of the same story includes a question not found in this version which highlights the superficiality of the brother's request for forgiveness. The old man asked the brother, "Tell me the truth, do you not justify yourself in your heart, saying you are making him an act of penitence, though actually . . . you are asking his pardon [only] in order to obey the commandment?"[56] It is clear why the other brother would not open the door to him: he had not really humiliated himself and sincerely asked for forgiveness. The concluding part of the story illustrates with delightful irony the *effectiveness* of humility put into action. The first brother, having finally realized what was required of him if he were to act with humility, went to ask forgiveness again. This second time, the sound of his knock on the door *alone* was enough to convince the brother inside of his sincerity. Before he could even speak, the second brother, from inside his cell asked the first for forgiveness. It was humility, realized in the first brother's genuine change of heart, that effected the reconciliation between the two brothers.

A simple, but genuine gesture of humility toward another human being could have astonishing revelatory power. A lifetime of struggle could be lifted in an instant by such an act of generosity, shedding new light on the meaning and purpose of one's life. One story tells of an old man who had practiced great fasting and asceticism for over seventy years. One day he asked God the meaning of a "word of Scripture" [ῥήματος τῆς γραφῆς], but God did not reveal it to him. At this the old man said to himself, " 'I have given myself so much affliction without obtaining anything, so I will go to see my brother and ask him.' But as he was closing the door behind him to go to see his brother, an angel of the Lord was sent to him who said, 'These seventy years you have fasted have not brought you near to God, but when you humiliated yourself [ἐταπείνωσας ἑαυτὸν] by going to see your brother, I was sent to tell you the meaning of this word.' "[57] Were this story merely an illustration of how the practice of humility had helped reveal the meaning of one particular saying from Scripture, it would be of some interest to us. But it goes further. The implication is that the old man had never really understood Scripture, or even the point of life in the desert up until this moment. By humiliating himself and breaking out of his isolation to seek help from his brother, the old man had begun, even at this late hour, on the road to wisdom. The story suggests the power inherent in the actual practice of the teaching of Scripture: it was the concrete act of self-humiliation which opened the doors of understanding. The fulfillment of the "first commandment" was the key that unlocked for the old man the meaning of the whole treasure of Scripture and the meaning of his own life.

The generosity implied in such an act of humility manifests itself vividly in the monks' willingness to endure, in silence and patience, unjust accusations sometimes brought against them. Sometimes the accusations were made by fellow monks; other times the elders were accused of wrongdoing by those living in the nearby villages. The stories relating such actions suggest that some monks had so realized the spirit of humility within themselves that it was possible to bear with such accusations graciously and generously. And, as we have already seen, the practice of such humility was perceived to have power and redemptive value. The connection between humility and the willingness to bear with unjust accusations is made clear in a story concerning a brother who was singled out as a focus for complaints by his fellow monks. He had made a habit of "taking upon himself all the brothers' accusations," and even of "accusing himself" of things he had not actually done. The complaints against him began to grow and become more vocal, some saying, "This person commits many sins and does not work." But one of the elders knew about the brother's practice, and said to the others, "I would rather have the single mat he makes with humility than all these you make with pride." Then, in a dramatic demonstration of the power of such humility, the elder instructed them all to bring their mats to him.

He lit a fire and threw all of their mats onto it. The only mat which did not burn was the one made "with humility." [58] We have seen the symbolism of fire in other stories. Like the precious book which extinguished a fire when it was thrown into its midst, the imperishable mat vividly conveys the power of the brother's humility. The story also communicates how deeply humility inheres in the brother's life: humility has been woven into his mat as carefully as it has been woven into his life.

We also find stories in the *Sayings* of monks unfairly accused by the local villagers of sexual misconduct. The cost of bearing with unjust accusations in such cases could include not only enduring the pain of knowing oneself as having been unfairly accused, but even severe physical abuse. The two stories which describe this most graphically concern Abba Macarius the Great and Abba Nicon, each of whom was blamed for an act which he did not commit—getting a girl pregnant. Abba Macarius relates that when the villagers heard that he was responsible for the girl's condition, "they came to seize me, led me to the village and hung pots black with soot and various other things round my neck and led me through the village in all directions, beating me . . . [T]hey beat me almost to death." Macarius's response? He accepted their accusations and set himself to work to begin earning a living for "his wife." [59] In the case of Abba Nicon, "they inflicted many blows upon him, and wanted to drive him away," but he asked them if he could be allowed to stay and "do penance" for the act for which he had been unjustly accused.[60] In both cases the truth was eventually discovered and the true perpetrator of the deed exposed; in the meantime, the one who was accused bore the accusation and the accompanying ridicule and abuse with humble silence. What emerges is a picture or image of humility realized under the severest of pressures. There is in these stories the conviction that truth—in this case the truth of humility—has an inherent power and will eventually emerge into the light of day. Whether this happened in every such case, we do not know. However, the desert fathers were apparently willing to take the personal risks that such a belief in truth required.

Abba John Colobos reminded those who might have faced similar abuse in their lives that they had good reason to be hopeful. Echoing the Beatitudes, he said: "Even if we are completely despised before men, let us rejoice that we are honored in the sight of God." [61] Apparently, he knew the meaning of these words, for he himself was revered throughout Scetis as one who had realized the call to humility. One of the elders asked, in astonishment: "Who is this John, who by his humility, has all Scetis hanging from his little finger?" [62] There is a striking irony here: the one who had entered into the deepest obscurity, who had realized humility in his own life to such a great degree, emerged with immense power.

Humility as Power

This power manifested itself most dramatically in the monk's capacity to overcome the haunting force of demonic attacks. This was a potent symbolic expression of the monk's mastery over the inner world: the person who had embraced obscurity, emptiness, and vulnerability wielded a dazzling confidence against those powers arrayed against him. Here, emptiness portended a presence, a fullness over which the demonic forces had no real power. And this sense of "presence in emptiness" had a striking effect on the way the elders approached the interpretation of Scripture. As we noted earlier, the monks' recitation or remembrance of certain texts from Scripture was often a source of encouragement in their struggles against the demonic forces that plagued them. Even more efficacious than this recitation of Scripture, however, and the end toward which all recitation of Scripture was meant to lead, was the realization of Scripture in one's life. The *realization* of humility was seen as giving the monks unusual power over the evil forces that plagued them.

In one instance a demon approached Macarius with a knife and tried to cut his foot. However, "because of [Macarius's] humility, he could not do so. He said to Macarius, 'All that you have, we have also; you are distinguished from us only by humility; by that you get the better of us.' "[63] Humility, the sign of lowliness and obscurity, was, by one of the ironies characteristic of the desert, a source of great power. It is about power that a demon asked Macarius on another occasion in which his assaults were repelled: "What is your power, Macarius, that it makes me powerless against you?" He did not have to wait for Macarius's response, for he already knew the answer. He ruefully admitted: "[I]t is your humility. Because of that, I can do nothing against you."[64]

Only those who had realized the power of humility within themselves could cast evil out of another. "A man possessed by the devil, who was foaming terribly at the mouth, struck a hermit-monk on the cheek. The old man turned and offered him the other. Then the devil, unable to bear the burning of humility [πύρωσιν τῆς ταπεινώσεως], disappeared immediately."[65] In another instance, an elder from the Thebaid went to cast a demon out of someone who was possessed. The demon said to the elder, " 'I am going to come out, but I am going to ask you a question, tell me, who are the goats and who are the sheep?' The old man said, 'I am one of the goats, but as for the sheep, God alone knows who they are.' When he heard this, the devil began to cry out with a loud voice, 'Because of your humility, I am going away,' and he departed at the same hour."[66] The common theme in all these stories is the presence of humility within the monk; it was the inherent quality of this virtue which gave the monks the power to drive the demons out.

Perhaps the best illustration of how this power worked in the life of the monk is seen in a story concerning a demon-possessed girl and the healing power of some anchorites. This story reflects the monks' conviction that such inherent power implied a profound interpretation of Scripture. The text most fully expressed its transforming power through being fulfilled or appropriated in the life of a holy person. The story recounts that a monk who knew the family of the girl told her father, ''No one can heal your daughter except some anchorites whom I know, but if you ask them to do so, they will not agree because of their humility.'' To get around this difficulty, he proposed a ruse: ''When they come to the market, you should look as though you want to buy their goods. When they come to receive the price, we will ask them to say a prayer and I believe she will be healed.'' The two men went to the market, where they found a disciple of the anchorites sitting down, selling their goods. They led him away with his baskets, ostensibly to pay him, but in reality to ask him to say the prayer. When they reached the house, their carefully laid plan suddenly came unraveled, for the demon-possessed girl ran from the house and slapped the disciple across the face. But,

> he only turned the other cheek, *according to the Lord's Command* [Mt 5:39]. The devil, tortured by this, cried out, ''What violence! The commandment of Jesus drives me out [ὂ Βία! ἡ ἐντολὴ τοῦ 'Ιησοῦ ἐκβάλλει με].'' Immediately, the woman was cleansed. When the [anchorites] came, they heard what had happened and glorified God saying, ''This is how the pride of the devil is brought low, through the humility of the commandment of Christ [ταπεινώσεως τῆς ἐντολῆς τοῦ Χριστοῦ].''[67]

This story reveals much about the presuppositions, purpose, and realization of the desert hermeneutic, particularly as it applies to the virtue of humility. It suggests that the authority and power which the anchorites were seen to possess was a direct expression of the purity and integrity of their lives. Those who knew the anchorites emphasized in the same breath both their power to heal the girl and their probable unwillingness to do so; they knew that the anchorites would not knowingly allow themselves to be drawn into a public display of their power. The anchorites' unwillingness to heal the girl is seen not as callousness but rather as a sign that their reputation for holiness is deserved. And as the action unfolds, we see the qualities for which the anchorites were known exemplified in the immediacy and single-mindedness with which the disciple of the anchorites responded to events.

It is significant, moreover, that these qualities are seen to flow from a deep appropriation of Scripture.

When the demon-possessed girl failed to play her part by waiting patiently for the plan to unfold but instead came running out and delivered a blow to the monk, he turned his other cheek immediately and in conformity with the Gospel command. Thus the demon was driven out by the commandment realized in action. The departure of the demon and the statement uttered upon his departure—"The commandment of Jesus drives me out"—serve as a reminder of what it meant for the elders to interpret a biblical text fully: the meaning of a text could only be realized completely through *applicatio*, action. The story as a whole suggests that for the desert fathers genuine interpretation of Scripture necessarily involved engaging in a concrete "hermeneutical action." Moreover, it shows that the power to engage in such an action depended in no small part on the purity of heart, or in this case, the humility, of the one acting. To have such power and purity of heart required one to have appropriated the text on a very deep level—in a sense to have become the text.

To realize humility in one's life implied ongoing sacrifice and endless small deaths to oneself for the sake of others. It meant, finally, opening oneself ever more deeply to the inexorable demands of love.

Notes

1. John of Thebes 1 [*PG* 65:233D] [RSV].
2. Robin Lane Fox, *Pagans and Christians* (New York: Knopf, 1987), 324; see also Harold Idris Bell, *Cults and Creeds in Graeco-Roman Egypt* (New York: Philosophical Library, 1953):

> Pagan thinkers might stress the inferiority of man, might warn against *hubris* and laud *aidos,* which demanded a humble attitude toward divinity, but paganism hardly regarded humility in general as a virtue. But if God had humbled himself to become man, if Christ had not 'abhorred the virgin's womb,' and lived as the son of the carpenter and died a shameful death, it was not wonderful that humility should be asked of man. (194)

3. Poemen 49 [*PG* 65:333B].
4. Syncletica 26 [Guy, *Recherches,* S9:35].
5. John Colobos 22 [*PG* 65:212D].
6. Theodora 6 [*PG* 65:204AB], [m].
7. Syncletica 16 [*PG* 65:425D–428A].
8. Isidore of Pelusia 5 [*PG* 65:224A].
9. Nau 222 [*ROC* 14:359].
10. Antony 7 [*PG* 65:77AB], [m].
11. Zeno 8 [*PG* 65:177CD].

12. Motius 1 [*PG* 65:300A].
13. Nau 323 [*ROC* 17:210].
14. Nau 332 [*ROC* 17:210].
15. Moses 18B [*PG* 65:288CD] [RSV].
16. Sisoes 42 [*PG* 65:405A], [m].
17. Poemen 81 [*PG* 65:341C].
18. Poemen 141 [*PG* 65:357A].
19. Syncletica 25 [Guy, *Recherches*, S7:35].
20. Nau 331 [*ROC* 17:210]; see also Or 13 [*PG* 65:440C].
21. Nau 309 [*ROC* 17:206].
22. Bessarion 9 [*PG* 65:141C], [m]; 1 Cor 10:13: "God is faithful and he will not let you be tempted beyond your strength, but with temptation will also provide the way of escape, that you may be able to endure it."
23. Poemen 44 [*PG* 65:332D].
24. Matoes 10 [*PG* 65:295A], [m].
25. Nilus 8 [*PG* 65:305C]; 1 Cor 4:13: "[W]e have become, and are now, as the refuse of the world, the offscouring of all things [πάντων περίψημα]." This is a strong term, meaning what is rubbed, washed off, a dirty vessel: scum. The word was used by the Greeks for the poor wretch who was sacrificed in order to free a city from an infection or plague that afflicted it. The same word was used of Christians who voluntarily incurred plague through tending the sick; see *PG* 20:689A.
26. Nau 324 [*ROC* 17:209]; Lk 18:32: "He [the Son of Man] will be delivered to the gentiles and will be mocked and shamefully treated [ὑβισθήσεται], and spat upon."
27. Serapion 4 [*PG* 65:417A].
28. Antony 15 [*PG* 65:80C]: ἀτιμία appears in Paul's writings as a necessary part of being restored to full honor and glory; see 2 Cor 6:8 (speaking of the way in which Christians serve God): "in honor and dishonor"; 1 Cor. 15:43 (speaking of the body): "It is sown in dishonor, it is raised in glory."
29. Arsenius 33 [*PG* 65:100 CD–101A].
30. John Colobos 21 [*PG* 65:212D]. Mt 11:30: "My yoke is easy, and my burden light [φορτίον μου ἐλαφρόν]"; Mt 23:4: "They [the scribes and pharisees] bind heavy burdens [φορτία βαρέα] and lay them on men's shoulders." On the importance of accusation of oneself, see Evagrius 8 [Guy, *Recherches*, S1:21]: "The beginning of salvation is the condemnation of oneself."
31. Hyperchius 8 [*PG* 65:432A].
32. Nau 143 [*ROC* 13:49].
33. Nau 203 [*ROC* 14:369], [m]
34. Moses 11 [*PG* 65:285CD].
35. Moses 12 [*PG* 65:285D]; see also Moses 11 [*PG* 65:285C]; see also Zeno 5 [*PG* 65:177A] for another possible allusion to the three days of Christ in the tomb. Abba Zeno, when he was living in Scetis, is said to have come out of his cell by night, and going in the direction of the marshes, spent "three days and three nights wandering at random."
36. Besides the two sayings already cited, see Moses 14, 15 [*PG* 65:288B], 18d

[*PG* 65:289ABC]. For an analysis of Moses' thoughts on "dying to one's neighbor" and its biblical sources, see Luciana Mortari, *Vita e detti dei padri del deserto*, vol. 2 (Rome: Città Nuova, 1971), 35, n. 46.

37. John Colobos 34 [*PG* 65:216AC].
38. Elias 7 [*PG* 65:184D–185A].
39. Isidore the Priest 5 [*PG* 65:220D–221A].
40. An Abba of Rome (Arsenius) 1 [*PG* 65:385C–389A], [m].
41. Pambo 8 [*PG* 65:369CD], [m].
42. Sisoes 14 [*PG* 65:396BC], [m].
43. John Colobos 23 [*PG* 65:212D–213A]; see also Arsenius 42 [*PG* 65:105D–108AB], Tithoes 1 [*PG* 65:428B], and Tithoes 6 [*PG* 65:428C], where it is especially clear that such a sigh or groan is associated with a deep religious experience.
44. Arsenius 3 [*PG* 65:88C].
45. Matoes 5 [*PG* 65:292A] (emphasis mine).
46. Nau 301 [*ROC* 17:204].
47. Apollo 3 [*PG* 65:136B], [m]; see also Nisterus 2 [*PG* 65:305D–308A].
48. Matoes 11 [*PG* 65:293B].
49. Nisterus the Cenobite 2 [*PG* 65:308D–309A].
50. John Colobos 20 [*PG* 65:212C].
51. Matoes 9 [*PG* 65:292C–293A].
52. Peter of Dios [*PG* 65:385C].
53. Poemen 4 [*PG* 65:317C–320A] (emphasis mine).
54. Nau 304 [*ROC* 17:205] (emphasis mine).
55. Nau 319 [*ROC* 17:206], [m] (emphasis mine).
56. Nau 334 [*ROC* 17:210].
57. Nau 314 [*ROC* 17:207], [m].
58. Nau 328 [*ROC* 17:209]
59. Macarius the Great 1 [*PG* 65:257CD–260B].
60. Nicon 1 [*PG* 65:309AC].
61. John Colobos 42 [Guy, *Recherches*, S2: 23], [m].
62. John Colobos 36 [*PG* 65:216C]. For a vivid portrait of this remarkable monk, see Lucien Regnault, "Le vrai visage d'un père du désert: Abba John Colobos," in *Les pères du désert à travers leurs Apophtegmes* (Sablé-sur-Sarthe: Solesmes, 1987), 37–53.
63. Macarius the Great 35 [*PG* 65:277CD]; see also Theodora 6 [*PG* 65:204B], where the demons claim, "nothing can overcome us, but only humility."
64. Macarius the Great 11 [*PG* 65:268BC].
65. Nau 298 [*ROC* 17:204].
66. Nau 307 [*ROC* 17:205–206].
67. Daniel 3 [*PG* 65:153C] (emphasis mine).

9

The Commandment of Love

Love was at the heart of the desert fathers' world. Whatever diverse motives may have first drawn them to the desert, whatever particular struggles occupied them during their sojourn there, the end of all their longings was ultimately expressed as love. The language, the attitudes, and the actions of the desert fathers were filled with this longing, with the desire to be touched and transformed by love. Nearly every significant act in the *Sayings* either moved toward or grew out of the commandment to love. It would not be an exaggeration to say that the biblical commandment to love, more than any other, defined and gave shape to the world in which the desert fathers lived. The memories of that world, preserved by later generations of monks, suggest that love was seen as the hallmark of early monastic life. A brother once asked an old man why in these [latter] days the monastic life did not bear the kind of fruit it had born in earlier days. The elder answered him simply and directly: "In those days there was charity."[1] The desire to remember the days when life in the desert was characterized by love accounts for the many stories preserved in the *Sayings* which portray the desert fathers' struggles to love.

The *Sayings* provides us with vivid glimpses of the monks' at work in the school of love. The first thing to note is that they were not at all glib or confident about the prospects for responding in love to God or to those around them. They recognized very clearly the cost of incorporating love into their lives, and how difficult it was to give of themselves so completely. Yet their desire to realize the commandment was such that they learned to be vigilant in their struggle against those passions, especially anger and judgment of others, which could kill the tender shoots of love. The *Sayings* reveals that some of the monks took the commandment very much to heart, eventually becoming, after long years of struggle, exemplars or bearers of love for others. This was the ultimate sign of holiness for the desert fathers and was the final act of interpretation—that their lives became transformed by love. As one would expect, the possibilities of its realization in a life

261

were virtually limitless. Sometimes one hears of the fulfillment of the commandment from the testimony of one who had accomplished it in his or her own life. Most often though, the interest was focused on the action, the deed or the gesture, whether dramatic or barely perceptible, of the one who had learned the meaning of love. It was here that the change wrought by love could be seen most clearly, and it was to these portraits of love that the desert fathers looked to learn how to realize the commandment of love in themselves.

The Way of Love

The Commandment

The language which the desert fathers used in speaking of the commandment to love reveals its authority in their lives. It was most often described simply as "the commandment" or "the law." As *the* central commandment in Scripture, it provided a point of reference for judging the relative importance of all the other ethical, moral, and ascetical imperatives which derived from Scripture. Difficult questions on this subject were often resolved simply and directly by recalling the example of the commandment. Such language provides an unambiguous expression of the hermeneutical center of gravity within the world of the desert fathers.

One can see evidence of the authority of the commandment to love in the distinction which is made between "the commandments" and "the commandment." There are numerous references in the *Sayings* to the commandments and the necessity of keeping or observing them. This expression is usually used in a general, undefined sense, rather than in reference to specific biblical texts. The elders referred to the commandments as a way of reminding the monks of the source of their moral obligations. Abba John Colobos told his disciples that they should "get up early every day and acquire the beginning of every virtue and every commandment of God."[2] Abba Isaac spoke of the importance of "keeping the commandments of God."[3] Elsewhere a brother expressed his quest for salvation in terms of his desire to "fulfill the commandments."[4] Beyond these commandments, however, there was *the* commandment. A brother worried aloud to Abba John Colobos that his lack of strength sometimes prevented him from joining in the common work and caused him to fail in his obligations to his brother. He asked what he should do "in order to fulfill *the* commandment [τὴν ἐντολήν]."[5] The meaning and significance of the latter expression as well as its practical implications, are illustrated well by a conversation between Abba Theodore of Pherme and a brother who questioned him:

"What is the work of the soul which we now consider to be secondary, and what is that which was secondary which has become our principal work?" The old man said, "Everything which is done because of the commandment of God [τὴν ἐντολὴν τοῦ θεοῦ] is the work of the soul; but to work and to gather goods together for one's own sake must be considered as secondary." Then the brother said, "Explain this matter to me." So the old man said, "Suppose you hear it said that I am ill and you ought to visit me; you say to yourself, 'Shall I leave my work and go now? No, I will finish my work and then go.' Then another idea comes along and perhaps you never go; or again, another brother says to you, 'Lend me a hand brother!' and you say, 'Shall I leave my own work and go and work with him?' If you do not go, you are leaving aside the commandment of God which is the work of the soul [ἀφίεις τὴν ἐντολὴν τοῦ θεοῦ ὅ ἐστι τὸ ἔργον τῆς ψυχῆς] and doing that which is secondary [τὸ πάρεργον], namely the work of your hands."[6]

This simple exchange reveals the importance attributed to the commandment in the spirituality of the desert and how it was meant to inform all choices and actions. The commandment—here referred to as "the work of the soul"—means the concrete, practical work of tending to the needs of another. Other considerations, however important or pressing they might seem, were to be relegated to a secondary status, as virtually an "odd job [τὸ πάρεργον]"[7] in comparison to the obligation to care for one who is sick or to help another person in any situation. The contrast was drawn by using what for Theodore was the strongest possible language: placing these lesser obligations at the forefront was tantamount to "leaving aside the commandment of God."

Particular biblical texts informed such thinking and influenced the behavior of the monks. Cassian relates that when he and Germanus went to visit an old man in Egypt and were offered hospitality, they asked him why he did not "keep the rule of fasting, when you receive visiting brothers, as we have received it in Palestine?" The old man replied to them, echoing Jesus' words:

Fasting is always [at] hand but you I cannot have with me always [Jn 12:8]. Fasting is certainly a useful and necessary thing, but it depends on our choice, while the law of God demands absolutely the fulfillment of charity [τὴν δὲ τῆς ἀγάπης πλήρωσιν ἐξ ἀνάγκης ἀπαιτεῖ ὁ τοῦ θεοῦ νόμος]. Thus receiving Christ in you [Mt 25], I ought to serve you with all diligence, but when I have taken leave of you, I can resume the rule of fasting again. For, "can the wedding guests fast while the bridegroom is with them? But when the bridegroom is taken from them, then they will fast on that day [Mt 9:15]."[8]

The message of this saying is clear: the law of charity takes precedence over any particular ascetical practices observed in the desert. The old man's use of Scripture reveals his practical understanding of the obligations of charity. He acknowledged in his allusion to Matthew 25 that his visitors are representations of Christ who deserve to be treated as Christ himself. And he amplified this by citing from Matthew 9, as if to remind them: whenever you appear the wedding feast of Christ is here.

John Colobos expressed the centrality of the commandment to love in terms which focus attention on the imperative to love one's neighbor. It is striking that he emphasized this in even stronger terms than one finds in the biblical texts themselves. He said to his disciples, "A house is not built by beginning at the top and working down. You must begin with the foundations in order to reach the top." When they asked him what he meant by this, he said, "The foundation is our neighbor, whom we must win, and that is the place to begin. For all the commandments of Christ depend on this one [Mt 22:39–40]."[9] While there is a clear allusion to the passage in Matthew's gospel here, John alters the sense of the text in a significant way. Instead of speaking of "all the law and the prophets" being dependent upon "these two commandments" (that is, love of God and love of neighbor), he says that "all the commandments of Christ" depend on "this *one*"—the love of neighbor. While there may be many commandments of Christ that require the careful consideration of those who have come to the desert, there should be no doubt as to which one forms the axis around which all the others revolve.

The Cost of Love

The elders were keenly aware, from their own personal experience, of the high cost of fulfilling the commandment to love. Their reading of Scripture served to confirm this sense and to encourage them to risk loving even under extreme circumstances. It is startling, as we listen to the monks talk about the requirements of love, how literally they took the words of Scripture. Poemen's interpretation of one Gospel text illustrates well the particular kind of demands love made upon the monks in their life in the desert, and how their reading of Scripture helped them to respond to these demands. As we noted earlier, gossip and slander were part of the everyday experience of the monks and could wound deeply. One way of fulfilling the commandment to love was to refuse to be drawn into vicious gossip or to respond to a personal attack in any way. Abba Poemen saw the text, "Greater love has no man than this, that a man lay down his life for his friends" (Jn 15:13) as referring to just such a situation: "If someone hears an evil saying, that is, one which harms him, and in his turn, he wants to repeat it, he must fight in order not to say it. Or if someone is taken advantage of and he bears it, without retaliating at all, then he is giving his life for his neighbor." [10]

Fulfilling the commandment, then, entailed having the courage to love in circumstances where one's natural response would lead one in precisely the opposite direction. Abba Or took these extreme demands of love seriously. For him, "loving one's enemies" was not a saying which the monk could afford to relegate to the status of a remote, abstract aphorism. Nearly every one of them *did* have enemies, as the numerous petty and not so petty disputes which we encounter in the *Sayings* reveal. Therefore, when Or asked the brothers one day how well they had "kept all the commandments," he pressed them especially on the question of love: "Have you," he asked, "loved your enemies [Mt 5:44] and been kind to them in their misfortunes?" [11] Love of this kind required a certain freedom from fear—fear that one would look foolish; fear that one would be consumed by another; fear of losing all that one had known. Such freedom is hinted at in a remarkable saying of Abba Agathon, which expresses the depth of self-giving he understood to be involved in fulfilling the commandment. He recalls a saying from the First Letter of John, "Perfect love casts out fear," and states what, for him, would be an expression of such love: "If I could meet a leper, give him my body, and take his, I should be very happy. That indeed is perfect charity [τελεία ἀγάπη] [1 Jn 4:18]." [12] This sense of the need for compassion toward the vulnerable is echoed elsewhere in the *Sayings*. Abba Epiphanius defined righteousness in terms of a willingness to extend an act of kindness toward someone in need: "God sells righteousness at a very low price to those who wish to buy it: a little piece of bread, a cloak of no value, a cup of cold water [Mt 10:42]." [13] Life in the desert provided no end of opportunities to practice this kind of love.

Life took its toll in different ways on those who came to the desert, and learning to love meant being sensitive to the particular needs of each person. Love could sometimes require one to summon up from within the capacity to extend oneself unexpectedly in response to the particular emotional condition of another. Calling to mind Jesus' words, "Those who are well have no need of a physician, but those who are sick" (Mt 9:12), Abba Poemen reminded his listeners, "[I]f you do a little good to the good brother, do twice as much for the other. For he is sick." [14] Another elder affirmed the need to sometimes go beyond what was expected in dealing with another. He cited a text from Matthew to indicate the lengths to which one should go in loving: "When someone asks something of you, even if you must do violence to yourself in giving it to him, your thought must take pleasure in the gift according to that which is written, 'If someone asks you to go a mile, go two miles with him' (Mt 5:41). That is, if someone asks something of you, give it to him with your whole heart and spirit.'' [15]

The elders did not make such declarations glibly, nor did they imagine it was a simple matter to put such sayings into practice. They knew how difficult it was to engage in even the smallest act of love, much less to allow the power of love to transform one. The *Sayings* is full of questions of how to overcome the legion of dark impulses within oneself which prevented one from loving. ''A brother asked Abba Joseph, saying, 'What should I do, for I do not have the strength to bear evil, nor to work for charity's sake?' The old man said, 'If you cannot do any of these things, at least guard your conscience from all evil with regard to your neighbor and you will be saved.' '' [16] This is an honest and revealing response. The elder recognized how inevitable it was that through weakness one would sometimes fail to rise to the demands of love. Yet, one could still ''guard the conscience,'' that is, learn to pay careful attention to the twisted patterns of one's thought and behavior which made love so difficult. In so doing, one could begin to break down the barriers to love and realize it in some way within oneself.

There was good reason why fulfilling the commandment to love was so difficult: the roots of those inner forces, or ''passions,'' which worked against love ran deep and strong. One could easily misjudge the extent to which such passions had been rooted out. We see this in the case of a certain monk who had fasted rigorously for some fifty years and who declared that he had finally managed to destroy the passion of vainglory within himself. Abba Abraham was surprised to hear him say this and when he next encountered him, put this question to him:

> ''Suppose you learn that of two brothers one loves you while the other hates you, and speaks evil of you; if they come to see you, will you receive them both with the same love?'' ''No,'' he replied, ''But I should struggle against my thoughts so as to be as kind towards the one who hates me as towards the one who loves me.'' Abba Abraham said to him, ''So, then, the passions continue to live; it is simply that they are controlled by the saints.'' [17]

This was a sobering reminder to the monks of the tenacity of the passions which lived within them. It was possible to learn how to love, to become, as Amma Theodora put it, ''a lover of souls.'' [18] But let no one underestimate the cost involved. It would require a lifetime of struggle against one's own worst tendencies, especially anger, judgment, and unwillingness to forgive others, to become tender enough to love.

Overcoming Anger

Even the most solitary monks were bound to other human beings. As such, they were called to test their commitment to love within the give-and-take of human relationships. These relationships were cultivated in different places and with varying degrees of intensity; they included the everyday life of the cell shared by a master and disciple, the weekly gatherings of the monks at the *synaxis*, the chance encounter with a visitor, and the commerce of the marketplace. Tensions invariably arose from time to time, exposing frayed nerves, long-held grudges, and boiling anger. The force with which this anger could explode and the havoc it could wreak on oneself and others led the monks to devote considerable energy toward overcoming this passion. They realized that unresolved anger and love could not coexist. The manifestation of anger in the life of the monk reflected a failure to love. On the other hand, the absence of anger in a person was one of the sure signs that love had begun to reign in the heart. The *Sayings* testifies to the various strategies the monks used and the biblical texts they drew upon to help them to resist anger and keep themselves from being overwhelmed by it. Occasionally, these stories convey the sense that it was possible to banish anger and so fulfill the commandment of love in one's life.

Abba Evagrius called anger "the most fierce passion." From his subtle description of how anger works, one can well understand why the monks felt that anger was potentially more destructive of love than any other passion. Anger, he said, is

> a boiling and stirring up of wrath against one who has given injury—or is thought to have done so. It constantly irritates the soul and above all at the time of prayer it seizes the mind and flashes a picture of the offensive person before one's eyes. Then there comes a time when it persists longer [and] is transformed into indignation. . . . This is succeeded by a general debility of the body, malnutrition with its attendant pallor, and the illusion of being attacked by poisonous wild beasts.[19]

If allowed to fester within in this way, anger could completely consume one, leading to emotional and physical exhaustion, even hallucinations. Its power, Evagrius cautions, should never be underestimated; it is a deep-rooted passion. Abba Ammonas's candid description of his long, grueling battle against anger suggests just how tenacious the grip of anger could be: "I have spent fourteen years in Scetis asking God night and day to grant me the victory over anger."[20] In equally stark terms, Abba Agathon expressed the danger of anger in the life of the monk and the seriousness with which the monk should struggle to overcome it. Alluding to the chapter on love in Paul's first letter to the Corinthians, he said: "A man who is angry, even if he were to raise the dead, is not acceptable to God [1 Cor 13:1–3]." [21] The noxious weed of anger had to be completely eliminated if the commandment of love was to take root in the soul.

The classic biblical text on the subject of anger comes from the letter to the Ephesians ("Do not let the sun go down on your anger." [Eph 4:26]) and the monks were deeply influenced by the simple exhortation contained there. In the *Vita Antonii* we hear that Antony urged the monks to

> take to heart the precepts in Scripture; to keep in mind the deeds of the saints, so that the soul, ever mindful of the commandments might be educated in their ardor. But he especially urged them to practice constantly the word of the Apostle, "Do not let the sun go down on your anger" (Eph 4:26), and to consider that this had been spoken with every commandment in mind—so that the sun should never set on anger nor on any other sin of ours. [22]

The importance Antony attributes to the need to practice this particular commandment suggests that it held the same authority as the commandment. That is, without refraining from anger, no progress could possibly be made in the school of love.

No one could possibly live entirely without anger, at least not in the beginning. Many monks expressed anxiety about their inability to stem the flow of anger within them. Amma Syncletica addressed this concern, noting that while anger did in fact overcome all of them from time to time, they should bear in mind the words of the Apostle and not lose heart: "It is not good to get angry, but if this should happen, the Apostle does not allow you a whole day for this passion, for he says: 'Let not the sun go down' (Eph 4:26)." She reminded them that this was not something they could put off dealing with indefinitely. "Will you wait till all your time is ended?" she asked them. [23]

The question of limits inevitably arose for some. How far were they to go in carrying out this command? How much would be required of them? A brother approached Abba Poemen with such a question, wanting to know, "What does it mean to be angry with your brother without cause [Mt 5:22]?" Poemen answered him, "If your brother hurts you by his arrogance and you are angry with him because of it, that is getting angry without cause." But it meant more than this. Poemen continued, offering a startling juxtaposition of biblical texts: "If he plucks out your right eye and cuts off your right hand [Mt 5:29–30], and you get angry with him, you are angry without cause." [24] By applying Jesus' words concerning adultery to the question of what it means to be angry without cause, Poemen dramatically heightens the stakes regarding how far one should go in rooting out anger. The message would have been clear: the temptation to give way to anger must be resisted at all costs.

Resistance to anger became, for some monks, a way of life. In these instances the exhortation from Ephesians was seen as being fulfilled. The relative importance of refraining from anger is illustrated in a conversation between Abba Hilarion and Abba Epiphanius, said to have taken place shortly before they died. Epiphanius invited Hilarion to visit him before they "departed from the body," and prepared some fowl for their meal. Hilarion, however, declined to eat it, saying, "Since I received the habit I have not eaten meat that has been killed." Epiphanius responded, "Since I took the habit, I have not allowed anyone to go to sleep with a complaint against me and I have not gone to rest with a complaint against anyone [Eph 4:26]." [25] Epiphanius's comment suggests that true asceticism involved more than engaging in great acts of physical privation but meant above all refraining from any expression of anger that could bring pain to another.

Abba Agathon, too, claimed to have learned to resist anger. He said, "I have never gone to sleep with a grievance against anyone, and as far as I could, I have never let anyone go to sleep with a grievance against me [Eph 4:26]." [26] He had a reputation for serenity, and some brothers came one day to see whether or not it was deserved. They tried to make him lose his temper, taunting him with all kinds of abuse: " 'Aren't you Agathon who is said to be a fornicator and a proud man?' 'Yes, it is very true,' he answered. They continued, 'Aren't you that Agathon who is always talking nonsense?' 'I am.' " [27] Agathon's refusal to be drawn by the brothers appears a modest achievement. Yet one can well imagine such a scene being replayed innumerable times in the desert: someone testing him, more often than not with some real slight or insult. The absolute refusal to respond in anger would loom ever larger when seen with the longer perspective of a whole lifetime.

A concrete expression of this resistance to anger was the refusal to retaliate. The biblical call to "not return evil for evil" (Rom 12:17; 1 Thes. 5:15) helped give shape and direction to the monks' aspirations to root out anger and live in love. Abba John Colobos cautioned that, "When you are insulted, do not get angry; be at peace, and do not render evil for evil [Rom 12:17]." [28] Rooting out the desire for revenge was not enough by itself, however; it had to be supported by positive action. Poemen spoke to this when he said, echoing Paul's letter to the Romans: "Wickedness does not do away with wickedness, but if someone does you wrong, do good to him, so that by your action you destroy his wickedness [Rom 12:21]." [29] Such a deed could not only help the one who had been wronged by compelling him to channel his energies into an act of kindness, but it could also help to diffuse the anger in the one who had wronged him.

If refraining from doing evil to another person was to become a way of life, it had to penetrate below the surface level and permeate one's whole being. Abba Isaiah, for one, knew that a person did not need to express his anger or discontent to another in so many words. Even the most subtle gesture, if it proceeded from an impure heart, could injure another: "When someone wishes to render evil for evil [Rom 12:17], he can injure his brother's soul even by a single nod of his head."[30] Abba Poemen offers an intriguing analysis of this, enabling us to observe the different levels at which anger can manifest itself. He suggests also what it means to clear up the sources within oneself which lead to the desire for retaliation. A brother questioned Poemen, asking:

"What does 'See that none of you repays evil for evil' (1 Thes. 5:15) mean?" The old man said to him, "Passions work in four stages—first, in the heart; secondly, in the face; thirdly, in words; and fourthly, it is essential not to render evil for evil in deeds. If you can purify your heart, passion will not come into your expression; but if it comes into your face, take care not to speak; but if you do speak, cut the conversation short in case you render evil for evil."[31]

Poemen's interpretation is intriguing because it cuts through all the levels of consciousness and behavior to reveal what is involved in giving this text meaning in practical terms. It also shows what kind of interpretation of a text can happen when one has experience or discernment. For Poemen, experience, "that which tests a person," is fundamental to the life in the desert.[32] It is the gift of discernment, born from experience, which makes it possible for him to understand many layers of meaning implicit in the text. To put this text into practice, one must become pure of heart, for only then will anger or resentment cease from welling up and unconsciously casting a shadow across the face. So too will words of bitterness and evil actions cease from pouring forth from the mouth. Poemen's discerning approach to interpretation encourages the brother to appropriate the meaning of the call "not to return evil for evil" at the depths of one's being and to let it bear fruit in all of one's actions. This approach also illustrates well the great moral cost exacted in interpreting a text with such integrity.

This careful consideration of the inner workings of anger had direct implications for the way the desert fathers thought about prayer. Abba Evagrius once defined prayer as "the seed of gentleness and the absence of anger."[33] That is, a monk could not learn to be without anger, to be free from the desire to retaliate against another, unless he practiced the art of prayer. However, the opposite was also true. The desire to retaliate against another could be so deeply imbedded within a person that any attempt at prayer would be futile; to be able to pray again, one would have to deal with the particular source of the anger. Evagrius addresses this twisted maze, especially the devastating effects that repressed anger, resentment, or desire for revenge could have on the soul and on one's ability to experience the presence of God in prayer, through an allusion to a text from Philippians: "If you want to pray as you ought," he said, "do not allow your soul to grieve or you will run in vain [Phil 2:16]." [34] This enigmatic comment should be compared to a parallel statement Evagrius makes in *Chapters on Prayer*. There, Evagrius says, "If you desire to pray as you ought, do not sadden anyone. Otherwise you run in vain." There are, as John Eudes Bamberger notes, definite moral considerations which lie behind these two sayings: "The thought of the injured brother will return at times of prayer and prevent [one] from drawing near to God in peace and with a pure conscience." [35] The implication is clear: any desire for retaliation against another, especially if it is realized, will sabotage the monk's attempt to pray. One cannot hold a grudge against another or withhold asking forgiveness to another and expect to enter God's presence in prayer. Evagrius makes it plain that there are certain ethical obligations on the way to pursuing the higher reaches of prayer.

A similar sentiment was expressed in relation to a different biblical text by Abba Zeno: "If a person wants God to hear his prayer quickly, then before he prays for anything else, even his own soul, when he stands and stretches out his hands towards God, he must pray with all his heart for his enemies [Mt 5:44; Lk 6:28]. Through this action, God will hear everything he asks." [36] Here, we see how prayer in the desert was conditioned by and rooted in the spirit of the Sermon on the Mount, especially its call to pray for one's enemies. Unwillingness to retaliate, refusal to bear grudges, wishing the best for one's enemies—these were all at the center of the process of learning how to live in love.

What did it mean, in concrete terms, to practice this asceticism, to fulfill the biblical injunction against retaliation? Several sayings indicate that, among other things, it meant "fleeing" from situations in which anger might arise. A brother asked Poemen what to do about fornication and anger, which warred against him. Poemen responded with an allegorical interpretation of an Old Testament text: "In this connection, David said: 'I will pierce the lion and slay the bear' (1 Sm 17:35–36); that is to say: I will cut off anger and I will crush fornication with hard labor." [37] Apparently the monks often did just that: they left anger behind. John Colobos tells of going up the road toward Scetis with some ropes to trade. He saw the camel driver talking, and what he said "moved me to anger. So, leaving my goods, I fled."[38] Another time, during the summer harvest, he "heard a brother speaking with anger toward his neighbor, saying, 'Ah, you too?' So, leaving the harvest, he fled."[39] In both cases, John was astute enough to realize that, if he sensed the passion of anger rising up in him, he ought to depart the scene before it could get a hold on him. Abba Isidore the Priest expresses a similar tenacity of purpose in relating what happened when he went to the market place to sell some small goods. "Seeing anger approaching me, I left the things and fled."[40] What is striking about these incidents is the *immediacy* with which the monks took flight, leaving the scene without any concern for the goods left behind. This flight was an expression not only of the sense of the ongoing danger that anger presented to the monk but also of a certain freedom from its power.

Freedom from the compulsion to retaliate was the result of a long process of purging anger from every level of one's being. The desert fathers were aware of the necessity of rooting out anger and its accompanying desire for vengeance at these deeper levels. This included refraining from anger both in words and in thoughts. Isidore, who fled when he saw anger coming near him, explained to a brother who asked why the demons were so afraid of him, that it was because "I have practiced asceticism since the day I became a monk, and not allowed anger to reach my lips."[41] For the call to refrain from anger to be fully realized, it had to penetrate beyond the level of words to the deeper level of thoughts. Isaac, Priest of the Cells, manifested this deeper realization. For him, not giving in to anger meant taking responsibility for his thoughts. Interestingly, he expressed this responsibility in spatial terms: "I have never allowed a thought against my brother who has grieved me to enter my cell; I have seen to it that no brother should return to his cell with a thought against me."[42] Thus, by care and vigilance, anger was shown to have been cleared up—even on the level of thoughts.

An example of where such deep realization of the call to refrain from anger could lead is seen in a story Theodora tells about a person who refused to be drawn into an argument. It concerns a devout man who happened to be insulted by someone but who responded to the one who had insulted him, saying, "I could say as much to you, but the commandment of God closes my mouth [ὁ νόμος τοῦ θεοῦ κλείει μου τὸ στόμα]."[43] This saying reveals the deep level at which anger was understood to be rooted out by those who had overcome it and the reason for this freedom from anger. In the matter-of-fact language characteristic of the *Sayings,* the man refuses to enter into the argument because the "commandment closes his mouth." Regardless of whether he is referring to the commandment of love or the more particular commandment to refrain from anger, this is a startling statement.

He does not say that he had pondered the meaning of the commandment and has decided it would be better not to speak. Rather, the commandment is seen to have been appropriated so completely that it shapes his behavior on the deepest level of his being.

Such stories provide hints that some of the monks did indeed come close to banishing anger from their lives. Some of the sayings, which might otherwise appear to be either wishful thinking or simply absurd, take on new meaning in light of this. For Poemen, there was a simple and stark equivalence between the monastic life and the absence of anger: "A monk," he said, "is not angry."[44] Elsewhere he compared a man without anger to "a stone pillar; hurt him and he does not get angry. . . ."[45] And the monks could whisper, in tones of respect, about those who had realized this freedom from anger within themselves. It was an astonishing thing to claim, as they did about Abba Ephrem, that "no one had ever seen him angry."[46] Here was a sign that love could come to reign in a life.

On Not Judging

Judgment of others could at times seem justified. Yet the desert fathers were convinced that judgment, like anger, was like a voracious appetite. If fed without moderation it would eventually turn vicious and destructive, consuming everything in its path. Refraining from judgment was not only a matter of avoiding certain kinds of behavior, however. It was inextricably bound up with the *ascesis* of dying to the self and being reborn in love. The desert fathers deepened this ascetical discipline by engaging in an ongoing dialogue with Scripture over the meaning of the commandment to refrain from anger. By a careful and imaginative reading of the texts in light of their own experience, the monks eventually came to a firmer grasp of the meaning of love in their lives.

The gravity and frequency with which the desert fathers talked about refraining from judgment reveal just how damaging they understood the action of judging others to be. Their own experience taught them this. Abba Xanthius noted with biting irony where his capacity for judging others placed him in relation to other, supposedly lower forms of life: "[A] dog is better than I am," he said, "for he has love, and he does not judge."[47] Aware of their capacity to reach such low levels, the monks devoted considerable attention to learning how to root out the desire to judge others. As though responding to Abba Xanthius's comment, another elder said, "If someone commits a sin in your presence, do not judge him, but consider yourself a worse sinner than he."[48] Abba Joseph held that not judging together with self-examination, were the two essential practices of the monk, and that refraining from judging was necessary if one hoped to find true peace in this life. When Poemen asked him how to become a monk, Joseph said, "If you want to find rest here below, and hereafter, in all circumstances, say, 'Who am I?' and do not judge anyone."[49] According to Abba Euprepius, the experience of the presence of God in the soul could only happen, if one "[did] not judge [$\mu\grave{\eta}$ $\kappa\rho\acute{\iota}\nu\epsilon\iota\nu$] others."[50]

The awareness of certain biblical texts also played an important part in forming the monks' attitudes and their practices regarding judgment. On at least two occasions, Abba Poemen used the classic text from Matthew's Gospel on not judging (Mt 7:3–5) to spell out for those living in the desert what it meant to refrain from judgment. Once, some monks who were quite rigorous in their ascetical practices asked Poemen how Abba Nisterus managed to bear so well with his disciple who, they implied, had not been a model of good behavior. Poemen said that if he had been in Nisterus's place, he would have gone even *further* in bearing with the brother, "placing a pillow under his head." Startled by this response, the brothers challenged Poemen to explain how he would have accounted to God for this soft treatment of the undisciplined brother. Poemen replied, "I would have said to him, 'You have said, "First take the log out of your own eye, then you will see clearly to take the speck out of your brother's eye" ' (Mt 7:5; Lk 6:42)."[51] Poemen's citation of this text served as an emphatic reminder to the brothers of the dangers of judging another. It was something only a hypocrite would do.

Abba Poemen used this same gospel text in another place to explore the relationship between not judging and hypocrisy. Someone asked him, "[W]hat is a hypocrite?" and he responded with what Lemaire calls a "véritable description phénoménologique." "A hypocrite," Poemen said, "is someone who teaches his neighbor something he makes no effort to do himself. It is written, 'Why do you see the speck that is in your neighbor's eye when there is a log in your own eye' (Mt 7:3–4; Lk 6:41)?"[52] The significance of Poemen's use of this text in this setting can be seen more clearly if one takes into account the verses immediately preceding these words in Luke's Gospel. There, Jesus asks, "Can a blind man lead a blind man? Will they not both fall into a pit? A disciple is not above his teacher, but every one when he is fully taught will be like his teacher" (Lk 6:39–40). Poemen expands the application of the biblical text from Jesus' narrow treatment of the relationship between master and disciple to include the much wider context of every person and his *neighbor*. The hypocrite is thus anyone who tries to teach or reprove his neighbor regarding something which he has not put into practice himself. Poemen makes this connection clear elsewhere:

"To teach your neighbor is the same thing as reproving him." [53] This saying expresses the realization that if a monk concentrated on his own sins and not on those of one's neighbor, he would not be tempted either to judge or teach others. [54] Abba Theodore of Pherme used slightly different language, also with rich biblical resonances, to drive home the importance of not judging: "There is no other virtue," he said, "than that of not being scornful [μὴ ἐξουθενεῖν]." [55] Such language recalls the words used by Paul in Romans where a scornful attitude is seen as the equivalent of judging: "Why do you pass judgment [κρίνεις] on your brother? Or you, why do you despise [ἐξουθενεῖς] your brother? For we shall all stand before the judgment seat of God" (Rom 14:10). The fact that the monks will themselves face judgment one day should remind them of the need to keep from scorning or judging others.

One measure of the seriousness with which the desert fathers took the need to refrain from judging is their comparison of judgment with other sins. Some of the monks saw sins of the flesh as so grievous that to identify and judge those who committed them was viewed as a useful and acceptable service to the rest of the monastic community. Abba Theodote used texts from Scripture to express his conviction that such thinking was fundamentally misguided: "If you are temperate," he tells his listeners, "do not judge the fornicator, for you would then transgress the law just as much. And he who said 'Do not commit fornication' also said, 'Do not judge [μὴ κρίνῃς]' [Jas 2:11]." Theodote, with an interesting gloss on the text from James, points out that yielding to the temptation to judge one who has fallen to fornication is an equally or possibly even more grievous transgression of the law than fornication itself. The text from James is set in a context which speaks about what it means to fulfill the whole law. James makes the point, using a dramatic analogy which is itself drawn from Scripture, that one cannot refrain from committing adultery and then kill someone, and imagine that one has kept the law. "For he who has said, 'Do not commit adultery' (Ex 20:13–14), also said, 'Do not kill' (Dt 5:17–18). If you do not commit adultery, but do kill, you have become a transgressor of the law (Jas 2:11)." Theodote shifts the ground somewhat and rereads the text from James in order to suggest that one cannot refrain from fornication, then judge someone who has committed fornication, and still imagine that one has kept the law. The implication regarding judging was clear: to judge another person was the moral equivalent of murder. [56]

If this was so, then how was one to keep from committing such a grievous crime? By practicing mercy and forgiveness in relations with others. Questions concerning the possibility of forgiveness of one's sins by God and the obligations of those who themselves had experienced forgiveness occupied the hearts and minds of the desert monks. And certain biblical texts shaped their thinking and practice. It was reported of Abba Isidore that "whenever he addressed the brothers in church, he said only one thing: 'Forgive your brother, so that you may also be forgiven' [Mt 6:14]." [57] Another elder also affirmed the reciprocal character of forgiveness in distinctly biblical terms: "If you say [to God], 'Have mercy on me,' God says to you, 'If you want me to have mercy on you, do you also have mercy on your brother; if you want me to forgive you, do you also forgive your neighbor' [Mt 6:14]." [58]

A basic question about forgiveness was whether one could be forgiven by God for one's sins. A story is told of a soldier who came to Abba Mius and asked him "if God accepted repentance." The old man responded to the soldier with great tenderness by putting a question to him in the soldier's own language: "Tell me, my dear [ἀγαπητέ], if your cloak is torn, do you throw it away? He replied, 'No, I mend it and use it again.' The old man said to him, 'If you are so careful about your cloak, will not God be equally careful about his creature' [Jon 4:10]?" [59] On another occasion, a brother, probably a new convert to Christianity, asked Abba Poemen a very similar question, "If a brother is involved in a sin and is converted, will God forgive him?" Poemen responded with a question of his own, "Will not God, who has commanded men to act thus, do as much himself and even more? For God commanded Peter to forgive till seventy times seven [Mt 18:22]." Poemen uses this text in response to the brother's question in order to assure him of the depth and certainty of God's forgiveness. At the same time, he links this assurance of God's mercy for human beings to the necessity for human beings to forgive one another. The extent of *God's* mercy, he suggests, can be seen by observing what he had commanded human beings to do. To drive this point home, he refers not to the well-known text on forgiveness—Mt 6:14: "If you forgive men their trespasses your heavenly Father also will forgive you." Rather, he cites the brief, concrete expression of Mt 18:22, which is more evocative and speaks more clearly to the imagination and the memory. If God has commanded human beings to forgive one another to such an extent—seventy times seven—*how much more* will God forgive human beings? [60]

Scripture could also be helpful for resolving tensions that arose among the monks and for helping to cultivate a spirit of love and forgiveness. Abba Bitimius put a very practical question to Abba Poemen, " 'If someone has a grievance against me, and I ask his pardon but cannot convince him, what is to be done?' The old man said to him, 'Take two other brothers with you and ask his pardon. If he is not satisfied, take five others. If he is still not satisfied by them, take a priest. If even so he is not satisfied, then pray to God without anxiety, that [God] may satisfy him, and do not worry about it.' '' Poemen draws upon the instruction on forgiveness found in Mt 18:15 ff. to indicate the way out of this impasse but also alters and extends the teaching of the text in some intriguing ways. The first change Poemen makes to the text has to do with who is at fault. According to Matthew, someone has "done you harm" and *you* are seeking satisfaction. In Poemen's saying it is that "someone has a grievance against me," and *he* is seeking satisfaction. Second, in Matthew's text, Jesus says that if one has done all one can to be reconciled and still cannot reach an understanding, then one should dismiss the person, treating him "like a pagan or a tax collector." By contrast, Poemen says that if one has done everything possible to become reconciled to the other person and has failed, the work of reconciliation should continue, albeit in a different manner. One should "pray to God without anxiety, that [God] may satisfy him and do not worry about it."[61] Poemen's resolution of the problem shows a greater level of detachment and compassion than the Gospel text itself and indicates how he envisioned such a text might be put in to practice in the desert.

The desert fathers realized, through practical experience, how easy it was to deceive oneself regarding the actions and motivations of another, and how destructive it could be to judge others carelessly. The *practice* or realization of this commandment was thus an important sign of the ascendency of love in one's life. The willingness to judge others, like the capacity to refrain from judgment, was often a matter of perception and perspective—how one saw things. In thinking about their endless capacity for judging others, and how to overcome this, the monks learned to pay attention to their perspective on things: what they looked at (others or themselves), how they saw things (from a perspective of superiority or empathy), and why they saw some things at all (the failings of others too often appeared crystal clear, while their own were invisible). There is an interesting irony in this visual metaphor. One of the signs of someone who had attained holiness was a refined perception, a keen vision, something the monks referred to as discernment. Yet when it came to judging others, precisely the opposite was true: blindness, a virtual incapacity to see fault in another person was one of the signs of a person who had become free from the compulsion to judge others, free to love.

A remarkable story told by Abba Poemen testifies to how misleading one's perception could be, especially when it was focused intently on another person's sin.

> "It is written," he said, " 'Give witness to that which your eyes have seen' (Prv 25:7); but I say to you even if you have touched with your hands, do not give witness. In truth a brother was deceived in this respect; he thought he saw his brother in the act of sinning with a woman; greatly incensed, he drew

near and kicked them (for he thought it was they), saying, 'Now stop; How much longer will you go on?' But it turned out that it was some sheaves of corn. That is the reason why I said to you: even if you touch with your hands, do not reprove.''[62]

This story vividly illustrates the dangers of relying on one's perception of things. It is interesting to note how Poemen uses the text from Proverbs to help him make his point. He implies that, while this dictum was reliable in most cases, there are extreme cases of self-deception where one must go beyond even the advice of Scripture. He alerts his listeners to this with his blunt statement of his own authority. Proverbs says one thing, "but *I* say to you. . . .'' The reason for his revision of the biblical text is clear: a brother had been utterly deceived by his own senses, had "seen" something which was not there, and as a result had been drawn into making a harsh judgment against another. As Graham Gould suggests, the point Poemen wants to make is not simply "that the brother's haste has led him to make a foolish mistake, that his action would not have been wrong had the sin been real, but that he has been the victim of a demonic deceit which has led him to commit the sin of judgment.''[63] The commandment of love thus required one to exercise real skepticism regarding one's own narrow vision of things, especially toward the actions of others.

The warning presented by this story was apparently taken seriously. The elders became convinced that the tendency to judge others could only be overcome by turning one's attention away from others and toward oneself. Abba Moses was one of the most insistent regarding the need to change the focus of one's attention. One should become indifferent toward the actions of another: "The monk must die to his neighbor and never judge him at all, in any way whatever.''[64] He noted that by looking at oneself, one would simply not be able to see what someone else was doing: "When someone is occupied with his own faults, he does not see those of his neighbor.''[65]

Abba Moses demonstrated his own grasp of this truth in a vivid symbolic action. He had been called to a council to judge a brother who had committed a fault. Moses at first refused to go, but after a brother came to tell him that the whole council was waiting for him, he reluctantly agreed to go. Setting off for the meeting, "He took a leaking jug, filled it with water and carried it with him. The others came out to meet him and said to him, 'What is this, Father?' The old man said to them, 'My sins run out behind me, and I do not see [οὐ βλέπω] them, and today I am coming to judge [κρῖναι] the errors of another.' When they heard that they said no more to the brother but forgave him.''[66] As this story demonstrates, refraining from judgment meant not only holding oneself from acting in a particular way, but also showing real solidarity with the other person. Once, when Abba Bessarion saw that a brother who had sinned was "turned out of the church by the priest, he got up and went with him, saying, 'I too am a sinner.' "[67]

Symbolic stories also served to communicate effectively the depth of one's refusal to judge in situations where others may have judged prematurely. When such parables were uttered by one of integrity, they had the potential to effect great change in those who heard them. In one instance, a brother was cast out of a monastery for "being tempted." He went to stay for a while with Abba Antony who, after a time, sent him back to his own monastery. But his brothers cast him out once again and this time Antony sent them a message, saying, "A boat was shipwrecked at sea and lost its cargo; with great difficulty it reached the shore; but you want to throw into the sea that which has found safe harbor on the shore." When the brothers realized that it was Abba Antony who had sent them this monk, they received him at once.[68] Another time, a brother who was falsely accused of fornication went off to see Abba Antony. The brothers followed him and in the presence of Antony engaged in a great argument over whether or not the brother was guilty. Abba Paphnutius, who was visiting with Antony at the time, listened and then told them this parable: "I have seen a man on the bank of the river buried up to his knees in mud and someone came to give him a hand to help him out, but they pushed him further in up to his neck." Then Abba Antony said about Abba Paphnutius, "Behold, a true man, who can heal souls and save them. All of those present were pierced to the heart by the words of the old man and they repented of what they had done to the brother."[69]

In both of these cases, words of power proceeding from elders who are pure of heart convey both the centrality of mercy and compassion and the genuine harm that can come from judging unjustly. The words of the parable *effect* what they say, piercing the hearts of those listening and bringing a painful, revelatory shock. In both stories, it is the reminder of the brothers' blindness, their limited perspective on things, which brings about their awakening. It is significant, moreover, that Antony expresses his approval of Paphnutius's parable not by commenting on the parable itself but by pointing to the qualities of the one who has uttered it. The story Paphnutius told shows him to be a "true man," one who, because of the depth of his compassion, can "heal souls and save them." It is the realization of the call to love in the life of the one who speaks that gives the words their healing and saving power.

Fulfilling the call to refrain from judgment meant learning to see the possibilities in a situation rather than simply the bare reality. Abba Mark the Egyptian, who had lived alone in his cell for thirty years, was in the habit of receiving communion from a certain priest. The devil, seeing Mark's remarkable endurance, decided to tempt him by enticing him to judge the priest. He sent him a demon-possessed man under the pretense of asking the elder for a blessing. The demon-possessed man used the opportunity to castigate the priest before Abba Mark, claiming that the priest "smelled of sin" and that Abba Mark should not allow him to come around any longer. But Mark rejected the temptation:

> [F]illed with the spirit of God, [he] said to [the demon], "My son, everyone rids himself of impurity, but you bring it. It is written: 'Judge not that you not be judged' (Mt 7:1). However, even if he is a sinner, the Lord will save him, for it is written: 'Pray for one another that you may be healed' (Jas 5:16)." When he had said this and when he had prayed, he drove the devil out of the man and sent him away healed.[70]

This story provides another instance of a "hermeneutical act," in which a person's fulfillment of a biblical text effects real change on those around him. Abba Mark may well have been tempted to believe the demoniac. He had no evidence to help him decide the case one way or another, yet he chose not to see this, and rejected the demoniac's suggestion that he judge the priest. It is interesting, moreover, that following his decision not to judge the priest—his fulfillment of the command to refrain from judging— the demon-possessed man was cleansed. The *act* of fulfilling the command interprets the text in a singularly powerful way: by choosing to look kindly toward the priest, he inadvertently helps to heal one who had been overcome by evil. The refusal to give way to the temptation to judge could also bear other kinds of fruit. Abba Agathon said, "Whenever his thoughts urged him to pass judgment on something which he saw, he would say to himself, 'Agathon, don't do this.' Thus his spirit was always recollected."[71]

For some, the refusal to judge others became a habit and bore fruit in an unwillingness or even inability to "see" sin or failure in others. In place of the kind of scrupulosity which some used as an excuse to watch the behavior of others and observe every mistake with careful attention, the desert fathers cultivated a spirituality of "knowing ignorance" motivated by compassion. When some brothers asked Poemen, "If we see someone committing a sin, do you think we ought to reprove him?" Poemen said to them, "[F]or my part, if I have to go out and I see someone committing a sin, I pass on my way without reproving him."[72] The same quality of "merciful ignorance" of sin is expressed in a story about Macarius the Great, who was revered in large part because he was "blind and deaf" to the faults of others. It was said of him that "he became, as it is written, a 'god upon earth,' because, just as God covers [σκεπάζων] the world, so Abba Macarius would cover the defects [σκεπάζων τὰ ἐλαττώματα] which he saw, as though he did not see them; and those which he heard, as though he did not hear them."

Macarius is said to have become a god upon the earth not because of any extraordinary power but because of the depth of his compassion.[73]

Perhaps more than any other elder, the one who had realized the command to refrain from judgment most deeply was Abba Ammonas. He was said to "have advanced to the point where his goodness was so great, he no longer took any notice of evil."[74] This is a telling statement, but one which could easily be misinterpreted. Ammonas's capacity to disregard evil was not a kind of moral imperviousness but rather a conscious choice to practice compassion toward others. And at times, this choice required him to extend himself considerably. This was especially true when people came to him for the express purpose of seeking a judgment on some matter. Because of the high esteem in which he was held, he was often approached to render judgments in disputes. But sometimes those who approached him simply wanted him to declare his judgment upon a sinner. Ammonas, though, refused to do so, even to the point of sacrificing his reputation. So intensely did Ammonas dislike rendering judgments on others, that "when some people came to be judged by him, he feigned madness [ἐμωροποίει]" in order to avoid doing so.[75] To keep from judging, he became like the "fools for Christ" spoken of in St. Paul's letters.

In another instance, someone brought him a young girl who was pregnant, saying,

> "See what this unhappy wretch has done; give her a penance." But, he, having marked the young girl's womb with the sign of the cross, commanded that six pairs of fine linen sheets should be given her, saying, "It is for fear that, when she comes to give birth, she may die, she or the child, and have nothing for the burial." But his accusers resumed, "Why did you do that? Give her a punishment." But he said to them, "Look, brothers, she is near to death; what am I to do?" Then he sent her away and no old man dared accuse anyone any more.[76]

The story is striking not only for the tenderness which Ammonas showed toward the young girl, but also for the tenacity he demonstrated in fending off her accusers. Refraining from judgment required at times like this not only tenderness, but uncommon courage and conviction.

These qualities were also in evidence when disputes arose within monastic circles. In one case, there was a "monk with a bad reputation" who had been accused by some brothers of keeping a woman in his cell. They wanted to drive him away and when they heard that Abba Ammonas was in that place, invited him to come with them to the monk's cell. The monk in question was in fact guilty of keeping a woman in his cell and when he heard that Abba Ammonas and the others were on their way to his place, he hurriedly hid the woman in a large cask which he kept nearby. Upon arriving at the brother's cell, "Abba Ammonas saw what was happening but for the sake of God he hid the deed." He came into the cell, seated himself on the cask and ordered the brothers to search the whole place. Then, seeing that the monks had searched everywhere without finding the woman, Ammonas reprimanded them for the harm they had caused the other brother, saying, "What is this? May God forgive you!" He prayed, and after making everyone else go out, took the brother by the hand and said, "Brother, watch yourself." [77] The tension between Ammonas's clear perception of the situation and his determination to protect the brother illustrates the power in a holy one of the realization of the commandment to refrain from judgment. It is not that he could not see, but that he *would not see* the sin of the brother. Ammonas's unwillingness to see evil illustrates how deeply certain of the desert fathers had interiorized the Gospel commands. Not judging another would always be a conscious choice, but it could also become part of the fabric of a person's life. And when this happened, it resulted in acts of compassion and tenderness towards others.

Compassion

Love as Bearing Burdens and Encouraging Others

Much of the language used to describe the fulfillment of the love commandment in the *Sayings* derives from the honesty with which the desert fathers faced up to the cost of love. They spoke in direct and realistic language about the need to "be with" others in their suffering, or even to "carry" part of their burden. Similarly, they understood that sometimes love required them to encourage—literally "give heart" to someone who was discouraged or depressed. This willingness to be in solidarity with other human beings in their sufferings was one of the ways the desert fathers brought the call of love to fruition in the desert.

The main word the desert fathers used to describe the action of "carrying" another in love was $\beta\alpha\sigma\tau\acute{\alpha}\zeta\omega$. It figures prominently in the New Testament, where it is used to describe Jesus' bearing of his cross, the need for the disciples to carry the cross in following Jesus, the need to bear others' burdens, and in particular the need to bear the failings of the weak. [78] While specific New Testament texts are not explicitly cited by the desert fathers, the way they use the language of bearing burdens suggests that they were conscious of trying to live out this dimension of the commandment to love. They understood the need to be discriminating about which burdens to carry, however. This is illustrated well by the sharp comment of a monk who saw someone carrying a dead person on a bier. He said to the monk, "Do you carry the dead? Go and carry the living [βάσταζε τοὺς ζῶντας]."[79] And among the living, Abba Daniel contended that it was especially the weak ones who should be the recipients of this compassion. He said that if someone "commits a sin through weakness, one must bear it [χρὴ βαστάζειν αὐτόν]."[80] One story that illustrates what it meant to "bear the weak" concerns a brother who was burdened by the weight of his sin but was afraid to acknowledge it to any of the elders. He approached Abba Lot to talk about what he had done but was so troubled and agitated that he could not even sit down. Instead, he paced nervously in and out of the cell and was unable to bring himself to say what was on his mind. Lot, realizing the great weight under which the brother was suffering, pleaded with him, saying, "Confess it to me and I will carry it [βαστάζω αὐτήν]." Encouraged by these words, the brother told Lot how he had committed fornication and sacrificed to idols in order to do it. Taking all this in his stride, Lot said to the brother, "Have confidence, repentance is possible. Go, sit in your cave . . . and I will carry half of your sin with you [βαστάζω μετὰ σοῦ τὸ ἥμισυ τῆς ἁμαρτίας]." We are told that God accepted the brother's repentance and that he became Lot's disciple.[81]

The commitment to carry those who are weak often expressed itself as an act of entering deeply into another person's experience and healing that person through encouragement born of real empathy. An example of someone "carrying another" by "comforting" them is conveyed in a story which makes use of a word play on the word "carry" to make its point. A brother complained to an old man that he was "worn out" and "afflicted" by the erratic behavior of his brother. The old man "comforted him [παρεκάλει αὐτὸν]" saying, "Bear with your brother [βάσταζον τὸν ἀδελφόν] and God, seeing the work of your forbearance, will bear him [φέρει αὐτὸν]." He noted that "it is not easy to bear someone through hardness . . . rather, bear him through kindness [τῇ χρηστότητι φέρεις αὐτὸν], for it is by encouragement that our God bears men [ὁ θεὸς ἡμῶν, τῇ παρακλήσει φέρει τοὺς ἀνθρώπους]." The old man went on to tell him a story of two brothers, one of whom became discouraged and wanted to return to 'the world.' An old man advised the other brother: "Go with him [back to the world], and because of the labor you are giving yourself, God will not let him fall."[82] "Going with" someone who was suffering or discouraged, "entering into" that experience through kindness and empathy, was one of the ways the desert fathers expressed their love.

Encouraging those who were weak sometimes meant that in one's dealings with others, the scales would not be completely even. One time three old men, one of whom had a bad reputation, came to see Abba Achilles and each one asked him to make him a fishing net. He refused the first two, saying he had no time, but to the third, the one with the bad reputation, he said, "For you, I will make one." When the two he had refused asked why he had treated them so unfairly, Achilles responded that he knew *they* would not be too disappointed if he did not make them a net; they would not take it personally because they understood that he did not have time. But with the other brother, it was different. "[I]f I had not made one for him, he would have said, "The old man has heard about my sin, and that is why he does not want to make me anything." This would have had the effect, Achilles claimed, of immediately "cutting the bond" between us. "But now," he said, "I have aroused his soul [διήγειρα . . . αὐτοῦ τὴν ψυχήν]." And, in an allusion to St. Paul's words, he explained that he acted this way toward the brother "so that he would not be overcome with grief [2 Cor 2:7]." [83] Discouragement of a very mundane kind frequently arose in the desert, and this too required the healing words or actions of the elders. Abba Ammonas was approached by some brothers who found life difficult where they were living. Having discerned that the difficulty they were experiencing would not bring "damage to the soul" but was merely a "human trial," he "comforted their hearts [παρακαλέσας αὐτῶν τὰς καρδίας]" and sent them back from where they had come. [84] A more serious case involved an anchorite who had been led into a grievous sin. He became so gloomy because of it, that he was considering giving up his life in the desert and returning to the world. His disciple, however, "encouraged [παρεκάλει]" the anchorite, who was so lifted by his kindness that he recovered his balance, remained in the desert, and intensified his way of life. [85]

In some cases, the sensitivity of the elders toward those who were lost in despair or confusion was such that they were willing to adopt whatever position necessary to lead the others out of their pain. In a story alluded to earlier, some old men who had heard of Abba Sisoes's reputation for wisdom came to consult him on the matter of the coming judgment. The first two cited texts having to do with eternal judgment, and the third, obviously troubled by the thought of this, asked: "Father, what shall I do, for the remembrance of the outer darkness is killing me." Sisoes himself was not troubled by these thoughts and tried to encourage the brothers by speaking of his own experience: "For my part, I do not keep in mind the remembrance of any of these things, for God is compassionate and I hope that he will show me his mercy." However, the old men were offended by this answer, which seemed to them to make light of the issue of the final judgment, and got up to leave. Realizing the effect that his response had had upon them, Sisoes quickly changed course, and said to them: "Blessed are you, my brothers; truly I envy you. The first speaks of the river of fire, the second of hell and the third of darkness. Now if your spirit is filled with such remembrances, it is impossible for you to sin. What shall I do then? I who am hard of heart and to whom it has not been granted so much as to know whether there is a punishment for men; no doubt it is because of this that I am sinning all the time." They prostrated themselves before him and said, "Now we have seen exactly that of which we have heard tell."[86] One could argue that Sisoes was being disingenuous with these old men. Did he really believe what he was telling them in his second response? In a sense, he did—he knew that a constant awareness of one's own sinfulness and the uncertainty of the judgment to come could kindle real moral acuity. Yet his response is more important for what it shows us about his capacity to empathize with his visitors' concerns. His desire to reach them and draw them out of their paralyzing fear about the final judgment was stronger than his attachment to any particular position about that judgment. It was Sisoes's willingness to move toward his visitors in love which touched them most deeply.

A common problem for younger monks in their relationship with the elders was knowing how often they should approach them with problems or questions. When inner warfare was specially intense or when a brother simply could not grasp the meaning of what an elder had to say, there was sometimes a need to return again and again. In such circumstances, there was an understandable reluctance to approach the elder, for fear of being a nuisance. One of the sure signs of compassion in the desert was a long-suffering kindness through which the elder was able to touch those who were uncertain of themselves or their position. In one such case, a brother who was severely attacked by lustful thoughts got up during the night, went to an old man, and told him about it. The old man "comforted him [παρεκάλεσεν αὐτὸν] and he returned to his cell strengthened." This happened many different times. Each time, "the old man did not reproach him, but spoke to him of what might help him [τὰ πρὸς ὠφέλειαν]. . . ."[87] This same compassionate acceptance of one who had "fallen" is illustrated in a story of a brother who sinned and was banished from the monastery on the orders of an old anchorite. The brother, we are told, fell into despair. Abba Poemen heard of the brother's plight and sent for him. When the brother arrived, Poemen, "seeing him so afflicted, arose and embraced him and was kind to him and invited him to eat." Then Poemen invited the old anchorite who had banished the brother to come and visit him. When the old man arrived Poemen told him this story: "Two men dwelt in one place and someone belonging to each of them died; the first one, leaving his own dead, went to weep over the other's. Hearing this, the old man was pierced

by the words [κατενύγη ἐπὶ τῷ λόγῳ]."[88] It was Poemen's words that
reached the old man and revealed to him how harshly he had treated the
brother. Yet the power of Poemen's words and their capacity to pierce the
old man's heart was directly linked to Poemen's own practice of compassion. Only one who had so realized within himself the call to love could
speak to others with such authority.

The very real sense which the monks had of Christ's boundless love for
them significantly affected their capacity to "bear with" others in their sufferings. In particular, they were able to share their experience of Christ as
the risen one and Christ as the one whose love sustained their lives with
those who especially needed encouragement. To one who asked her about
the manner and meaning of the resurrection of the dead, Amma Theodora
found it sufficient simply to point to the sign and source of their hope: "As
pledge, example, and as prototype we have him who died for us and is
risen, Christ our God."[89] This sense of Christ's presence as risen and living
within them could be especially helpful in responding to an annoying or
troublesome person. We see an instance of this with someone who was said
to have been "very austere of body, but not very clear in his thoughts." He
went to ask Abba John Colobos for help with his problem of "forgetfulness" but, having received the word, he returned to his cell and promptly
forgot what John had said to him. He repeated this pattern many times.
Later, when he met Abba John, he conceded that he had yet again forgotten
the word he had given him. "But I did not want to overburden you, so I
did not come back." John did not rebuke him but instructed him to carry
out a simple task: to go light a lamp, and then light another one from it.
After the brother had done this, John asked him: "Has the lamp suffered
any loss from the fact that other lamps have been lit from it?" The brother
responded, "No." The old man continued, "So it is with John; even if the
whole of Scetis came to see me, they would not separate me from the love
of Christ. Consequently, whenever you want to, come to me without hesitation."[90] This was a simple, and in some ways modest, gesture of love.
Yet to be able to respond with kindness to the continuous, often nagging
requests for help day in and day out required no small reservoir of love.
John's sense of living in communion with the love of Christ reveals the
ultimate source of that love. And it helps us to see the truth of Poemen's
comment about John, that he had realized within himself the commandment
to love: "When a brother went to see Abba John Colobos, he offered him
that charity of which the apostle speaks, 'Charity suffers long and is kind.' "[91]
Instances such as these confirm one in the belief that for the monks, "the
study of Scripture [was] undertaken to know Christ and to keep him in the
centre of the heart before God."[92]

The willingness to "be with" another in an experience of suffering and to redeem that person through this action is one of the most striking aspects of the practice of compassion found in the desert. One of the chief causes of such suffering was the depression and despair that could overcome one after committing some sin which seemed to put one beyond the pale. To share in the suffering of such a person could be the beginning of the process of redemption. Once, when two brothers were at market, one of them "fell" into fornication and was so ashamed of what he had done that he refused at first to return to his cell with the other brother. But the other persisted, and, "wishing to win him over, said to him, '[T]he same thing happened to me too . . . come, let *us* go and do strict penance and God will forgive us.' . . . [T]hen one of the brothers did penance for the other *as though he had sinned himself.* [B]ecause of the great love of the brother who had not sinned," the one who had sinned was forgiven.[93] Such love for another could even require allowing oneself to become completely overwhelmed by the pain of another. In one such instance, a brother found that someone he knew was possessed by a demon. The brother, "being as it is written 'moved by the love of God' " prayed that the devil might "pass into himself and that the other might be liberated. God heard his prayer . . . [and] . . . the ascetic was overwhelmed by the devil. . . . Finally, because of his love, God drove the devil away from him after a few days."[94] The personal cost of such action was high. Yet for the sake of a friend suffering in this way, it was a cost the brother was willing to pay. And, as we have seen earlier, real power was seen to reside in those who realized the commandments of Scripture in their lives. In this case, the cathartic act of banishing the devil was accomplished not by the idea of love, but by the *realization* of love within the brother's life.

Love as Tenderness

It is surprising in some ways, given how harsh life in the desert could be, that the final word in desert spirituality is tenderness. The long and hard effort of the monks to realize within themselves the meaning of the commandment to love resulted in a certain tenderness, even sweetness in their behavior and demeanor. The number of stories preserved by the monks referring to tiny, seemingly insignificant acts of kindness and tenderness is quite revealing. Such acts of tenderness toward others were preserved because the monks were convinced that it was here above all that one could see the fruit of the long years spent struggling in the desert. Such gestures were treasured as much as more heroic deeds of love, for they showed the elders to be bearers of the mercy, kindness, and tenderness of God. The

spontaneity of such acts, the freedom with which love was given revealed
the possibility of an existence transformed by love.

A practical question over which the monks often struggled was how to
balance the requirements of their ascetic rule and the requirements of love.
Should one, in the event of having visitors, keep the rule—involving solitude, silence, fasting—or break it for the sake of the higher law of charity
and hospitality? In spite of the seriousness with which the monks took their
ascetical regime, it is apparent that the commandment had a greater weight
in these circumstances. The willingness to override the lesser imperatives of
human commandments, personal customs, or local rules to provide refreshment [ἀνάπαυσις] of both a material and a spiritual kind for those in need
was one expression of the realization of the commandment to love among
those in the desert. One story tells how during a period of fasting at Scetis
some visitors came to see Abba Moses and he cooked some food for them.
Seeing the smoke rising from his cell, some of the brothers said to the
ministers, "Look, Moses has broken the commandment and has cooked
something in his cell." The ministers agreed that when Moses came to join
them for the Saturday *synaxis* they would speak to him about what he had
done. However, when the time came, the ministers, who knew of Abba
Moses' "magnificent way of life," chose not to condemn him for what he
had done, but to praise him instead. They declared, "O Abba Moses, you
broke the commandment of men, and kept the commandment of God."[95]
One of the interesting things about this story is how the ministers came to
the conclusion about the character of Moses' behavior. It was not simply on
the merits of the present case that they knew that Moses had broken a lesser
commandment in order to keep a higher one. Rather, because they knew of
his magnificent way of life, they recognized in his behavior the sure signs
of an act motivated by love. We see a similar motivation at work in two
other stories. In the first, two brothers came to see an old man whose custom
it was "not to eat every day." When [the elder] saw the brothers, "he
rejoiced, and said, 'Fasting brings its reward, but he who eats again through
charity, fulfills two commandments, for he gives up his own will and he
fulfills the commandment.' And he refreshed the brothers."[96] We see here
another example of the monks' willingness to suspend mere customs—whether
personal or local—in any situation which called for an expression of generosity or love. "Eating again through charity," while clearly compromising
the elder's strict ascetical regime, became a means of fulfilling the commandment. Another story tells of a brother who went to see an anchorite,
apparently causing the old man to break his fast in order to tend to the needs
of the brother. As he was leaving the brother asked forgiveness from the old
man "for having taken you away from your rule." But the anchorite showed

himself to be utterly unconcerned with this perceived breach of his ascetical regime and told the brother, "My rule is to refresh you [ἀναπύσω σε] and send you away in peace." [97]

Misplaced emphasis on ascetical rigor was not restricted to the issue of fasting but also manifested itself in other ways. One of the signs of this tenderness was a rejection of this rigor. For instance, some rather stern brothers once asked Abba Poemen, "[W]hen we see brothers who are dozing at the *synaxis*, shall we rouse them so that they will be watchful?" He responded: "For my part, when I see a brother who is dozing, I put his head on my knees and let him rest." [98] Similarly, Abba Arsenius once pretended to have fallen asleep during the vigil so that his companions who had fallen asleep would not feel foolish or ashamed. [99] Such tenderness was extended especially to those who were in pain or trouble of any kind. On one occasion, when some brothers were traveling to Scetis, the guide who was leading them there became confused and lost his way. In order not to embarrass him, John Colobos pretended to be ill so they could stay there until dawn. [100]

The tenderness of the desert fathers could also express itself in spontaneous and extravagant gestures of love. This can be seen in a story concerning the reconciliation between Abba Motius and a brother with whom he had had a falling out. We are told that the brother, under the instigation of the devil, had "opposed him and persecuted him," causing Motius to withdraw and live as a recluse. Sometime later the same brother was part of a group of monks which came to visit Abba Motius. "As soon as [Motius] heard the name of the brother who had distressed him, in his joy the old man took a hatchet, battered down the door and came running out to where the brother was. He went to him . . . and made a prostration to him and embraced him." [101] What is striking about this episode is the immediacy and urgency with which Motius responded to the voice of his beloved friend. There was not a moment's hesitation when he heard that the young man was near, nor could he tolerate another moment without being reconciled with his friend. Love was often expressed in such concrete and intimate terms in the desert.

In addition, there are numerous stories of brothers looking after those who are ill and showing them great acts of kindness. One time a brother came upon an old man living in a distant desert, who had become ill and was unable to care for himself. The brother "looked after him, washed him, cooked some of the provisions he had brought, and offered them to him to eat." [102] In another case, a brother served a sick elder at great personal cost to himself, tending his open sores, and looking after all his needs. Many times he was tempted to flee, but he stayed, "suffered and went on serving the old man, and seeing the brother's labor, God healed the old man." [103]

One time a brother heard of an old man who was ill and who was longing for some fresh bread. The brother gathered some loaves of dry bread, ran a great distance to a town where he could get fresh bread and brought them back for the old man while they were still warm.[104] Other times love extended into the domain of the work place and involved placing one's own interests behind those of the others. Three brothers were harvesting together when one fell ill and could not continue working. The other two brothers decided that with increased effort they could do the extra work for the sick brother. They did so, collected the wages for the three of them, and paid the sick brother his share.[105] In another instance, a brother heard one of his companions telling how he had no handles to put on his baskets and that he was concerned because market day was approaching. So he gave the other one his own handles and "caused his brother's work to succeed by neglecting his own."[106]

Such seemingly insignificant acts of kindness fill the *Sayings*. Although they make for less dramatic reading than the recitation of great ascetical feats, the frequency with which they are recounted serves as an indication of the significance attached to them by the desert fathers. For those who sought to understand how to proceed in the way of holiness in the desert, the innumerable small words, gestures, and acts of the holy ones were precious reminders of the possibilities that lay before them. Nor should the significance of these gestures be underestimated. What Patricia Cox has noted about ancient biographies of holy men and women is also true of these sayings. Their "aim was to evoke, and thus to reveal the interior geography of the hero's life. . . . [T]hus when they sought to 'capture the gesture,' they were negotiating the intersection of the human and the divine."[107] The gestures and images of the holy ones which we find in the *Sayings* also capture something else: the attempt on the part of the monks to bring to life the Scriptures which formed the basis of their life. The *Sayings* provides visual evidence of the power of Scripture to create new life in the desert; it suggests that for the desert fathers *the* place where the "surplus of meaning" of Scripture came to realization was in the transformed lives of the holy ones. Those who wished to learn from the holy ones could look to their words or to their teachings. But above all, they looked to the holy ones themselves, to the ones who had drunk so deeply from the well of Scripture that they had become new living texts.

We see this in the stories describing the visages of some of the greatest of the elders; they were seen to reflect the light of the great biblical exemplars. Because of his shining countenance, Abba Pambo was said to be "like Moses, who received the image of the glory of Adam when his face

shone."[108] Abba Arsenius's "appearance was angelic, like that of Jacob.
. . ."[109] Abba Nisterus was also said to have reflected the glory of Moses,
though indirectly. He was likened to "the serpent of brass which Moses
made for the healing of the people [Nm 21:8–9]: he possessed all virtue and
without speaking he healed everyone."[110] The comparison is striking in that
it picks up a central Old Testament symbol of healing to communicate elo-
quently the silent healing power which Nisterus possessed. Many of those
listening to this comparison would have been immediately reminded of that
one whose healing power was said to have surpassed that of Moses' serpent
(Jn 3:14; 19:37). The presence of the refracted light of biblical exemplars
in the faces of the desert fathers indicates a kind of spiritual trajectory in the
desert: the exemplars of Scripture showed the way to live, and the desert
fathers, by imitating them, became new exemplars. This was not only an
important part of the monks' own self-understanding, it also explains much
of their appeal to their contemporaries: "To be a 'man of God' was to
revive, on the banks of the Nile, all other 'men of God' in all other ages.
. . . Little wonder that strong millennial hopes flickered around the persons
of the holy men and around the walled monasteries of the Nile."[111] Yet, in
the end these hopes were focused on something obscure and utterly unspectacular: the quiet, forceful *presence* of one who had become a bearer of
compassion. We can see this best in a story told about three elders who used
to visit Antony every year. Two of them would discuss their thoughts and
the salvation of their souls with him, but the third always remained silent,
not asking him anything. Antony finally asked him why it was that he always came with the others but did not ask him anything. He replied simply,
"It is enough for me to see you, Father."[112]

Notes

1. Nau 349 [*ROC* 17:298].
2. John Colobos 34 [*PG* 65:216A].
3. Isaac, Priest of the Cells 11 [*PG* 65:225D].
4. Theodore of Pherme 18 [*PG* 65:192AB].
5. John Colobos 19 [*PG* 65:212BC].
6. Theodore of Pherme 11 [*PG* 65:189CD], [m]. Reflecting the differences of
opinion on the relative merits of asceticism and practical charity, one story, Nau 355
[*ROC* 17:300], tells of two brothers, one of whom lived a solitary life for six days
a week, giving himself much pain, while the other served the sick. The question was
raised, "Whose work does God accept with greater favor?" The old man replied,
"Even if the one who withdraws for six days were to hang himself up by the nostrils,
he could not equal the one who serves the sick."

7. So Lampe defines παρέργιον, in *PGL*, 1033.

8. Cassian 1 [*PG* 65:244AB], [m].

9. John Colobos 39 [*PG* 65:217A] (emphasis mine).

10. Poemen 116 [*PG* 65:352B]. Poemen says elsewhere that the three things which are the most helpful are: "fear of the Lord, prayer, and doing good to one's neighbor" (1 Thes 5:15). See also Poemen 160 [*PG* 65:361A].

11. Or 11 [*PG* 65:440B].

12. Agathon 26 [*PG* 65:116C].

13. Epiphanius 16 [*PG* 65:168A].

14. Poemen 70 [*PG* 65:337D–340A].

15. Nau 345 [*ROC* 17:297].

16. Joseph of Panephysis 4 [*PG* 65:229B].

17. Abraham 1 [*PG* 65:129D–132B].

18. Theodora 5 [*PG* 65:204A].

19. *Praktikos* 11; trans. John Eudes Bamberger, *The Praktikos and Chapters on Prayer* (Kalamazoo, MI: Cistercian Publications, 1978), 18. Bamberger, himself trained as a psychiatrist, comments on the accuracy of Evagrius's description of anger, even by contemporary standards: "This interesting description of the dynamics of disproportionate anger will be appreciated for its accuracy perhaps only by those who have carefully followed the progression of certain forms of schizophrenia." On the monastic perspective on the debilitating effects of anger, especially in the thought of Evagrius, see T. Špidlík, *The Spirituality of the Christian East: A Systematic Handbook*, trans. A. P. Gythiel (Kalamazoo, MI: Cistercian Publications, 1986), 251–52.

20. Ammonas 3 [*PG* 65:120B].

21. Agathon 19 [*PG* 65:113C]. Other sayings confirm the danger of anger in slightly different terms. Cf. Poemen 68 [*PG* 65:337C]: anger is "contrary to nature"; Pityrion [*PG* 65:376A]: "the devil accompanies anger."

22. *VA* 55 [*PG* 26:921B], trans. R. C. Gregg, *The Life of Antony and the Letter to Marcellinus* (New York: Paulist Press, 1980), 72.

23. Syncletica 3 [*PG* 65:425C].

24. Poemen 118 [*PG* 65:352CD].

25. Epiphanius 4 [*PG* 65:164C]. Another version of the same saying occurs in Cassian 4: "Abba John, abbot of a great monastery, went to Abba Paësius who had been living for forty years very far off in the desert. As he was very fond of him, and could therefore speak freely with him, he said to him, 'What good have you done by living here in retreat for so long, and not being easily disturbed by anyone?' He replied, 'Since I lived in solitude, the sun has never seen me eating.' Abba John said to him, 'As for me, it has never seen me angry.' " See also Poemen 203 [Guy, *Recherches,* S16:30], where Poemen speaks of a similar contrast: "[He] heard of someone who had gone all week without eating and then had lost his temper. The old man said, 'He could do without food for six days, but he could not cast out anger.' "

26. Agathon 4 [*PG* 65:109B].

27. Agathon 5 [*PG* 65:109C].

28. John Colobos 34 [*PG* 65:216AC].

29. Poemen 177 [*PG* 65:365A]; Rom 12:21: "Do not be overcome by evil, but overcome evil with good."
30. Isaiah 8 [*PG* 65:181D].
31. Poemen 34 [*PG* 65:332AB].
32. Poemen 24 [*PG* 65:328C].
33. Nilus 2 [*PG* 65:305B].
34. Nilus 6 [*PG* 65:305B].
35. Evagrius, *Chapters on Prayer*, 20; Trans. Bamberger, *The Praktikos and Chapters on Prayer*, 58, n. 21; see also I. Hausherr, S. J., *Les leçons d'un Contemplatif: Le traité de l'oraison d'Evagre le Pontique* (Paris: Beauchesne, 1960), who cites another text of Evagrius's which affirms this relationship: "Anger dissipates contemplation, but long-suffering gathers it" (35).
36. Zeno 7 [*PG* 65:177BC].
37. Poemen 115 [*PG* 65:352B].
38. John Colobos 5 [*PG* 65:205B], [m].
39. John Colobos 6 [*PG* 65:205B], [m].
40. Isidore the Priest 7 [*PG* 65:221B], [m].
41. Isidore the Priest 2 [*PG* 65:220C].
42. Isaac, Priest of the Cells 9 [*PG* 65:225C].
43. Theodora 4 [*PG* 65:201D–204A].
44. Poemen 91 [*PG* 65:344C].
45. Poemen 198 [Guy, *Recherches*, S11:30].
46. Ephrem 3 [*PG* 65:168CD].
47. Xanthius 3 [*PG* 65:315C].
48. Nau 327 [*ROC* 17:209].
49. Joseph of Panephysis 2 [*PG* 65:228C].
50. Euprepius 5 [*PG* 65:172C].
51. Poemen 131 [*PG* 65:356A], [m] [RSV].
52. Poemen 117 [*PG* 65:352C]. Poemen joins the beginning of Mt 7:3 to the end of Mt 7:4.
53. Poemen 157 [*PG* 65:360D].
54. See J. P. Lemaire, "L'abbé Poemen et la Sainte Écriture" (licentiate thesis, University of Freiburg, 1971), 50.
55. Theodore of Pherme 13 [*PG* 65:189D]. Several other biblical texts use the word ἐξουθενέω to convey a particularly contemptible treatment of other human beings. Lk 18:9 (introducing the parable of the pharisee and the tax collector): "He also told this parable to some who trusted in themselves that they were righteous and despised [ἐξουθενοῦντας] others"; Rom 14:3: "Let not him who eats despise him who abstains. . . ." It is also used specifically in reference to Jesus to describe the contempt with which he was treated: see Acts 4:11; Lk 23:11; Mk 9:12.
56. Theodote 2 [Guy, *Recherches*, S1:22].
57. Isidore the Priest 10 [Guy, *Recherches*, S1:24–25]. This also echoes 1 John 4:7: "Beloved, let us love one another."
58. Nau 226 [*ROC* 14:360].
59. Mius 3 [*PG* 65:301D–304A]. The suggestion that Mius may be alluding to

the text from Jonah is based not on verbal similarities but on a similarity in ideas. In the text from Jonah, God compares Jonah's relatively minor concern about a castor oil plant to God's great sorrow and compassion for the inhabitants of the city of Nineveh.

60. Poemen 86 [*PG* 65:341D]; see Lemaire, "L'Abbé Poemen," 31.

61. Poemen 156 [*PG* 65:360CD].

62. Poemen 114 [*PG* 65:352AB] ὃ εἶδον οἱ ὀφθαλμοί σου, ταῦτα διαμαρτύριου Prv 25:7 *[LXX]:* ἃ εἶδον οἱ ὀφθαλμοί σου, λέγε.

63. Graham Gould, "The Desert Fathers on Personal Relationships" (Ph.D. diss., Cambridge University, 1988), 175.

64. Moses 14 [*PG* 65:288B].

65. Moses 16 [*PG* 65:288B]; see also Moses 18 [*PG* 65:289B]: "If we are on the watch to see our own faults, we shall not see those of our neighbor."

66. Moses 2 [*PG* 65:281D–284A]; see also Pior 3 [*PG* 65:373CD–376A], which relates a similar episode.

67. Bessarion 7 [*PG* 65:141BC].

68. Antony 21 [*PG* 65:81D–84A].

69. Antony 29 [*PG* 65:85AB], [m].

70. Mark the Egyptian [*PG* 65:304ABC].

71. Agathon 18 [*PG* 65:113C].

72. Poemen 113 [*PG* 65:352A].

73. Macarius the Great 32 [*PG* 65:273D], [m]. The citation comes from the *Apostolic Constitutions* II, 26, 4; on God as protecting the world, see I Clement 60:3: "So shall we be sheltered by thy mighty hand"; see also Barsanuphius 239, *Barsanuphe et Jean de Gaza: Corréspondance* (Sablé-sur-Sarthe: Solesmes, 1971), where he writes to a scatterbrained younger brother, "After God I have spread my wings over you till this day. I bear your burdens and your misconduct . . . your thoughtlessness. I have seen and covered all that, just as God sees and overlooks our faults" (189–90).

74. Ammonas 8 [*PG* 65:121BC].

75. Ammonas 9 [*PG* 65:121C]; on being a "fool for Christ," see 1 Cor 3:18: "If anyone among you thinks he is wise in this age, let him become a fool [μωρὸς] that he may become wise"; 1 Cor. 4:10: "We are fools for Christ's sake [μωροὶ διὰ χριστόν]."

76. Ammonas 8 [*PG* 65:121BC].

77. Ammonas 10 [*PG* 65:121D–124A], [m].

78. On Jesus carrying the cross, see Jn 19:17; on the need for disciples to carry the cross in following Jesus, see Lk 14:27; on bearing one another's burdens, see Gal 6:2; on bearing with the failings of the weak, see Rom 15:1.

79. Nau 335 [*ROC* 17:294].

80. Daniel 6 [*PG* 65:156BC].

81. Lot 2 [*PG* 65:256B], [m]; see also Nau 346 [*ROC* 17:297–98]. In an interesting parallel, two letters of Barsanuphius (Letters 72 and 73) indicate the kind of burdens that the monks are willing to bear for one another. Barsanuphius makes a distinction between the ability to carry *half* of someone else's burden (something that

is actually manageable) and *all* of another's burden (something only the "perfect" can do). See *Barsanuphe et Jean de Gaza: Corréspondance*, 72–73. Lot's willingness to carry *half* the brother's burden seems to be an indication of his genuine humility.

82. Nau 180 [*ROC* 13:270], [m].

83. Achilles 1 [*PG* 65:124BC], [m]; 2 Cor 2:7: "You should rather turn to forgive and comfort him, or he may be overwhelmed by excessive sorrow."

84. Ammonas 5 [*PG* 65:120C].

85. Nau 176 [*ROC* 13:268–69].

86. Sisoes 19 [*PG* 65:397D–400A].

87. Nau 164 [*ROC* 13:53–54].

88. Poemen 6 [*PG* 65:320BCD], [m].

89. Theodora 10 [Guy, *Recherches*, S3:23].

90. John Colobos 18 [*PG* 65:209D–212B].

91. Poemen 74 [*PG* 65:340C].

92. B. Lindars, "The Bible and the Call: The Biblical Roots of the Monastic Life in History and Today," *Bulletin of John Rylands Library* 66 (1983–1984):239.

93. Nau 179 [*ROC* 13:270] (emphasis mine).

94. Nau 354 [*ROC* 17:300].

95. Moses 5 [*PG* 65:284BC].

96. Nau 288 [*ROC* 14:375], [m].

97. Nau 283 [*ROC* 14:372].

98. Poemen 92 [*PG* 65:344C].

99. Arsenius 43 [*PG* 65:108BC].

100. John Colobos 17 [*PG* 65:209CD].

101. Motius 2 [*PG* 65:300BCD], [m].

102. Nau 157 [*ROC* 13:52].

103. Nau 356 [*ROC* 17:300].

104. Nau 348 [*ROC* 17:298].

105. Nau 350 [*ROC* 17:298–99].

106. Nau 347 [*ROC* 17:298].

107. Patricia Cox, *Biography in Late Antiquity: A Quest for the Holy Man* (Berkeley: University of California Press, 1983), xi.

108. Pambo 12 [*PG* 65:372A].

109. Arsenius 42 [*PG* 65:106A]. Scripture nowhere attributes this quality to Jacob. It is possible that such a comparison is found in an apocryphal text or another ancient tradition. See Luciana Mortari, *Vita e detti dei padri del deserto*, vol. 1 (Rome: Città Nuova, 1971), 111, n. 55.

110. Nisterus the Cenobite 1 [*PG* 65:308D–309A].

111. Peter Brown, "The Saint as Exemplar in Late Antiquity," in *Saints and Virtues*, ed. J. S. Hawley (Berkeley: University of California Press, 1987), 11.

112. Antony 27 [*PG* 65:84C].

Epilogue

It is now possible to see with renewed clarity the profound way in which Scripture shaped the spirituality of the early Christian monks. This is significant on at least three levels. First, it sheds new light on our historical understanding of early monasticism, establishing the depth at which Scripture permeated the experience of the early desert monks. Second, it focuses attention on hermeneutical questions, suggesting that the diverse, creative hermeneutical strategies at work in the desert contributed significantly to the monks' capacity to make sense of and live within the world of Scripture. Finally, it provides a new way of thinking about the meaning of the desert fathers' quest for holiness and the shape of their spirituality, suggesting that their continuous rumination upon Scripture, their desire to embody the texts in their lives, was a primary source of the compelling spirituality that emerged from the desert.

Any attempt to understand the history of early monasticism must take into account the central role that Scripture played in the life of the monks. Whether it was *the* primary force behind the rise and development of early monasticism is uncertain; but it was surely among the key influences shaping the early monks' life and spirituality. An appreciation of this element of early monasticism can help to fill out our understanding of early monastic asceticism, complementing recent studies that have focused on such issues as the social and economic dimensions of asceticism, the role of the body in the ascetical life, the relationship between different ascetical "schools," and the historical origins of asceticism. Any conclusions drawn about the role of Scripture in early monasticism must be seen as fitting into the increasingly rich and complex picture of early asceticism that has arisen from this work. At the same time, the role of sacred texts in forming the early monastic communities deserves to be taken seriously on its own terms and to be seen as a crucial part of the ascetical life of the monks.

For example, while there were almost certainly multiple and even conflicting motives behind the rise to monasticism, there are good reasons for thinking that Scripture may have played a central role in this process. What we know of early Egyptian Christianity and the ascetical impulse of that period from the monastic sources as well as from papyrological evidence makes it entirely plausible that certain key biblical texts may have influenced the growth of early monasticism. Still, there is much in this early period that remains hidden from our view. What is utterly clear, on the other hand, is the pulsing life the sacred texts gave to the daily existence of the early monks: the texts were proclaimed, recited (in solitude and in community), memorized, ruminated upon, and discussed. They served as a basic frame of reference and primary source of sustenance to the early monastics. (It is noteworthy that Peter Brown, in reevaluating his own groundbreaking work on the role and function of the holy man in late antiquity, has pointed to the need to take more seriously "the crucial role of liturgical prayer" in shaping the early monks' experience.) If we are to understand the particular cultural and spiritual achievements of these desert ascetics, we must take seriously this fundamental element in their monastic existence.

The constant reference to biblical texts in the lives of the monks does not mean that there was always complete agreement about how to understand them. We find in the *Sayings* numerous conflicts over how to approach and interpret the texts in general and over the understanding of particular texts. The presence of these hermeneutical tensions in the *Sayings* reveals to us some of the fault lines running through the early monastic world and points to the ambiguous, often conflicting character of much early monastic world-building. We see, for example, certain tensions emerging from the different assumptions about language on the part of literate and non-literate members of the early monastic communities. Elsewhere, we find Scripture becoming part of a debate between cenobitic and eremitical monks regarding the nature of the ascetical life. And often, Scripture acts as a mirror, held up by an elder before a disciple to reveal the monk to himself. Much of the drama of the early monastic world was played out on a stage where delicately textured light, color, and sound were provided by the sacred texts.

A distinct but related issue addressed by this study concerns hermeneutics, the role played by the monks' creative interpretive strategies in giving rise to and sustaining the early monastic world. There was little that was original in the particular hermeneutical approaches of the desert fathers, something that perhaps helps to account for the neglect of the early monastic herme- neutic in the standard histories of biblical interpretation. What we do find in the *Sayings* is dramatic evidence, in stories and anecdotes, of the influence interpretive questions had on the moral and spiritual life of an entire community. Focusing on contemporary hermeneutical categories illuminates the rich, multifaceted character of this ancient hermeneutic.

We have seen, for example, that the desert fathers were acutely aware of the disclosive power of language, and that their encounters with words— whether those of an elder or of Scripture—often had the character of "word events." Similarly, the assumptions or prejudices the elders brought to the texts were vital to the sense or understanding they derived from them. The monks' belief that the sacred texts were inherently powerful, a source of holiness, with a capacity to transform their lives, may have arisen from the largely oral culture of which they were a part; or it may have been an assumption that was particularly strong within their ascetic culture. Whatever the precise source for such an attitude, there can be no doubt that these attitudes about language had a profound effect on the monks' practical hermeneutic and on their spirituality. In the solitary acts of memorization, rumination, and meditation of Scripture, words penetrated the deepest recesses of the soul and created new possibilities and challenges. In the ethical relationship between elder and disciple, words spoke forcefully and demanded an often costly response. The monks were drawn into a hermeneutical circle, in which the words of Scripture and the elder elicited from them increasingly incisive responses of moral honesty and commitment. And the words themselves were experienced as infinitely elastic, growing with the monks' own growth and struggle, drawing them ever more deeply into the mystery revealed through the words.

Finally interpretation, understood as a means to transformation and holiness, was fundamental to the desert fathers' spirituality. While the monks we meet in the *Sayings* are generally reticent to speak of their spiritual experience, we can nevertheless glimpse substantial traces of their spirituality through their interpretation of Scripture. They saw the sacred texts as projecting worlds of possible meaning that they were called upon to enter. To ruminate on Scripture was to embark upon a deeply personal drama that the monks referred to as the quest for purity of heart. Interpretation of Scripture in this context meant allowing the text to strip away the accumulated layers of self-deception, self-hatred, fear, and insecurity that were exposed in the desert solitude and in the tension of human interaction. It also meant opening oneself to the new possibilities of meaning offered by these texts, realizing this meaning within oneself, and being transformed by this realization. While the avenues opened up by the texts were as diverse as the texts themselves and the questions the monks put to them, a certain consensus emerged among the desert fathers in the *Sayings* regarding what is at the heart of Scripture and thus at the center of their spiritual quest.

The central themes in the spirituality of the desert fathers noted in the latter half of this book, such as eschatology, *penthos,* and the struggle against evil; renunciation, freedom from care, and the recovery of paradise; humility and love, emerged from the monks' unceasing rumination on Scripture. Their desire to enter into the worlds projected by the sacred texts took on concrete shape as they confronted the particular demands and possibilities proposed by Scripture. The episodes contained in the *Sayings* refer again and again to the attempts by various monks to take into themselves a particular text, to make it part of their souls and their lives. Interpretation and misinterpretation of Scripture in the desert had little to do with doctrinal orthodoxy; rather, the aim of interpretation was moral purity and integrity and through this, the experience of God. Holiness for the desert fathers was expressed as personal transformation arising from the realization of Scripture within oneself. It is clear from the *Sayings* that the desert fathers exemplified in their own lives qualities that they absorbed from Scripture. They became "Christ-bearers," mediators of God to humanity. The ultimate expression of the desert hermeneutic was a *person,* one who embodied the sacred texts and who drew others out of themselves into a world of infinite possibilities.

Appendix: Biblical Texts

Cited in Cotelier's Greek Text and in Modern Translations of the *Sayings*

Old Testament

	Cotelier	Ward	Regnault	Mortari
Genesis	6	4	20	52
Exodus	3	2	5	19
Leviticus				1
Numbers			1	7
Deuteronomy	1	1	2	7
Joshua	1	1	2	4
I Samuel		1	5	6
II Samuel			2	6
I Kings	4		2	4
II Kings	2	2	2	9
Tobit				1
II Macabees				1
Job	3	2	4	7
Psalms	26	23	26	70
Proverbs	5	3	6	9
Ecclesiastes	1		1	2
Wisdom			1	1
Sirach	1		3	3

Old Testament

	Cotelier	Ward	Regnault	Mortari
Isaiah	11	3	10	25
Jeremiah	2	2	2	5
Ezekiel	3	2	2	10
Daniel	1		2	6
Joel				8
Amos				1
Jonah				1
Zechariah				2
Malachi				1
TOTAL	70	45	98	269

New Testament

	Cotelier	Ward	Regnault	Mortari
Matthew	29	21	46	162
Mark	3	1	3	14
Luke	10	5	19	74
John	4	3	4	70
Acts	1	1	6	16
Romans	1		4	22
I Corinthians	4	2	7	39
II Corinthians	1	2	2	22
Galatians			1	7
Ephesians	3	2	4	16
Philippians	1	1	1	15
Colossians	2	1	2	8
I Thessalonians	3	1	6	9
II Thessalonians			2	4
I Timothy	3	2	4	5
II Timothy	1			9
Titus	1	1	1	4
Hebrews	3	2	5	18
James	2	2	3	16
I Peter	2	1	4	9
II Peter	1	1	5	

New Testament

	Cotelier	Ward	Regnault	Mortari
I John			1	7
Jude				1
Revelation				11
TOTAL	75	48	126	563
TOTAL OT/NT	145	93	224	832

Selected Bibliography

Primary Sources

THE SAYINGS

Apophthegmata Patrum: Alphabetico-Anonymous collection

Greek Alphabetical collection, Jean Baptiste Cotelier, ed. *Ecclesiae Graecae monumenta, I.* Paris: Muguet, 1677. Reprinted in J. P. Migne. *PG* 65:72–440; Supplemented by Jean-Claude Guy in *Recherches sur la tradition Grecque des Apophthegmata Patrum. Subsidia Hagiographica* 36. Brussels: Société des Bollandistes, 1962.

Greek Anonymous collection. F. Nau, ed. "Histoire des solitaires égyptiens (MS Coislin 126, fol. 158f.)." Nos. 133–369. *Revue d'Orient Chrétien* 13 (1908):47–57, 266–83; 14 (1909):357–79; 17 (1912):204–11, 294–301; 18 (1913):137–40.

Latin Systematic collection. Heribert Rosweyde, ed. *Verba Seniorum* [*Vitae Patrum, books V–VIII*]. Antwerp: Plantin, 1616. Reprinted in J. P. Migne. *PL* 73:851–1062.

Apophthegmata Patrum: Versions and Translations

Amélineau, A. *Monuments pour servir à l'histoire de l'Égypte chrétienne: Histoire des monastères de la Basse-Égypte.* Annales du Musée Guimet. Vol. 25. Paris: Leroux, 1894.

Budge, E. A. Wallis. *The Book of Paradise, Being the Histories and Sayings of the Monks and Ascetics of the Égyptian Desert according to the Rescension of "Anan-Isho" of Beth Abbe.* Vol. 2. London: Printed for Lady Mieux by Drugulin, 1904.

Chadwick, Owen. *Western Asceticism.* Philadelphia: Westminster Press, 1958.

Chaîne, M. *Le manuscrit de la version copte en dialecte sahidique des "Apophthegmata Patrum."* Bibliothèque d'études coptes 6. Cairo: L'institut français d'archéologie Orientale, 1960.

———. "Le texte originale des Apophthègmes des pères." *Mélanges de la faculté orientale.* Vol. 5, pt. 2. Beirut: Université St. Joseph, 1912.

Collectio Monastica. Ethiopian text and Latin translation by Victor Arras. *CSCO* 238–39. Louvain: CSCO, 1963.

Dion, Jean and Guy Oury. *Les sentences des pères du désert: Recueil de Pélage et Jean.* Introduction by Lucien Regnault. Sablé-sur-Sarthe: Solesmes, 1966.

Duensing, H. ed. *Christlich-palästinisch-aramäische Texte und Fragmente.* Göttingen, 1906.

———. "Neue christlich-palästinisch-aramäische Fragmente." *Nachrichten von der Akademie der Wissenschaften in Göttingen aus dem Jahre 1944.* Philologisch-historische Klasse. Göttingen: Vandenhoeck and Ruprecht, 1944.

Dvali, M. *Anciennes traductions georgiennes de récits du moyen âge.* Vol. 1: *Traduction par Euthyme l'Hagiorite d'une ancienne recension du Patericon, d'après un manuscrit du XIe siècle.* Tiflis: Institut des Manuscrits, 1966.

Ethiopian Paterikon. Ethiopian text and Latin translation by Victor Arras. *CSCO* 277–78. Louvain: CSCO, 1967.

Guy, Jean-Claude. *Les Apophtegmes des pères du désert.* Spiritualité orientale et vie monastique 1. Bégrolles-en-Mauges: Bellefontaine, 1968.

Leloir, Louis. *Paterica Armeniaca a P. P. Mechitaristis edita (1855) nunc latine redditat.* *CSCO* 353, 361, 371, 379. Louvain: CSCO, 1974–1976.

Mortari, Luciana. *Vita e detti dei padri del deserto.* 2 vols. Rome: Città Nuova, 1971.

Regnault, Lucien. *Les sentences des pères du désert.* Sablé-sur-Sarthe: Solesmes, 1981.

———. *Les sentences des pères du désert: Nouveau recueil.* 2d ed. Sablé-sur-Sarthe: Solesmes, 1977.

———. *Les sentences des pères du désert: Série des anonymes.* Sablé-sur-Sarthe/Bégrolles-en-Mauges: Solesmes/Bellefontaine, 1985.

———. *Les sentences des pères du désert: Troisième recueil and tables.* Sablé-sur-Sarthe: Solesmes, 1976.

Sauget, J. M. "La collection d'Apophtegmes du ms. 4225 de la Bibliothèque de Strasbourg." *OCP* 30 (1974).

———. "Le Paterikon du ms. Mingana Christian Arabic 120a." *OCP* 28 (1962).

Ward, Benedicta. *The Sayings of the Desert Fathers: The Alphabetical Collection.* London: Mowbrays, 1975.

———. *The Wisdom of the Desert Fathers: Apophthegmata Patrum from the Anonymous Series.* Oxford: SLG Press, 1975.

OTHER PRIMARY SOURCES

Athanasius. *Vita Antonii.* PG 26:838–976. English translation: R. C. Gregg. *The Life of Antony and the Letter to Marcellinus.* New York: Paulist Press, 1980. Robert T. Meyer. *The Life of Saint Antony.* London Westminster, MD: Longman, Green and Co. Newman Press, 1950. Syriac *Life:* R. Draguet, ed. *La vie primitive de S. Antoine conservée en syriaque.* CSCO 417, *Scriptores Syri* 184. Louvain: CSCO, 1980.

Augustine. *Confessions*. PL 32:659–868. English translation: R. S. Pine-Coffin. *The Confessions*. Baltimore: Penguin Books, 1961.

Barsanuphe et Jean de Gaza: Correspondance. Translated from Greek by Lucien Regnault and Philippe Lemaire or from Georgian by Bernard Outier. Sablé-sur-Sarthe: Solesmes, 1971.

Benedict. *The Rule of St. Benedict*. Edited by T. Fry. In Latin and English with notes. Collegeville, MN: The Liturgical Press, 1981.

Cassian, John. *Collationes. Conférences*. Edited and translated by E. Pichery. Sources chrétiennes 42, 54, 64. Paris: Cerf, 1955, 1958, 1959. English translation: Edgar C. S. Gibson. *A Select Library of Nicene and Post-Nicene Fathers*, n.s., no. 11 Oxford: Parker and Co., 1894. Reprint. Grand Rapids, MI: Eerdmans, 1973. Owen Chadwick, *Western Asceticism*. Philadelphia: Westminister, 1958. Colm Luibheid, *John Cassian: Conferences* New York Paulist Press, 1985.

———. *De Institutis coenobiorum*. In *Institutions Cénobitiques*. Edited and translated by Jean-Claude Guy. Paris: Cerf, 1965.

Eusebius of Caesarea. *Historia ecclesiastica*. 2 vols. Greek text with English translation by Kirsopp Lake and J. E. L. Oulton. Loeb Classical Library. London/Cambridge, MA: Heinemann/Harvard University Press, 1926–1932.

Evagrius Ponticus. *Praktikos. Évagre le Pontique, traité pratique ou le moine,* edited by A. and C. Guillaumont. Sources chrétiennes 170–71. Paris: Cerf, 1971. English translation: John Eudes Bamberger. *The Praktikos and Chapters on Prayer*. Kalamazoo, MI: Cistercian Publications, 1978.

Historia Monachorum in Aegypto. Critical edition of the Greek text, edited by André Marie Jean Festugière. Brussels: Societé des Bollandistes, 1961. English translation: Norman Russell. *The Lives of the Desert Fathers*. Introduction by Benedicta Ward. London: Mowbray, 1980.

Abba Isaiah. *Asceticon*. Edited by René Draguet. *Les cinq recensions de l'ascéticon syriaque d'Abba Isaïe I: Introduction au problème isaïen. Version des logoi I–XIII avec des parallèles grecs et latins*. CSCO 293, Scriptores Syri 122 (Louvain: CSCO, 1968).

Jerome. *Selected Letters of St. Jerome*. Translated by F. A. Wright. London: Heinemann, 1933.

Lives of Pachomius. Edited by F. Halkin: *Sancti Pachomii vitae graecae*. (In Greek). Subsidia hagiographica 19. Brussels: Société des Bollandistes, 1932. English translation: A. Veilleux. *Pachomian Koinonia. The Lives, Rules, and Other Writings of Saint Pachomius and His Disciples*. Vol. 1: *The Life of Saint Pachomius and His Disciples*. Cistercian Studies no. 45. Kalamazoo, MI: Cistercian Publications, 1980. French translation: A. M. J. Festugière. *La première vie greque de saint Pachôme, introduction critique et traduction*. Vol. 4, pt. 2 of *Les Moines d'Orient*. Paris: Cerf, 1965.

Palladius. *The Lausiac History [Historia Lausiaca] of Palladius. A Critical Discussion, Together with Notes on Early Monachism*. Edited and with an introduction by C. Butler. Texts and Studies, vol. 6, pts. 1 and 2. Cambridge: Cambridge University Press, 1989–1904. English translation: Robert T. Meyer. *The Lausiac History*. Westminister, MD: Newman Press, 1965.

Philostratus and Eunapius. *The Lives of the Sophists*. English translation by W. C. Wright. London: William Heinemann, 1922.

Plotinus. *The Enneads*, with Porphyry, *Life of Plotinus*. Translated by S. Mackenna. London: Faber and Faber, 1963.

Socrates. *Historia ecclesiastica*. *PG* 67:29–842. English translation: In A. C. Zenos, ed. *Library of Nicene and Post-Nicene Fathers*. Ser. 2, vol. 2. Grand Rapids, MI: Eerdmans, 1979.

Sozomen, *Historia ecclesiastica*. Edited by Joseph Bidez. *Kirchengeschichte Sozomenus*. Berlin: Akademie-Verlag, 1960. Also in *PG* 67:853–1629. English translation: In A. C. Zenos, ed. *Library of Nicene and Post-Nicene Fathers*. Ser. 2, vol. 2. Grand Rapids, MI: Eerdmans, 1979.

Synesius of Cyrene. *Essays and Hymns: Letters*. Edited by N. Terzagh. English translation by A. Fitzgerald. London: Oxford University Press, 1930.

Secondary Works

Ackroyd, P. R. and C. F. Evans. *The Cambridge History of the Bible*. Vol 1. *From the Beginnings to Jerome*. Cambridge: Cambridge University Press, 1970.

Allchin, A. M. *The Silent Rebellion: Anglican Religious Communities, 1845–1900*. London: SCM Press, 1958.

Allenbach, J. et al. *Biblia Patristica: Index des citations et allusions bibliques dans la littérature patristique*. Paris: Editions du Centre nationale de la recherche scientifique, 1975–1982.

Anson, P. F. *The Call of the Desert: The Solitary Life in the Christian Church*. London: SPCK, 1973.

Armstrong, A. H. "The Ancient and Continuing Pieties of the Greek World." In *Classical and Mediterranean Spirituality*, edited by A. H. Armstrong. New York: Crossroad, 1986.

———, ed. *Classical and Mediterranean Spirituality*. New York: Crossroad, 1986.

Bacht, Heinrich. "L'importance de l'idéal monastique de saint Pachôme pour l'histoire du monachisme chrétien." *Revue d'ascétique et. de mystique* 26 (1950).

———. "Pakhôme et ses disciples." In *Théologie de la vie monastique*. Études sur la tradition patristique. Paris: Aubier, 1961.

———. "Vom Umgang mit der Bibel im ältesten Mönchtum." *Theologie und Philosophie* 41 (1966).

———. *Das Vermächtnis des Ursprungs*. Studien zum frühen Mönchtum 1. Würzburg: Echter, 1972.

Barnard, L. W. "Some Liturgical Elements in Athanasius' Festal Epistles." *Studia Patristica* 13 (1975).

Barnes, T. D. "Angel of Light or Mystic Initiate? The Problem of the *Life of Antony*." *Journal of Theological Studies*, n.s., 37 (1986).

————. *Constantine and Eusebius.* Cambridge: Harvard University Press, 1981.

Baur, F. "Die heilige schrift bei den ältesten Mënchen des Christlicher Altertums." *Theologie und Glaube* 17 (1925).

Bauer, Walter. *Orthodoxy and Heresy in Earliest Christianity.* Translated and edited by R. A. Kraft and G. Krodel. Philadelphia: Fortress Press, 1971.

Baynes, A. C. "St. Anthony and the Demons." *Journal of Egyptian Archaeology* 40 (1954).

Baynes, N. H. *Constantine the Great and the Christian Church.* 2d ed. Preface by H. Chadwick. New York: Oxford University Press, 1972.

————. *The Thought World of East Rome.* London: Oxford University Press, 1947.

Bell, Harold Idris. *Cults and Creeds in Graeco-Roman Egypt.* New York: Philosophical Library, 1953.

————. *Egypt from Alexander the Great to the Arab Conquest: A Study in the Diffusion and Decay of Hellenism.* Gregynog Lectures, 1946. Oxford: Clarendon Press, 1948.

Benz, E. "Littérature du désert chez les Evangéliques allemandes et les Piétistes de Pennsylvanie." *Irénikon* 51 (1978).

Biarne, J. "La Bible dans la vie monastique." In *Le monde latin antique et la Bible,* edited by Jacques Fontaine and Charles Pietri. Paris: Beauchesne, 1985.

La Bible et les Pères. Colloque de Strasbourg, 1–3 October, 1969. Paris: Presses Universitaires de France, 1971.

Binns, J. R. "The Early Monasteries." *Medieval History* 1 (1991).

Black, M. *Models and Metaphors.* Ithaca, NY: Cornell University Press, 1962.

Bloch, Marc. *The Historian's Craft.* New York: Vintage Books, 1953.

Boak, A. E. R. "An Egyptian Farmer of the Age of Diocletian and Constantine." *Byzantina Metabyzantina* 1 (1946).

————. "Village Liturgies in Fourth-Century Karanis." In *Akten des VIII Internationalen Kongresses für Papyrologie. Wein 1955.* Vienna: Rudolf M. Rohner, 1956.

Bondi, R. *To Love as God Loves: Conversations with the Early Church.* Philadelphia: Fortress Press, 1987.

Bousset, W. *Apophthegmata. Studien zur Geschichte des ältesten Mönchtums.* Tübingen: Mohr, 1923.

Bouyer, L. *The Spirituality of the New Testament and the Fathers.* New York: Seabury Press, 1982.

————. *La vie de S. Antoine: Essaie sur la spiritualité du monachisme primitif.* Bégrolles-en-Mauges: Bellefontaine, 1977.

Bowersock, G. W. *Hellenism in Late Antiquity.* Ann Arbor: University of Michigan Press, 1990.

Bregman, Jay. *Synesius of Cyrene.* Berkeley: University of California Press, 1982.

Brennan, Brian. "Athanasius' *Vita Antonii:* A Sociological Interpretation." *Vigiliae Christianae* 39 (1985).

Brisson, L. et al., eds. *Porphyre: La vie de Plotin, travaux préliminaires.* Paris: J. Vrin, 1982.

Brock, S. P. "Early Syrian Asceticism." *Numen* 20 (1973).

Brown, Peter. "Approaches to the Religious Crisis of the Third Century A.D." *English Historical Review* 83 (1968).

———. *The Body and Society: Men, Women and Sexual Renunciation in Early Christianity.* New York: Columbia University Press, 1988.

———. *The Making of Late Antiquity.* Cambridge: Harvard University Press, 1978.

———. "The Philosopher and Society in Late Antiquity." Colloquy 34. Center for Hermeneutical Studies, Berkeley: 1978.

———. "The Rise and Function of the Holy Man in Late Antiquity." *Journal of Roman Studies* 61 (1971). Reprinted with revisions in idem, *Society and the Holy in Late Antiquity.* Berkeley: University of California Press, 1982.

———. "The Saint as Exemplar in Late Antiquity." In *Saints and Virtues,* edited by J. Stratton Hawley. Berkeley: University of California Press, 1987.

———. "A Social Context to the Religious Crisis of the Third Century A.D." Colloquy 14. Center for Hermeneutical Studies, Berkeley, 1975.

———. *Society and the Holy in Late Antiquity.* Berkeley: University of California Press, 1982.

———. *The World of Late Antiquity.* London: Thames and Hudson, 1971.

Buck, D. F. "The Structure of the Lausiac History." *Byzantinische Zeitschrift* 45 (1976).

Cadoux, C. J. *The Early Church and the World: A History of the Christian Attitude to Pagan Society and the State Down to the Time of Constantius.* New York: Charles Scribner's Sons, 1925.

Camelot, P.-Th. "L'Évangile au désert?" *La Vie Spirituelle* 140 (1986).

Camille de la Grâce-Dieu. "Jean Cassien: La sainte écriture dans la vie du moine." *Tamié 79. La Lectio divina. Rencontre des Père-Maîtres et Mère-Maîtresses bénédictins et cisterciens du Nord et de l'Est de la France à l'Abbaye de Tamié (Savoie) du 22 an 27 janvier, 1979.*

Cavallera, F. "Apophtegmes." *DS.* Vol. 1.

Chadwick, Henry. "The Ascetic Ideal in the Early Church." In *Monks, Hermits and the Ascetic Tradition,* edited by W. J. Sheils. Oxford: Blackwell, 1985.

———. *The Early Church.* Harmondsworth: Penguin, 1967.

———. "Pachomios and the Idea of Sanctity." In *The Byzantine Saint: University of Birmingham Fourteenth Spring Symposium of Byzantine Studies (1980). Studies Supplementary to Sobornost* 5, edited by Sergei Hackel. London: Fellowship of St. Alban and St. Sergius, 1981.

Chadwick, Owen. *John Cassian.* 2d ed. Cambridge: Cambridge University Press, 1968.

Chaleur, S. "Le culte de St. Antoine." *Bulletin de l'Institut des études coptes* 1 (1958).

Chitty, Derwas J. "Abba Isaiah." *Journal of Theological Studies,* n.s., 22 (1971).

———. "The Books of the Old Men." *Eastern Churches Review* 6 (1974).

———. *The Desert a City.* Oxford: Blackwell, 1966. Reprint. London: Mowbrays, 1977.

Colombás, G. "La Biblia en la espiritualidad del monacato primitivo." *Yermo* 1 (1963); 2 (1964).

Couilleau, G. "La liberté d'Antoine." In *Commandements du Seigneur et libération évangélique,* edited by Jean Gribomont, O.S.B. Studia Anselmiana 70. Rome: Anselmiana, 1977.

Cox, Patricia. *Biography in Late Antiquity: A Quest for the Holy Man.* Berkeley: University of California Press, 1983.

Creed, J. M. "Egypt and the Christian Church." In *The Legacy of Egypt,* edited by S. R. K. Glanville. Oxford: Clarendon Press, 1942.

Crouzel, H. "Origène, précurseur de monachisme." In *Théologie de la vie monastique: Études sur la tradition patristique,* edited by G. LeMaître. Paris: Aubier, 1961.

Daniélou, J. *Gospel Message and Hellenistic Culture.* Translated and edited by J. A. Baker. London/Philadelphia: Darton, Longman and Todd/Westminster, 1973.

Daniélou, J. and H. Marrou. *The Christian Centuries.* Vol. 1: *The First Six Hundred Years.* Translated by V. Cronin. New York: McGraw-Hill, 1964.

Davril, A., O.S.B. "La psalmodie chez les pères du désert." *Collectanea Cisterciensia* 49 (1987).

Deseille, Placide. "Le père spirituel dans le monachisme primitif." *Axes* 6 (1974).

Devilliers, N. *Saint Antoine le Grande, père des moines.* Bégrolles-en-Mauges: Textes Monastiques, 1971.

Dictionnaire de spiritualité ascétique et mystique, doctrine et histoire. Edited by Marcel Viller, F. Cavallera, and J. de Guibert. Paris: Beauchesne, 1937–.

Dodds, E. R. *Pagan and Christian in an Age of Anxiety.* New York: W. W. Norton, 1965.

———. "Tradition and Personal Achievement in Plotinus." *Journal of Roman Studies* 50 (1960).

Dörries, H. "Die Bibel in ältesten Mönchtum." *Theologische Literaturzeitung* 72 (1947).

———. *Wort und Stunde,* vol. 1. Göttingen: Vandenhoeck and Ruprecht, 1966.

Draguet, R. "Le 'Histoire Lausiaque,' une oeuvre écrite dans l'esprit d'Evagre." *Revue d'Histoire Ecclésiastique* 41 (1946); 42 (1947).

Driscoll, J., O.S.B. *The 'Ad Monachos" of Evagrius Ponticus: Its Structure and a Select Commentary.* Rome: Studia Anselmiana, 1991.

Ebeling, W. *Word and Faith.* Translated by J. W. Leitch. Philadelphia: Fortress Press, 1963.

———. "Word of God and the New Hermeneutic." In *The New Hermeneutic,* edited by J. M. Robinson and J. B. Cobb, Jr. New York: Harper and Row, 1964.

Ehrman, Bart D. "The New Testament Canon of Didymus the Blind." *Vigiliae Christianae* 37 (1983).

Entralgo, P. Lain. *The Therapy of the Word in Classical Antiquity.* New Haven: Yale University Press, 1970.

Esbroeck, Michael van. "Les apophtegmes dans les versions orientales." *Analecta Bollandiana* 93 (1975).

Evdokimov, Paul. *The Struggle with God.* Glenn Rock, NJ: Paulist, 1966.

Evelyn-White, H. G. *The Monasteries of the Wâdi 'n Natrûn.* Pt. 2: *The History of the Monasteries of Nitria and Scetis.* New York: Metropolitan Museum of Art, 1932.

Fernández Marcos, Natalio. "La Biblia y los orígenes del monaquismo." *Miscelánea Comillas* 41 (1983).

Festugière, A.-J. *Antioche païenne et chrétienne. Libanius, Chrysostome et les moines de Syrie.* Paris: E. de Boccard, 1959.

———. *Les moines d'Orient.* Vol. 1: *Culture ou sainteté. Introduction au monachisme oriental* Paris: Éditions du Cerf, 1961.

Fisher, C. N. "Pain as Purgation: The Role of Pathologizing in the Life of the Mystic." *Pastoral Psychology* 27 (1978).

Flaubert, G. *La tentation de saint Antoine.* Edited by R. Dumesnil. Paris: Les Belles-Lettres, 1940.

Fontaine, Jacques and Charles Pietri, eds. *Le monde latin antique et la Bible.* Paris: Beauchesne, 1985.

Fowden, Garth. "The Pagan Holy Man in Late Antique Society." *Journal of Hellenic Studies* 52 (1982).

Frazer, Ruth. "The Morphology of Desert Wisdom in the *Apophthegmata Patrum.*" Ph.D. dissertation, University of Chicago, 1977.

French, R. M., trans. *The Way of the Pilgrim.* New York: Seabury Press, 1965.

Frend, W. H. C. "Religion and Social Change in the Late Roman Empire." *The Cambridge Journal* 2 (1939).

———. *The Rise of Christianity.* Philadelphia: Fortress Press, 1984.

Froehlich, K. *Biblical Interpretation in the Early Church.* Philadelphia: Fortress Press, 1984.

Funk, Robert. *Language, Hermeneutic and the Word of God.* New York: Harper and Row, 1966.

Gadamer, H.-G. *Philosophical Hermeneutics.* Berkeley: University of California Press, 1976.

———. *Truth and Method.* New York: Crossroad, 1975.

Garido-Bonaño, Manuel. "Fundamentos bíblicos de la caridad en las reglas monásticas." *Burgense* 14 (1973).

Geffken, Johannes. *The Last Days of Greco-Roman Paganism.* Translated by Sabine MacCormack. Amsterdam: North Holland Publishing Company, 1978.

Gibbon, E. *The History of the Decline and Fall of the Roman Empire.* 7 Vols. Edited by J. B. Bury. London: Methuen, 1896–1900.

Gill, S. D. "Nonliterate Traditions and Holy Books." In *The Holy Book in Comparative Perspective,* edited by F. M. Denny and R. L. Taylor. Columbia: University of South Carolina Press, 1985.

Gnolfo, P. "Pedagogia Pacomiana." *Salesianum* 10 (1948).

Goehring, J. E. "New Frontiers in Pachomian Studies." In *The Roots of Egyptian*

Christianity, edited by B. A. Pearson and J. E. Goehring. Philadelphia: Fortress Press, 1986.

———. "The World Engaged: The Social and Economic World of Early Egyptian Monasticism." In *Gnosticism and the Early Christian World: In Honor of James M. Robinson,* edited by J. E. Goehring et al. Sonoma, CA: Polebridge, 1990.

González-Cobos, Aurora M. "Sobre los condicionamientos sociales de los orígenes del monacato." *Hispania Antiqua* 3 (1973).

Gould, Graham. "The Desert Fathers on Personal Relationships." Ph.D. dissertation. Cambridge University, 1988.

———. "Early Egyptian Monasticism and the Church." In *Monastic Studies: The Continuity of Tradition,* edited by J. Loades. Bangor: Headstart History, 1989.

———. "The *Life of Antony* and the Origins of Christian Monasticism in Fourth-Century Egypt." *Medieval History* 1 (1991).

———. "A Note on the *Apophthegmata Patrum.*" *Journal of Theological Studies,* n.s., 37 (1986).

Goulet-Cazé, Marie-Odile. "Plotin, Professeur de philosophie." In *Porphyre: La vie de Plotin, travaux préliminaires,* edited by L. Brisson et al. Paris: J. Vrin, 1982.

Graham, William A. *Beyond the Written Word: Oral Aspects of Scripture in the History of Religion.* Cambridge: Cambridge University Press, 1987.

Grant, R. M. *Early Christianity and Society.* New York: Harper and Row, 1977.

———. "The New Testament Canon." In *The Cambridge History of the Bible,* vol. I edited by P. R. Ackroyd and C. F. Evans. Cambridge: Cambridge University Press, 1970.

Grant, R. M., with D. Tracy. *A Short History of the Interpretation of the Bible.* 2d ed., rev., enl. Philadelphia: Fortress Press, 1984.

Green, H. A. "The Socio-Economic Background of Christianity in Egypt." In *The Roots of Egyptian Christianity,* edited by B. A. Pearson and J. E. Goehring. Philadelphia: Fortress Press, 1986.

Gregg, R. and D. Groh. *Early Arianism: A View of Salvation.* Philadelphia: Fortress Press, 1981.

Gribomont, Jean, O.S.B., ed. *Commandments du Seigneur et libération évangélique. Études monastiques proposées et discutées à Saint-Anselme.* Studia Anselmiana 70. Rome: Anselmiana, 1977.

———. "Monasticism and Asceticism—Eastern Christianity." In *Christian Spirituality: Origins to the Twelfth Century,* edited by B. McGinn, J. Meyendorff, and J. Leclercq. New York: Crossroad, 1985.

Griggs, C. Wilfred. *Early Egyptian Christianity: From Its Origins to 451 C.E.* Leiden: E. J. Brill, 1990.

Guillaumont, A. *Aux origines du monachisme chrétien. Pour une phénoménologie du monachisme.* Spiritualité orientale et vie monastique 30. Bégrolles-en-Mauges: Bellefontaine, 1979.

———. "La conception du désert chez les moines d'Egypte." In *Aux origines du monachisme chrétien.* Bégrolles-en-Mauges: Bellefontaine, 1979.

————. "Le dépaysement comme forme d'ascèse dans le monachisme ancien." *École pratique des hautes études.* V section: *Sciences religieuses, Annuaire 1968–69* 76 (1968).

————. "Esquisse d'une phénoménologie du monachisme." *Numen* 25 (1978).

————. "The Jesus Prayer among the Monks of Egypt." *Eastern Churches Review* 6 (1974).

————. "Monachisme et éthique judéo-chrétienne." *Judeó-Christianisme, Recherches historiques et théologiques offertes en hommage au Cardinal Daniélou, Recherches de Sciences Religieuses* 60 (1972).

————. "Le problème des deux Macaires dans les *Apophthegmata Patrum.*" *Irénikon* 48 (1975).

Guy, Jean-Claude. "Les *Apophthegmata Patrum.*" In *Théologie de la vie monastique,* edited by G. LeMaître. Paris: Aubier, 1961.

————. "Écriture sainte et vie spirituelle." *DS.* Vol. 4.

————. "Educational Innovation in the Desert Fathers." *Eastern Churches Review* 6 (1974).

————. *Jean Cassien: Vie et doctrine spirituelle.* Paris: P. Lethielleux, 1961.

————. "Note sur l'evolution du genre apophthegmatique." *Revue d'ascétique et de mystique* 32 (1956).

————. *Recherches sur la tradition grecque des Apophthegmata Patrum.* Subsidia Hagiographica 36. Brussels: Société des Bollandistes, 1962.

————. "Remarques sur le texte des *Apophthegmata Patrum.*" *RSR* 63 (1955).

————. "Un dialogue monastique inédit." *Revue d'ascétique et de mystique* 33 (1957).

Gwyn Griffiths, J. "The Faith of the Pharaonic Period." In *Classical Mediterranean Spirituality,* edited by A. H. Armstrong. New York: Crossroad, 1986.

Hadot, Pierre. *Exercices spirituels et philosophie antique.* Paris: Études Augustiniennes, 1981.

————. *Plotin, ou la simplicité du regard.* Paris: Librairie Plon, 1963.

Halkin, François. *Saints moines d'orient.* London: Variorum Reprints, 1973.

Hamilton, Andrew. "Spiritual Direction in the Apophthegmata." *Colloquium* 15 (1983).

Hanson, R. P. C. "Biblical Exegesis in the Early Church." In *The Cambridge History of the Bible,* vol. 1, edited by P. R. Ackroyd and C. F. Evans. Cambridge: Cambridge University Press, 1970.

Hardy, E. R. *Christian Egypt: Church and People.* New York: Oxford University Press, 1952.

Harnack, A. *The Mission and Expansion of Christianity in the First Three Centuries.* Translated and edited by J. Moffatt. 2d rev. ed. Vol. 2. New York: Putnam, 1908.

Hart, Ray. *Unfinished Man and the Imagination,* New York: Seabury Press, 1979.

Hausherr, I., S.J. *Direction spirituelle en orient d'autrefois.* Orientalia Christiana Analecta 144. Rome: Pontificium Institutum Studiorum Orientalium, 1955.

————. *Études de spiritualité orientale.* Orientalia Christiana Analecta. Rome: Pontificium Institutum Studiorum Orientalium, 1969.

————. "The Great Currents of Eastern Spirituality." *The Eastern Churches Quarterly* 2 (1937).

————. *Hésychasme et prière*. Rome: Pontificium Institutum Orientalium Studiorum, 1966.

————. "L'hésychasme: Étude de spiritualité." *Orientalia Christiana Peroidica* 22 (1956).

————. *Les leçons d'un contemplatif: Le traité de l'oraison d'Evagre le Pontique*. Paris: Beauchesne, 1960.

————. *Penthos: The Doctrine of Compunction in the Christian East*. Translated by Anselm Hufstader, O.S.B. Kalamazoo, MI: Cistercian Publications, 1982.

————. "Pour comprendre l'orient chrétien: La primauté du spirituel." *OCP* 33 (1967).

Heidegger, M. *Introduction to Metaphysics*. Translated by R. Manheim. New Haven: Yale University Press, 1959.

————. *Poetry, Language and Thought*. Translated by A. Hofstadter. New York: Harper and Row, 1971.

Henne, H. "Documents et travaux sur l'anachôrèsis." In *Akten des VIII Internationalen Kongresses für Papyrologie. Wien 1955*. Vienna: Rudolf M. Rohner, 1956.

Heussi, K. *Der Ursprung des Mönchtums*. Tubingen: Mohr, 1936.

Iswolsky, H. *Christ in Russia*. Milwaukee: Bruce, 1960.

Jaeger, Werner, *Early Christianity and Greek Paideia*. London: Oxford University Press, 1961.

Jeanrond, W. G. *Text and Interpretation as Categories of Theological Thinking*. Translated by T. J. Wilson. New York: Crossroad, 1988.

Jones, A. *Soul Making: The Desert Way of Spirituality*. San Francisco: Harper and Row, 1985.

Jones, A. H. M. "Egypt." With revisions by J. David Thomas. In *The Cities of the East Roman Provinces*, by A. H. M. Jones. 2d ed. rev. Oxford: Clarendon Press, 1971.

————. *The Later Roman Empire*. 4 vols. Oxford: Blackwell, 1964.

————. "The Social Background of the Struggle between Paganism and Christianity." In *The Conflict between Paganism and Christianity in the Fourth Century*, edited by A. Momigliano. Oxford: Clarendon Press, 1963.

Judge, E. A. "The Earliest Use of Monachos for 'Monk' (P. Coll. Youtie 77) and the Origins of Monasticism." Jahrbuch für Antike und Christentum 20 (1977).

————. "Fourth-Century Monasticism in the Papyri." In *Proceedings of the Sixteenth International Congress of Papyrologists*, edited by R. S. Bagnall et al. Chico, CA: Scholar's Press, 1981.

Kannengiesser, C. *Early Christian Spirituality*. Philadelphia: Fortress Press, 1986.

Keiner, L. "L'horreur des Égyptiens pour les démons du désert." *Bulletin de l'Institut d'Égypte* 26 (1943–1944).

Kelber, W. H. *The Oral and Written Gospel*. Philadelphia: Fortress Press, 1983.

Kirschner, Robert. "The Vocation of Holiness in Late Antiquity." *Vigiliae Christianae* 38 (1984).

Klijn, A. F. J. "Jewish Christianity in Egypt." In *The Roots of Egyptian Christianity*, edited by B. A. Pearson and J. E. Goehring. Philadelphia: Fortress Press, 1986.

Kristensen, A. "Cassian's Use of Scripture." *American Benedictine Review* 28 (1977).

Kugel, J. and R. A. Greer. *Early Biblical Interpretation.* Philadelphia: Westminister Press, 1986.

Lane Fox, Robin. *Pagans and Christians.* New York: Knopf, 1987.

Lecky, W. E. H. *History of European Morals.* 3rd ed., rev. New York: D. Appleton, 1895.

Leclercq, Jean, O.S.B. "S. Antoine dans la tradition monastique médiévale." *Studia Anselmiana* 38 (1956).

———. "Évangile et culture dans l'histoire de l'autorité monastique." *Collectanea Cisterciensia* 34 (1972).

———. *The Love of Learning and the Desire for God.* New York: Fordham University Press, 1961.

Leloir, Louis. *Désert et communion: témoignage des Pères du Désert, recueillis à partir des "Paterica" arméniens.* Bégrolles-en-Mauges: Bellefontaine, 1978.

———. "Lectio Divina and the Desert Fathers." *Liturgy* 23 (1989).

———. "La lecture de l'Écriture selon les anciens Pères." *Revue d'ascétique et de mystique* 47 (1971).

———. "Les orientations essentielles de la spiritualité des pères du désert d'apres le paterica Arméniens." *Revue de théologie et de philosophie* 24 (1975).

———. "Les Pères du Desert et la Bible." *La Vie Spirituelle* 140 (1986).

———. "La sagesse des anciens moines." *Studia Missionalia* 28 (1979).

———. "Solitude et sollicitude: Le moine loin et près du monde, d'après paterica Arméniens." *Irénikon* 47 (1974).

Lemaire, J.-P. "L'abbé Poemen et la Sainte Écriture." Licentiate thesis, University of Freiburg, 1971.

LeMaître, G., ed. *Théologie de la vie monastique: études sur la tradition patristique.* Paris: Aubier, 1961.

Leroy, Julien. "Experience of God and Primitive Cenobitism." *Monastic Studies* 9 (1972).

Lewis, Naphtali. *Life in Egypt under Roman Rule.* Oxford: Clarendon Press, 1983.

Lialine, Clément. "Érémitisme en orient." In *DS.* Vol. 4.

Lienhard, Joseph T. "On 'Discernment of Spirits' in the Early Church." *Theological Studies* 41 (1980).

Lietzmann, Hans. *A History of the Early Church.* Vol. 4: *The Era of the Church Fathers.* Translated by B. L. Woolf. London: Lutterworth, 1951.

Lilienfeld, Fairy von. "Anthropos Pneumatikos—Pater Pneumatophoros: Neues Testament und Apophthegmata Patrum." *Studia Patristica* 5, *TU* 80. Berlin: Akademie Verlag, 1962.

———. "Die Christliche Unterweisung der Apophthegmata Patrum." *Bulletin de la Société d'Archéologie Copte* 20 (1971).

———. "Jesus-Logion und Vaterspruch." In *Studia Byzantina.* Edited by Johannes Irmscher. Halled-Wittenberg, 1966.

————. "Paulus-Zitate und Paulinische Gedanken in den *Apophthegmata Patrum.*" *Studia Evangelica* 5, *TU* 103. Berlin: Akademie-Verlag. 1968.

Lindars, B. "The Bible and the Call: The Biblical Roots of the Monastic Life in History and Today." *Bulletin of John Rylands Library* 66 (1983–1984).

Louf, André. "Ascèse et prière." *Collectanea Cisterciensia* 33 (1971).

————. "Spiritual Fatherhood in the Literature of the Desert." In *Abba,* edited by John R. Sommerfeldt. Kalamazoo, MI: Cistercian Publications, 1982.

————. "The Word beyond the Liturgy." *Cistercian Studies* 6 (1971); 7 (1972).

Louth, A. "St. Athanasius and the Greek *Life of Antony.*" *Journal of Theological Studies,* n.s., 39 (1988).

————. *The Wilderness of God.* London: Darton, Longman and Todd, 1991.

————. "The Pachomian Experience." *Review for Religious* 35 (1976).

McFague, S. *Metaphorical Theology.* Philadelphia: Fortress Press, 1982.

————. *Models of God.* Philadelphia: Fortress Press, 1987.

McMurry, J. "The Scriptures and Monastic Prayer." *Cistercian Studies* 2 (1967).

Malherbe, A. J. *Moral Exhortation: A Greco-Roman Sourcebook.* Philadelphia: Westminster Press, 1986.

Malone, Edward E. *The Monk and the Martyr: The Monk as the Successor of the Martyr.* Studies in Christian Antiquity 12. Washington, D.C.: Catholic University of America Press, 1950.

Margerie, B., S.J. *Introduction à l'histoire de l'exégèse.* Vol. 1: *Les pères grecs et orientaux.* Paris: Cerf, 1980.

Markus, R. A. *The End of Ancient Christianity.* Cambridge: Cambridge University Press, 1991.

————. "Paganism, Christianity and the Latin Classics in the Fourth Century." In *Latin Literature of the Fourth Century,* edited by J. W. Binns. Boston: Routledge and Kegan Paul, 1974.

Marrou, H. I. *A History of Education in Antiquity.* Translated by G. Lamb. Madison: University of Wisconsin Press, 1982.

————. "Jean Cassien à Marseille." *Patristique et Humanisme.* Paris: Éditions du Seuil, 1976.

Martin, Annick. "L'église et la khôra égyptienne au ive siècle." *Revue des Études Augustihiennes* 26 (1979).

Matthew the Poor. *The Communion of Love.* Introduction by H. Nouwen. New York: St. Vladimir, 1984.

Mazzarino, S. *The End of the Ancient World.* Translated by G. Holmes. London: Faber & Faber, 1966.

Meinardus, O. *Monks and Monasteries of the Egyptian Desert.* Cairo: The American University of Cairo Press, 1961.

Meredith, A. "Asceticism—Christian and Greek." *Journal of Theological Studies,* n.s., 27 (1976).

Merton, Thomas. "The Spiritual Father in the Desert Tradition." *Cistercian Studies* 3 (1968).

————. *The Wisdom of the Desert.* New York: New Directions, 1960.

————. *Zen and the Birds of Appetite.* New York: New Directions, 1968.

Metzger, Bruce M. *The Early Versions of the New Testament: Their Origin, Transmission, and Limitations.* Oxford: Clarendon Press, 1977.

Meyer, Robert T. "Lectio Divina in Palladius." In *Kuriakon: Festschrift Johannes Quasten,* edited by P. Granfield and J. A. Jungman. Munster: Verlag Aschendorff, 1970.

———. "Palladius and Early Christian Spirituality." *Studia Patristica* 10 (1970).

———. "Palladius and the Study of Scripture." *Studia Patristica* 13 (1971).

Miller, Fergus. *The Roman Empire and Its Neighbours.* London: Weidenfeld and Nicolson, 1967.

Miquel, Pierre, O.S.B. *Lexique du désert.* Bégrolles-en-Mauges: Bellefontaine, 1986.

Mondésert, C., ed. *Le monde grec ancien et la Bible.* Paris: Beauchesne, 1984.

Montalembert, Charles Forbes René de Tryon, comte de. *The Monks of the West from St. Benedict to St. Bernard.* New York: Kennedy, 1912.

Morard, F. E. "Monachos, une importation sémitique en Égypte? Quelques aperçus nouveaux." *Studia Patristica* 12 (1971).

Munz, P. "John Cassian." *Journal of Ecclesiastical History* 11 (1960).

Murray, R. "The Exhortation to Candidates for Ascetical Vows at Baptism in the Ancient Syrian Churches." *New Testament Studies* 21 (1974).

———. *Symbols of Church and Kingdom: A Study in Early Syriac Tradition.* Cambridge University Press, 1975.

Nagel, P. "Action-Parables in Earliest Monasticism: An Examination of the Apophthegmata Patrum." *Hallel* 5 (Winter 1977–1978).

Naldini, Mario. *Il christianesimo in Egitto: Lettere private nei papiri dei secoli II–IV.* Florence: Le Monnier, 1968.

Neyt, François. "A Form of Charismatic Authority." *Eastern Churches Review* 6 (1974).

Niebuhr, Richard R. "The Strife of Interpreting: The Moral Burden of Imagination." *Parabola* 10 (1985).

Nock, A. D. *Conversion.* London: Oxford University Press, 1933.

———. *Essays on Religion and the Ancient World.* 2 vols. Edited by Zeph Stewart. Oxford: Clarendon Press, 1972.

Nouwen, H. *The Way of the Heart.* New York: Ballantine Books, 1981.

Novelli, E. "Littérature du désert dans le renouveau catholique au début de l'époque moderne." *Irénikon* 51 (1978).

O'Neill, J. C. "The Origins of Monasticism." In *The Making of Orthodoxy: Essays in Honor of Henry Chadwick,* edited by Cambridge: Cambridge University Press, 1989.

Ong, Walter J. *Orality and Literacy: The Technologizing of the Word.* London: Methuen, 1982.

Orlandi, Tito. "Coptic Literature." In *The Roots of Egyptian Christianity,* edited by B. A. Pearson and J. E. Goehring. Philadelphia: Fortress Press, 1986.

Palmer R. *Hermeneutics: Interpretation Theory in Schleiermacher, Dilthey, Heidegger, and Gadamer.* Evanston, IL: Northwestern University Press, 1969.

Pearson, B. A. "Earliest Christianity in Egypt: Some Observations." In *The Roots of Egyptian Christianity,* edited by B. A. Pearson and J. E. Goehring. Philadelphia: Fortress Press, 1986.

————. *Gnosticism, Judaism, and Egyptian Christianity*. Philadelphia: Fortress Press, 1990.

Peifer, Claude. "The Biblical Foundations of Monasticism." *Cistercian Studies* 12 (1972).

Pelikan, J. *The Excellent Empire*. San Francisco: Harper and Row, 1987.

Plumley, J. Martin. "Early Christianity in Egypt." *Palestine Exploration Quarterly* 89 (1957).

Poswick, F. "Les apophthegmes d'Hyperchios. L'ascèse du moine, méditation des Éritures" *Collectanea Cisterciensia* 32 (1970).

Priestly, G. M. "Some Jungian Parallels to the Sayings of the Desert fathers." *Cistercian Studies* 11 (1976).

Raasch, J. "The Monastic Concept of Purity of Heart and its Sources." *Studia Monastica* 12 (1970).

Regnault, Lucien. "Les Apophtegmes des pères en Palestine aux 5e–6e siècles." *Irénikon* 54 (1981).

————. "The Beatitudes in the Apophthegmata Patrum." *Eastern Churches Review* 6 (1974).

————. "Des pères toujours vivants." *La Vie Spirituelle* 669 (1986).

————. *Les pères du désert à travers leurs Apophtegmes* (Sablé-sur-Sarthe: Solesmes, 1987.

————. "La prière continuelle 'monologistos' dans les apophtegmes des Pères." *Irénikon* 47 (1974).

————. "La prière de Jésus dans quelques apophtegmes conservés en arabe." *Irénikon* 52 (1979).

————. *La vie quotidienne des pères du désert en Égypte au IVe siècle*. (Paris: Hachette, 1990).

Religions en Égypte hellenistique et romaine. Colloque de Strasbourg, 16–18 Mai 1967. Centre d'études supérieures specialisé de l'histoire des religions de Strasbourg. Paris: Presses Universitaires de France, 1969.

Ricoeur, P. *Essays in Biblical Interpretation*. Edited with an introduction by Lewis S. Mudge Philadelphia: Fortress Press, 1980.

————. "The Hermeneutical Function of Distanciation." In *Hermeneutics and the Human Sciences*, edited, translated, and introduced by J. Thompson. Cambridge: Cambridge University Press, 1981.

————. *Interpretation Theory: Discourse and the Surplus of Meaning*. Forth Worth: Texas Christian University Press, 1976.

————. "The Model of the Text: Meaningful Action Considered as a Text." In *Hermeneutics and the Human Sciences*, edited, translated, and introduced by J. Thompson. Cambridge: Cambridge University Press, 1981.

————. "Naming God." *Union Theological Seminary Quarterly Review* 34 (1979).

Roberts, C. H. "The Codex." *Proceedings of the British Academy* 40 (1954).

————. *Manuscript, Society and Belief in Early Christian Egypt*. London: Oxford University Press, 1979.

Roberts, C. H. and T. C. Skeat. *The Birth of the Codex*. London: Oxford University Press, 1983.

Rostovtzeff, M. *The Social and Economic History of the Roman Empire.* 2d ed., rev. by P. M. Fraser. Oxford: Clarendon Press, 1957.

Rousse, Jacques. "Lectio Divina." *DS.* Vol. 9.

Rousseau, Philip. *Ascetics, Authority, and the Church in the Age of Jerome and Cassian.* Oxford Historical Monographs. Oxford: Oxford University Press, 1978.

————. *Pachomius: The Making of a Community in Fourth-Century Egypt.* Berkeley: University of California Press, 1985.

Rubenson, S. *The Letters of St. Antony: Origenist Theology, Monastic Tradition and the Making of a Saint.* Lund: Lund University Press, 1990.

Schneiders, S. M. "Scripture and Spirituality." In *Christian Spirituality: Origins to the Twelfth Century,* edited by B. McGinn, J. Meyendorff, and J. Leclercq. New York: Fortress Press, 1985.

Severus, E. von. "Zu den biblischen Grundlagen des benediktinischer Mönchtums. *Geist und Leben* 26 (1953).

Skeat, T. C. "Early Christian Book Production: Papyri and Manuscripts." In *The Cambridge History of the Bible. Vol. 2: The West from the Fathers to the Reformation,* edited by G. W. H. Lampe, Cambridge: Cambridge University Press, 1969.

Špidlík, T. *The Spirituality of the Christian East: A Systematic Handbook.* Translated by A. P. Gythiel. Kalamazoo, MI: Cistercian Publications, 1986.

Steidle, B., ed. *Antonius Magnus Eremita.* Studia Anselmiana 38. Rome: Orbis Catholicus, 1956.

Steiner, George. *Real Presences.* Chicago: University of Chicago Press, 1989.

Steinmetz, David, C. "The Superiority of Pre-Critical Exegesis." *Theology Today* 37 (1980).

Taft, Robert, S.J. *The Liturgy of the Hours in East and West.* Collegeville, MN: The Liturgical Press, 1986.

Tamburrino, P. "Les saints de l'ancien testament dans la catéchèse de saint Pachôme." *Melito* 4 (1968).

Torjeson, Karen. *Hermeneutical Method and Theological Structure in Origen's Exegesis.* Berlin, NY: de Gruyter, 1986.

————. "Review of *Early Christian Spirituality.*" *Patristics* 16 (1988).

Tracy, David. *The Analogical Imagination.* New York: Crossroad, 1981.

Veilleux, Armand. "Holy Scripture in the Pachomian Koinonia." *Monastic Studies* 10 (1974).

————. *La liturgie dans le cénobitisme pachômien au quatrième siècle.* Studia Anselmiana 57. Rome: Herder, 1968.

————. "Monasticism and Gnosis in Egypt." In *The Roots of Egyptian Christianity,* edited by B. A. Pearson and J. E. Goehring. Philadelphia: Fortress Press, 1986.

Vogüé, A. de. :"Les deux fonctions de la méditation dans la règles monastiques anciennes." *Revue d'Histoire de la Spiritualité* 51 (1975).

————. "To Study the Early Monks." *Monastic Studies* 12 (1976).

Vööbus, A. *A History of Asceticism in the Syrian Orient.* CSCO 184, Subsidia 14 Louvain: CSCO, 1958.

Wagenaar, C. "Prière de Jésus et sentences des pères." *Collectanea Cisterciensia* 46 (1984).

Wakefield, G. "La littérature du désert chez John Wesley." *Irénikon* 51 (1978).

Walsh, W. L., S.J. "Reality Therapy and Spiritual Direction." *Review for Religious* 35 (1976).

Ward, Benedicta. "Signs and Wonders: Miracles in the Desert Tradition." *Studia Patristics* 17 (1982).

————. "Spiritual Direction in the Desert Fathers." *The Way* (January 1984).

Ware, Kallistos. *The Power of the Name.* Oxford: Fairacres, 1974.

————. "Pray without Ceasing: The Ideal of Continual Prayer in Eastern Monasticism." *Eastern Churches Review* 2 (1969).

Wilder, A. "The Word as Address and the Word as Meaning." In *The New Hermeneutic,* edited by J. M. Robinson and J. B. Cobb, Jr. New York: Harper and Row, 1964.

Wilken, R. *The Christians as the Romans Saw Them.* New Haven: Yale University Press, 1984.

Williams, C. S. C. "The History of the Text and Canon of the New Testament to Jerome." In *The Cambridge History of the Bible.* Vol 2: *The West from the Fathers to the Reformation,* edited by G. W. H. Lampe. Cambridge: Cambridge University Press, 1969.

Wilson, Stephen, ed. *Saints and Their Cults.* Cambridge: Cambridge University Press, 1985.

Wisse, F. "Gnosticism and Early Monasticism in Egypt." In *Gnosis: Festschrift für Hans Jonas,* edited by B. Aland. Gottingen: Vandenhoeck and Ruprecht, 1978.

Zander, V. *St. Seraphim of Sarov.* London: SPCK, 1975.

Index of Biblical Citations

OLD TESTAMENT

Genesis
2:15 190
18 168, 250
23 189
23:2 189
37:27–36 250
39:7ff. 202
42:36 38, 169
46:3 123

Exodus
3:1–17 196
14:14 197
15:2 200
20:13–14 275

Leviticus
19:18 249

Numbers
20:17 195
21:8–9 291

Deuteronomy
5:17–18 275
10:17 183

Joshua
5:14 249

1 Samuel
5:1–5 202–3
17:35 194
17:35–36 271
18:23 168
20:14 187, 209n23

1 Kings
17:5 168

2 Kings
4:8–17 206

Job
1:21 228

Psalms
7:17 199, 211n60
18:29 219
42:1 201
48:5 234n40
54:23 222–23
58:6 200
65:12 200
69:2 128
72:22–23 250
74:16 119
94:6 187, 209n23
104:19 202
117:18 200
132:4 196

Proverbs
4:23 160, 168
25:7 277

Wisdom
7:26 187
12:22 187, 209n24

Isaiah
1:16–18 191
10:15 202
30:15 203
30:18 239
66:24 183

Daniel
7:10 183

Joel
1:13 208n17
2:12–13 208n17

Jonah
4:10 276

323

NEW TESTAMENT

General Index

327

DATE DUE